Conflict of Interest
in American Public Life

Conflict of Interest
in American Public Life

ANDREW STARK

Harvard University Press

Cambridge, Massachusetts, and London, England   2000

Library of Congress Cataloging-in-Publication Data

Stark, Andrew, 1956–
    Conflict of interest in American public life/Andrew Stark.
    p. cm.
    Includes bibliographical references and index.
    ISBN 0-674-00233-4
    1. Conflict of interests—United States. I. Title.
JK468.E7 S73   2000
172'.2—dc21   99-088225

For Deborah,
who at first was conflicted
but then became interested

CONTENTS

ACKNOWLEDGMENTS

I began work on this book as a guest scholar at the Brookings Institution (1990–91), continuing it as a fellow in the Harvard Program in Ethics and the Professions (1991–92), a faculty member at the University of Toronto (beginning in 1992), and a fellow at the Woodrow Wilson International Center for Scholars (1994–95). I am grateful to all four institutions for the various kinds of material and intellectual support they provided, as well as to the Social Sciences and Humanities Research Council of Canada, the Smith Richardson Foundation, the Earhart Foundation, the Connaught Fund of the University of Toronto, and the Division of Management, University of Toronto at Scarborough, for additional financial assistance.

Kathleen Clark, Stuart Gilman, Don Herzog, Mark Lilla, Stephen Wasby, and Alan Wertheimer read the entire manuscript and offered valuable comments. Tyler Cowen, Stéphane Dion, Joseph Gangloff, Patti Goldman, Moshe Halbertal, Alan Houston, Rob Howse, Mike Krashinsky, Keith Krehbiel, Will Kymlicka, John Rohr, Amélie Rorty, Frederick Schauer, Tracy Strong, Dennis Thompson, Paul Thompson, Melissa Williams, and Kenneth Winston read parts of the manuscript in article form and offered constructive suggestions. I presented two papers that eventually made their way into the book in the 1991–92 Harvard Ethics Program Fellows' weekly seminar; I am grateful to participants not only for their comments on my essays, but also for—over the course of the year—providing innumerable insights that helped shape my thinking on many issues of applied ethics. At vital moments, Barbara Jafelice, Wladyslaw Pleszczynski, and Gary Ruskin provided hard-to-get information above and beyond the call of duty. Christopher Blackburn ably prepared the index. My parents, Lois and Marvin Stark, encouraged me to pursue my academic interests and follow the often circuitous paths of contemplation. My daughters, Rachel and Zoe, urged me to cut to the chase and enjoy the pleasures of completion. And my wife, Deborah, with her usual perfect pitch, maintained exactly the right balance in supporting both impulses. I am indebted to them all.

*　　*　　*

Portions of Part I appeared as "Beyond Quid Pro Quo: What's Wrong with Private Gain from Public Office?" *American Political Science Review* 91 (1997), pp. 108–120; of Part II as "Limousine Liberals, Welfare Conservatives: On Belief, Interest, and Inconsistency in Democratic Discourse," *Political Theory* 25 (1997), pp. 475–501; "It Wasn't Because He Didn't Want to Get High," *Times Literary Supplement,* February 14, 1997, p. 14; "Don't Change the Subject: Interpreting American Public Discourse over Quid Pro Quo," *Business Ethics Quarterly* 7 (1997), pp. 93–116; and "Legislators with Interests: Better Advocates but Worse Judges?" *Public Integrity Annual* 2 (1997), pp. 53–57; of Part III as "The Appearance of Official Impropriety and the Concept of Political Crime," *Ethics* 105 (1995), pp. 326–351; and of Part IV as "What Is a Balanced Committee? Democratic Theory, Public Law, and the Question of Fair Representation on Quasi-Legislative Bodies," Ian Shapiro and Will Kymlicka, eds., *NOMOS* 39 (1997), *Ethnicity and Group Rights* (New York: New York University Press, 1997), pp. 377–418; "Public Knowledge, Private Knowledge," *The Antioch Review* 48 (1990), pp. 439–448; and "The Man Who Knew Too Little," *Washington Post,* April 1, 1990, p. C5.

Conflict of Interest
in American Public Life

Introduction

On April 22, 1994, Hillary Clinton met the national press in the White House State Dining Room and for an hour and a half parried questions about her financial past. The inquiries were minute, detailed, excruciating, iterative. Many concerned the lucrative commodities trading Mrs. Clinton had conducted, in the late 1970s, with the assistance of Arkansas attorney James Blair. At the time Bill Clinton was the state's governor; Blair was chief counsel for an Arkansas-based corporation, Tyson Foods, which had been aggressively seeking regulatory, tax, and financial concessions from the state government. The questioners, unabashedly expectant that they would catch the First Lady in a contradiction, focused on her allegedly "shifting explanations," "shifting accounts," or other seeming inconsistencies. In this particular quest, the assembled reporters met with failure. A headline in the next-day's *Washington Post* read, "First Lady—On the Spot—and Hitting It."

But in fact, although it passed without notice, there *was* a 180-degree turn in Hillary Clinton's remarks, one that she executed literally within the space of two sentences. Concerning her relationship with Blair, a reporter asked: "Did it concern you at the time that, because of [Blair's] position with the company that he represented, there was an ethical question raised by your accepting that level of assistance in a financial matter from him?"

And the First Lady responded: "No, it did not. And the reason it didn't is that he and his wife are among our very best friends. My husband performed their marriage ceremony. I was the best person at the wedding. We are very close friends. And I found it surprising that anyone would suggest [such a thing] because in 1980, right during the time this was all going on, when my husband ran for reelection, [Blair's client] Tyson supported his opponent."[1]

The First Lady, in other words, located Blair in the camp of both "friend"—one of her husband's most faithful companions—and "opponent"—the chief instrument of her husband's most influential enemy, representing its views, advancing its interests, and executing its agenda. Any contradiction here, of course, is not factual. This kind of friend/opponent

1

combination happens (all the time). But what was the point Hillary Clinton was trying to make about her relationship with Blair? And how could she have hoped to establish it by calling attention to diametrically antithetical details of his biography, pointing out the ways in which he had picked up the characteristics of both friend and foe? Wouldn't whatever followed from the fact that Blair was a loyal compadre necessarily be undermined by noting that, in effect, the interests he was seeking to advance belonged to their most powerful antagonist?

The point Hillary Clinton wanted to make was that her husband's judgment as governor of Arkansas could not possibly have been impaired by her dealings with Jim Blair, that those dealings had placed Bill Clinton in no conflict of interest. If on the one hand Blair was already the Clintons' close friend, then his helping Hillary Clinton was unlikely to have made the governor feel especially beholden to reciprocate, say with an official favor for Blair's client. Instead, Bill Clinton would have interpreted Blair's assistance as a gesture of personal affection, a gesture for which Blair anticipated nothing by way of recompense. A little bit of help for his novice wife on the commodities exchange, in the governor's mind, would have appeared simply as one more strand in a web of ongoing expressions of genuine mutual regard between the Clintons and the Blairs, not a particular *quid* to be recompensed through an official *quo*. Federal conflict-of-interest regulations allow officials to accept certain kinds of gifts from friends—theater tickets, invitations to golf tournaments, meals, and hospitality—that they prohibit officials taking from anyone else. The assumption, here as in Hillary Clinton's remarks, is that everyone has friendships, ties, and allegiances. They cannot, as Blair himself said, be "weeded out."[2] And a gift from a friend will not independently affect an official's judgment or make him any more disposed toward the friend than he or she unavoidably is.

But on the other hand, Blair was also an enemy. An energetic representative of his client Tyson, Blair's personal interests were deeply entangled with the company's interests at a time when Tyson strenuously opposed Clinton's candidacy and several of his key policies. And so if it turned out that, once reelected, Clinton actively helped the company—as he did—then it must have been because he determined it was in the public interest for him to do so. Certainly, it was not because he bore Tyson any personal feelings of partiality, affection, or gratitude. Indeed, to have helped his old enemy Tyson, Clinton would have had to turn the other cheek, demonstrably and admirably overcoming a personal animus that might otherwise have encumbered his official judgment.

For Hillary Clinton, then, the fact that Blair had assumed the status of both friend and enemy triangulated Bill Clinton's political judgment, allowing her to pronounce it unimpaired. The problem, though, is that precisely the opposite interpretation is available. If Blair was a personal friend, then wouldn't Bill Clinton's affection for him have skewed the governor's judgment far more than any simple trading favor ever could have done? Wouldn't their deep connectedness—far from somehow defanging Blair's trading assistance of the ability to impair Clinton's judgment—actually have compounded any partiality the governor felt and made him even more likely to assist his friend's client? And if that client itself happened to be an opponent of the governor's, wouldn't Clinton's ultimate aid also smack of a betrayal of principle, a compromise of judgment? Among other things, Tyson had been seeking lenient new environmental regulations, regulations that Clinton had opposed in the 1980 gubernatorial campaign. But it was precisely such regulatory reform that Clinton then advanced, once reelected, at Blair's behest. Helping an opponent under such circumstances shows not that the governor rose above a judgment-encumbering personal animus, but that—to recompense Blair's favors to his wife—he acted against his better judgment as to where laid the public interest. Or so the Clintons' critics suggested.[3]

Hillary Clinton's comment shows that conflict of interest is not just conflict of interest anymore. We have come to demand reassurance from officeholders that their official judgment is unencumbered in ways that require increasingly sophisticated excursions into their (and often our own) moral psychologies. The following pages and chapters explore the last several decades of public discourse over conflict of interest in American public life, discourse that embraces questions such as: Should we penalize officeholders for allowing the mere appearance of impropriety to arise surrounding their official activities, even if they have engaged in no actual wrongdoing? Should we investigate officials' personal character on the assumption that doing so will shed light on their public performance? Should we curtail public financial disclosure as an affront to officials' privacy or, alternatively, rely on it as the only remedy necessary for conflict of interest? Should we punish officeholders for profiting privately from public office even if they could not possibly have compromised their official performance in the process? Should we regard officials who take positions inconsistent with their personal interests as courageous or, alternatively, as hypocrites? Should we treat those who adopt views compatible with their interests as self-serving or as reassuringly genuine? Should we encourage congressmen to share pecuniary interests with their constituents on the grounds that their doing so will make them better representatives? Should we worry that officials' beliefs, predispositions, and commitments can, under some circumstances, be every bit as encumbering of their judgment as their pecuniary interests? Should we restrict the careers of officials' spouses in any way, and if so why? Should we visit particularly heavy restrictions on officials who leave government to work for foreign as opposed to domestic-owned businesses, and if so, why? All of these questions—and many more—have come to bear on our ongoing enterprise of determining whether official judgment is encumbered.

Connecting each of these questions is a central issue to which I frequently return. Over the past thirty years something transforming has indeed happened to our understanding of conflict of interest. In fact, two things have happened—one to our conception of "conflict," the other to our notion of "interest." We have come to take a distinctly *objective* approach to conflict. And we have evolved a deeply *subjective* understanding of interest.

To explain: The "conflict" in "conflict of interest" takes place entirely in the mind. The term "conflicted" refers exclusively to the official's impaired capacity for judgment. The problem, though, is that we cannot directly peer into an officeholder's mental state as she comes to judgment, cannot gauge the extent to which she remained admirably impervious to—or else was all-too-fallibly mindful of—her own interests. Since no law could effectively forbid officials from becoming judgmentally impaired by their own interests—which of course is the real evil—conflict-of-interest regulation instead prohibits the holding of certain kinds of interests altogether. Or, to take another example, because we could not enforce a law that forbade officials from becoming psychologically beholden to those who give them gifts, conflict-of-interest rules prohibit the very act of receiving gifts under certain kinds of circumstances. Because we cannot directly view mental states, in other words, conflict-of-interest strictures remain concerned not with what "actually happened" in the official's mind but with "what might have happened"; they make it illegal not to "succumb to temptation" but "to enter into relationships which are fraught with temptation."[4]

Over time, American conflict-of-interest regimes have thus moved away from hortatory strictures requiring certain inner states-of-mind—in the plaintive words of one senator, "I just wish we could pass a law . . . mandat[ing] good judgment"[5]—and toward prophylactic laws that prohibit external circumstances or actions that *might lead* to impaired mental states, to conflicted judgment. In fact, this movement is probably as much analytical as historical, replaying itself in the verbal reasoning, the "thinking out loud," of innumerable legislators, judges, and journalists.

One can put all of this in slightly different language. According to Melvin Aron Eisenberg, a legal principle "lies at the objective end of [the] spectrum if its application depends on a directly observable state of the world, and at the subjective end if its application depends on a mental state."[6] If so, then in the realm of "conflict," we have come to eschew a subjective approach and adopt an objective one. Or, as the legal scholar Bayless Manning put the point as long as thirty years ago, in conflict-of-interest law "subjective intent is not important . . . If the wrong kind of outside interest is held no amount of leaning over backward or purity of soul will satisfy [a confirmation] Committee or the statutes. The governing principle is objective . . . in the mechanical way that we associate with primitive law."[7]

But what constitutes the "wrong kind of interest?" For a long time, and certainly up until the middle of the 1960s, the type of private "interest" that conflict-of-interest discourse addressed remained largely pecuniary—hence "objective"—and amenable to regulation. The term *interest,* Bayless Manning insisted in 1964, should not be understood to embrace "subjective" impairments on judgment such as "loyalties, biases, affiliations, and experiences."[8] Along similar lines, Manning elsewhere observed that "conflict of interest regulation is innocent of any touch of theories of history or behavioristic psychology. Once a Defense Department official has sold his stock, for example, he is considered shriven, and it is out of order to question whether his past associations, his social identification, or his commercial loyalties continue to operate, or to affect his conduct."[9]

Yet even as Manning wrote, the public debate of the latter 1960s and early '70s was beginning to lend to "interest" precisely those "subjective," psychological connotations that he and other legal scholars of his era had excluded (or had wished to exclude). Congressmen, lobbyists, legal counsel in the Department of Justice, and others all began speaking of the need to deal, somehow, with what can generically be termed "ideological" biases: various "associational" and "partisan" attachments, for example, and diverse other "influences," "loyalties," "concerns," "emotions," "predispositions," "prejudgments," and "animuses"—even "moral" beliefs and "aesthetic" positions—all of which, arguably, can encumber an official's judgment every bit as much as her financial holdings can.[10]

Any objective reticence toward interpreting "interest" no further than the pecuniary has thus, over time, evolved into a more subjective approach, one that brings within its compass a variety of putative ideological and psychological impairments to judgment. In fact, in a kind of inversion of economic reductionism, an officeholder's economic interests now attain significance largely because they are thought to betoken a far more critical range of underlying ideological postures. As Hubert Humphrey said to secretary of agriculture-designate Earl Butz at the latter's 1971 confirmation hearings, "You can put your [stocks and bonds] in escrow, but I don't think you can put your philosophy in escrow."[11] Again, this movement is certainly historical. But even more it is personal, evident in the individual reasoning of legislators, judges, and commentators, who call for the divestiture of pecuniary interests and then, in the very text of their arguments, work themselves around,

Humphrey-style, to the position that such divestiture will hardly deal with the vast *sub rosa* realm of psychological bias.

When we speak of "conflict," then, our focus has shifted from subjective mental states themselves—on the grounds that trying to "accurately predict the subjective propensity to corruption of each individual official would be futile"—to a series of objective, prophylactic proxies for such mental states.[12] Because we cannot measure the different subjective effects any particular interest might have on different minds, in other words, if we are going to prohibit that interest in one case then we must objectively do so in all.[13] Yet when it comes to classifying those interests themselves, our gaze has moved from a narrow class of objective, pecuniary encumbrances to the broad range of subjective, ideological impairments they are thought to betoken.

To see what this means, consider the differing confirmation experiences of two secretaries-of-defense-designate, Charles E. Wilson in 1953 and John Tower in 1989. Wilson had been president of General Motors and was still, at the time of his confirmation, a major stockholder in the company. "No one," as Walter Goodman recounts, "argued that Wilson's attitudes toward life and toward General Motors would be transformed by [the] mere transfer of stock" that the Senate had required of him, and yet "not even Mr. Wilson's severest critics suggested that had he kept the stock, he would have been tempted to flood his old company with Defense Department contracts."[14] In 1953, in other words, senators were willing to accept that a required divestiture of the secretary-designate's objective pecuniary interests would suffice to resolve any problems posed by his deeper "attitudes," because it was additionally felt—on the basis of a considered assessment of Wilson's particular subjective mental states and habits—that his attitudes would have had no encumbering effect on his judgment while in office.

But for John Tower, things took a very different turn. Notwithstanding that at the time of his unsuccessful confirmation hearings, Tower had already severed all objective pecuniary relationships with defense contractors, senators nevertheless feared that he still harbored favorable attitudes toward them. Further, senators refused to use their personal knowledge of Tower to come to an individualized determination as to whether such attitudes were, in fact, likely to render *his* particular judgment conflicted. Instead, senators concluded that their mere objective presence sufficed to place his mental state in question.

The many consequences of these "two ships passing"—of conflict heading in an objective and interest in a subjective direction—form the book's central theme. I elaborate on it and several additional sub-themes throughout the volume, which is divided into four parts. Part I, "Conflict," explores the implications of our objective approach to conflict. I focus here very much on legal issues, on the nitty-gritty of conflict-of-interest law. My goal is to expose the normative impulses that underlie our efforts to regulate the various categories of conflict—often, they are in competition with one another—and critically trace their ultimate resolution in the kinds of legal principles that govern in American conflict-of-interest regimes. In Part I, in other words, I operate as much in an anthropological as in a philosophical mode, in which—so it often seemed to me as I was writing Part I—I assume the role of an interpreter of a vast and frequently esoteric culture, searching for some rhyme and reason that I can communicate to the outside world.

Part I begins with a discussion of the perils and paradoxes of prophylactic law and then offers a taxonomy of several distinct situations in which we deem officials to be in conflict—situations which are often confused or conflated. My purpose is to distinguish them but also to place them in a coherent relationship with one another—a topography—and to explore their differing legal and ethical complexities. Principal among them are "self-dealing"—where an official has the straightforward capacity to affect her own interests—and bribery/*quid pro quo*—where the official has the capacity to affect the interests of a private party who gives her something of value, hence becoming beholden to perform an official act by way of recompense.

But beyond these two relatively better-known conflict categories are several others, some of which have only recently come to the fore. For example, I examine our increasing preoccupation with what is often called "abuse of office." Here, an official—although taking something of value from a private party whose interests he can affect in office—nevertheless provides full *private-market* services in consideration. His doing so, the official will argue, ought to quell any fear that he will feel beholden to perform a favorable *official act* in return. Consider the case of Congressman Mario Biaggi, who had the official capacity to favorably affect the interests of Wedtech Corporation but who claimed not to be under its hold because—in return for payments he received from the company—his law firm rendered the company full-value legal services. What Biaggi and others in similar situations have done disturbs us, but it is not so easy to say why.

I also examine the converse set of circumstances—what might be called "private payment for public acts"—where an officeholder receives payment from a private party which he fails to recompense with private-market services, but whose interests he has *no* official capacity to affect. This situation crops up when officeholders—often part-time, without–compensation, or private-public executive exchange officials—get their public salaries underwritten by private companies, albeit companies whose fortunes they have no official capacity to affect one way or the other. The problem, if there is one, is that these private entities might, by usurping Congress's monopoly in controlling government's pursestrings, subtly shape the policy agenda—even if in ways that don't directly serve their interests.

Or, to take another example, consider our ballooning debate over "private gain from public office." Private gain from public office can provoke normative concern even where officials are incapable of affecting the interests of the paying private party *and* provide full private market consideration for whatever payment they receive. Think of the former secretary of state who receives a lucrative contract from a publisher—an entity whose interests he could not have affected through his foreign-policy role—to write his memoirs, hence offering full private-market value in return for the publisher's payment. The secretary may nonetheless court criticism for using the experiences and stature of his public role to profit privately. But, again, isolating what's wrong with his doing so is trickier than it might seem.

All of these and other conflict situations raise legal, moral, and political perplexities which I scrutinize. Then the final sections of Part I turn to postemployment "revolving-door" conflicts affecting not current but former officials, in which debates over the meaning of influence, ingratiation, disloyalty, and profiteering abound. Such disputes have grown exceedingly complex of late, as a whole new cast of characters who abide in the revolving door between public and private life have emerged to configure them in new ways: government consultants, presidential transition-team members, special kinds of defense procurement officials, and former officeholders who lobby for foreign interests, to name just a few. Again, my aim in each case is to look at the controlling legal regime and search for principles that account for its particular size and shape.

Part II, "Interest," turns to the consequences of our increasingly subjective approach to interest, where we virulently debate whether a host of psychological commitments, predispositions, and ideologies might not be just as encumbering of official judgment as pecuniary holdings are. Of course, we cannnot expect officeholders to divest themselves of all such commitments and predispositions. Nor do we always view them as encumbrances on judgment. Often, in fact, such beliefs and commitments seem to us to constitute the very faculty of official judgment, precisely the type of mental apparatus we do expect officeholders to bring to bear in making their decisions. To Hubert Humphrey's invitation that he place his philosophy in escrow, Earl Butz demurred. For Butz, it would have been eminently appropriate for him to make judgments in office on the grounds that they served his convictions and beliefs (although certainly not his pecuniary interests).

Part II begins by examining this pervasive debate, focusing on the accusations of hypocrisy and protestations of sincerity that fly fast and thick in American public discourse. It is in such exchanges, more than anywhere else, that officials and citizens debate the principles on which we should parse self-serving from genuinely considered political judgments and utterances. The book then turns to America's ongoing struggle over the "character" issue. When it comes right down to it, I argue, our disputes over the personal behavior of officials often disguise a deeper disagreement over whether the pursuit of office is better understood as a selfish, vainglorious thing—much like an encumbering pecuniary interest—or, alternatively, as a means of realizing one's most genuinely felt convictions concerning the public good.

All of these various putative impairments on judgment—predispositions, commitments, beliefs, ideologies, prejudgments, animuses, and the pursuit of office—fall into the class of internally generated as opposed to externally imposed. They act from *within* the official. But another set of encumbrances, which is examined in the second half of Part II, are externally imposed, imposed by others who act *on* the official: salary-earning spouses, agenda-harboring official colleagues, and interest-bearing businesspeople, lobbyists, and groups. Here a different set of issues emerges, having to do with the nature of marital attachment, the concerns we should have when officials engage in *ex parte* contacts with colleagues or agencies harbor conflicting prosecutorial and judging functions, and—most prominently—the kinds of *quid pro quo* relationships that so dominate public debate but elude legal regulation.

Finally in Part II, after having explored whether various beliefs, prejudgments, animuses, relationships, contacts, or engagements impair official judgment, the book returns to the notion of pecuniary interest and asks whether it remains encumbering for officials whose roles require them not to judge but to advocate. Here I hold the "interest" constant—it remains in the realm of the pecuniary—but I vary the official role, from decisional to representational, and I explore the perennial claim that legislators who share financial interests with constituents—oil-baron senators from Oklahoma, say—are better able to advocate for their electors in an effective, empathetic way (even if they are perhaps less able to judge the national interest in a detached, impartial way). Part II concludes with an examination of the debate over whether some pecuniary interests can grow so minimal or trivial that they cease to pose a conflict at all, and if so, how we should draw the line.

If the kinds of conflict that engross us have moved beyond straightforward bribery and even self-dealing, if the kinds of interests or encumbrances that now exercise us far outstrip the pecuniary and the financial, then it should not be surprising that—on top of all of this—we are agitated not only by realities but appearances. Part III, "Appearances," analyzes the mushrooming debate over the appearance of conflict of interest, that is, the question of whether we should penalize officials for improper appearances even assuming they are not, actually, in any *real* conflict of interest. Those who object to the appearance standard maintain that it violates two legal norms. First, they say, it involves an element of *factual prejudgment*. To apply the appearance standard is to penalize an officeholder in advance of—indeed, regardless of—any legal determination as to whether she committed an actual impropriety, and certainly in advance of any full consideration of the (often mitigating) facts and realities of the situation. And in the second place, the appearance standard is said to involve a significant element of *legal retroactivity*. By definition appearance violations consist of situations other than those captured by any established ethics law. Otherwise they would be *real* violations. Consequently, the substance of what the standard prohibits can be known only after the situation has arisen, depending as it does on whether an unacceptable "appearance" has registered in the mind of the public.

Fundamental norms of legal justice, however, require that an individual be punished only *after the fact*, that is, after the actuality of a real crime has been established. And legal norms also hold that the substance of an offense be defined *before the fact* so that an individual will know in advance whether a particular situation is prohibited by law. "The principle of legality," as Judith N. Shklar has written, holds "that there shall be no punishment without crime . . . and no crime without law"—a bipartite precept which the appearance standard, so its critics argue, violates.[15] But the appearance standard has its enthusiastic defenders too. However *legalistically* transgressive the appearance standard may be, they argue, penalizing officials for appearance violations serves an overriding *political* purpose: the preservation of public confidence in government.

Part IV turns to debate over the four principal remedies for conflict of interest—and "debate" is precisely the right word. For in several cross-cutting ways, the four compete with—even contradict—one another, each tapping into its own legal-political tradition. Up until the middle of the 1960s, two of the four were more prominent: recusal (which aims to remove the interested officeholder from any conflicting official roles) and divestiture-blind trust (which aims to remove any conflicting interests from the in-role officeholder). Both remedies have roots in legal practice broadly construed—recusal in the practice of the judiciary, divestiture in the concept of the fiduciary. The late 1960s, however, saw the ascendancy of two rather more "political" remedies for conflict of interest: balance of interests and public disclosure.

In a sense—and Part IV explores this—each of the two more venerable legal remedies, recusal and divestiture-blind trust, finds itself inverted by one or the other of the two more recent political remedies, balance and public disclosure. Balance of interests rests on the principle that strongly interested officeholders are precisely what we may want in certain collective decision-making situations, because—provided the interests they represent are diverse and appropriately counterpoised—interest will counter interest, issuing forth in the public good: conflicts of interest as remedy for conflict of interest. As such, balance is a relatively more suitable remedy for officials exercising quasi-legislative policy-making functions, whereas its reliance on pluralistic interest clashes would be inapt for the bench or other quasi-judicial processes. Recusal, conversely, *is* a relatively appropriate remedy for officeholders performing quasi-judicial functions, since in most cases one judge can easily replace another. But it remains ill-suited for those executing quasi-legislative responsibilities. As the legal scholar Peter Strauss puts it, recusal "may, by changing [a] commission's balance, disturb an intended and legitimate political judgment of the President and the Senate."[16]

As for divestiture/blind trust, it makes an official's interests as irrelevant or invisible to the official herself as they are to the public. In so doing, it runs directly athwart public-disclosure's governing principle, on which the official's interests should be made as visible and apparent to the public as they are to the official herself. While divestiture/blind trust has roots in fiduciary or trustee understandings of public office, disclosure has obvious affinities with contrary "delegate" or "agency" conceptions, on which citizens are deemed competent to judge not just the decisions but the motives of officeholders. Thus it is that variants of political concepts such as pluralism (in the case of balance) and accountability (in the case of disclosure) have intruded on the remedial domain once occupied exclusively by derivations from the law—the judiciary in the case of recusal, the fiduciary in the case of divestiture/blind trust. Part IV devotes the bulk of our attention to the two remedies of more recent vintage, balance and disclosure, and to the broad political issues of representation and privacy they provoke.

Conflict of Interest in American Public Life is not a narrative or historical but rather a critical and analytical work, one that explores the last fifty years of debate over encumbered official judgment in America, its causes and its implications. And it is very much *public* discourse I examine. Although my analysis is informed by over fifty interviews I conducted with congressional ethics staff, departmental and agency ethics officials, former White House Counsel, Office of Government Ethics (OGE) personnel, and others, everything I cite is on the public record: congressional hearings, investigations, and reports; executive-branch letters, advisory opinions, and interpretations; bar association opinions; case law; independent reports and studies; and academic and journalistic commentary.

I concentrate throughout on conflict of interest at the federal level in the two political branches, drawing distinctions between the issues confronting presidential appointees and career officials, and between executive and legislative officeholders wherever they diverge—as they do, for example, in debates over undue influence, private gain from public office, and various kinds of remedies. Often, for purposes of contrast, I discuss related issues as they emerge in the judicial branch. I emphasize, though, that wherever officials have some kind of discretion, some kind of capacity to exercise independent judgment, the issues and arguments are generally similar regardless of branch, function (quasi-legislative versus quasi-judicial) or rank. They transmute only as an official's level descends to the point where she exercises rote "ministerial" responsibilities that wholly constrain her use of discretion, or where her responsibilities move heavily toward the judicial, where—unlike most executive or legislative policy decisions, in which competing versions of the public interest clash—there may exist some independently right result (for example, actual guilt or innocence) against which to measure her use of discretion.[17] Where useful for comparison or illumination, I also draw on relevant state-, municipal-, and foreign-governmental material, and on issues of conflict of interest as they arise in other professions, particularly law, medicine, and business. And I focus throughout on America's manifold and intertwined debates over the meaning of impaired official judgment—which, after all, is conflict of interest's central question—and only peripherally on issues, important in their own right but handled well elsewhere, of ethics education, investigation, and enforcement. This book is about impairment, not impeachment.

In fact, if one is going to write a critical or analytical work on conflict of interest, there is a sense in which the product necessarily will *not* be particularly narrative or historical in its approach. Notwithstanding the evolution in our understanding of conflict from subjective to objective, and in our understanding of interest from objective to subjective, public discourse over conflict of interest has changed very little in the last fifty years. While it is true that many of the situations that now dominate our concerns—conflicts that sweep beyond bribery/*quid pro quo* and self-dealing, interests that far outstrip the pecuniary—loom larger than they once did, they were never wholly absent, and the same sorts of arguments were made about them fifty years ago as today. In what follows, I range freely over cases drawn from the last many decades, noting differences in context where necessary, but focusing on arguments that plainly have not changed and debates that clearly have not resolved themselves in half a century.

The fact that these debates have failed to resolve themselves over decades suggests that they are inveterate in democratic discourse—perhaps even timeless—but certainly not amenable to closure any time soon. This is not to deny that concerning at least some of the issues I discuss here, we have available some pertinent empirical evidence that bears on the matter. But any such data faces three potential blockages whenever it seeks to enter the bloodstream of public debate over conflict of interest, dominated as it is by legal, political, and moral modes of argument.

First, social-science findings—whether they consist of sociological analyses of lobbying networks or psychological inquiries into biased judgment—rarely rise to a level where they can be incorporated into *legal* argumentation. Because courts cannot cognize most such facts, their bearing on legal briefs and decisions in the realm of conflict of interest has been minimal. *Political* argumentation, for its part, tends to use what facts there are for its own combative purposes. Where the issues are deeply contested, as they are here, there are always "facts" available for all sides to marshal. Some will point to studies showing no connection between congressional votes and campaign contributions, others to scholarship that purports to demonstrate such a link, and the debate simply reproduces itself. As for *moral* argumentation, even where the fact of the matter is well established, the problems captured under the (in)famous "is-ought distinction" imply that often, no moral conclusion *necessarily* follows. Suppose we know that extensive lobbying networks do exist for ex-officials. Although that information bears on the question, it still cannot tell us whether such lobbying is *wrong*. Because legal argumentation is limited in its capacity for factual cognition, political argumentation in its capacity for factual consensus, and moral argumentation in its capacity for factual conclusoriness, empirical data—even where it exists—is unable finally to resolve many of the disagreements that make up debate over conflict of interest in American public life.

This ultimate imperviousness to empirical resolution, of course, does not stop politicians, journalists, and academics from taking strong normative stances within conflict of interest's many disputes. Books and essays appear continuously to either sharply attack the "appearance standard" or just as resolutely defend it, to denounce private gain from public office or to deny anything at all wrong with the practice, to insist that officeholders' private lives are crucially relevant to an assessment of their official conduct, or to scorn any such notion. In what follows, I have chosen for the most part not to take these kinds of cut-and-dried stands, and I owe the reader an explanation as to why not and a brief account as to what kind of book this is.

At this stage in conflict-of-interest discourse—in what is now an entrenched set of debates central to democratic politics—the benefits of yet another volume boosting this traditional side over that one may be limited. Indeed, contemporary books, articles, or speeches that do take one or another venerable stance in conflict of interest's many disputes invariably get criticized for "round[ing] up the usual suspects," providing analyses that are "hardly news," or offering prescriptions that are "somewhat one-sided."[18]

Consequently, I have tried to step back from partisan positions and instead elucidate and then critically analyze the structure of debate as a whole, explaining its intractability and situating it within American democratic theory and practice. In doing so, I draw distinctions between legal and moral concepts that are frequently blurred, show where two opposing arguments share a common assumption or where well-known positions rest on incompatible premises, juxtapose strands of debate that are typically segregated but in fact are mutually relevant, and probe the jurisprudential, ethical, and political-philosophical underpinnings of different longstanding claims. Although I didn't deliberately set out to provide what Ronald Dworkin calls "constructive interpretation"—someone "interpreting a social practice, according to that view, proposes value for the practice by describing some scheme of interests or goals or principles the practice can be taken to serve or express or exemplify"—in fact, this is largely what I have done.[19] I have tried to find principles that render intelligible a mass of often vexatiously confusing practices and debates, which isn't to say for a moment that those principles themselves are beyond criticism. Indeed, I often criticize them.

It is noteworthy that towering above many of the books and articles authored on the topic over the last forty years are two landmark works—Roswell Perkins's *Conflict of Interest and Federal Service* (1960) and Bayless Manning's *Federal Conflict of Interest Law* (1964)—which even today get cited more often than any other. Both books have survived precisely because, as Manning explicitly noted, neither took predictable stands.[20] Rather, they painted luminous, yet close-to-the-ground portraits of discourse, portraits that made coherent a vast morass of regulatory and policy debate and situated it within broader themes in American law and politics. I should emphasize that while Perkins and Manning, both legal scholars, concentrated on legal issues, my book adopts a legal-, moral-, and political-philosophical approach, by turns, where appropriate. For example, Part I is primarily devoted to legal issues—attempting a "rational reconstruction of the law [to] reveal the implicit logic of the legal categories behind the necessary flux of judicial practice"[21]—while Parts II and III examine preponderantly moral and political questions. But as did Perkins and Manning, in looking at any given debate I either delineate the differing circumstances in which each of the competing positions finds itself resting on the strongest ground, or else show how all are misconceived. Rarely do I totally uphold one over the rest. Given that the arguments I analyze rest on ultimately contestable legal, moral, and political premises, such an approach seems best suited to the topic. As A. B. Atkinson notes, it can often prove more fruitful when our concern lies with "'the grammar of arguments about policy,' not with the advocacy of policies themselves."[22]

My approach, then, compels me to resist taking one or another position along the horizontal axes (so to speak) of the debates I examine, while on the vertical axis I stay much closer to the ground of discourse—to the multiple and sprawling problems of practice as politicians, journalists, and citizens conceive them—than to the realm of high theory. In recent years, scholars interested in the philosophical analysis of policy issues have explored and then announced their preference for the kind of method I adopt here. Michael Walzer, for example, defends a style of social criticism that resists imposing a "moral yardstick" on discourse. Instead, Walzer contends, it can be far more fruitful to operate in "an interpretive mode," one that "struggles to find meaning in the 'text' of public discourse," in "the way in which people explain and justify what they do, the stories they tell," knowing that "any given interpretation will be contentious" and will not necessarily bring "definitive closure" to the debate.[23]

I emphasize, though, that a book written in this tradition—one that stays close to the ground of public discourse—need by no means totally forswear the use of political, legal, and moral theory. Thus at various points I include discussions not only of political and legal liberalism, but also of theoretical perspectives on hypocrisy and sincerity, representation, pluralism, *mens rea* and strict liability, the law of contract, official fiduciary responsibility, civic virtue, political trials, privacy, neutrality, and more. But although I make use of such theory throughout, my doing so is guided solely by the need to illuminate whatever practical conundrum is at hand; I try to position myself, on the vertical axis, closer to the ground of the concrete than the heights of the abstract.

Equally, a book that—on the horizontal axis—takes few traditional positions in the debates it analyzes need not be bereft of a central theme, a prescriptive aim, or a critical edge. *Conflict of Interest in American Public Life* does indeed have a central theme, the consequences of which it explores in detail: Conflict has migrated from a subjective, internal approach to an objective, prophylactic one, just as interest has moved from an objective, pecuniary understanding to a subjective ideological one. This is a theme, however, that concerns the structure of debate itself, not one that advances a favored position within it. In the conclusion, the book also makes prescriptive recommendations. But, again, they are recommendations about how we should rhetorically conduct a debate that I believe will never end, not how we might ameliorate or even resolve it with a particular policy fix. And throughout the book, I do make normative judgments. Again, though, they are judgments about the structure of particular disputes, judgments that implicate both sides rather than vindicate one over the other.

There is a final reason why debate eludes closure—why conflict-of-interest discourse is so irascible and intractable—apart from its recalcitrance to empirical findings. One can best understand what really drives and envenoms conflict-of-interest discourse, and why its legal, political, and moral perplexities are so tenacious, by coming at it from an angle at which it is not often viewed, one that places it alongside three other major American policy debates.

Consider that American public discourse divides itself into three great streams, one centering on foreign-policy issues, a second on constitutional matters, and a third on domestic questions. In debate over foreign policy, moral and political considerations traditionally struggle for primacy, while legal considerations—because the status of international law remains controversial at best—have always played a smaller supporting role. In the constitutional arena, Americans are heir to a tradition in which legal and moral arguments contend, but in which considerations that are essentially political—what does the majority want? how can we best compromise the competing interests at hand?—are at the very least muted and disguised, if not totally absent. And in discourse over central domestic policy issues, where we devise laws to respond to conflicting political demands—from welfare to education to abortion—the language of law and politics predominates, while controversial moral argumentation (how should people lead their personal lives? what is the content of "virtue," "vice," and "the good"?) often assumes a more ambiguous, perhaps even a suspect, role. As Amy Gutmann and Dennis Thompson note, we "preclude fundamental moral conflict" in domestic politics "by denying certain reasons moral standing in the policy-making process."[24]

For many reasons, American public debate has evolved so that in each of these major streams of discourse—foreign, constitutional, and domestic—at least one particular kind of normative consideration, whether legal, political, or moral, has always been *in some way* secondary to the other two. I do not mean to be wholly categorical about this. Antirealists in foreign policy, for example, would question whether legal arguments really do (or at any rate, should) occupy a secondary role in foreign-policy debate. Critical-legal scholars, among others, doubt whether certain types of political considerations really are debarred from constitutional discourse, and even whether they should be. And communitarians of various stripe dispute whether fundamental moral concerns can, in fact, be so easily abstracted out of domestic debate.

Without in any way dismissing the merits of their various positions, I would suggest that simply to name these groups is to underscore the fact that they occupy a distinctly minoritarian position within American public debate. Their very existence as critics testifies to the continuing dominance of a certain kind of liberalism in American public deliberation, a liberalism which—in order to function—requires the tactful retreat of at least one of the three normative approaches in any given question of major controversy. Pause to reflect, for example, on how much more overwrought our foreign-policy debates would be if legal considerations had to be fully factored in, how much more divisive our constitutional wrangles would be if political considerations also demanded a full reckoning, how much more fractious our domestic-policy disagreements would be if full-blown moralistic arguments held an equal place at the table.

Perhaps there is an embodied wisdom here. At least, so one might conclude from the experience of what is now emerging as a fourth major realm of American public discourse, debate over the ethics of officials—and conflict of interest in particular. For in debate over official ethics, and indeed *only* in debate over official ethics, do legal, political, and moral considerations come together as unbridled equals, no one of them taking any kind of an institutionalized "back seat" to the other two. Not only are legal considerations central in the resolution of government-ethics issues, but the federal conflict-of-interest laws themselves are among the very few criminal statutes that come with attendant regulations (hundreds of pages of them). Not only are political considerations often pivotal, but it is deemed appropriate to legally and morally penalize officials for mishandling political optics as well as political realities, for allowing questionable appearances to arise, and for neglecting to consider "how things look." Not only are moral considerations crucial in the realm of government ethics, but they routinely and legitimately embrace the most excruciating inquiries into officials' virtue, character, and personal morality of a sort we hesitate to import into other areas of public discussion.

After establishing this proposition in many ways throughout, I return to it in the book's conclusion. There, I argue that if we are to lower the temperature of debate over the ethics of officials—to narrow the controversies if not achieve total closure—we must strategically leech out legal, moral, and political considerations, by turns, from various strands of our deliberation over conflict of interest, strands where one or another of them has become too dominant. Some conflict-of-interest situations best lend themselves to purely legal remedies unfreighted with moralistic condemnation and political assault. Others are essentially moral problems, defying both legalistic solutions through the judicial system *and* political redress through the electoral system. And still others, really, are political problems and should not be dealt with legally; nor do they even lend themselves, ultimately, to moralistic approval or disapproval. Drawing these distinctions—and making them stick— offers the best hope, I argue, of making our discourse over conflict of interest in public life less venomous for officials and more lucid for citizens.

I

CONFLICT

1

The Perils of
Prophylactic Law

In America, if a citizen believes that an official act exceeds legitimate bounds, he can ask a court to strike it down. Courts judge such cases, at least in principle, by referring to applicable constitutional, statutory, or regulatory standards governing the limits of official discretion. Wherever a governmental act does fall within the legitimate scope of official discretion, it is then left to citizens themselves to judge. Citizens fulfill this function, at least in principle, by referring to their own conceptions of the public interest. But that courts should have anything to say about official conduct that otherwise falls unquestionably within the bounds of constitutional, statutory, or regulatory discretion—much less that they should pass such judgments against the standards of criminal law—is a peculiar jurisprudential and political notion. And yet, just such a notion has come to configure much of American public life.[1]

Conflict-of-interest law, unique among American legal codes, requires courts and other (quasi-) judicial tribunals to pass judgment in a realm where we are more accustomed to thinking of the citizen as the ultimate arbiter: the realm of official acts that fall uncontroversially within the legitimate bounds of official discretion. The aim of conflict-of-interest law is to ensure that such discretion, such official judgment, is exercised in an unimpaired way. But in carrying out this task, courts face a couple of monumental challenges.

First, in any area where an official commands the constitutional, statutory, and regulatory freedom to act, courts are incapable of measuring the extent to which her decisions deviate from the true public interest, and then using that deviation as an indicator—a proxy—of the extent to which her judgment may have been impaired. Certainly, a court can take notice that a trade official holds a private interest in a domestic timber mill. But how is a court to know whether it contravened the public interest when she recommended a tariff on imported lumber? Likewise, a court can take notice that a senator possesses private oil interests. But how is it to determine whether her vote to increase the oil-depletion allowance abrogated the public interest? And if it cannot, how can it use the senator's ultimate conduct to say whether her antecedent judgment was distorted? Once we are operating within the constitutionally, statutorily, and regulatorily vouchsafed realm of official discretion—where officials legitimately make law, policy, and rules—there exists no prior standard of the public interest to which courts can refer when judging official conduct. Indeed, the question, "where lies the public interest?" is precisely what remains to be worked out in the act of law-, policy-, or rule-making at hand.

Of course, while a court cannot normatively assess a particular tariff or subsidy, it can normatively censure an official who took into account her own private lumber or oil holdings when deciding a tariff or subsidy issue—regardless of whether, by some standard of the public interest inaccessible to the court, she ultimately made a good or a bad decision.[2] Or, as a law review article put the point over three decades ago, "if the courts are judging [official] ethical conduct," then "intention and motives rather than the external act should be the basic consideration," for "the acts themselves fall into a [normative] grey area."[3]

Here, though, a second problem crops up. True, skewed intentions and biasing motives are normatively objectionable. But they lie beyond the realm of factual determination. No court could cognize such tainted mental states with sufficient precision such that—even though they may rise to the level of *mala in se*, wrongs in themselves—they could realistically constitute the *actus reus* itself of a legal offense. Of course, intentions and motives that constitute the "*mens rea* vis a vis [an] *actus reus*"—the intentions or motives with which an individual commits some other, cognizable act such as killing or stealing—*are* presumed accessible to courts.[4] But in conflict-of-interest law, the problem, to quote Blackstone, is that since "no temporal tribunal can . . . fathom the intentions of the mind otherwise than as they are demonstrated by outward actions, it cannot punish for what it cannot know."[5] If the conflict-of-interest laws attempted to govern officials' states of mind directly—if they literally prohibited officials from "taking notice" of their own interests in official transactions, becoming "beholden" to those bestowing gifts or payments, exercising "undue influence" in a private capacity on official colleagues, or using their office to "ingratiate themselves" with prospective private employers—the laws would be vague and unenforceable. Certainly, "taking notice," "feeling beholden," "exerting or experiencing influence," and "ingratiating oneself" all directly describe the "evils" to be guarded against. All of them constitute *mala in se*, things that are bad in themselves. But they are also all terms of highly contestable legal meaning having to do with mental dispositions, and liberal legalism cannot countenance the direct regulation of states-of-mind.[6] Such impaired mental states are normatively troubling—that is why they can be deemed *mala in se*, wrongs in themselves—but they are insufficiently factually accessible to constitute the object of regulation and sanction. Hence they too lie beyond the reach of the law.

We have, though, already seen that official acts posterior to the *malum in se* mental states—the "ultimate conduct" to which those mental states give rise—are also unregulable. A court may take factual notice of such external acts, of the imposition of a tariff or the introduction of a subsidy, but it is incapable of according them normative appraisal. And it can normatively condemn an official whose judgment was impaired by her sawmill-holdings or encumbered by her oil stocks, but it cannot factually cognize such inner impairments or encumbrances for the purposes of penalizing them. Hence, in identifying the regulable offense, conflict-of-interest law is forced to take yet a further step backward, from the *mala in se* states-of-mind themselves to a set of acts *anterior* to those states of mind. Conflict-of-interest law ultimately does, then, focus on external acts, but on those acts that give rise *to* encumbered states of mind, not the ultimate acts which flow from them.

So: Because we cannot prevent officials from mentally taking notice of their own interests, we prohibit the act of holding certain kinds of interests in the first place. Because we cannot prohibit officials from becoming mentally beholden to those who give them gifts, we prohibit the very act of receiving gifts under certain kinds of circumstances. Because we cannot prevent officials from being mentally influenced or ingratiating, we forbid them the acts of contacting official colleagues (former or current) or private employers (prospective and previous) in particular situations. The conflict-of-interest laws are thus, by and large, prophylactic in nature.[7] They prohibit officials from taking certain factually cognizable but normatively innocuous actions—*mala prohibita* that are not in themselves wrong, such as holding certain interests or contacting particular individuals—because those actions might lead to normatively troubling but factually incognizable encumbered states of mind, the *mala in se*.[8] When in the midst of a 1986 ethics-law hearing, Senator Joseph Biden declared, "I just wish we could pass a law . . . mandat[ing] good judgment," he was expressing the regret he felt, as a lawmaker, on being compelled to push the law back from the true *malum in se*, impaired judgment, to regulate a host of acts not wrong in themselves.[9]

Conflict-of-interest law thus does two things: It takes the official's tainted mental state, and not whatever ultimate official conduct that mental state occasions, as the *malum in se,* the actual harm to be prevented. And it takes the personal conduct that occasions officials' tainted mental states—particular interest-holdings, personal interactions, and so forth—and not those states-of-mind themselves, as the object of regulation, the *malum prohibitum.* Most laws require the *malum in se* to center on ultimate acts, not states-of-mind. And most laws equate the *malum prohibitum* with the *malum in se.* But here, the absence of a conception of the public interest against which to judge officials' ultimate acts pushes the *malum in se* back to the underlying state-of-mind. And the impossibility of punishing mental states directly pushes the *malum prohibitum* back to a point where it covers acts antecedent to those states-of-mind.[10]

Neither characteristic of conflict-of-interest law abides without controversy. Some critics of the law, to begin with, seek to move the *malum prohibitum* forward from antecedent conduct—the mere possession of interests, gifts, or contacts—so that the regulation centers directly on *malum in se* states-of-mind, on the mental partiality, the beholdenness, and the encumbering inner influences such antecedent conduct can create.[11] Even the American Civil Liberties Union (ACLU) has endorsed this effort. Rules that directly prohibit an official from being partial to her own interests or unduly influenced by the importunings of her former colleagues, however vague and therefore potentially "chilling" they may be, would at least be tailored to the *malum in se* state-of-mind, the real evil to be expunged. Such rules would not rise to the level of prior restraint, as prophylactic law does by prohibiting the mere holding of certain interests or the making of certain contacts.[12] The ACLU, at least in some situations, prefers vague rules that focus on tainted states-of-mind *in se*—and all the better if such rules are simply hortatory and nonenforceable—to clear law that punishes conduct *per se*.

Among critics of conflict-of-interest law there are also those who take the next step. According to them, we should not simply move the *malum prohibitum* up from the antecedent acts so that it more directly overlays *malum in se* states-of-mind. We should reframe our understanding of the *malum in se* itself, recognizing that the evil to be expunged is not a partial or encumbered state-of-mind that may never be given effect but is only any such ultimate act—a bad official decision or harmful official conduct—those states-of-mind actually happen to cause. Bayless Manning, observing that "it is not conflicts of interest as such that we are trying to prevent, but rather those acts that we fear a man is likely to do if he has a conflict of interest," himself expresses a preference for keeping the focus on those actual ultimate deeds, not the precipitating mental states.[13] Others, along identical lines, urge that conflict-of-interest law confine itself only to actual "behavior which deviates from the normal duties of a public role because of private-regarding . . . pecuniary status or gains,"[14] or to "official conduct" that in the event "conflicts . . . with . . . cognizable public interests."[15] The American Bar Association (ABA), in this vein, prohibits a lawyer "who holds public office [from using] his position to obtain . . . special advantage in legislative matters for himself or for a client under circumstances *where . . . such action is not in the public interest*."[16] The vocabulary is telling, betraying not only a focus on ultimate "acts," "behavior," and "conduct," but an assumption that we can assess such conduct against a "cognizable," relatively uncontested conception of the "public interest," or of what it means for an official to fulfill the "normal duties" of her "public role." If such ultimate conduct or behavior runs afoul of the public interest, then we may assume that it was diverted by the official's private interest. But the mere presence of a private interest, and a state-of-mind impaired by cognizance of it, ought not attract our regulatory concern. On this view, it is the ultimate conduct, not the precipitating state of mind, that ought to constitute the *malum in se*.[17]

Both criticisms—the one that would push the *malum prohibitum* forward from antecedent acts to consequent states-of-mind, and the one that would push the *malum in se* forward from states-of-mind to ultimate conduct—have failed to win through. They remain, however, prominent in discourse. Those who, like the ACLU, would keep the *malum prohibitum* focused on states-of-mind—and not the antecedent conduct that occasions them—show a marked tolerance for the vagueness most such injunctions would display. Those who—like the ABA—would keep the *malum in se* focused on ultimate official conduct, and not the underlying states-of-mind that occasion it, show a notable indifference to the unavailability of uncontroversial standards of the public interest against which to measure that conduct. Neither assumption has shown itself sufficiently tenable to bear the burden of the legal structure. Conflict-of-interest law has moved the offense inexorably and definitively toward before-the-fact conduct, toward the realm of the prophylactic.

Appearances and Temptation

One point of clarification: Many claim that the law's prophylactic character is meant to prevent even the *appearance* of a conflict of interest. If the chief federal banking regulator takes out a loan from a federally regulated bank, on this argument, the problem is that he might appear to be judgmentally impaired when it comes to that bank, even if he really isn't.[18] This notion is mistaken.

Part III discusses the "appearance standard" in much greater detail, but consider here the case of Comptroller of the Currency Robert Clarke. In 1991, Clarke was reprimanded for allowing "the appearance" of a conflict of interest to arise because, among other things, he had been taking out loans from *state*-chartered banks. As a *federal* banking regulator, Clarke actually had no capacity to favorably affect the interests of the state banks in question, so he was in no real conflict of interest. But to the public—whom the Treasury Department general counsel doubted would make fine distinctions between federally and state-chartered banks—it might have *appeared* as if he was in a conflict of interest.[19]

In sanctioning Clarke for the appearance of a conflict of interest, the general counsel in effect penalized a mere partial *malum prohibitum*—a federal banking regulator with a bank loan of *some sort*—on the grounds that the appearance of a full *malum prohibitum,* a federal banking official with a *federal* bank loan, might nevertheless have materialized in the public mind. This is a far cry from what the "real" conflict-of-interest laws themselves are meant to accomplish. They penalize only full *mala prohibita*—a federal banking official with a federal bank loan—on the grounds that a *malum in se,* a real encumbrance, might otherwise arise in the official's mind.

Let me develop this a little further. While it is possible to understand the laws prohibiting real conflict of interest as an effort to inhibit *temptation,* it would be impossible to so construe the laws prohibiting the appearance of conflict of interest. It makes sense to prevent a federal banking regulator from taking out a loan from a federally chartered bank—as the real conflict-of-interest laws do—because he might be tempted to favor that bank in his official role and hence slip into an impaired mental state. It would make no sense to prevent a federal banking regulator from taking out a loan from a state-chartered bank—as the appearance standard might do—on the grounds that his doing so might someday tempt him to take out a loan from a federally chartered bank, let alone tempt him to favor that state-chartered bank in his official role as a federal bank regulator. The appearance standard, in other words, is not a prophylactic law.

Take another example. Consider the case of a federal agency official who, after having been observed flying first-class by an agency client, gets reprimanded for appearing as if he might have been using government funds for first-class travel. In fact, he was on a personal trip for which he was paying personally. Whatever one thinks of the justice of such a penalty, it would be even less tenable—hence even more unjust—to say that his flying first-class personally might have tempted the official to fly first-class with government monies and should therefore be prophylactically prohibited. While it is reasonable to describe the conflict-of-interest law itself as a prophylactic—as an attempt to prevent temptation—it would be implausible to so describe the appearance standard.

By the same token, while it is obviously possible to explain the appearance standard as an effort to prevent disturbing appearances, it is inapt to so describe the prophylactic conflict-of-interest laws. Appearances are things that are corrigible, parasitical on the deeper reality they obscure. The more one knows of an appearance situation, the more the appearance itself disappears and the reality—whether a real impropriety or instead something completely innocent—emerges. In Clarke's case, for example, the more the public knew about his bank loan, the further the loan would have moved, in the public mind, from the category "possibly federal" toward "definitely state." The more, in other words, any appearance of impropriety would have dissolved into the reality of propriety.[20]

But now assume that Clarke, while occupying a federal banking role, held a *federal* bank loan—the situation prohibited by the laws against an actual conflict of interest. We could not have known any more than that. Any consequent impaired mental state would have remained permanently hidden, beyond the realm of cognizable reality, let alone corrigible appearances. Hence to speak of such a role/interest combination—federal banking regulator plus federally chartered bank loan—as the *appearance* of some deeper mental impairment is, at least in one sense, inapt. For this kind of appearance is one that will never give way to a reality; it already goes to the very limits of what we can know. Any such external "appearance" is incorrigible and the inner "reality," whether impairment or nonimpairment, is beyond our ever finally discovering. In metaphysics that might work. But in politics, appearances are corrigible, realities cognizable. The prophylactic ethics laws, going as they do to the limits of whatever we can know, prohibit what for our purposes are real, not apparent, conflicts of interest.[21]

To sum up: *Appearance* is a term that characterizes the relationship between one set of external facts and another set of external facts. A federal bank regulator with a state bank loan might *look* like a federal bank regulator with a federal bank loan, but he will not be tempted to become one. *Temptation*, by contrast, is a term that applies to the relationship between one set of external facts and an inner mental state. A federal bank regulator with a federal bank loan might be tempted to favor the bank, and thus his judgment might become clouded. But such a set of external facts—federal bank regulator with federal bank loan—constitutes the total knowable reality, not the further corrigible appearance, of a conflict of interest. Appearances are outer, while temptation works inwardly. The prophylactic conflict-of-interest laws are meant to deal with inner temptation and the appearance standard, with outward appearances.

Prophylaxis, Intent, and Strict Liability

When it comes to defining the kind of offense that conflict-of-interest law could conceivably regulate, the spectrum of possibilities ranges from ultimate conduct to the underlying states-of-mind that may occasion it, and from those states-of-mind to the prior conduct that may precipitate them. On this spectrum, for reasons set forth, conflict-of-interest law pushes the offense toward the "prior conduct" end. But this is only half (indeed, the more famous half) of the story. For in addition to the question of where along the spectrum flowing from "ultimate conduct to states of mind to antecedent conduct" we should locate the acts that constitute the offense, there is also the question of where along the spectrum from "strict liability" to "general intent" to "specific intent" we should locate the *mens rea* of the offender. Some criminal laws impose strict liability on an offender.[22] Others require a general *mens rea*—a basic knowledge on the part of the offender that he was committing the acts that constitute the offense. And still others demand various forms of specific intent, a heightened awareness of particular facts or norms that go beyond the offender's mere consciousness that he was engaging in a certain kind of conduct.[23]

In the domain of conflict-of-interest, these two spectrums—the one concerning the acts that constitute the offense, the other concerning the *mens rea* of the offender—interact in a dynamic, in fact an ironic way. The dynamic is this: To the extent that conflict-of-interest law removes the offensive acts it regulates from beyond even shouting distance of the *malum in se* of encumbered judgment, moving them instead toward the prophylactic class of pure *mala prohibita* antecedent acts, pressure will build to move the *mens rea* required of the offender away from the strict-liability or even the general-intent end of the spectrum and toward some form of heightened knowledge or awareness.

This might seem paradoxical. Precisely because they are bereft of moral content, most prophylactic laws—such as those prohibiting speeding or the use of outdoor barbecues or other conduct not harmful in itself—impose strict liability on the offender. Since a violation of such laws bespeaks nothing about the moral character of the violator—since prophylactic speeding laws, say, are meant simply to promote public safety or preserve a certain kind of public order—we feel comfortable imposing strict liability on offenders. But the conflict-of-interest statutes are *criminal* prophylactic laws.[24] Here, the fact that the acts which compose the offense are devoid of moral content tacks in exactly the opposite direction. It requires, in many cases, that the *mens rea* of the offender go well beyond strict liability; indeed, beyond even mere general intent.

Consider: It has become a staple of conflict-of-interest discourse to criticize the ethics laws, and in particular their prophylactic quality, for requiring officials to comport themselves in ways that they could not possibly intuit with ordinary moral reason. Moral intuition will never lead a Food and Drug Administration (FDA) inspector to conclude that it is wrong for him to accept a sandwich, but not a cup of coffee, while touring a plant. But precisely for this reason, to hold an official liable as long as he was simply aware of eating a sandwich—without some additional knowledge of the elements of the offense—is troubling. "[U]nless the law accord[s] with justice and morality, one [cannot] hold all men to it . . . 'no authority, however great, will ever be able to persuade mankind, that penal laws ought to constitute a science merely of memory, and not of reason.'"[25] Perhaps it is fitting that the phrase *ethical lapse*—with its resonance of *memory lapse*—has become the term of choice for those explaining ethics-law violations.[26] Officials, of course, may labor under a greater onus than citizens to know the law in detail regardless of its "accordance with justice and morality," and the Office of Government Ethics is available to assist them in this task.[27] But, overwhelmingly, as the acts that constitute conflict-of-interest offenses have become more and more prophylactic, roaming ever farther away from the *malum in se*, it has *for that reason* become necessary to move the offender farther and farther away from strict liability, to show, in fact, that he had at least some heightened understanding of his conduct beyond the bare minimum, some specific intent beyond the general.[28]

Here, though, is the irony. Much of the point of shifting the "offense" to a class of prophylactic *mala prohibita* in the first place is to avoid the need, in the area of conflict-of-interest law, to inquire into officials' states-of-mind, states-of-mind which of course are the real loci for the *mala in se*. Yet the effect of then moving the category of "offender" away from those strictly liable, and toward only those who meet some kind of intent requirement, is simply to reimport vexing inquiries into officials' states-of-mind. The twist is that the states-of-mind reimported are not the ones from which the law initially recoiled. Hence, the difficulty of having to parse officials' states-of-mind reemerges, without the redeeming feature of our bringing the offense any closer to the *malum in se*.

Take, for example, the evolution of the federal postemployment laws, clustered in 18 U.S.C. §207. In the case of 18 U.S.C. §207(a)(2), which came into effect in 1962, the *malum in se* to be prevented is the possibility that an ex-official might make use of knowledge gained in office to now lobby her former colleagues. Of course, any such *malum in se*—any quantum of improperly used insider knowledge—would exist only in the mind of the ex-official. States of mind being near-impossible to establish, they remain directly regulable only through intolerably vague strictures. Hence 18 U.S.C. §207(a)(2) prophylactically makes it an offensive act for ex-officials to lobby on *any* matter that had been under their official responsibility, regardless of what their knowledge of it might have been. After all, it is easier to tell whether a matter came under an ex-officeholder's official responsibility than to say whether it entered her mind; although obviously, for officials in very high positions, the range of matters under their official responsibility will far exceed the set with which they may have had some personal acquaintance. With the 1989 amendments to 18 U.S.C. §207, however, the status of the offender's mental state moved from the realm of general intent—where it had lodged for decades—to embrace some specific knowledge, a mental state beyond basic mental competence. The statute now stipulates that in order to violate 18 U.S.C. §207(a)(2), it is not sufficient for an official simply to lobby on a matter that had been under her responsibility. She must also *know* that it had been under her responsibility. In other words, the prosecution must now prove that the official had a heightened knowledge or understanding of what she was doing, since otherwise the official would be strictly or generally liable for the commission of a legal offense totally removed from anything she might morally intuit.

Whether it is possible for an ex-official to have no knowledge *of* a particular matter that was under her responsibility—a possibility consistent with there being a prophylactic-style offense—while still knowing *that* the matter was under her official responsibility—as she now must for her to be an intending offender—is a nice question but a secondary one. The primary issue is this: What was precluded by moving the offense from *malum in se* to *malum prohibitum,* namely the need to probe the official's state-of-mind, is now re-introduced by moving the offender back from the domain of strict or basic criminal liability to a point where her specific knowledge is required. But it is a different state-of-mind: not the state-of-mind necessary for there to be an *in se* offense of using insider information (knowledge *of* the matter under her official responsibility), but the state-of-mind necessary for there to be an intending offender (knowledge *that* the matter was under her official responsibility). Such a maneuver brings the law no closer to the *malum in se,* while, as Common Cause has noted, making "enforcement . . . exceedingly difficult."[29]

In similar fashion, Congress in 1978 passed 18 U.S.C. §207(c), a prophylactic ban on any senior ex-official lobbying her former agency for one year after leaving office. At the time, the ban covered lobbying on any matter pending under the agency's jurisdiction during that postemployment year, regardless of whether it had concerned the agency at all during the ex-official's time in office, let alone whether it had fallen under her official responsibility, let alone whether she had gathered any first-hand knowledge of it. Here, the *malum in se* mental state to be "got at" is the distorted judgment the ex-official's *former colleagues* might develop, on an issue currently under their discretion, as a result of being importuned by an old superior. But the *malum prohibitum*—the behavior nearest the *malum in se* on which the law was capable of seizing as an offense—comprises any representations at all made by a senior ex-official on a pending matter to her former subordinates, regardless of whether such representations would distort (who could say for sure?) their judgmental processes.

The problem, however, is that such a *malum prohibitum*—mere representations *per se*—is itself morally innocuous. In many and perhaps most cases, it leads to no harm. Because the ex-official's ordinary moral intuitions could not necessarily be expected to alert her that such representations in-and-of-themselves would constitute the *actus reus* of an offense, the new statute eschewed not only strict liability but even general intent when it came to the *mens rea* of the offender. Instead, it required proof that the ex-official—in order for her to be deemed an offender—was aware that, during the time she was making her representations, the topic of her lobbying was indeed pending before, was of live interest to, her former agency and colleagues.

Hence, with 18 U.S.C. §207(c), an inquiry into the state-of-mind of the ex-official doing the influencing had become necessary in order to determine whether she was an offending actor. And it had become necessary precisely *because*, in defining the offensive act, the law sought to avoid an inquiry into the states-of-mind of the officials being influenced, which of course is the real issue. But there is no reason why the first sort of state-of-mind inquiry—into the mental states, the knowledge and awareness, of the ex-official doing the influencing—should be any less vexing than the second sort, into the mental pressures felt by the influenced officials. And, to boot, the first type of mental state has nothing directly to do with the *malum in se*. Hence, Lyn Nofziger, at one time a senior White House aide in the Reagan administration, was acquitted in 1989 of a charge under 18 U.S.C. §207(c). The prosecution was unable to prove that Nofziger knew the White House had a contemporaneous "direct and substantial interest" in the subject of his lobbying—one of the elements of the offense—and it was unable to do so precisely because states of mind are difficult to prove.[30]

Beyond Average Officials

The *Nofziger* case displays one further wrinkle. Grant that to attain the status of a conflict-of-interest offender, specific knowledge of certain elements of the offense—a heightened *mens rea*—is required. One might still have asked whether Nofziger himself actually knew of those elements; whether he knew, for example, that the matter was of concern to the White House—or, simply, whether an average or reasonable official in Nofziger's position would have so known. And if an average or reasonable official would have so known, then the court would convict. If not, it would acquit. But since it is possible that Nofziger himself might actually not have known of the White House's interest where an average or reasonable ex-official would have—perhaps for idiosyncratic personal reasons having to do with Nofziger's level of awareness, focus, or engagedness—the "average-reasonable official" standard is a higher one. Using it would produce more liable officials than would a standard that forces us to look at what the accused individual official, in all his inattention and ignorance, may or may not have actually known. Or, put another way, the criterion that requires an exploration into the individualized psychology of the particular ex-official accused, as opposed to holding her to the standard of an average or reasonable ex-official, is in practice a more lenient one. It occupies a point on the spectrum of *mens rea* that much further away from strict liability.[31]

And it is precisely toward this point that conflict-of-interest law has tended, by stipulating what is necessary to deem someone an offender. The *Nofziger* court set out to determine whether Nofziger *actually* knew, not whether an average or reasonable ex-official in Nofziger's situation would have known, of specific elements of the offense. Conflict-of-interest jurisprudence, in other words, not only forswears a strict-liability approach, on which it would be the commission of the act alone, and not the accused's mental state, that determines whether she is an offender. Given the need to determine the accused's mental state, it goes the distance and asks not simply whether an average or reasonable official would have had the requisite mental state, but whether the accused official actually had the requisite mental state. Even within the category of "mental states," where the concern is with the intent or knowledge of the offender, one could still settle on those either nearer or farther to the strictly liable. And the tendency, in conflict-of-interest law, has been to come to rest at a farther, considerably more lenient point.

But if we have taken a relatively lenient approach to determining the *mens rea* of the offender, a kind of reverse dynamic has operated when it comes to defining the acts that constitute a prophylactic conflict-of-interest offense. Over time, they have moved from the kinds of acts sufficient to substantially impair the judgment of the *average* official, to antecedent acts that might possibly impair the judgment of *anyone,* even the most susceptible officeholder. Although the prospect of a two-hundred-dollar capital gain might not affect the judgment of an average official, much less the judgment of the particular official in question, it nevertheless could affect the judgment of *some* official, and hence must in most regimes be disclosed if not divested.[32] Historically, the offense—the *malum prohibitum*—has migrated from the holding of interests "likely" to lead to a "substantial" loss of independence and impartiality to the holding of interests that merely "might" or "could" lead to anything other than "complete" and "total" independence and impartiality.[33]

As the historical record suggests, it is in the nature of an objective, prophylactic approach to conflict that it define the offense down in this way. Consider that in 1953, when a subjective approach to conflict was uncontroversial, a Senate legal counsel report was able to declare that "a showing of an . . . interest of such magnitude as to demonstrate a probable influence upon the official actions of the officer concerned would seem to be" required to predicate an offense. Further, it noted that "the sufficiency of proof of such influence necessarily presents a question to be determined from the evidence in each individual case, and any endeavor to state a generalization applicable to all cases would seem to be inadvisable."[34] Such a standard would have allowed us to enter the mind of each individual official concerned, determining—on a case-by-case basis—whether he was subjectively capable of overcoming whatever encumbering circumstances he faced; whether, that is, he was able to avoid conflict. A mere ten years later, however, Roswell Perkins heralded a change toward the objective, criticizing the subjective method for taking on "the flavor of a character rating of the official seeking [to hold a particular interest] . . . a rating on the scale of imperviousness to motives of personal gain. The higher the rating of character, the more severe the outside interest may be."[35] Even if we could somehow peer into their minds and accurately gauge what magnitude of interest would compromise which official, thus allowing some officials to hold interests of a certain size while denying the privilege to others—simply on the basis of the different senses we have of their subjective capacities to resist encumbrances on their judgment—it would be invidious.

Accordingly, conflict-of-interest law has featured a race to the bottom, where whatever situations would place the least psychologically resistant in conflict are prohibited to all. One might sympathize with Anthony Lewis, who—bristling at the conflict-of-interest charges leveled against then-United Nations ambassador-designate Richard Holbrooke—insisted that "[e]veryone knows Richard Holbrooke is ambitious—but not for money. The notion that he would try to gain improperly from the use of a [rent-free] room in a friend's house is laughable, as is the idea that he had financial motives when he met American diplomats abroad."[36] But Lewis isn't saying the same thing about the innumerable other, more minor officials who get caught up in the same kinds of charges. Do they, by implication, have a lower threshold of resistance to encumbrance? Because the notion of graduating the law's application to officials based on our sense of their subjective capacities to rise above their encumbering circumstances—to avoid conflict—is offensive to democratic norms, we have inexorably moved toward the lowest common denominator, prohibiting all but *de minimis* impairments on judgment. The ill-conceived and ill-fated decision to lower the federal honorarium ban from a prohibition on honoraria above $2,000 to a proscription on all honoraria—and the tortured debate it provoked—offers the most evocative recent illustration of this slippery slope.[37] Hence, even within the category of *mala prohibita*, where the concern is to prohibit certain kinds of conduct antecedent to *mala in se* states of mind, one could still settle on conduct—certain kinds of interest-holdings or financial relationships—nearer to or farther from the *malum in se* for most officials. And the dynamic has been to come to rest, heavily, at a farther, more draconian point.

*　　*　　*

To sum up: What I have offered here, by way of prologue, is a "best-fit" interpretation of the legal-moral structure of conflict-of-interest law. The major theme is this: Conflict-of-interest law has evolved—and continues to evolve—in the direction where the offense centers on a set of antecedent *mala prohibita* acts, not on the consequent impaired mental states that constitute the true *mala in se*. But it has also moved in the direction where the offender must harbor a heightened mental state vis à vis those acts and not simply have committed them. It has moved toward specific intent of some form, far away from the pole of strict liability or even general intent.

Indeed, even within these two spectrums, the movements have tended toward their respective extremes. The offensive acts consist not only of prophylactically defined conduct or situations. Within that class, they tend toward *minimal* sets of acts or situations that would trigger impaired mental states only in the most susceptible, easily corruptible official imaginable—and not the more substantial sort necessary to impair an "average" official with, presumably, some ability to protect his judgment from certain above-minimal kinds of encumbrance. As for the offender's *mens rea*, it has to consist not only of a particular mental state of heightened understanding and awareness. Given that requirement, we must also show that the actual official herself—who may well have been idiosyncratically disengaged and inattentive—had knowledge of certain elements of the offense. It would not suffice to show that an average official would have had such knowledge. Over the past thirty years, these twin dynamics of offensive act and offender's *mens rea* have become intimately connected in conflict-of-interest jurisprudence and interminably controversial. This is not to say that all conflict-of-interest offenses are prophylactic, nor that every single one requires an intending offender—and I will account for the exceptions below. But far and away, this is the tendency.

Prophylaxis, Criminal Punishment, and Civil Penalties: A Coda on the Future

In addition to "prophylactic versus nonprophylactic offenses" and "strictly liable versus non-strictly liable offenders," the statutory conflict-of-interest laws array themselves along one other spectrum: criminal versus civil penalties. In 1989, Congress for the first time attached civil penalties to many of the criminal conflict-of-interest statutes. It did so because the laws were so prophylactically removed from any real moral wrong that criminal prosecutors were failing to win convictions on all but the most egregious cases.[38] In return for the less stigmatizing civil penalty, Congress felt, the offense would become easier for prosecutors to establish: "Civil rather than criminal enforcement," Professor William Eskridge told a 1993 hearing, "avoid[s] the rule of lenity and burden of proof problems that plague criminal cases." Less onerous civil penalties would also allow for settlements in which, for a greater number of elements in the offense, some offenders could be held strictly liable.[39]

In any event, only a handful of civil conflict-of-interest cases have been brought under the federal statutes since 1989, although of course no one knows how many erstwhile violations the new civil penalties may have deterred.[40] Why the sparse take-up? In part, the answer is this: Conflict-of-interest violations rarely result in measurable economic losses to the government. Therefore, the Department of Justice's civil division has shown little interest in pursuing them. These violations remain with the criminal division, which is unlikely to pursue even a civil penalty unless a case rises to criminal standards.

But there may be a deeper dynamic at work here, having to do with the complex way in which the three dimensions—criminal/civil penalty, prophylactic/nonprophylactic offense, and strictly liable/intending offender—interact with one another. Consider what happens when civil penalties supplement the criminal, as they did in 1989. First (as noted), with the more lenient civil penalty, it becomes easier to move at least some offenders in the direction of strict liability. But second, less onerous civil penalties—by allowing for a lower burden of proof and a diminished reliance on lenity—make it easier to move the offense, the *malum prohibitum,* even further from the true *malum in se.* If even fewer facts need be established (reduced burden of proof), or if what facts are established need not fit as tightly into the statutory definition (reduced lenity), then—in effect—the law's prophylactic circumference has been widened. The offense has moved even farther away from the actual harm to be prevented.

Up until a few years ago, then, as the acts that constitute a conflict-of-interest offense moved toward the prophylactic, the mental state required of the offender moved further away from strict or even general-intent liability. But the more recently inaugurated criminal-civil dimension introduces a third variable beyond offensive act and offender's *mens rea,* that of penalty. And as the penalty moves from criminal to civil, its tendency is to make the offense more prophylactic *and* take the offender nearer the realm of strict liability. Perhaps it is because it thus thwarts the inverse relationship between prophylaxis and strict liability—a relationship lying at the core of conflict-of-interest law—that the civil penalty has not entirely taken off.

2

The Topography of Conflict

Over time, it is often observed, conflict of interest (a relatively subtle form of transgression) has replaced bribery, kickbacks, office-buying, and other gross forms of corruption as the principal malfeasance in American public life.[1] But in fact—and this counts as one of the more striking developments in the last many decades of public discourse over ethics in government—our concerns have moved beyond not only bribery, but conflict of interest itself, where conflict-of-interest is understood as the prototypical "self-dealing" transgression wherein an officeholder straightforwardly has the capacity, in her official role, to affect a personal interest. Instead, if we are talking broadly of our current debate and preoccupations, we are just as likely to be concerned with one of four distinct but related situations beyond both bribery *and* self-dealing, or else with various hybrids between them. The distinctions and connections between these various classes of conflict, including self-dealing, and the question as to what exactly is wrong with them, cause enormous confusion in public discourse. The following "topography" attempts to sketch out those distinctions and connections; the chapters that follow explore each type of conflict's particular moral perplexities.

The first category of conflict beyond self-dealing, to borrow the term most often applied in discourse, is "undue influence." Recall that self-dealing involves a single official, along with a (financial) interest she both possesses personally and can affect officially. Undue influence, by contrast, involves *two* officials and one interest. One of the officials, A, has the capacity to affect the interest in question through her official role, but it is not she who possesses it. The other official, B, possesses—or, more accurately, is associated with—the external interest but does not have the capacity to affect it in her own particular official role. Undue influence occurs when official B, personally associated with the interest but incapable of officially affecting it, seeks favorable treatment for it from official A, who is not associated with the interest but *is* capable of officially affecting it.

For example, a public-affairs officer for Agency X might, as a part-time principal in a company that provides audio-visual services, seek a contract for his firm from the technology officials at Agency Y.[2] Or consider the case of Peter Strobel who, though having just become President Eisenhower's public buildings commissioner, assiduously pursued a contract on behalf of his engineering firm, Strobel and Salzman, with the Army Corps of Engineers' procurement officer, Lyn Hench.[3] Ever since the Civil War period, two federal conflict-of-interest statutes, now codifed as 18 U.S.C. §203 and 205, have prohibited officials, acting outside of their official roles on behalf of private interests, from influencing other officials to affect those interests in a favorable way.

A second type of conflict beyond self-dealing usually falls under the rubric "abuse of office," perhaps for want of a better term. Where undue influence involves two officials and one private interest, abuse of office typically involves one official and two private interests. Here, the official may have the capacity to affect one of the interests (call it interest "C") in her official role, but it is not an interest with which she is any way personally associated. The other interest, D, is one which the official does possess, but she has no capacity to affect it through her office. "Abuse of office" arises when C—the interest the official can affect but does not possess—enters a business relationship with D, the interest the official possesses but cannot affect. Consider the 1990 trial of Congressmen Mario Biaggi. Among the clients of his private law firm—a firm whose interests Biaggi could not directly have affected as a congressman—was a private company, Wedtech, in which he held no interests but whose fortunes he *was* able to affect in office. Or consider the case of President Nixon's interior secretary, Walter Hickel, whose Hickel Investment Company—a company Hickel had no official capacity to affect—received a one-million-dollar contract from Atlantic Richfield (ARCO) at a time when ARCO cared every much about "decisons Hickel would be making as secretary of the interior."[4] Similarly, in 1955 Air Force Secretary Harold Talbott was forced to resign because among the clients of his private consulting firm—a firm with which the Air Force itself would have had no interest in contracting—were several major engineering companies, companies very much interested in contracting with the Air Force. Abuse of office, as does undue influence, represents an extension, or an unfolding, of self-dealing. But where undue influence elaborates on self-dealing by adding a second public official, abuse of office complicates it by adding a second private interest.

One might wonder what distinguishes abuse of office not only from bribery, but from *quid pro quo* understood even in its most sweeping terms. In its broadest incarnation, a *quid pro quo* arises whenever an officeholder (a) has the official capacity to affect the interests of a private party that transfers value to her, but (b) to whom she provides no equivalent private economic consideration in return. Hence, we fear that the officeholder might have become beholden to that private party to perform some kind of official act by way of recompense. (As I shall show shortly, a bribe is simply a *quid pro quo* that meets criminal-legal levels of factual proof and normative lenity; and in neither bribery nor *quid pro quo* need the recompensing official act have been performed or even specified.) Abuse of office, for its part, centers on situations where an officeholder likewise has the capacity to affect the interests of a private party that transfers something of value to her, but to whom—because she *does* provide equivalent private economic consideration in return—she is arguably not beholden. According to Harold Talbott, since his firm furnished full consideration to client Air Force contractors in the form of private-market consulting services, he was in no way beholden to them to perform a favorable official act. Had an Air Force contractor showered him with gifts—free trips, expensive meals, theater tickets—and especially if he had not repriocated with gifts of his own, the situation would have entered the realm of *quid pro quo*. But, Talbott pointed out, that is not what happened.[5]

I shall examine this argument further later. I raise it here, though, because it provides a convenient point of entry into the third conflict domain beyond bribery/*quid pro quo* and self-dealing, the domain of "private payment for public acts." Private payment for public acts inverts the structure of abuse of office. It upends the situation where an officeholder has the official capacity to affect the interests of a private party that transfers value to her, but to which—because she provides equivalent private-market consideration in recompense—she claims not to be beholden. In the realm of private payment for public acts, the official receives unrecompensed value from a private interest—and hence becomes beholden to it—but has no official capacity to affect that interest. "Unlike other conflict-of-interest laws," Beth Nolan observes, 18 U.S.C. §209—the federal statute governing private payment for public acts—does "not require any connection between the payor and the government agency in which the payee work[s], or the specific government work performed by the payee."[6] Certainly, some believe 18 U.S.C. §209 and comparable laws are "honored more in the breach" and hedged with exceptions, especially when it comes to situations where private businesses underwrite the salaries of without-compensation or part-time government employees. Nevertheless, in prohibiting private payment for official acts *regardless* of whether the official can affect the interests of the private payor, 18 U.S.C. §209 is not meant to prohibit *quid pro quo per se*—many other regulations do that—so much as prevent public decision-making from being controlled by any private party, even one whose interests may not remotely be at stake.

Abuse of office on the one hand, and private payment for public acts on the other, each represent one-half but not the other of a bribery/*quid pro quo* situation. Bribery/*quid pro quo,* as I have suggested, arises whenever (a) a private party whose interests an official can affect, (b) transfers value to the official for which she fails to provide compensating private-market acts, and so she becomes beholden. But in abuse of office, the official does provide compensating nonofficial acts. And in private payments for public acts, the official has no capacity to affect the private party's interests.

A fourth and final category of conflict beyond bribery/*quid pro quo* and self-dealing, "private gain from public office," looms ever larger in contemporary conflict-of-interest discourse. "Private gain from public office," in its most generic form, refers to situations where officials draw on knowledge, skills, experiences, stature, or prestige derived from their public offices to reap some form of private gain: a corporate-board membership, a fee for a professional service, an honorarium for an appearance, an expense-paid invitation to a charitable golf tournament. Conceptually, private gain from public office is independent (and, in practice, often arises in the absence) of both characteristics of *quid pro quo.* It can arise, that is, even if the officeholder is (a) incapable of officially affecting the fortunes of the private interest from which she is reaping the gain, and (b) not in any way beholden to it, having provided full private-market recompense for the payment.

Consider, for example, the former secretary of state who makes a fortune publishing his memoirs. Although earning his payment from a publishing firm whose interests he had no official capacity to affect, and although providing ample private-market consideration—a best-selling book—for whatever he receives, he may still come under attack for exploiting his office for private gain. Private gain from public office thus occupies a realm not only beyond self-dealing, but beyond *quid pro quo* as well—meaning that the official's in-role judgment need in no way be compromised, impaired, or encumbered as a result. As the landmark New York Bar Association study noted in 1960, "it is possible to imagine an official who acts impartially, does not play favorites, and is a model of public decorum," but who nevertheless falls afoul of injunctions against "the use of public office for private gain, an independent and specific objective involved in the field of conflicts of interest."[7]

There is, then, a topography—a lay of the land—to the various conflicts in "conflict of interest." And what it reveals is that our concerns have moved not only beyond bribery/*quid pro quo*—where an official can affect the interests of another party to whom she is beholden—but self-dealing as well, where an official can affect her own interests. Or, in Table 1, we have moved from the top toward the bottom row. I say *toward* the bottom row because, in fact, pure self-dealing still occurs; and while criminal bribery is rare, gray-area *quid pro quo*s—which for either factual or normative reasons fail to rise

Table 1 The Topography of Conflict

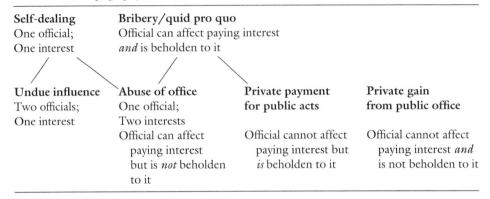

Self-dealing	Bribery/quid pro quo		
One official;	Official can affect paying interest		
One interest	*and* is beholden to it		

Undue influence	Abuse of office	Private payment for public acts	Private gain from public office
Two officials;	One official;		
One interest	Two interests		
	Official can affect paying interest but is *not* beholden to it	Official cannot affect paying interest but *is* beholden to it	Official cannot affect paying interest *and* is not beholden to it

to the level of legally actionable bribery—have become enormously controversial in American public discourse. I defer discussion of this vast domain of "chiaroscuro" *quid pro quo* until later—to examine the issues it raises, I require some of the ideas I set forth at the beginning of Part II—and I here explore, in turn, self-dealing, undue influence, abuse of office, private payment for public acts, and private gain from public office. In each case, I attempt to pinpoint exactly how conflicted judgment occurs—which is not always evident on the surface—and to articulate the principles that account for the often contorted shape of the law.

3

Self-Dealing

In self-dealing, an officeholder's official role allows her to affect one or more of her own personal interests. That the interests are *personal* means that they originate out-of-role, in the official's private financial holdings, and not in-role, in "the interests [she may have in her] grade, salary or other matter arising solely from government employment."[1] Although they do figure in some of the other conflict-of-interest categories, an officeholder's in-role or professional interests—in her official remuneration, public-service career, pet projects, and bureaucratic glory—have no place in self-dealing. The reason is simple: Next to everything an official does in her role affects them.[2] Neither recusal nor divestiture, let alone disclosure or balance-of-interests, would offer effective remedies to self-dealing understood as the officeholder's official capacity to affect her in-role interests.

Just as the *interest* in self-dealing cases must originate out-of-role, not in-role, the *conflict* in self-dealing lies wholly with obligations that originate in-role, not out-of-role. An official who is in a position to steal government funds without being caught, as Thomas L. Carson observes, is not in a conflict situation. "Refraining from stealing money is not a duty which one has in virtue of occupying an office or position," Carson notes, "it is an obligation all people have independently of their roles and positions."[3] So in self-dealing, the interests must come from outside the official's role; the conflict must originate inside it. This is not to deny that an official who hires a mediocre applicant to diminish possible career competition—like one who steals supplies from the government—violates norms. But he does not self-deal.

The *malum in se* in self-dealing resembles the *malum in se* in all the other conflict-of-interest domains: It consists of an impaired mental state, specifically, the impaired inner state that could result whenever an officeholder has the official capacity to affect her own private interests. But the *malum prohibitum* in self-dealing—the set of external, legally cognizable facts that defines the offense—is in one important way unlike any of the others.

Many self-dealing laws prohibit officials not only from affecting their own interests, but from even being in a position to affect their own interests. They go beyond preventing a particular act and preempt instead an entire state of existence. It would be extremely difficult for any of the other conflict-of-interest laws to do the same. The undue-influence strictures, for example, could not prophylactically prevent an out-of-role official—say a Buildings Commissioner Peter Strobel—from being in a *position* to influence another, a Lyn Hench of the Army Corps of Engineers. Likewise, it would be impossible for the abuse-of-office strictures to prevent a Harold Talbott's consulting company from being in a *position* to provide services to a paying private client, an Air Force contractor, whose interests Talbott could affect. Nor could the rules against private gain from public office prevent a secretary of state from being in a *position* to write his memoirs.

The reason is that in these other conflict-of-interest realms, at least some of the key actions—a Peter Strobel making representations on behalf of his company to a Lyn Hench, a Harold Talbott's consulting company performing private services for an Air Force contractor, a former secretary of state writing his memoirs—take place out-of-role. And it would be impossible to prophylactically prevent individuals or firms, in private life, from being in a *position* to do these things. Any such law would be unenforceable. In self-dealing, by contrast, the only key action—the official's executing an official act that affects his personal interests—takes place within role, within an institutional structure. "The special character" of the self-dealing law, Roswell Perkins has written, "is that it restricts official activities rather than private activities; [i]t is aimed directly at the public role of the government employee."[4] And, consequently, in self-dealing the logic of prophylaxis is able to extend beyond merely prohibiting an official from acting to affect her interests, to prevent her from being even in a position to affect her interests—precisely because there *is* a role, a position, from which to bar her. Definable roles exist for officeholders when they engage in their official work, roles that can poise them to act in specified ways even if they have not yet done so. Hence the Supreme Court was able to declare, in 1965, that if an official "must be apprehended in the act . . . before steps can be taken to prevent [self-dealing], there is little or nothing left of the preventive or prophylactic function."[5]

Notwithstanding the active voice of the term "self-dealing," then, what the prophylactic self-dealing laws prevent falls more into the class of "being" than "doing"—a situation, not an action.[6] The problem, though, is that it is simply much more difficult to say whether a particular *situation* falls into the class contemplated in a legal prohibition, at least in most instances, than it is to say whether a particular *act* is the one prohibited by the law. Hence, the perimeters of the self-dealing rules are extraordinarily ambiguous and the law notably uncertain and controversial in its application.

To see this further, consider that even where the self-dealing laws fail literally to go beyond prohibiting actions to prohibit situations, they do in effect. In the other categories of conflict-of-interest—undue influence, say, or abuse of office or private gain from public office—the out-of-role acts that constitute the offense are straightforward and easy to specify: an out-of-role official contacts an in-role official, or contracts to perform private services for a private party, or reaps out-of-role gain based on her government stature. But in self-dealing, the act that defines the offense, mediated as it is through the structure of role, becomes refracted and imprecise. After all, for any given official act the structure of role might dictate that the officeholder collaborate with many others or perform the act solo, involve herself centrally or tangentially, engage at a very preliminary stage or a pivotal one, participate in a "chain of causation [that is] attenuated" or else confined, and so on.[7] Officials' in-role acts are just more complex, and less easily specified, than their out-of-role acts—certainly in the realm of conflict of interest.

The federal self-dealing laws, accordingly, prohibit an officeholder not simply from affecting a particular personal interest, but from "personally and substantially" affecting "any particular matter," if her doing so will have a "direct and predictable effect" on her "financial interests."[8] Not surprisingly, enormous legal controversy surrounds the self-dealing provisions, as prosecutors and accused alike debate the meaning of various terms. What, in any given case, does it mean for an official to "personally and substantially" affect a "particular matter" that has a "direct and predictable" effect on her "financial interest?" By contrast, there can be far less debate over whether one official has contacted another, or whether a private party has transacted business with an official's private interest, or whether a private party has supplemented an official's public salary—the concrete actions necessary to break the rules against undue influence, abuse of office, and private payment for public acts. As Justice Department attorney George Allen Carver, Jr., told a 1986 hearing, "there are issues under 208 [the self-dealing statute] that have arisen and that are recurring issues . . . One of them involves the meaning of the term 'particular matter.' One of them involves the meaning of the term 'financial interest.' . . . Now if we seek precise definition, aren't we always going to eventually face a defense from any good lawyer when we reach the line that the statute is void for vagueness as applied? . . . We can't avoid that. No matter how we define the terms, eventually we get to that point."[9]

None of this is to deny that situations of unambiguous self-dealing can happen. But because the remedies of recusal and divestiture usually snap into effect beforehand, these situations are rare. Almost every case of self-dealing that actually escapes prevention thus has a vagueness about it. Consequently, there are almost always two ways of describing it.

Consider the 1962 case of *Smith* v. *U.S.*, where a Department of Agriculture bureau headed by Smith contracted with a warehouse in which he held an interest—although Smith himself in no way participated in the decision. One might, on the one hand, deem this a case of self-dealing in spirit if not literally, a violation of "the spirit of the [law] *in its prophylactic sense.*"[10] After all, if preventing an official from personally and substantially participating in the award of a government contract to his own warehouse is meant to prophylactically preempt encumbered judgment, then preventing the entire bureau that he heads from doing the same will, with an abundance of caution, simply erect an even more airtight prophylaxis. Even if the prophylactic self-dealing law does not *literally* concern itself with the possibility that his mere presence in the agency might have some intangible effect on the decision, it does in spirit; and some element of self-dealing—along with the deeper danger of impaired official judgment—is, on this interpretation, every bit as real. To violate the spirit of a prophylactic law "in its prophylactic sense," then, is to do something arguably implied—but not literally stated—in the *malum prohibitum.* (To violate the spirit of a prophylactic law in its *non*prophylactic sense, by contrast, one would simply have to commit the *malum in se*—which of course remains legally incognizable.)

But there is another way of conceiving this situation. It is not that the official somehow participated, if ineffably and intangibly, in the decision—thereby violating the self-dealing law in spirit. It is not that official decision-making was in any way encumbered; that's just too remote a possibility. Rather, the problem was that the public, unable to digest all of the facts, might have mistakenly believed that Smith was personally and substantially involved when in fact he wasn't—meaning that he violated the self-dealing law in appearance. Or, as the *Smith* court put it, the public at a distance might reasonably conclude that Smith, as bureau chief, "ordered, directed, authorized or consented to the dealings which his subordinates carried on with the business entity"—even if he actually had nothing to do with it.[11] Smith was found guilty, but it is unclear which of the two lines of reasoning accounted for the verdict. Did he violate the self-dealing laws in spirit? Or in appearance?

Because of this structural ambiguity, most cases of self-dealing fall into a penumbra realm where those two ghostly entities, spirit and appearance, meet and mingle.[12] Indeed, in the Office of Government Ethics' (OGE) compilation of its first decade of advisory letters, 1979–1988, the substantial majority of cases that fall under the index's self-dealing heading also fall under the appearance heading. It would seem OGE itself cannot make up its mind whether most such instances constitute literal/spiritual or else apparent self-dealing, whether they come closer to violating the prophylactic self-dealing laws or the appearance standard. Such uncertainty arises because—unique among the conflict-of-interest offenses—the *malum prohibitum,* the external situation that the self-dealing law prohibits, is hedged with vague terms, becoming almost as ineffable as the *malum in se,* the inner tainted state-of-mind itself.

I will say much more about appearances themselves in Part III. Here, my concern is with self-dealing and with how quickly it becomes contestable by disintegrating into violations in spirit and then in appearance. But it becomes contestable in another way as well. For not only does self-dealing quickly blur into its own penumbra realm, but its borders with the other major conflict categories—especially undue influence and abuse of office—are notoriously indistinct. Where self-dealing does *not* bleed into appearances, it often exists only in hybrid with one of the other types of conflict.[13]

Self-Dealing and Undue Influence

Consider first how self-dealing blurs into undue influence. Undue influence occurs when an official's role denies her the capacity to affect her own interests, but—acting *out-of-role*—she nevertheless influences another official who does command such a capacity. Self-dealing, by contrast, occurs when her own role does afford the official the capacity to affect her private interests.

But the two begin to meld. For an official's *role* might require her not just to take various kinds of direct action that could affect her own interests, but simply to "recommend or advise"—to influence—other official colleagues to take various kinds of action, some of which could affect her interests.[14] In "positions of administrative leadership" in particular, Marver H. Bernstein has written, the "need to mind someone else's business in order to mind one's own opens up possibilities for undue influence" *in-role.*[15] As long as any particular activity of influencing still arguably falls within the bounds of the officeholder's official role, however, then (assuming her own interests are at stake) the law is more likely to deem the situation "self-dealing" than "undue influence."[16] A county supervisor who recuses himself on a matter affecting a personal interest does not necessarily "cure the evil" of self-dealing; "the influence upon his fellow members is the same" as if he had been voting himself.[17] In such circumstances, "everybody knows what he thinks about it and he sits there with his interest and he looks at you while he is not voting and that is the loudest not-vote you ever heard."[18]

There comes a point, though, where it is unclear whether an interested official is exerting influence on her colleagues from inside rather than outside her role. This is precisely where self-dealing blurs with undue influence. Consider the recent case of an officeholder who, outside of his official role, directed a nonprofit organization that was seeking a grant administered by other officials in his own agency. The officeholder attended an agency meeting dealing with the issue but said nothing, although it was unclear whether "he had discussed the issue or exercised influence outside of the meeting" and (more important) "unclear whether he would have been acting as an official or executive director of the charity" in doing so.[19] As an official, he would have been self-dealing; as executive director of the charity, he would have been exercising undue influence.

Sometimes this kind of ambiguity, this netherworld where it is unclear whether the influence being exerted abides in-role or out-of-role, allows officials to fall between the stools of self-dealing and undue influence. In *State v. Bennett*, the Milwaukee school board decided to buy a plot of land owned by Bennett, the city engineer, for a school site. There was no evidence that Bennett, within the metes and bounds of his official role as city engineer, did anything that would remotely qualify as an attempt to influence his official colleagues on the school board to purchase his property. Bennett did, however, join a nonofficial citizens' committee to recommend possible purchase sites. Because the court deemed Bennett to have exercised influence *outside* of his role, it did not find him guilty of the self-dealing charge that had been brought against him. Because Milwaukee had no strictures against out-of-role influence exercised by officials—of the sort covered at the federal level by 18 U.S.C. §203 and 205—Bennett violated no law.[20]

On the other hand, consider the case of *U.S.* v. *Reisley*, in which Reisley, a Veterans' Administration (VA) official, was acquitted of a charge under the undue-influence statutes. Reisley had come across the record of Barile, who—unbeknownst to Barile himself—had an outstanding claim for disability benefits against the VA. Instead of passing Barile's record on to the adjudication department as he was bound to do in the normal course of business, Reisley withheld it. Pretending to be a physician, Reisley then contacted Barile, offering to secure Barile a "new" disability award if Barile paid him three hundred dollars. Upon Barile's agreement to pay, Reisley released the file to his departmental colleagues and it was duly processed. Opining that Reisley really should have been charged with self-dealing—with using his own role to advance a personal interest—the court acquitted him of undue influence. The "gravamen" of undue influence, the court said, would be that

the defendant received compensation for services rendered to Barile before the Veteran's Administration. There was no evidence that the defendant rendered services to Barile, in the sense of advancing his claim, before the Veterans' Administration . . . If no other government official knows of the defendant's interest in the matter at hand, if the latter argues no claim, appears before no department or governmental body on behalf of the one who pays him, makes no appearance . . . it is obvious that he has not utilized . . . his influence with his co-workers to serve the claimant who has paid him.[21]

The boundary of official role, then, can grow sufficiently indistinct that officeholders such as Bennett who are prosecuted for self-dealing—for exercising influence *as an official* to affect personal interests—should actually have been charged with exercising undue influence *out-of*-role. Conversely, some officials charged with exerting undue influence out-of-role, such as Reisley, should, so courts have said, instead have been charged with in-role self-dealing.

Self-Dealing and Abuse of Office

Self-dealing also bleeds into abuse of office. Recall that self-dealing involves an official and a single interest she both possesses and can affect, while abuse of office involves an official and two business interests. One of these interests the official possesses but cannot affect; the other she can affect but does not possess; and the possibilities for abuse increase with the possibilities for a business arrangement between the two interests. Self-dealing blurs into abuse, then, at the point where it is unclear whether one business interest or two separate interests are involved—unclear, that is, whether the business links between the two have become so tight that, for all intents and purposes, they are as one.[22]

Consider the Harold Talbott situation. As Air Force secretary, Talbott had the capacity to affect the interests of Air Force contractors—among them Avco Manufacturing, Olin Industries, and Greyhound Corporation—which, in turn, were in a position to retain a consulting firm, the Paul Mulligan Company, in which Talbott partnered with Mulligan.[23] On the one hand, the Mulligan Company's relationship with Avco (say) might have been relatively tight and integrated. The two businesses might have adopted a long-term contractual or contingency fee arrangement. Or, to ratchet up the degree of mutual integration one notch, say they had embarked on some kind of joint venture or governance structure. In other words, assume the relationship was not so much externalized in the marketplace as internalized in a common organizational configuration or contract-nexus.[24] In such a situation, Talbott's case would have begun to fall on the self-dealing, rather than the abuse-of-office, side of the line. For whatever might have promoted the health and well-being of Avco would have directly redounded to the health and well-being of Mulligan, or, at least, the health and well-being of Mulligan would have varied directly with that of Avco.[25]

But now, suppose that the relationship between Avco and Mulligan was relatively unintegrated and arms-length. Say it took the form of a simple retainer that Avco could have canceled at its discretion; say it assumed the guise much more of an external-market than an internal-organizational link. Such a situation would have fallen more on the abuse-of-office than the self-dealing side of the line. After all, the fortunes of Avco and Mulligan would have covaried far less in such circumstances. The evil that would most have attracted our attention is not the possibility that Talbott might somehow have directly enriched *himself* by awarding a contract to Avco. Rather, it is the possibility that Avco's discretion in choosing to do business with the Mulligan Company might have been affected—manipulated, prevailed-upon, or coerced—by Talbott's official capacity to affect Avco's interests: in other words, abuse of office. To the extent that the second-party interest, Avco, appears as an independent actor with its own discretion that might be preyed upon—its own interests that might be compromised—as opposed to a frictionless conduit or cipher through which the official can channel benefits to *his own* interests, we have a situation of abuse of office, not self-dealing. Of course, the borders between an external-market relationship and an internal organizational one can blur, meaning that it will often be unclear whether a situation qualifies as abuse or self-dealing—just as the boundaries between out-of-role and in-role influence can blur, meaning that it will often be unclear whether a situation qualifies as undue influence or self-dealing.[26]

How Serious Is Self-Dealing?

The boundaries of self-dealing, then, are indistinct. On the one hand, many instances of self-dealing quickly evaporate into a penumbra realm of appearances. On the other, self-dealing tends to meld into one of the neighboring categories of undue influence or abuse of office. But there is something else. There is a sense in which self-dealing raises less serious normative concerns than either undue influence or abuse of office, notwithstanding its location at the conceptual center of conflict of interest.

To see this, let me begin by drawing a distinction between undue influence and abuse of office on the one hand, and a form of corruption—bribery—more normatively troubling than they are on the other. In undue-influence situations, the out-of-role official doing the influencing is the one charged under the law. The influenced official, the one whose judgment is actually impaired, commits no violation. Eisenhower's buildings commissioner Peter Strobel, the official doing the influencing, had to resign. The Army Corps' Lyn Hench, the influenced official, was treated as more put-upon than co-conspirator. In bribery, by contrast, it is not just the individual doing the bribing but the bribed official, too, who is culpable.

Now compare abuse of office and bribery: In abuse situations, the official abusing his office is of course penalized. But the private party involved, the one that engages the official's business interest knowing of the official's capacity to affect its fortunes, is rarely charged. Eisenhower's Air Force secretary Harold Talbott, the abusing official, had to resign. But Air Force contractor Avco, his consulting firm's paying client, seemed more preyed upon than predator. In bribery, by contrast, it is not just the bribed official but the private firm doing the bribing who will be prosecuted.

So, to summarize, in undue-influence situations the influenced (the "second") official—and in abuse-of-office situations the "abused" (the "second") private interest—appear as relatively innocent parties. Yet while undue influence and abuse of office are in one respect less normatively loaded than bribery, they are—along precisely the same dimension—more normatively charged than self-dealing. For in both undue influence and abuse of office, there is an identifiable victim.

As a law-review note pointed out about undue influence long ago, "while any wholly honest public official may by force of circumstance find himself in the typical [self-dealing] situation and so [himself] be more victim than villain, the administrative persuader"—the undue influencer—engages in a "more conscious attempt to subvert governmental processes"; consequently his "attempt[ing] to exert his influence upon others seems primarily a function of his general character and integrity, rather than the nature of his specific interests."[27] Consider a telling difference in the regulatory treatment accorded self-dealing and undue influence. While the statutory *self-dealing* provisions in 18 U.S.C. §208 prohibit an official from letting a contract to herself, and some agency self-dealing regulations—with an abundance of prophylactic caution—forbid an official from contracting with her own agency, no self-dealing laws preclude an official from holding a contract with any other government department. The *undue-influence* statutes, by contrast, prohibit an official from influencing officeholders in any government agency, her own or any other, to award contracts to interests with which she may be aligned. In self-dealing she can be "victimized" only by those personal interests her role affects; but in undue influence, she can make a victim out of anyone anywhere in government. Because undue influence, unlike self-dealing, involves another person, it consigns violators to the status of "subverter," "persuader," or victimizer.

If in undue influence, the influencing official "subverts" or "persuades" other officials, in abuse of office, she "coerces" or "extorts" other private parties who might do business with her own private interests. Consider three differences in the regulatory treatment accorded self-dealing and abuse of office, one from each of the branches. The Office of Government Ethics permits a university to name a chair after a high executive branch official—one who presumably could affect the university's (hence her own) interests—but positively forbids the official from lending his name to the university's fund-raising activities, where contributions might be sought from other parties whose interests the official could affect.[28] The House of Representatives' ethics rules, to take a legislative example, allow a congressman to become a member of an organization whose interests he can affect but not to recruit other parties—whose interests he might also be able to affect—to join it.[29]

Judges, on assuming office, are not routinely required to divest themselves of private interests in which they passively invest. But they *are* expected to absent themselves from all private business activities in which they are actively involved. Passive investments at most create the possibility of self-dealing, should the judge find herself docketed with a case where they are at stake. In such instances straightforward recusal will deal with the problem. Active business involvement, however, creates the capacity for abuse. As Steven Lubet notes, judges who are actively engaged with their enterprises will "not only be more visible to the public, but also more knowledgeable about the business' customers and patrons than will be passive investors." They will thus be in a far stronger position to "coerce . . . lawyers or litigants to patronize their enterprises [and hence] become the beneficiaries of economic favoritism."[30]

In undue influence, the influencing official is a manipulator and a subverter. In abuse of office, she is an extorter or a coercer. The self-dealer is neither. But I do not want to press this too far. For in many ways, ways I am about to explore, undue influence and abuse of office—and beyond them, private payment for public acts and private gain from public office—occupy a complex normative realm, a realm of moral *chiaroscuro*, to use Dennis Thompson's term. Notwithstanding the putative inveigling and coercing, the finagling and extorting, it is not at all clear what is wrong with them.

4

Undue Influence

"Evidently," opined the first Justice John Marshall Harlan in 1906, the statutes now codified as 18 U.S.C. §203 and 205 have for their "main object" to protect "executive [officials] against undue influence"; specifically, undue influence exerted by *other* government officials.[1] In 1953, for example, Peter Strobel—President Eisenhower's commissioner of public buildings—fell afoul of the statutes by contacting Lyn Hench, an official at the Army Corps of Engineers, to get an overdue bill paid to his private construction firm.[2] Or, to borrow an example from the federal regulations themselves, a White House official may not represent a client, even *pro bono,* in a hearing before the Social Security Administration.[3]

Undue influence, as understood here, arises in the interaction between two officials. One, acting outside of her official role but representing a private interest, attempts to influence another, who has no private connection with the interest but *is* capable of affecting it in his official role. The "influencing official" can be a member of either the executive or the legislative branches—and discourse treats the two circumstances in very different ways—while the "influenced official" must, generally, be one capable of "executive action" (out-of-role executive officials are not comparably regulated in their dealings with the legislative branch).[4]

Executive Officials

In situations of undue influence, it is debatable whether either official, influencing or influenced, actually is in a conflict of interest *per se.* The official exerting the influence (and it is her conduct the law regulates) *is* linked to an interest: consider Buildings Commissioner Strobel representing his construction firm, or the White House adviser interceding on behalf of the Social Security recipient. But it is not clear in what way she may be in conflict. After all, she acts entirely outside of her official role and so cannot be impaired—conflicted—in the exercise of it. The official being influenced, by contrast, is in conflict. It is he—say, the Army Corps of Engineers official, the Social Security Administration judge—who remains in-role, and it is his judgment that risks impairment from the influence exerted by the out-of-role official. But here, it is not clear in what way, if any, such conflict is posed by an "interest" the influenced official has. By definition, he has no personal stake in the matter. In the kind of undue influence exerted by official on official, the idea of conflict of interest thus becomes elastic, depositing some of its features but not others with each of the two parties. Any conflict of interest would seem to be shouldered by the two in a kind of division of labor. Understandably, some have gone so far as to deny that undue influence is a species of conflict of interest; more generally, commentators have criticized the two federal statutes governing undue influence for incoherence.[5]

In fact, undue influence's one major difference with every other conflict-of-interest domain is both profound and easily isolated. Because the conflict of interest here reaches across two officials instead of abiding within one, it cannot (and does not) consist in a single, self-contained mental state. Rather, its carrier is, and must be, an external act, the act of influence that connects the two officials. And this makes all the difference—for the moral status of both the influencing and the influenced official.

Consider first the influencing official—a Public Buildings commissioner such as Peter Strobel who, acting out-of-role, lobbies on a contract with the Army Corps of Engineers, or a White House official who, again out of role, importunes the Social Security Administration. Since Peter Strobel is acting out-of-role, not fulfilling part of his official function, a prophylactic requirement that he preserve a certain state-of-mind would be wholly inapt. All that the law can reasonably ask of such an out-of-role official, and all that it does ask, is that he refrain from a particular kind of ultimate act: an act of influence, an attempt to move, alter, or divert government from the path it might otherwise take.

But the undue-influence law then goes a step further. To see this, consider yet another point of contrast with self-dealing. According to the law-review analysis discussed in the previous chapter, "any wholly honest public official may by force of circumstance find himself in the typical [self-dealing] situation, and so be more victim than villain." After all, the offense of self-dealing operates at considerable prophylactic remove from the *malum in se*. But in undue influence, the influencing official engages in "a more conscious attempt to subvert governmental processes," and this "attempt to exert influence upon others" seems, more naturally, "a function of his general character and integrity, rather than the nature of his specific interests." In the realm of undue influence, as contrasted with self-dealing, the analysis thus concludes, "we are more likely to be dealing with a knowing and calculated course of action."[6] To commit the offense of undue influence—unlike the offense of self-dealing—the influencing official must *ipso facto* have had the requisite knowledge and intent to be an offender. Also, self-dealing has a passive quality—the official might simply "find himself" in a position where he can affect his interests—whereas an act of influence is, obviously, active.

Thus, over time, ethics officials have come to treat the undue-influence strictures, unlike the self-dealing or postemployment statutes, as strict liability laws—at least when reckoning with the influencing official. To prove the offensive act is to prove the offending actor. The undue-influence laws, as a couple of Office of Government Ethics letters put it, "prohibit . . . absolutely certain forms of conduct" on the part of the influencing official "which have been determined to be harmful per se"—without requiring further "proof of consciousness of wrongdoing or bad purpose to disobey or disregard the law."[7]

By focusing on the influencing official's acts, not her state of mind, 18 U.S.C. §203 and 205 convert her into a strictly liable actor. But this is only half the story: the other half concerns the influenc*ed* official, the put-upon Army Corps or Social Security officials in our examples. And here, the statutory focus is very much on state-of-mind. The influenced official is the one in conflict, after all. Yet not only is the influenced official not held strictly liable under the statutes, he is not in any sense considered an offender. What impairs his judgment are not his own personal interests but the importunings—the acts of influence—of others, fellow officials, for which he cannot reasonably be held responsible. In *Burton,* Justice Harlan offered a somewhat more exacting rendition of the kind of conflict under which such importunings place the influenced official: "The main purpose of the statutes," Harlan wrote, "is to secure the integrity of executive action against undue influence [by those] whose favor might have much to do with the appointment to, or retention in, public position of those whose official action it is sought to control or direct."[8] More generally, the statutes protect "the integrity of executive action" against out-of-role influence by officials whose in-role actions—at one point or another—could have a bearing on the career of the executive official subject to pressure.[9] Although the influenced official has no out-of-role pecuniary interest at stake, she may possess a series of in-role professional interests—in her progress through the ranks, her departmental budget, her favorite projects—over any of which the influencing official may at some point be able to exert control. Who knows when the Army Corps of Engineers might need the Public Building commissioner's help, or the Social Security Administration and the White House might have a difficult encounter?

What all of this means, though, is that where the prophylactic imperative does enter into the undue-influence laws—as it must, since there is a state-of-mind to protect, in this case the influenced official's—its reach is greatly magnified, extending (at the federal level) government-wide.[10] True, it is hard to imagine what kind of influence a postal clerk could exercise over an interior secretary; hard to imagine, to return to Justice Harlan's principle, how a low-level ministerial official could ever manipulate a cabinet officer's in-role interests in career, budget, and programs. But an injunction against undue influence, if it is truly prophylactic, will necessarily apply even in situations where the importuning official actually has no influence—just as the prophylactic self-dealing statutes apply even in situations where an official's private interests actually wouldn't encumber his judgment.[11] As William G. Buss, Jr., wrote of the Massachusetts undue-influence law, "the rule is a prophylactic one. Because it is impossible to articulate a standard by which one can distinguish between employees in a position to influence and those who are not, *all* will be treated as though they have influence."[12]

On this point, a 1990 OGE advisory letter pierced the prophylactic veil in an instructive way. The letter permitted an out-of-role official to appear before a regulatory commission in an agency other than the one that employed her—to lobby for a commercial license—as long as she did not disclose to the commission that she was a government official.[13] One can interpret this ruling as suggesting a form of remedy for undue influence, a kind of blind trust which—instead of preventing a decision-making official from knowing his own out-of-role interests, as would a blind-trust remedy for self-dealing— prevents the influenced official from knowing of the influencing official's in-role capacities. Indeed, on the Harlan argument, that is what poses the impairment in undue-influence situations.[14]

The undue-influence statutes are thus a case study in what happens when one conflict of interest distributes itself between two officials. Because the influencing official is not in conflict—Strobel's mental state is of no concern since he operates out-of-role—the law instead focuses on his external acts, the acts of influence he exerts on colleagues. And, just for this reason, it is able to make him strictly liable. Because the influenced official (say the Army Corps procurement officer Hench) has no self-generated out-of-role pecuniary interests at stake, the law focuses instead on the in-role encumbrances imposed upon him by other officials. And, just for this reason, the prophylaxis expands to become government-wide. Far from being confined to the personal portfolio of out-of-role interests he could conceivably affect, as it is in self-dealing, the prophylaxis in undue influence stretches to cover anyone who could conceivably affect his in-role interests. In the domain of undue influence—where one conflict of interest is shared by two—the whole is emphatically *not* less than the sum of its parts. Rather, the offender could not be more strictly liable, nor the offense more dramatically prophylactic.

Some critics of the federal undue-influence statutes, noting that most officials command nothing near government-wide influence, have suggested reining in the law's prophylactic extremity by prohibiting out-of-role officials from influencing only those in-role officials within their own agencies or departments. Many state laws have done just this, allowing out-of-role officials to make representations before agencies other than their own, where their ties with the influenced official are likely to be attenuated at best.[15] Even so, the most modest undue-influence laws in the U.S.—those that extend merely agency-wide, not government-wide—are coextensive with the most expansive self-dealing laws, a few of which prohibit officials from holding interests which their agencies can affect, although most stop simply at forbidding an official from holding interests which her own role touches. Federal undue-influence law has, however, mitigated its own prophylactic extremity in a different, twofold, way—a way that, when it is taken as a whole, makes considerable sense.

First, under the statutes, undue influence can occur only in matters where the out-of-role official acts on behalf of the interests of *other* persons or entities—including, in most cases, businesses in which she might have a stake. Undue influence does not occur when the out-of-role official represents her own interests as an individual, whether on a broad policy issue or on a specific administrative matter that affects her personally. Those who drafted the undue-influence laws in the Civil War era, and reaffirmed them in 1962 and 1979, harbored a constitutionally borne reticence to obtrude on any citizen's capacity—and this obviously includes the capacity of an executive official-out-of-role—to communicate her own views to government.[16]

Second, 18 U.S.C. §203 and 205 state that undue influence can occur only in matters where the United States is a "party or has a direct or indirect interest." Out-of-role officials, in other words, are free to influence the government in proceedings where the contending parties are entirely private—as when a corporation and a union argue before the National Labor Relations Board—and where the United States has no interest at all.[17] Undue-influence statutes, then, cease to operate where the government itself has no definable interest, or where the influencing official has a very personal interest. They cease to govern, in other words, as the penumbra of her official role recedes and her out-of-role civic self emerges.

Legislators

While the "law of undue [legislative] influence is a still evolving, difficult to define area of jurisprudence [with a] relatively small body of case[s]," one can nevertheless coax out of it discernible norms separating acceptable from unacceptable forms of legislative-executive contact.[18] And, as it turns out, the norms of engagement for legislators seeking to influence departments or agencies differ, almost in mirror-image, from those applicable to executive-branch influencers.

While undue influence in the executive branch offers a case study in prophylaxis *in extremis,* undue influence in the legislative context—almost unique among the various conflict-of-interest realms I discuss—is wholly *un*amenable to any kind of prophylactic regulation. It is not possible to prophylactically bar legislators from representing the interests of others (no matter whom) in their dealings with government, nor from contacting executive officials (no matter whom) in the process.[19] Representing the interests of others before departments and agencies may fall "out-of-role" for most executive officials, but it is central to the official role of all legislators.

Of course, debates persist about whether (if no absolute barriers are possible) some partial barriers ought to obtain. Perhaps a legislator should be confined to representing only her own constituents before the executive branch. Maybe she should be prohibited from lobbying agencies over which she exercises committee-oversight responsibilities.[20] But even in light of these oft-proposed partial strictures, which are far from uncontroversial, the absence of anything near a complete prophylactic barrier to the legislator's exercise of influence with the executive branch has had a signal effect. This absence means that any norms governing undue influence exerted by legislators will require some inquiry into the states-of-mind of those involved, whether they be the influencing legislator, the influenced executive official, or the represented party. The only question is: Who should conduct such inquiries? And here there can be only one answer: the legislator herself.

On the one hand, because legislators are not prophylactically barred from representing any (nonpaying) party before government, they are under an onus to inquire into the case—and this often means the motives—of those whose interests they seek to represent. On the other hand, because legislators are not prophylactically barred from contacting any executive official at all, they are under an onus to anticipate the reaction—and this essentially means the mental state—of the official whose decisions they seek to influence.[21] Thus Congress requires that members "not endorse the claims of [those they represent] without checking them" and eschew any "irrelevant or extraneous" promises, threats, or arm-twisting—any "overt coercion or threats of reprisals or promises of favoritism or reward to administrators."[22] This notably vague set of standards goes straight to issues of mental state—to whether the represented party has good reasons for making a case, the executive official has good reasons for deciding it, and the legislator has taken good care on either score.[23]

Consider the Keating Five's relationship both with the interest they represented—Charles Keating's Lincoln Savings and Loan—and with the officials they influenced, those at the Federal Home Loan Bank Board. On the one hand, the senators' attachment to Keating seemed, in the eyes of many, to resemble more a lawyer-client than a representative-constituent relationship. The senators, in other words, did not feel bound to concern themselves with the policy merits of Keating's case nor the extent to which their carrying his brief was in the public interest; they did not concern themselves with his motives. As one observer put the point, "Today, too many lawmakers see their job as being similar to that of a lawyer—represent the client, no matter what the cost."[24]

But if the senators intruded a legal approach into a situation in which they should have behaved as representatives, they also intruded as representatives into a realm that should have been vouchsafed to the law. They politically interfered—they brought to bear a show of political force—in an ongoing regulatory law-enforcement proceeding against Charles Keating, one which should have been governed strictly by the legal merits. Behaving as if they were lawyers when they should have been political in the best sense, and intruding as politicians in a realm which should have been governed exclusively by legal considerations, the Keating Five illustrated the perils of legislative influence in pure form. No precise rule could have been fashioned to prevent the *malum in se*—to specify the lines that cannot be crossed in a way that would clearly apply to all cases—and anything prophylactic, any broader *malum prohibitum*, would have impeded the legislative role.

While legislators who represent *others* before departments and agencies should—and in fact do—command far greater latitude than executive officials who do the same, legislators who seek to represent their *own* personal interests should—and do—command far less latitude than executive branch officials. The House rules, for example, "restrict the official duties of [legislators and legislative] employees . . . they may not contact other government agencies with respect to non-legislative matters affecting their own significant interests."[25] That the legislator's role encompasses regular interventions with the executive branch explains not only the greater latitude we accord her to represent *others* before agencies and departments, but the tighter restrictions we place on her capacity to represent herself. For legislators, self-representation becomes a form of self-dealing. The legislator risks abusing a role, a trust, we have explicitly given her to exercise exclusively on behalf of others.[26]

Consider a final difference between the boundaries of legislative and executive branch undue influence. Recall that executive officials are prophylactically prohibited from attempting to influence departments and agencies only where U.S. interests are at stake. Where the United States is not a party or possessed of a discernible interest, then any representation the out-of-role executive official might care to make—even one that attacks governing legislation and regulations—is within bounds. The situation in the legislative case is substantially the reverse. Legislators may represent causes antithetical to the "U.S. interest"—that is, the interests being pursued by the executive branch—but they must do so in a way strictly consistent with governing "statutes, regulations or considerations of equity and public policy" (if in the Senate) or with "governing law and regulations" or congressional "intent" (if in the House).[27] Indeed, legislators must positively assure the executive officials they contact—even when challenging U.S. interests as defined by the executive branch—that they seek nothing other than a resolution consonant with existing law or the intent of the legislative branch.

This distinction, too, between the treatments accorded legislative and executive influencers displays its own rhyme and reason. A legislator, in effect, must ensure that her interventions with the executive remain compatible with her legislative role, which means that those interventions must explicitly reinforce the letter and spirit of the laws, regulations, and rules that her branch has promulgated and overseen—even if she vigorously takes issue with the interests of the executive branch as a partisan. The onus on the executive official-cum-influencer is the reverse. She must be careful not to act where the branch in which she occupies a role has partisan interests at stake. But she has no similar obligation to the legislative branch, whenever a controversy involves questions of legislative intent, or the meaning and validity of a law more generally.

One of the reasons legislators want to represent others before the executive is that they thereby become better lawmakers. While each individual legislative representation must remain consistent with existing law, such representations—summed over a sufficient number—can also cue legislators to the need to change a law. As Senator Paul Douglas put the point, "the cumulation of individual complaints" that legislators bring before the executive branch "gives them an insight into the weaknesses of laws."[28] Casework activities, Robert Klonoff observes, "create a major potential source of information concerning recurrent agency malfunctions."[29] If so, then it is easy to see what troubles us about Senator Tom Daschle's interventions with the U.S. Forest Service on behalf his constituent Murl Bellew, whose local airline fleet continually failed to meet Forest Service standards. Ultimately unsuccessful in his representations on Bellew's behalf, Daschle introduced legislative amendments that would have stripped the Forest Service of the ability to inspect such aircraft, thus encouraging the bureau to adopt such a change itself through regulation. Subsequently, on February 24, 1994, one of Bellew's planes crashed, killing four people. "[W]hen a constituent has a problem,"

Daschle said, "I don't say how many others are there like you? I don't take a poll. If it's right, it's right. I said to Murl, 'You make a good case.'"[30] Paul Douglas thought that legislators ought to make representations that are explicitly consistent with existing law or, based only on a "cumulation" of cases that suggest a problem, change it. The difficulty with Daschle's interventions, by contrast, was that they confronted executive officials with a change of the law based, explicitly, on one case.[31]

Notwithstanding the apparent morass, there is indeed a comprehensible normative structure to undue-influence law and discourse, one which configures itself in a strikingly inverse fashion between the executive and legislative branches. Executive officials are prophylactically barred from (a) representing all others (b) before all departments and agencies, but are allowed to represent (c) their own personal interests or (d) the interests of others where challenges to U.S. interests are not involved. Legislators, by contrast, are in vague terms permitted to (a) represent all others provided those others have meritorious cases (b) before all agencies and departments provided they do so on the merits, but legislators may not (c) represent their own personal interests or (d) get involved in challenges to U.S. law. The contours of undue influence in the two branches are starkly different. Indeed, they invert one another—testimony to the ways in which normative structures take on the configuration of institutional imperatives.

5

Abuse of Office

The words *abuse of office* appear in no federal statute or regulation. Often used as an umbrella phrase—as an equivalent for corruption or malfeasance—the term would seem to embrace not only conflict of interest but other forms of official wrongdoing as well. Yet despite being bereft of legal definition and burdened with generic connotation, abuse of office has been consigned by discourse to a particular domain within the conflict-of-interest universe. "[A]buse of office is coercion by a government official, however subtle, to induce private advantage for himself or his associates"; "abuse of office [occurs when officials] use their offices to coerce . . . other persons to provide any financial benefits to themselves, their families or business or financial connections."[1] Secretary of the Air Force Harold Talbott provided one of the most prominent postwar cases of abuse of office when his private consulting business performed remunerative services for several major Air Force contractors. More recently, the Bronx law firm of Biaggi and Ehrlich—which retained Congressman Mario Biaggi as senior counsel—courted abuse-of-office accusations when it executed paid legal services for Wedtech Corporation, whose dealings with the federal government Biaggi had the capacity to abet or retard.[2] Or, more hypothetically and timelessly, consider the "wardheeler" who, in Paul Douglas's telling, operates a private insurance business while remaining in a position to affect, in his official capacity, the interests of scores of actual and potential clients.[3]

Structurally—and the Talbott, Biaggi, and wardheeler cases all illustrate this in pure form—abuse of office involves one official and two private business interests. One of the interests belongs to the official (Talbott's consulting business, Biaggi's law firm, the wardheeler's insurance practice), but it is not the one that he can affect in his official role. The other does not belong to him, but he *is* capable of affecting it in-role: the interest of an aerospace firm such as Avco in getting an Air Force contract, the interests of a Wedtech in getting federal assistance, the interests of a ward construction firm in a zoning variance or permit. The possibility of abuse of office emerges with the possibility of a business link between the two interests.

The word *coercion* often appears in definitions or discussions of abuse of office. It would be a mistake, though, to interpret its pervasiveness to mean that abuse necessarily entails the solicitation or wresting of benefits—business opportunities—*by* an official *from* private parties whose interests he can affect. Abuse of office may seem to involve an initiating official and a reacting private party, much as bribery is colloquially thought to involve the reverse— an initiating private party and a reacting official. But in fact in either case, bribery/*quid pro quo* or abuse of office, the chain of cause and effect can go in the reverse direction. An official can solicit a bribe, and a private party can initiate a business relationship with an official's firm in hopes that the official will abuse his position in a favorable way—which, of course, is not to deny that the private party might feel coerced. The distinction between bribery/ *quid pro quo* and abuse of office consists in something other than a difference in the initiating party.

In an archetypal situation of bribery/*quid pro quo,* an officeholder either receives or solicits something of economic value from a private party, one whose interests he has the official capacity to affect. Having not reciprocated by providing equivalent private-market services, the implication looms large that the officeholder will furnish consideration through some form of official act, whether past, present or future. In situations of abuse of office, the officeholder *does* recompense the paying private party through the market, usually via services rendered, thereby (arguably) obliterating any implication that he may be beholden to reciprocate with an official act. Talbott did not take a fee from Air Force contractor Avco in return for using his office to grant the company contracts. He, or rather his firm, took a fee in return for providing professional services. In Paul Douglas's rendering, the wardheeler does not take a fee in exchange for using his offices to grant the payor a zoning variation. He takes a fee in exchange for using his insurance office to write the payor a mutual policy. And, as the court noted in *Biaggi,* "this case is not the garden variety of extortion/bribery in which a payment is made to a public official who has no colorably lawful claim to it, [for] a payment to a law firm is normally a legitimate payment for services rendered . . . A client paying his law firm's legal fee does not commit bribery simply because a Congressman is 'of counsel' to the firm and the client hopes the Congressman will some day be helpful."[4] All of which affords Talbott, Biaggi, and the wardheeler the opportunity to deny the possibility of any consequent impairment of their official judgment: Each owes nothing public or official to the private party, because each provides complete private, economic consideration in return for the benefit received. In Paul Douglas's hypothetical example, the wardheeler cites the fact that there is no "price differential between the insurance" he provides and that offered by competitors to suggest that he is unlikely to feel beholden to his customers.

Not all abuse situations are "pure" in this way. Many bleed into some version of *quid pro quo*.[5] Often, there is a genuine question as to whether the official has in fact offered sufficient private-market consideration for the value he has received, or whether he indeed "owes" something more. Notions of consideration are elastic. In the case of Jim Wright, former Speaker of the House of Representatives, considerable debate arose over the decision of Fort Worth developer George Mallick—whose interests Wright was able to further as Speaker—to hire the Speaker's wife, Betty, at $18,000 a year for four years. Some argued that the private-market consideration Betty Wright rendered for her salary was inadequate. She was insufficiently equipped to deliver suitable business services in exchange, and in fact worked only twelve days during the four years. Therefore, many observers concluded, a portion of Mallick's payments must have gone to buy public, official acts from her husband. As William Safire wrote at the time, the "issue is not . . . a public official's influence in getting a spouse a job; the ethical transgression is to pay a spouse who does not work, or corruptly to overpay a spouse to contribute to an official's support."[6]

But others—those more reluctant to parse the question of whether Betty Wright provided services commensurate with her remuneration—expressed concern about the Speaker's wife securing a job from an interest the Speaker could affect *even if* Betty Wright had rendered full consideration in return.[7] Both sides drew a distinction between abuse of office and *quid pro quo* but disagreed as to which term more aptly described the Betty Wright situation; the disagreement between the two hinged on assessments of consideration.

It is worth noting—and this is documented in some detail in Part II—that there is a sense in which those who assume a relatively harsh posture toward officials in *quid pro quo* situations adopt a very *broad* understanding of what constitutes consideration. Take as an example an official who participates in granting a multimillion-dollar contract to a firm which, some time earlier, had sent him two tickets to a baseball game. The official, typically, will use the value differential between the private *quid* and the public *quo* to deny the possibility of any *pro;* the lack of any equivalency between the two, he will argue, gainsays the possibility that they were undertaken even partly in exchange for one another. "[Mike] Espy's defenders," notes columnist David Frum, referring to the former secretary of agriculture, "argue that the very smallness of the sums at stake proves his innocence: You can't buy a cabinet secretary with free tickets to the U.S. Open."[8] The official's critics, however, will insist that *quid* and *quo* need not exhibit anything near equivalence for the relationship between them to have been one of exchange, for the one to have figured as consideration for the other.

But when we move from *quid pro quo* to abuse of office—where what the official gives in return for the payment takes the form of private-market services, not an official act—the doctrinal positions are reversed. Here, critics of officials take a narrow, proportionalist view of consideration, using any inequivalency between what the official gives and what he gets to *deny* that the official offered consideration for what he received, so as to then push the offense from the less clearly troubling category of "abuse of office" to the more clearly troubling class of *quid pro quo*. In defending themselves, by contrast, officials are much more inclined to adopt a latitudinarian, all-encompassing notion of consideration—one in which, as in the Betty Wright case, a few periodic phone calls on behalf of Mallick sufficed as consideration for an $18,000 annual salary.

Any given case, then, will cross the boundary from *quid pro quo* to abuse of office when there is no question but that the official did indeed render adequate private-market consideration for what he received. Just to round this out, if abuse borders *quid pro quo* on the one side, it also (as noted previously) borders self-dealing on the other. Abuse bleeds into self-dealing as the incentives increase for some form of regularized relationship to be established between the interest the official can affect and the one he possesses, such that it becomes more apt to refer to them as one interest, not two. Such incentives normally increase with the transaction costs accompanying the economic exchanges between the two interests, to the point where it makes sense for them to begin "internalizing" the relationship in embedded contractual or joint-organizational form, as opposed to their repeatedly encountering one another in the external marketplace.[9] In sum, abuse of office is most likely to arise in "ordinary market" situations, where the relationship between the parties has neither transcended the realm of market exchange altogether—as when the private party pays an above-market price and we have entered a situation of bribery/*quid pro quo*—nor been substantially internalized *from* the marketplace, as when transaction costs mount and self-dealing might be the ultimate result.

There is another sense in which an "ordinary market" situation is necessary for abuse to occur. I have been assuming that the private party who engages the official's business enterprise is in fact in the market—is a candidate—for the kind of goods or services the official's business enterprise supplies. I have been assuming, in other words, that the possibility of a normal business relationship exists between the private party whose interests the official can affect and the official's business enterprise. However, this need not always be the case. Say, for example, that the official owns a tractor emporium. While in office, he can affect the interests of high-tech firms. Conceivably, one such high-tech firm could place an order for tractors from the official's emporium and get ample consideration in the form of top-of-the-line tractors for whatever it pays. But the issue here would center on the fact that it was not just the firm's choice of the official's company with which to do business, but its decision to do this kind of business at all, that might have been influenced by the official's in-role capacity to affect its interests. In such cases—where the high-tech firm is influenced not just in its choice of actor (that is, in its choice of tractor vendor) but in its choice to act at all (to buy tractors in the first place)—abuse of office transmutes into "shakedown." It becomes reminiscent of the stereotypical attempt to sell "protection" or "insurance" to merchants who do not need it, purveyed by individuals who are in a position, legally or illegally, to affect the interests of those merchants. So for purposes of abuse of office—in order to cabin the concept in a way faithful to discourse—I assume that the private party is one for whom there exists the *possibility* of a normal business relationship with the official's private enterprise, whatever it may be.

But now if these are the boundaries of abuse of office—if this is pure abuse of office—then what is wrong with it? The very point of a transgression called "abuse of office"—the reason why it occupies its own substantial expanse in the topography of conflict—is that even where there is an acceptable level of consideration between the two interests, something troubling may have occurred. The presence of consideration does not mean the absence of a problem. The question remains: What exactly is the problem?

In a situation of pure abuse, we would hesitate to say that the official, having rendered full value in consideration for what he has received, remains beholden to the paying private party concerned—as we would in a case of *quid pro quo*. Even so, we might describe the official as being *grateful to* or *appreciative of* the private party. Assume a relatively competitive market, where the official's business enterprise is only one of a number of private economic entities that could have performed the task at hand—provided consideration in the way of consulting, legal, or insurance services—in return for the private party's payment. Yet in the face of such an array of choice, the paying private party (an Avco, a Wedtech, a local construction company) nevertheless purchased its services from the official's enterprise (Talbott's consulting company, Biaggi's law firm, the wardheeler's insurance practice) when it could, presumably, have gone elsewhere. Any such decision would bring value to the official, for which we could then reasonably assume him to be appreciative—not beholden in the sense that he owes a debt (for he has furnished private-market services in recompense) but grateful in the sense that he may want to dispense a gratuity, through his public office, for having been chosen.

Of course, such a presumption may be inaccurate in certain cases. To the extent that the official's business interest occupies an oligopolistic or monopolistic market position, the private party would have had little or no choice but to do business with it—certainly not if it wanted the kind of private-market goods and services the official's firm provides. To the extent that the official knows his firm would have captured the market on pure business criteria anyway, he is less likely to exhibit gratitude in his official role. But otherwise, in most abuse situations, while the official may in no way feel beholden to the private party to perform a particular public act, he may nevertheless feel grateful for having been chosen to provide the private-market service.

In *quid pro quo* situations, beholdenness and gratitude assume exactly the reverse emphasis. That is, while an official who receives a *quid* would be beholden to the private party paying it, he is unlikely to be grateful to that party for bribing *him* to perform the contemplated public act—in the way in which, in abuse situations, an official might be grateful to an affected private party, an Avco or a Wedtech, for choosing *his* firm to perform private economic services. And this is because the private party would have had no choice but to bribe that particular official, certainly not if it wanted that particular public act performed. *In-role,* there is often only one or at most a very few officeholders who can perform any particular official act, at least if such acts go beyond the purely ministerial. We thus rarely think of a bribed or gifted official as being grateful that he, and not another official, received the bribe or gift. In a *quid pro quo* situation, our concern is that the official is beholden for an act, not grateful for being the actor. In abuse of office, the reverse is the case.

In an abuse-of-office situation, there remains, though, one question: How grateful is the official? In *quid pro quo,* we can measure an official's beholdenness in an arguably objective way, by reference to the magnitude of the private payment he receives. The larger the payment, the more substantial we suppose the recompensing official act will be. But in abuse of office—because the official has already recompensed the private payment through market services rendered—the magnitude of his gratitude is bereft of a market measure. Instead, it will correspond to the producer surplus or rent he or his firm earns, if any, in supplying the service. Rent or surplus, of course, occurs in a variety of market circumstances. It arises whenever any given producer—a consulting business, a law firm, an insurance company—finds itself offering its services at a market price (say $100 per hour), set by the marginal firm that demand calls forth, which exceeds the price (say $75) at which *it* would have been willing to render the service, for whatever reason—perhaps because of its greater efficiencies, perhaps because of its greater desire for the business. The magnitude of this difference—rent or surplus of various description— will differ for each firm, but it has no direct or explicit market representation. And it is precisely because rent differs unknowably for each producer that the consumer—an Avco, a Wedtech, a local construction firm—is likely to feel coerced. For absent some form of explicit agreement which would take us into the realm of bribery, an Avco will never be able to tell whether a Talbott will be extremely grateful, just a little grateful, or not at all grateful for its business.

In *U.S. v. Gorman* (1986) the court came closest to explicitly grappling with this point.[10] Paul Gorman, an assistant U.S. attorney, had acquired a loan from Merle Weber, a creditor's representative whose interests in an Illinois bankruptcy Gorman had the capacity to advance. Having repaid the loan with interest, Gorman contended that he had "merely entered into an economic exchange, receiving something for which he had paid a fair price." Conceding that Gorman's argument was "logical," the court nevertheless noted that Gorman was in "severe financial difficulties during the time period in question" and concluded that while Gorman might not have been "objectively" beholden to Weber, he had reason to be "subjectively" grateful. For in addition to its "objective" value, the court opined, the loan would have had a "subjective value to Gorman over and above [its] market price." Weber, of course, would have had no way of measuring that "subjective value."

Of course, while the paying private party might have no way of knowing what subjective valuation the official places on the payment, he nevertheless will assign it his own subjective valuation. And this offers accused officials an alternative gambit, one well illustrated by Sherman Adams, President Eisenhower's chief of staff. Bernard Goldfine, a Boston businessman whom Adams had assisted in his dealings with the federal government, on one occasion paid Adams's hotel bills and on another (more famously) gave him a vicuna coat. Adams denied that these gifts constituted a bribe, because although they possessed considerable objective market value, they were of no subjective value not necessarily to Adams himself but to Goldfine. Goldfine kept the Boston hotel room as an apartment. And since Goldfine's family manufactured vicuna coats, the gift's marginal cost to Goldfine was next to nil. Goldfine, on Adams' account, had furnished Adams with nothing of value to Goldfine; therefore Adams owed nothing (official) in return.[11]

So in any given case where an official can affect the interests of a private party with which she or her firm is doing business, the extent of her gratitude is the constructive measure of the abuse taking place. Such an official is most likely to feel gratitude where her own private interest, her consulting or law or insurance firm in our examples, operates vulnerably in a competitive market, such that customers—whether an Avco, a Wedtech, or a local insurance-purchasing construction firm—*could* have gone to other service suppliers. And the official is also more likely to feel gratitude where her firm garners some kind of rent or surplus in the transaction. Of course, these two circumstances may not arise at the same time; indeed, to some extent the magnitude of competition and the magnitude of rent are in tension. To the extent that a market is actually a competitive one—meaning that the official may feel gratitude for her firm's having been chosen—it might also be one in which, precisely because competitors will beat the price down, it earns little or no rent.

On the other hand, to the extent that the official's firm enjoys some market dominance—an oligopolistic or even monopolistic position—her firm is likely to earn a sizable rent. But precisely to the extent that her firm enjoys some market dominance—such that customers have little choice but to come to her—she may feel less grateful, less called upon to dispense a "gratuity" by way of an official act.[12]

During the time when literary agent Lynn Chu was auctioning a book proposal of Newt Gingrich, former Speaker of the House, Gingrich had sufficiently segmented the market that he had become a monopolist, the sole provider of the product, a "book by the most influential political figure in America." Chu cited Gingrich's market dominance as proof that he need not have felt grateful to the winning bidder, HarperCollins. After all, had Harper-Collins not offered Gingrich $4.5 million, another publisher would have. "You don't reach those numbers if a number of publishers aren't involved," Chu said.[13] True. But precisely to that extent, they collectively bid the price up far above the level that would have been necessary to induce Gingrich to produce the work in the first place, as was ultimately revealed when Gingrich himself, under political pressure, reworked his price downward.

Abuse of office, then, is an offense that presumes a particular kind of market situation: First, the costs of the transactions between the official's business interest and the paying business interest must be low enough to justify an ordinary external market relationship between them. If transaction costs are sufficiently high, the two may begin merging into one interest, thus converting the situation into self-dealing. Second, the amount paid by the private party must not rise above the market price typically charged for the service the official's firm renders, else the situation bleeds into *quid pro quo*. Assuming negligible transaction costs and no above-market pricing, the stage then begins to set for abuse. But still, more is needed. For abuse additionally requires that the official's firm both face at least some competition and earn at least some rent from the transaction, so that the official becomes grateful to the private payor for having entered into a market relationship with her firm. If competition is so severe that rent is wiped out, or if the rent itself results from the official's firm's enjoying a monopolistic or oligopolistic market position, then the measure of her gratitude will fall.

But given all of these circumstances—in other words, given a fairly typical market situation of no-cost market-price transactions and moderate (neither perfect nor monopolistic) competition, what bothers us about pure abuse of office begins to emerge. An official feels grateful for having been chosen to perform the private-market service in question, and the private party feels coerced—or threatened, uneasy—because he has no way of knowing what value the official places on having been chosen.

6

Private Payment for Public Acts

In pure abuse of office, a private party transfers value to an officeholder, who then provides full private-market consideration in return. Hence, although the officeholder may be in a position to officially favor the private party, she claims not to be beholden to it. So described, the structure of abuse readily suggests the possibility of its inversion. Specifically, it suggests the possibility of a private party who has a hold on a public official—having transferred value to the official for which the official has provided *no* private-market consideration in return—but where the official cannot in any way affect the private party's interests.

Indeed, there does exist just such a domain within American conflict-of-interest discourse, one with its own governing law and cases. It addresses situations in which an official neither provides compensating out-of-role consideration to a paying private party nor has the in-role capacity to affect its interests. At the federal level, 18 U.S.C. §209 prohibits "private payment for public acts"—private payments "as compensation for [an official's] services as an officer or employee of the executive branch"—regardless of whether such public acts or services in any way affect the interests of the private-party payor.[1] In practice, the statute is concerned with two situations. In the first, individuals on the brink of entering government receive what seem to be generous termination bonuses, pension cash-outs, or other lump-sum payments from a private employer for which they have (arguably) rendered inadequate private-market consideration as employees. Here, "[w]here no commensurate past services can be shown, the inference will be virtually inescapable that the [pension or severance] rights accruing to the employee during his government service are [being paid] 'in connection with his government service'"—even if the employee has recused herself from all matters involving her former employer.[2] In the second "private payment for public acts" situation, individuals, once in government—for example, dollar-a-year men or without-compensation officials—receive private supplements for their inadequate, low, or nonexistent public salaries.

Many mistakenly believe that 18 U.S.C. §209 in fact does require an official to be in a position to affect the interests of the private payor. But of course if it did, it would essentially collapse into some variant of a bribery or gratuity statute.[3] As a 1960 New York Bar Association study notes, if the "outside compensation rule is to add anything to the general rule requiring personal disqualification, it must apply to outside compensation from any source, not just a sensitive source"[4]—although the Bar adds that, so understood, 18 U.S.C. §209 is "in the strictest sense . . . not a conflict-of-interest statute. The employee does not have to do anything improper in his office to violate the statute. His receipt of the outside salary for his government work, coupled with his status as a government employee, is all that is required."[5]

So what, then, could be wrong with private payment for public acts?

Private payment for public acts becomes controversial, as noted, in two circumstances: when private companies offer generous lump-sum payments or bonuses to employees about to enter government, or when private firms supplement officials' meager dollar-a-year (or otherwise inadequate) public salaries once they have entered government. In the first type of case, litigants and courts debate whether a particular severance payment represents fair compensation for services the employeee rendered the company over her career, or whether, on a more credible reading, those payments include a premium for future government service. Typically, in such situations, employees departing for government service and their private employers—seeking to elude the reach of 18 U.S.C. §209—take an exceedingly broad view as to what constitutes consideration. For them, the most generous termination bonuses can constitute fair recompense for the most minimal services rendered by the employee, relieving any fear that the employee—now an official—might remain beholden to the private employer. However, critics—those who seek to bring officials to heel under Section 209—adopt a far narrower definition of fair consideration: If the official received a private payment even marginally in excess of the private services she rendered her old firm, this would be a sign that she will be beholden for further, *public* acts once in office.[6]

In the second type of "private payment for public acts" case, legislators and commentators debate the wisdom of exempting part-time executive employees or full-time "volunteers"—dollar-a-year men, without-compensation employees, or generally anyone whose official salary is inadequate or below-market—from the statutory prohibitions on private payment for public acts. In 1962, part-time and volunteer employees did win exemption from 18 U.S.C. §209's strictures against privately sourced salary supplementation (although some commentators still think this was a bad idea), while those full-time officials whose salaries otherwise seem low or inadequate are not exempt (although many believe they should be).[7]

Of course, the question of what constitutes an adequate or market-level official salary is an open one. Here, interestingly, it is the recipient official's critics—those who seek strong Section 209 enforcement—who adopt an exceedingly broad view of consideration, in which even the most meager official salary constitutes fair recompense for the most copious and diligent public services. Hence, any private salary supplementation is unnecessary and represents a windfall to the official: "[w]hen additional pay or perquisites are accepted by a public officer for performance of duties germane to his office, a taxpayer has a right to insist that the funds wrongfully received shall be returned to the public treasury. And this right is not nullified by the fact that the reasonable value of the services exceeded the amount received."[8]

By contrast, officials themselves—those who seek to escape Section 209's reach—here take a much stricter, narrower view of the necessary proportionality between official salary and services. For them, if the value of the public services the official renders is obviously greater than her official salary, then privately sourced salary supplements do not represent a gratuity or windfall, but rather they simply ensure that the official is getting remuneration equivalent to what she gives.

The most interesting debates over private payment for public acts, however, arise when there is no doubt that the official's actual salary is not adequate compensation. They take place against the shared assumption (indeed, what is preponderantly the case) that government salaries are below-market, that they are insufficient to compensate officials for their services. And the question then is: Why, as many have urged, should we prevent an official whose salary is concededly below-market—or, as some still urge, a without-compensation or dollar-a-year official—from receiving outside salary supplementation? Why pass an 18 U.S.C. §209? Of dollar-a-year men, Woodrow Wilson, during whose presidency the original statute came into existence, argued that when officials "serve the government without remuneration," it is because "Americanism [is] their only motive."[9] An official, goes the Wilsonian view, "ought not be fully rewarded by financial means to leave some room for the public-service motive."[10]

Wilson (and others who subsequently argued in the same vein) never denied that official salaries are inadequate. What they claimed is that the demonstrable shortfall between low official salaries and prodigious official workload ought to be made up by the official's own public-spiritedness, and not by various kinds of private salary supplementation. One way of recasting the Wilsonian argument is to say that public service generates its own psychic income that augments whatever meager official salary it offers. Or, as Senator William Proxmire put it with remarkable precision, "[t]here is a lot of psychic income in this business that I would estimate to be worth at least

$150,000."[11] The combination of admittedly low official salary but generous psychic income should, defenders of Section 209 argue, be enough to compensate the official for the services she renders. Any additional private salary supplementation would, consequently, bring her total remuneration to a level *in excess* of whatever she delivers by way of public service, leaving her beholden to the private payor. Private salary supplements, on this argument, would indeed represent a rent or windfall to the official, because she would have performed the public services in question anyway, having willingly supplemented inadequate wages out of her own psychic pocket. Thus it is that those who oppose private payments for public acts—those who assume private payors will exert a hold even on low-paid public officials—are also those who believe officials are (or should be) motivated to perform their official tasks by a healthy modicum of gratuitous public-spiritedness, civic-mindedness, magnanimity, and "Americanism."[12]

No such presumption lurks beneath the rhetoric of those who have inscribed 18 U.S.C. §209 with numerous exceptions and hedged it with waivers over the years. For them, not only is the official salary that a government job generates pitifully low, so is the psychic income it offers. In many cases, then, private salary supplements promise the only means of bringing an official's total remuneration up to a level adequate to recompense her for the official services she renders. Private payments should therefore exert *no* hold on the official, for she will still be giving amply—by way of public service—for whatever combination of low official salary, nonexistent psychic income, and gap-filling private supplementation she happens to receive. Any such private supplementation would not represent a tip or a perk, a rent or a reward, for doing something she would have done anyway. Rather, absent such privately underwritten salary subventions, many officials would just as happily have remained outside of government, given the low public salary and psychic income otherwise offered. Hence as the political scientist Steven Kelman acknowledges, those "who will work for government only if salaries are fully competitive" and who otherwise "lack any commitment to public service" will not, absent private-sector support, be attracted to government.[13] If indeed the erstwhile official can earn more than a low government salary elsewhere, a private salary supplement that simply makes good the difference would provide her no "rent," nor give the payor any hold over her, assuming she is indifferent to government service itself.[14]

In fact, if such private payments do any entity a favor, it is not the official but the government, which would otherwise be unable to retain her.[15] Hence, defenders of private payments to officials rarely talk of the psychic income public service itself provides. Rather, they portray government service as a burden for which adequate monetary consideration must be paid through (if need be) a combination of public and private sources. "Our society [wrongly] assumes that the 'psychic income' of public service will compensate executives for [the] loss" of private income, as Alexander Trowbridge puts it.[16]

Let us now accept the Wilsonian premise that justifies strictures prohibiting private payments for public acts. Let us assume, in other words, that officials should (or do) make good the gap between their low official salary and their high level of public service with their own internally generated psychic income, and hence should not and need not rely on outside private supplements. On such an assumption, any private salary supplementation the official did receive would be supererogatory, a premium or windfall, something that could put a hold on the official. But—again, assuming that the official cannot affect the interests of the private payor—where exactly would the problem lie? Where precisely is the conflict?

Those who are bothered by such a practice, who see it as posing a conflict, make one further assumption. They assume that a private payor with a hold on a public official might exert that hold, might be interested in seeking action from the official, even in matters that *go beyond* those affecting the payor's own interests. To remain unperturbed by "pure private-payment-for-public-acts" situations, one would have to believe that private actors, and certainly private payors in Section 209 circumstances, are actuated only by matters in which their own pecuniary interests are at stake and not by any broader political program or other-regarding considerations. Consider the following rationale for 18 U.S.C. §209 that the New York Bar Association study, headed by Roswell Perkins, offered in 1960:

> [O]pen channels for policymaking are frustrated when an official appears to perform an ordinary role but is in fact responding to the demands of others to whom he is secretly economically tied. It is not simply that he or the outside group make money out of it. They may not. It is that the public processes of government are being subverted while policy is made silently by forces not known or responsive to the electorate.[17]

The use of the words policy, policymaking, and public processes of government suggest a private payor with a broad agenda—an ideology—who might well use his hold on the official to direct her in areas that range far beyond his own personal interests.[18] Indeed, 18 U.S.C. §209's origins lie in the trend, during World War I, for nonprofit associations—which had no direct interests at stake—to encourage government studies of social issues by underwriting the salaries of officials involved. More recently, Robert Wallach, having paid some of the legal bills that Attorney General Ed Meese incurred in office, found himself accused of being a freelance policy advisor when he counseled Meese on foreign and domestic policy matters ranging far afield from any in which he might have had a personal, private interest.[19]

It is thus the Wilsons and the Perkinses—those who believe in officials with deep public spirits and payors with broad public interests—who most oppose private payments for public acts. By contrast, an official solely motivated by private pecuniary interests—who derives no psychic income from government work—will be giving far more in official services than she is getting personally out of her low-paying official job; hence, any private salary supplementation will not put a hold on her (indeed, without it *she* will be the one who feels owed). And a private payor motivated solely by his own private pecuniary interests—one who sticks to his own knitting—is unlikely to want to exert his hold on an official who cannot affect them. Pure "private payment for public acts," then, is a peculiar kind of conflict of interest. The more public-spirited officials are assumed to be, and the more publicly motivated payors are thought to be, the more likely we are to be troubled by situations of pure private payment for public acts.

7

Private Gain from
Public Office

As the various categories of conflict of interest fan out from self-dealing, a
subtle shift in the nature of conflict sets in. In self-dealing it is, straightforwardly, the official's own pecuniary interests that create the impairment. But
in each of the three conflict categories beyond self-dealing, the pecuniary imperative—while evident—actually plays a secondary role, ceding the title of
"actual impairment" to a new set of elements. In undue influence, on the
best jurisprudential authority we have, the influenced official's judgment is
impaired by her own professional, collegial, or in-role interests, those she
fears that the influencing official could manipulate, either as reward or as
punishment. In abuse of office, the abusing official's judgment is impaired by
a sense of gratitude proportional to the immeasurable—indeed, subjective—
rent or surplus she enjoys in supplying a service or good in the marketplace.
In private payment for public acts, the official's impairment is proportional to
the psychic income the official enjoys from—or the "public service" motive
she brings to—her government work, which the private payor enables and
tops up. Professional bureaucratic interests, private producer surplus, public-
service psychic income—these are the added imponderable ingredients in the
fields of conflict beyond the pecuniary interest at stake in self-dealing; indeed,
they are the agents that make for conflict itself.

The origins of the fourth conflict category beyond self-dealing, private
gain from public office, lie in yet another mental terrain—in the skills and
stature an official derives from office and then turns to private account,
whether through fees for services rendered or boards joined, honoraria for
speeches delivered or advances for books written, expense-paid trips to conferences or free weekends at charity golf tournaments. Whatever the particu-
lars, in private gain from public office the official's in-role judgment or performance need not in any way be encumbered; after all, neither element of
quid pro quo need be present. Private gain from public office can provoke
normative concern even when officials are incapable of affecting the fortunes
of the paying private interest in question *and* are in no way beholden to it.

Consider, for example, an Environmental Protection Agency (EPA) official who teaches a university course on a policy issue related to her government work, or a Navy procurement officer who contracts with a publisher to write a manual on how to do business with his bureau. In neither case does the official—the EPA program supervisor, the Navy procurement official—have the capacity to affect the paying private interest, the university or the publisher. Nor, having rendered compensating private-market consideration (a course or manual) are the officials beholden. Certainly, cases of *im*pure private gain from public office can arise, as they would were the EPA official to offer the course, or the Navy official to sell the manual, directly to entities whose interests they could affect or at inflated prices. But even in such cases, something else would bother us beyond the various elements of *quid pro quo*. What would bother us is the sight, as the House Ethics Manual puts it, of officeholders "cash[ing] in on official position."[1]

Whether in fact or in concept, private gain from public office is thus an evil (if it is an evil) that arises separate and apart from any conflicted mental state. As the "Topography of Conflict" chart suggests, it is an outlier, reposing beyond the very realm of conflict itself. Not surprisingly, then, of all the categories I have analyzed thus far it is the only one that is a *non*prophylactic offense. Private gain from public office is both the *malum prohibitum*—it is the very thing that we directly, if somewhat vaguely, prohibit—and the *malum in se,* the harm (such as it is) in itself.

But what kind of harm? In what follows, I attempt to identify what it is that troubles us about pure private gain from public office, even where the official otherwise acts "impartially, does not play favorites, and is a model of public decorum."[2] For of all the realms of conflict, private gain from public office is perhaps the most normatively contested. Some officials or scholars find it untroubling: As Dennis F. Thompson says, "despite the strong condemnations of private gain in most codes of government ethics, there is nothing *in itself* wrong with personally benefiting from holding public office".[3] Others, however—usually government agencies or political commentators—view it is a significant offense: "I have always believed it was improper," the journalist Haynes Johnson has written, "for people to hold high positions in the government and use that position for profit."[4] But before exploring the normative question as to what, if anything, is *wrong* with private gain from public office, it is necessary to examine the no less strenuously debated conceptual question, "What *is* private gain from public office?"

Not all instances of ethical transgression that fall outside the realm of impaired official judgment need fall inside the parameters of private gain from public office, as wide as they are. For example, the private use of confidential or classified information derived from government service is prohibited under its own class of regulations and poses no difficult normative (if sometimes exquisitely difficult factual) questions.

Nor is an official found guilty of receiving an illegal gratuity under 18 U.S.C. §201 necessarily also guilty of private gain from public office. True, as with situations of private gain from public office—although unlike bribery/*quid pro quo*—gratuities need not have any encumbering effect on the official's judgment or performance. "Payments to a public official for [official] acts that would have been performed in any event," the court said in *U.S.* v. *Campbell,* "are probably illegal gratuities rather than bribes."[5] Although the officeholder may execute a favorable official act, in other words, it is not done *in consideration for* the gratuity; for whenever an act would have been performed anyway, it cannot count as consideration for any other. Unlike in situations of private gain from public office, however—and like bribery/*quid pro quo*—the gratuity-receiving official also renders no *private*-market service in consideration for the payment received. In fact, he executes no private-market act at all. As Bayless Manning put it in a different context, "'[g]ratuity' is an odd word to use where it is given 'in consideration of' something," as the payment is in private gain from public office.[6] In gratuity cases, then, the official gains. Yet she has performed neither official acts, as in bribery/*quid pro quo,* nor private-market services, as in private gain from public office, in return.

Conceptual Issues

"Private gain" and "public office"—the two concepts at play here—are each ambiguous in meaning. And it is the exploration and exploitation of their ambiguity that, largely, structures debate over the conceptual question, "what *is* private gain from public office?" *Private gain* signifies that culpable officials, in seeking or enjoying the gain in question, are doing so outside of their official roles. The modifier *private* suggests a kind of gain—a trip on a corporate jet, attending an association meeting at a resort, an all-expense paid trip to a charity event—that does not, or ought not, or need not, redound to the official as part of his or her job. If the official's responsibilities required the official to board the corporate aircraft, or be present at the association meeting, or attend the charity event, then there would be no "private" gain, just the exercise of office. But assume now that the activity in question is emphatically not part of an official's role, that it therefore uncontroversially does constitute private gain. To then say that such private gain flows from *public office* implies that the official enjoys such gain only because she happens to occupy that official role. The invitation to the charity event or, more diffusely, the knowledge, skills, and stature which now attract business, would not have evolved had the official never held that office.

Faced with the charge of using public office for private gain, implicated officials will deny either that the gain is private or else that it results from anything public. Thus on the one hand, implicated officials will insist that their boarding the corporate jet, or attending the association's meeting, or even participating in the charitable event was part of their job—something they had to do in-role anyway—and hence constitutes something neither private nor gain. It represents no new net augmentation to their psychic or economic utility; it is in no way an "extra" but simply "all in a day's work." On the other hand, conceding that a trip, meal, or invitation does constitute private gain and not official duty, officials—pointing to facets of their out-of-role selves such as a personal association with the charity, or innate talents or skills—will then deny that it flows to them because of their public offices.

For the concept of "private gain from public office" to be coherent, it must arise in a realm outside the borders of official role (otherwise there can be no private gain), but where the role nevertheless casts some sort of penumbra-shadow (otherwise the gain fails to result from public office). Implicated officials, for their part, want either to expand the borders of the role (so that there has been no private gain, only the undertaking of public responsibilities), or else contract the penumbra into nothingness (so that any private gain results from privately, not publicly, rooted capacities). But the need to simultaneously expand and contract the realms of public and private—a need which besets argument on both sides if in inverse ways—places each side, implicated officials and those accusing them, in internal tension.

Private Gain or the Execution of Office?

In 1991, a North Carolina environmental group invited William Sanjour, an EPA employee, to address its members (expenses paid) on the dangers of locating a hazardous waste incinerator in Northampton County. Sanjour, an in-house critic of EPA's willingness to allow such projects, was forced to decline the invitation, citing the rules against private gain from public office. Sanjour and a colleague then launched an action against EPA in District of Columbia District and subsequently Circuit Court, seeking to contest the rules covering private gain from public office, at least as applied to his prototypical kind of case. *Sanjour* v. *EPA* and the attendant congressional hearings emblematize one of the key conceptual debates at play in private gain from public office: Accused officials, citing those qualities of their challenged activities that had a "public" or "official" quality, will claim they were operating in-role. Accusing agencies or departments, while denying that the official was operating in-role, will cite those same "public" characteristics as evidence that the official's role extended into and enabled the private gain in question.[7]

Agencies and departments, to begin with, have a strong incentive (to the extent that there is any ambiguity or leeway to the issue) to categorize the activity in question—in Sanjour's case, speaking to the North Carolina environmental group—as private or unofficial, not as an exercise of office. To the extent that the activity does fall under the official's in-role responsibilities, then its subvention by private sources risks falling afoul of 18 U.S.C. §209, which prohibits private payments for official acts. Because the acts in question are official, there exists the presumption that they have already been paid for, or ought ultimately to be paid for, by the public treasury.[8] Agencies thus have reason to nudge any given privately underwritten act in the direction of the private, to offload it into the unofficial—for if official, the agency itself could be expected to come up with the funds to defray it.

As a consequence of their conflicting imperatives, there has emerged a gray area of activities which each party—agency and official—conveniently describe as both public and private, both official and personal. Or, more exactly, they each conveniently ascribe to these activities the least problematic features of both the public and the private. In this realm, acts are sufficiently unofficial so that the agency can disclaim the responsibility to provide them itself, but sufficiently official that the officeholder him- or herself can deny a charge that they constitute private gain. The U.S. OGE, piecemeal in its rulings, has evolved a category of activities that are not considered part of an agency's "functions" but that may nevertheless lie within its sphere of "interests."[9] That an activity—say a particular kind of speaking engagement to a private group—lies outside the agency's functions means that the agency is not itself required to underwrite it.[10] But that an official's engaging in the activity falls within the agency's realm of interests means that the official, in having his or her expenses privately underwritten to do it, is not being personally enriched.[11]

In Sanjour's case, however, the EPA determined that the activity in question—Sanjour's expense-paid attendance at the North Carolina event—did not fall even within the agency's sphere of interests. It could not in any way be classed as an official activity and hence would necessarily constitute private gain—private, because the agency would not have sent him anyway as part of his job; Sanjour, moreover, would have been advancing his own views, not those of EPA. And the trip would have constituted gain because the travel and lodging themselves were of some value. There being nothing wrong with private gain in and of itself, the agency further contended that such gain could have resulted only from Sanjour's holding public office. Sanjour would not have been invited had he not been an EPA official; his talk would have drawn on knowledge derived from his job and dealt with agency-related subject matter; the group, in inviting Sanjour, may well have been under some illusion that he would be speaking in an official capacity; indeed the invitation was directed to him at the office. All of which suggested to the agency that while Sanjour's speech would have constituted a private act, it would have accrued to him because of his public office and not (as EPA regulations put it) his "individual knowledge and accomplishments."[12]

The very same observations, however, suggested something quite different to Sanjour. Specifically, they suggested *not* that it was by virtue of his public office, and his public office alone, that he would have found himself privately enriched by a trip to North Carolina. Rather, these observations—that the group's invitation was addressed to Sanjour at EPA, that the group may plausibly have thought he would be speaking in an official capacity, that his talk would have drawn on knowledge derived from his official role and would have dealt with agency-related subject matter—all went to suggest, for Sanjour, that his proposed trip resembled far more the exercise of his public office than an instance of private activity or gain. The agency may not have regarded the activity in question as "official" but some segment of the public, in addressing the invitation to him at the agency and welcoming him as an EPA spokesman, obviously did—and why should the agency's construction of his official role be controlling? Sanjour further affirmed that the knowledge and information upon which he would have drawn for his speech were indeed derived from his public office—conceding the very point that in other contexts implicated officials are loath to do—but for Sanjour, once again, the public derivation of his activity suggested that it was, in fact, a public activity. The taxpayer, Sanjour urged, had subsidized his acquisition of knowledge and was therefore entitled to its fruits. His environmental insights belonged to the citizen and it was part of his role to disseminate them. Likewise, the fact that the subject matter of his speech related to his official duties further buttressed, for Sanjour, the claim that delivering it would have been an in-role, not a personal, act.

What for the agency constituted evidence that Sanjour's trip (while private gain) was occasioned by his public role—invitations to the office, drawing on officially derived knowledge, concerned with official subject matter—was for Sanjour evidence that the trip was indeed part of his public role, not supererogatory private gain. What for the agency indicated that an official's role casts a shadow far outside its boundary, for Sanjour signified territory well within the boundaries of role.

Sanjour prevailed, but on First Amendment grounds. That is, he argued that any regulation prohibiting such a trip—the purpose of which was to enable him to speak on a public issue—would have interfered with his freedom of speech. In agreeing, the *Sanjour* court was able to avoid the crucial question of how to determine the borders between public role and private activity, and so left debate over private gain from public office very much open.

In this way, *Sanjour* represents another in a line of cases that have restored to officials, albeit haltingly, their constitutional rights when those rights conflict with other goods Congress seeks to promote. Examples include the Supreme Court striking down the honorarium ban prohibiting remunerative speech, or the various Hatch Act cases concerning officials' political activities.[13] But in those instances, the evil the government was seeking to prevent—the financial or partisan corruption of the civil service—is at least conceptually and normatively comprehensible. Here, the principal question is to what extent "private gain from public office" represents an evil in the first place, let alone one whose preclusion would justify any attendant impairment on the constitutional rights of officials. Moreover, political speech constitutes only a confined subset of acts—others include attending events, or rendering professional services—that could constitute private gain from public office. In most cases of private gain from public office, officials' First Amendment rights are simply not implicated, which (among other reasons) is why *Sanjour* settled little.[14]

Private Payments, Public Payments

When the term "private gain from public office" is used in discourse, what makes a gain "private" is not that it comes from a private payor, although it usually does. What makes a gain private is that it accrues to a private activity the official undertakes (hence Sanjour's attempt to expand the boundaries of his role and the agency's attempt to contract them). Private gain can arise, then, when an official bills out-of-role trips or expenses to the public treasury, not just to a private individual or group. During his tenure as George Bush's White House chief of staff, for example, John Sununu sought reimbursement from the public treasury for what arguably were nonofficial acts. Sununu flew to New Hampshire on a government plane, where, while conducting some government business, he attended his son's high-school graduation. Sununu also billed the government for travel and hotel costs he incurred attending a New Hampshire celebrity charity ski event for the Christa McAuliffe Sabbatical Trust.[15]

Where do such incidents fit in the spectrum of private gain from public office, or in the spectrum of ethical transgressions more generally? In cases of private gain from public office, the official's occupancy of a public role has a gainful effect on his private, out-of-role activities. While there is an element of that in the Sununu-type case, the overlaying problem is actually a more traditional form of conflict of interest, where the official's private interests affect his public, in-role activities. Sununu's in-role activities—his deployment of his own time and other official resources—was altered, in part, by his private needs. The test of conflict of interest *per se* is whether the official might have done something in-role that he or she otherwise would not have done in order to advance a private interest. Sununu's acts met this test; they constituted a form of self-dealing, if not misappropriation of government property.

The debate surrounding Sununu's ventures, however, illustrates a larger point. Sununu felt compelled to argue, in each case, that the activity concerned *was* official. Sununu claimed that he would not have attended his son's graduation had he not been in Boston anyway on official business (thereby choosing, perhaps, to place one facet of his personal virtuousness in question in order to shore up his public rectitude). And if he would not have gone on such a trip anyway—that is, for personal reasons—Sununu argued, then he must have undertaken it for official reasons, and its being underwritten by the treasury would not be classifiable as private gain. Sununu likewise designated his attendance at the Christa McAuliffe event an official act, since the McAuliffe programs had been classified as an example of President Bush's "Points of Light" initiative. In fact, Sununu contended that his every act was official, if *official* is defined as "what is in the interests of the administration." The White House counsel, however, took a different view, as did most commentators. For example, although the Points of Light initiative was indeed an official program, it was an official program explicitly devoted to the recognition of private institutions that had taken over public functions from the state. Sununu's argument contravened the program's spirit, even as it highlighted the ambiguities of the public-private distinction.[16]

Notably, while officeholders argue for a very expansive interpretation of their official role in order to rebut charges of private gain from public office, they often argue for a far narrower interpretation in order to refute charges of *quid pro quo*: after all, if their role would not affect a payor's interest, it's not *quid pro quo*. Obviously, a dilemma arises for officials in cases that combine elements of private gain from public office and *quid pro quo*. Or, more graphically, consider former Agriculture Secretary Mike Espy's insistence that his attendance at the Superbowl as the guest of Atlanta's Fernbank Museum was part of his official responsibilities—hence constituted no private gain—but that his acceptance of football tickets from Tyson Foods did not constitute *quid pro quo,* since his role did not lead him to directly oversee meat and poultry inspection.[17]

From Public Office or Personal Abilities?

Whether the funds underwriting an act—a speech, a trip, attendance at a charity event—come from a private party or the government, the officeholder (wherever there is any ambiguity involved) has incentive to classify the act as official; the agency to classify it as private and hence as gain. But this is only one-half of the structure of debate over private gain from public office. For there comes a point sufficiently far along the spectrum where the official, as well as the agency, accepts that the acts in question are uncontroversially private. Here the implicated official—seeking to deny that the private gain had anything to do with his or her occupancy of public office—will reverse strategy. She will insist that the invitation did not in fact go to the office, that her benefactors were in no way interested in or even cognizant of her official role, and that the knowledge and information on which she drew were personal and private, based on her own "individual accomplishments"—all just the opposite of Sanjour's line of argument. A couple of cases illustrate the argumentative hazards this strand of discourse imposes on its participants: the first centers on the paradoxes it imposes on officials; the second on those it places on government agencies.

In 1992, Washington Mayor Sharon Pratt Kelly spoke to a Chicago meeting of the Municipal Bond Investors Assurance Company, which paid her an honorarium and hotel expenses. When the media inquired about the trip, the mayor's spokespeople gave "conflicting information about whether she was representing the District." One of Kelly's staff members, Vada Manager, said the mayor was indeed representing the city; Ellen O'Connor, deputy mayor for finance, added that the District stood "to benefit from the mayor's meeting with the three hundred investors, analysts and bankers" assembled and from her "encouraging them to do business with the city." But the mayor's interim chief of staff, Karen Tramontano, stated that Kelly's comments at the meeting "were not made in her official capacity as mayor, nor did she seek to secure benefits for the District." Instead, Kelly was in attendance as a "nationally recognized figure," and her "conduct was in complete accord with the letter and spirit of the applicable law."[18]

The dichotomy in Kelly's response illustrates the competing imperatives officials face in "private gain from public office" situations. On the one hand, they are impelled to classify the act—a trip to Chicago to speak to the Bond Assurers—as an official responsibility (Kelly was invited in her role as mayor), in which case it does not constitute supererogatory private gain. On the other, officials are impelled to insist that their capacity to perform the act results from purely private, personal accomplishments (Kelly was invited because she is a nationally recognized figure in her own right), and hence does not derive from public office. Officials will try to argue either that they are acting in-role—well within the bounds of their public office—in which case there is no private gain or, conceding that they do act out-of-role, they will insist that their capacity to do so has absolutely nothing to do with their public office. Instead, they attribute it exclusively to their own private talents. But the very arguments that suggest the mayor was invited because of her personal stature, not her public office—she did not attend in her capacity as mayor; she did not seek to secure benefits for the District—undermine the contention that her attendance was part of her official responsibility, and hence in no way constituted private gain.

In the same way, Sununu was motivated to insist that his attendance at the McAuliffe Foundation event fell within his official responsibilities—he would not otherwise have made the trip on his own personal initiative—hence his going at taxpayer's expense would have represented no private gain. That argument failed when the White House counsel formally deemed the McAuliffe trip to fall outside his official responsibilities. But in doing so, it left open the possibility that if the government could not reimburse Sununu for his McAuliffe travel and lodging, the foundation itself could—assuming, of course, that Sununu had not been invited because of his official role but because of who he was outside of his role. Accordingly, Sununu reversed himself. He pointed out that he had attended the McAuliffe event for a number of years prior to becoming the president's chief of staff, so as to suggest that he would therefore have been invited anyway separate and apart from his role. Sununu, in other words, intimated that the invitation came to him not as a result of his public office but as a consequence of his personal qualities, traits and history, and personal links to and support for the charity.[19] But in thus observing that he had regularly gone for many years anyway (and that his attendance this year would therefore have had to do with who he was as a private individual and not his public office), Sununu effectively subverted his earlier claim that he would *not* have gone anyway (and that his attendance would therefore have had to do with his public office, hence could not have represented private gain). The same piece of evidence—his habitual attendance patterns—went to determining both whether the act constituted private gain *and* whether it resulted from public office; it helped define the border between public and private in either case.

Kelly and Sununu display an argumentative tension the reverse of Sanjour's. Sanjour, recall, courted the danger that whatever for him constituted evidence that his trip was an official act and not private gain (the invitation went to the office; he would have drawn on officially derived knowledge) for the agency constituted evidence that, though an unofficial act, Sanjour's capacity to undertake it resulted from his public office, from his in-role knowledge and stature. Conversely, for Kelly and Sununu, whatever shows that they in no way drew on public office when going to Chicago or New Hampshire—on in-role experiences and stature—also undermined any conjoint claim that the trip was in fact an official responsibility and therefore could not have represented private gain.

Government agencies run into the same set of argumentative constraints, although they face a different kind of internal strategic dilemma. For example, a 1990 OGE letter dealt with an official who, in his private capacity, wanted (expenses privately paid) to lead a delegation of businesspeople to

Europe.[20] "[O]n close examination," OGE ruled, "the connection between [his] proposed activity and his agency responsibility is so fundamental that characterizing it as private would be impossible." Here it was the government, not the officeholder, that sought to push the expense-paid trip in the direction of the "official," so as to attribute the officeholder's receipt of it to the public office he held. There was sufficient proximity between the purposes of the trip on the one hand, and the kind of in-role responsibilities the officeholder possessed on the other, that in inviting him his hosts may have thought they would benefit from official support and capacities on their trip. Hence, OGE was able to stamp the trip "*misuse of office* for . . . private gain."

Yet recognizing that the very argument it mounted to show that the trip redounded to public office (not the employee's personal talents) could also be used to classify it as an official responsibility (hence not private gain), the opinion was careful to say: Even though the employee's "proposed activity might more appropriately be characterized as official, that can occur only if it is specifically determined by the agency to be appropriate involvement in an official capacity." Aware that the exact claims supporting its case on the one hand weakened it on the other, OGE had to carve out a realm between the official and the unofficial where such a thing as *private* gain from *public* office is possible. OGE wanted to preempt any argument the official might make that the trip-invitation resulted from purely private, personal aptitudes—as opposed to public office—without giving him the opportunity to then stamp it as an official responsibility—as opposed to private gain.

Role Differences: Legislative and Executive

It is necessary to distinguish between the kind of private gain that flows from (a) the knowledge or skills officials derive from their public roles and (b) the prestige or stature those roles provide them. Both may be sources of "private gain from public office,"[21] but in fact important distinctions between them do emerge, depending largely on whether the official holds legislative or executive office.

Consider two principal—and, taken together, apparently puzzling—differences between the two branches' norms covering private gain from public office. Historically—up until the honorarium ban of 1989—the chair of the Senate Armed Services Committee, say, could receive an honorarium for delivering a speech on defense issues or other matters "related" to his role. But the secretary of defense was forbidden from doing so, even if the group extending the invitation was not one whose interests he could have affected through his office. Even now, legislators and their staff who engage in penumbra activities—those not integral to their jobs but "related" or "connected" to them—can get the associated travel or lodging expenses privately underwritten with greater ease, and in a larger number of circumstances, than can executive officials. As the journalist Lars-Erik Nelson puts it, private parties can defray legislative missions "like Newt Gingrich's $24,000 trip to London in 1997 [while an] executive-branch official would go to prison for accepting identical hospitality."[22] In sum, by taking reimbursements or remuneration for private activities that are fairly proximate to their roles, executive officials sooner court charges of "private gain from public office" than do legislators.[23]

But as we move from private activities relatively closely related to official role—speaking on defense matters, going on fact-finding trips—to those less closely related—attending social or charity events or engaging in various kinds of business activities—the poles reverse. Here, legislators court a greater risk of "private gain from public office" than do executive officials (and, again, just to isolate the "private gain from public office" element, I am assuming that the expense-payor is one whose interests the legislator or executive official cannot affect). Thus, the administrator of the EPA may attend, expenses paid, a "showing of a new adventure movie", and a White House employee can attend a cocktail party "given by a Washington hostess . . . even though he has only recently been introduced to the hostess and suspects that he may have been invited because of his official position"—regardless of how widely attended the event is, or where it is held.[24] Senate and House rules would forbid similar activity.

Likewise, while legislators are prohibited "from accepting reimbursement for transportation or lodging in connection with any charity event,"[25] high-level executive officials (provided they do not accept reimbursement from interests they can affect) labor under fewer restrictions when engaged in charitable fundraising activities.[26] And while Senate staff earning more than $25,000 may not serve on the boards of public corporations or affiliate with professional firms—again, even where the staff member could have no impact on the business's interests—most executive officials at comparable levels face no analogous strictures.[27] The question is: What could account for the greater leniency accorded legislative officials in the first set of instances—where the out-of-role activities remain relatively close to role—and the greater leniency accorded executive officials in the second, where the out-of-role activities rest at a greater remove from official role?

What may be pertinent here is a particular kind of difference between the knowledge or skills (on the one hand) and the prestige or stature (on the other) that officials in the two branches draw from their roles. Consider knowledge and skills first. Legislators, as distinct from executive officials, are thought (indeed, expected) to derive relatively more of their knowledge and understanding from out-of-role experience than from role-engendered expertise. Legislative facts are deemed more universally accessible, and to arrive through many more personal avenues, than those that undergird many kinds of executive branch decisions. When it comes to activities proximate to an official's role but that nevertheless represent private gain—such as an expense-paid speaking trip on defense issues not strictly required by an official's role-responsibilities—the legislative ethics committees are thus more likely to attribute the legislator's capacity to perform them to her personal capabilities and qualities, and less to abilities or understandings she derived exclusively within role. Legislators, so the different norms seem to presume, glean more of their knowledge and skills out-of-role as citizens and less of it in-role as professionals.[28]

On the other hand, more of a legislator's in-role prestige and status extends out-of-role than is the case for executive officials. It's worth noting that prior to the 1996 rules changes, which forbade legislators from accepting travel and lodging reimbursement to attend charity events, the legislative ethics committees would determine whether the legislator was a celebrity before entering Congress. If she was not, the committees would attribute her capacity to provide consideration (by drawing a crowd) to her official role, not her personal stature, and she would be prohibited from accepting paid expenses. In the rare situation where the legislator was a celebrity in another life, she would be allowed to reap whatever material gain is entailed in attending an expense-paid charity event.

More generally, when it comes to private gain that redounds to activities *not* relatively proximate to a legislative official's role—whether charitable, social, or business enterprises—we are more likely to attribute such gain to the prestige and stature of role than would be the case in analogous executive branch situations.[29] At the lower levels, anonymous executive officials simply enjoy less celebrity—or, at least, less of a public profile—than do most legislative employees. Thus, executive officials may engage in certain kinds of business or professional activities forbidden to even low-level legislative employees, for whom the mantle of official role is less easily shucked in out-of-role situations. At cabinet and subcabinet levels, a greater proportion of the celebrity executive officials enjoy is more likely to have adhered to them prior to their assuming office—rooted as it often is in out-of-role accomplishments—than is the case with most legislators. Thus, even relatively high-ranking executive officials, such as the EPA administrator, may accept certain kinds of social or charitable invitations that legislators must refuse.

In sum: To the extent that legislators act as citizens and executive officials operate as professionals, a certain kind of private gain—that redounding to knowledge or skills—is more readily attributed to legislators' personal talents, insights, and experience and less readily to their official role. But to the extent that legislators are public persons and most executive officials possess larger private spheres, other kinds of private gain—those having to do with prestige or stature—are more readily attributed to the legislator's official role than to anything developed personally or *sui generis*. Once again, legal distinctions take on the configuration of interbranch differences.

Normative Issues

It is one thing to confront the thorny conceptual issue of the extent to which, in any given case, an official acting out-of-role (itself a contested enough concept) benefits from drawing on aspects of the self—knowledge, skills, expertise, relationships, stature, prestige—developed in-role. It is another to address the no-less difficult normative question as to what, exactly, is wrong with an out-of-role official drawing remuneratively on in-role talents and prestige, assuming of course that the official is neither beholden to nor can affect the interests of those providing the remuneration. Private gain from public office seems to occupy a realm not only conceptually ambiguous but normatively innocuous.

Two kinds of answers are available for this question. One runs along these lines: There may be nothing wrong, *per se,* with officials gaining privately from their roles and especially from skills, stature, and capacities they developed while occupying them. We do, however, want to discourage people from serving in government if part of their motivation for doing so is ultimately to profit privately from public office. The second normative objection has it that there *is* something wrong when officials profit out-of-role from what they have become in-role, regardless of whether their motivation is, or ever was, to do so.

Why would we not want in office those who (as the first objection would have it) are motivated to draw on their government experience and stature for private gain regardless of whether they are actually successful doing so?[30] One answer seems to dominate: We can readily imagine officials so motivated conducting themselves, in office, in ways they would not otherwise were their motivations more public-spirited. Officials determined to use their time in government to acquire marketable skills and capacities might work more preponderantly on certain files, spend more time cultivating certain kinds of contacts, and devote more energy to acquiring a certain kind of reputation than they would otherwise. That being the case, however, the motivational problem would seem closely to resemble—perhaps it even collapses into—a more traditional conflict-of-interest problem involving altered or impaired in-role judgment and performance, where ill and real consequences could follow, in-role, from an official's encumbered state-of-mind. After all, motivation goes to state-of-mind. Officials motivated by possibilities for private gain to enter or serve in public office have a conflict (their in-role decisions and actions could be affected) of interest (by their desire to optimize possibilities for private gain). If our concern is with officials motivated to profit personally from government service (regardless of whether or not they actually do so), then our problem lies not with private gain from public office *per se*, but with conflict of interest. It lies with the extension of private motivations into the role, not with the extension of role into private activities.

If, however, our concern lies with an official profiting privately from government service regardless of whether he or she was ever motivated to do so—regardless of any conflict of interest or impaired official performance—then we must look elsewhere for normative sustenance. Any objection to "pure" private gain from public office—gain that occurs in the absence of any possibility of encumbered judgment—must be rooted in some kind of fiduciary notion of office. As Ernest Weinrib observes, the fiduciary has two obligations: "[H]is duty must not conflict with his interest, and he must not profit from his position."[31] Fiduciary law thus explicitly distinguishes profiting from position *per se*, separate and apart from any conflict of interest or encumbrance on judgment, as an impropriety to be guarded against. Doing so would seem to afford the most promising conceptual vehicle available for exploring the normative issues of private gain from public office. But if fiduciary law in general (or, more exactly, fiduciary law as applied to the professions of law and business) is fairly well-developed, on the profession of government in particular it is less so. This is not to say that notions of "trusteeship," "stewardship," and "custodianship" are not evident in scholarship surrounding the obligations of officials.[32] But no explicit, dominant theory of official fiduciary obligation has entered and suffused public discourse.

Rather than formulating and then imposing my own theory of official fiduciary obligation, by referring to public debate, I will identify the particular understanding of fiduciary obligation that undergirds the objection to private gain from public office, along with a competing fiduciary notion on which such an objection would be ill-founded. Because fiduciary concepts are better developed in the other major professions—law, business, and medicine—it is best to draw on them to lend definition and distinctiveness to the notions of official fiduciary obligation implicit in discourse about private gain from public office.

To begin with, consider a fundamental way in which the fiduciary concept, when applied to government, inverts the structure it assumes in most other professions. This inversion is equally manifest in the argument mounted by those normatively troubled *and* by those normatively unperturbed by private gain from public office; it constitutes a shared assumption of discourse. In law, business, and medicine, on the most common conceptions, the professional—the lawyer, manager, or doctor—is thought to have "fiduciary" or "role-moral" obligations (I use the terms interchangeably) to pursue and protect certain interests possessed by a defined, identifiable set of principals: clients, shareholders, patients. Additionally, on this understanding, the professional is thought to have a sometimes conflicting set of "ordinary-moral" obligations to the interests of a broader public—society at large. "Role-moral" obligations—the ones the professional possesses toward his or her principal—are heightened duties of singular commitment and devotion. They allow the professional to show a keen partiality toward the interests of his or her clients, patients, or shareholders, subject to certain ordinary-moral obligations. Those ordinary-moral obligations—the ones the professional owes toward all others, an undifferentiated public, or society as a whole—include minimalist or baseline duties, duties to be fair and decent of the kind we bear toward anyone, including those with whom we have no special relationship.[33]

The situation of government reverses that of other professions in one key respect. If the government official has any kind of fiduciary or role-moral obligation, it redounds precisely to the undifferentiated public, to society as a whole. It is the public itself—and not, generally, particular agency clients, stakeholders, and so forth—that constitutes the official's principal, the entity to whose interests the official is primarily or singularly committed. Accordingly, the kind of obligations the official bears toward those specific agency "client groups" with whom the official deals on behalf of the public-principal—welfare recipients, business contractors, broadcast licensees—would fall into the "ordinary moral" class. The official does not bear these client groups fiduciary obligations (those are reserved for the public), although the official does bear them ordinary-moral obligations of baseline fairness and decency of the sort she harbors toward anyone. In government, the imposition of a fiduciary construct would thus direct the official's role-moral obligations toward the *public,* and the official's ordinary-moral obligations toward particular *clients or groups.* The reverse is the case for other professions.

This is a simple distinction, and one could quibble with it on any number of dimensions. It glosses over, for example, the question of whether the official's fiduciary obligation is in fact directed toward her agency, or even toward the government in general, rather than to the public at large. Analogous questions, however, surface in business—over the much-debated issue of whether the manager's role-moral obligations flow toward the corporation instead of the shareholder—and in law—over the question of whether the lawyer's role-moral obligations flow to the court as well as to the client.

Along another dimension, some might argue that officials have role-moral, fiduciary obligations not just to the public but also to particular clients (welfare officers, on this argument, have fiduciary obligations to the particular individuals whose cases they handle). On similar lines, however, some have urged that managers have "multifiduciary" obligations, obligations not just to shareholders but others—customers, suppliers, and so forth.[34]

Precisely because equivalent disputes appear in other professions, I will abstract from them here. The central point, which survives these complications, is that officials' role-moral obligations direct them *relatively* more toward the public, and their ordinary-moral obligations *relatively* more toward client groups; whereas in other professions, role-moral obligations are generally owed to a client and ordinary-moral obligations to the public.[35] In any case, almost all public-administration scholars who deal with these issues—who analyze the official's varied obligations to agency clients, the agency itself, other government bodies, discrete subpublics, the laws, and the constitution—nevertheless ultimately situate those obligations within, or else derive them from, their own conceptions of a more fundamental fiduciary obligation to the public.[36]

What do these distinctions—between the fiduciary concept as applied to government and as applied to the other professions—imply for the normative assessment of private gain from public office? To answer, we need to explore some further elaborations, the first of which shapes the fiduciary concept as deployed by those who *oppose* private gain from public office. Any particular client or other group to which an official need show only ordinary-moral regard—a welfare recipient, an agency contractor, a broadcast licensee—is also part of the public, part of the very principal to whom the official owes role-moral obligations. Discourse over recent federal procurement reforms shows what this can mean. Companies selling to government expect agencies to not only observe ordinary-moral obligations of private contractual fairness in dealing with them, of the sort that any customer ought accord a supplier, but they also expect government to observe fiduciary or role-moral obligations of due process in dealing with them, of the sort the state accords all citizens. So, for example, in objecting to the proposed injection of market-oriented reforms into the public procurement system, some government contractors refuse to view government as an arm's-length customer, obligated to accord them only their ordinary-moral due while looking after, first and foremost, the interests of its principal, the public. Rather, as constituents of the public, contractors regard government officials as being *fiduciarily* obligated—obligated in-role—to take heed, in dealings with them, of their own business interests: their interests in profits, employment, market share, and firm survival.[37]

When officials, acting in-role, take insufficient heed of their agency-clients' interests, those clients (regardless of how the public is otherwise served) might well complain that they are shown inadequate fiduciary regard. Similarly, when officials acting out-of-role gain from their public office, it is those whose interests are harmed—namely their private-sector competitors—who complain that the officials involved are violating their fiduciary commitments. It is not, in other words, the public at large or those speaking in *its* name—it is not the principal itself *in toto*—that claims to have been harmed by private gain from public office. Instead, if officials use skills or stature they derive from office to supply various goods or services on the private market, it is competing suppliers who will protest. If ex-officials, for example, use knowledge or prestige drawn from their public role to aid them in devising or implementing corporate strategy for Ford or General Motors, Chrysler might object that its tax dollars have gone to subsidize or underwrite intellectual or reputational capital made available to the competition.[38]

Hence, while the public as a whole *might* claim to have been wronged by private gain from public office, it is particular parts of it that actually *do* claim to have been wronged. But theirs is not an ordinary-moral complaint about overly aggressive competition, one that they could launch equally against any private-market competitor, one rooted in a sense of unfairness. Rather, their complaint is that a fiduciary, role-moral obligation has been violated—one they could launch only against an official or former official, one rooted in a sense of betrayal. They react not as agency clients, nor as mere business adversaries whose interests are harmed by the official's competitive behavior, but as taxpayers and citizens—principals—whose trust the official has breached.

Hence it is that normative criticisms of private gain from public office almost always take the form of accusations of unfair competition. The public-as-principal, as a whole, cannot launch such a complaint; only individual members of the public can sensibly do so. Edwin McElwain and James Vorenberg perhaps came closest to articulating the chief grievance raised in cases of private gain from public office when they reframed and sharpened, for the government context, the dichotomy Ernest Weinrib discerned within the professional's fiduciary obligation. "The conflict-of-interest statutes reflect two essential principles," they wrote in 1952, "impartiality in government service" and that "no government employee is entitled to an advantage over private persons in the conduct of business . . . by virtue of their position."[39] It is not profiting by their position *per se*—that is too broad—but rather gaining advantage over private persons by virtue of their position that constitutes the harm done.

This is the nub of most normative complaints concerning private gain from public office. But how should we evaluate this kind of claim? Or, put another way, what fiduciary understandings lie behind the contrary case, oft-made in discourse, that private gain from public office represents no normative wrong?

Consider two further ways of subdividing the four professions of law, medicine, business, and government. First, in law and medicine—as distinct from business and government—the professional does not, or at least need not in the regular conduct of practice, face conflicts of interest between different principals to whom he or she is role-obligated. Of course, lawyers often encounter circumstances where the interests of different clients could come into conflict, but such inter-principal legal conflicts of interest are straightforwardly prohibited, or at the least are amenable to a variety of remedies. It is even less likely, because of its nonadversarial nature, that the practice of medicine will place an individual physician in a similar situation, where the interests of different patients conflict. Certainly, scarce medical resources may increasingly bring the interests of different patients into collision. But to what extent should the capacity to reconcile such inter-patient conflicts rest with various social institutions—legislatures, insurance companies, HMOs—and to what extent with individual physicians? This intensely controversial dilemma is only now just beginning to be fully debated. It could be argued that while physicians practicing in managed settings owe fiduciary obligations to their patients as physicians, they also owe fiduciary obligations to their business superiors—their shareholders—not as physicians but as any hired manager might. But so described, the situation is a conflict between their professional roles as physicians and managers, not between principals to whom they owe fiduciary obligations as physicians.

Conflicts between the interests of different principals are, by contrast, far more integral to and accepted in the regular practice of both business and government. Shareholders conflict over a range of issues concerning which managers are role-obligated to promote equally interests belonging to each of them; citizens likewise conflict with respect to officials. This is why majorities and minorities exist among shareholders and citizens but not medical patients and legal clients. But the fact that in business and government the interests of different principals may conflict often means that there is no univocal course of fiduciary action. Such conflicts between principals allow both the manager and the official a particular kind of fiduciary autonomy—"business judgment" and "official discretion"—that does not exist in law and medicine.

Now reconfigure the four professions and consider a way in which government resembles medicine while remaining distinct from both law and business. In law and business, the fiduciary is less likely to have to deal with intraprincipal conflicts of interest. This is because in both law and business, the practitioner is far more frequently obligated, in a fiduciary way, to serve only one particular interest of any individual principal's: pecuniary wealth in the case of the shareholder, legal victory for the client. This is not the case to nearly the same extent in government or medicine, where the diverse interests of the same principal may come into internal conflict within the domain where the official or physician is fiduciarily responsible. The possibility that officials' roles may require them to reconcile the manifold different interests that any individual member of the public-principal harbors—in economic growth and consumer safety, for example—is well-known. Physicians, too, derive much of their (increasingly controversial) autonomy not from inter-patient but intra-patient conflict, where, for example, a patient's interest in being told the truth conflicts with her interest in retaining peace of mind, or a patient's interest in being cured or surviving conflicts with his interest in avoiding suffering, disfigurement, or risky treatment. The fiduciary responsibilities of government and medicine thus extend *relatively* more (if not in entirety) to the total individual, and hence not just to one but to a range of interests a particular principal may have. As do physicians, officials must participate—and in practice they often dominate—in the reconciliation of the internally conflicting interests of their principals, which is why paternalism is a charge leveled more often against officials and physicians than against lawyers and managers.[40]

The sum and substance of all of this is that the official's role-moral responsibilities are exceptionally complex and diluted because in government the principal comprises the entire public—both a large class of persons and many of their interests. The interests for which the official bears *fiduciary* responsibility come into conflict both between individual principals and within individual principals. The former is not true in law and medicine; the latter is not true in law and business. And this particular understanding of official fiduciary obligation emerges in sharpest relief only in comparative professional context.[41]

What does such an understanding imply for the normative evaluation of private gain from public office? If the principal is so multifarious and riven, the official's fiduciary obligations are by no means univocal. True, there is a sense in which some interests of some part of the principal, some part of the public, may find themselves harmed by any given instance of private gain from public office. But there is also a sense in which another part of the principal might be helped, and indeed those harmed in respect of some of their interests may be helped in respect of others. In its recruitment advertisements for the U.S. Army (most famously) and other services and agencies, the government promises precisely *to* provide training, skills, and stature in-role that the official can then use remuneratively out-of-role. In other words, it promises that public office *will* lead to private gain, and it views such a happenstance as beneficial to (some large section of) the public—even as it may also harm some of the interests of other citizens, namely competitors who must acquire those skills and stature on their own.[42]

A fiduciary understanding of public office can thus support both the condemnation and the exoneration of private gain from public office. However, in many situations, it might lend relatively greater support to the one as opposed to the other. Consider an official who, perhaps while in office but more likely after leaving it, writes and sells a memoir of his or her official experience. Most observers would neither prohibit nor condemn such activity. The question, though (assuming the memoir discloses no commercially confidential or officially classified information), is why? Why are official memoirs not generally criticized for representing private gain from public office?[43] It is true that memoirs *may* assume a form far more personal than official, in the sense that the official's in-role experiences may be filtered heavily through her personal subjectivity and her own particular perspective and worldview, and the work as a whole may partake largely of insights and understandings formed outside, not inside, the role. A manual on how to deal with the official's agency, or a course on a policy issue related to the employee's department, may by contrast seem relatively less personal or out-of-role, and more official or in-role, in origin. Even if true, however, this is a matter of degree. And in fact it is usually not true. In most cases it is precisely the official's role-derived experiences or stature that constitute a memoir's selling point. The official—Henry Kissinger, to take an obvious example—would not be a bestseller had he not occupied his role.

Perhaps the more compelling reason why memoirs seem relatively unobjectionable on pure "private gain from public office" grounds is this: Memoirs *are* "personal," but not in the sense that they are subjective, not in the sense that the capacity to produce and sell them results more from the out-of-role person than the office. Rather, memoirs are personal in the sense that they are singular, so that no part of the public-principal is harmed by their production, no matter how much their success owes to the official's public experiences, knowledge, and stature. It is hard to imagine who among the public was competitively disadvantaged, hence fiduciarily betrayed, by Henry Kissinger's publication of his memoirs—in the way in which a rival handbook publishing house might be, were officials to produce a manual on how to deal with their agencies.[44] An analogous part of the public—that competing part of the principal that has been harmed—would seem not to exist in the case of memoirists. Similarly, the legal scholar Thomas Morgan notes that "[a] book such as Chief Justice Rehnquist's recent account of the workings of the Supreme Court, for example, could be written only by someone in his position"—an observation which, for Morgan, dissipates any objection one could have to Rehnquist's profiting from it, since no one else could have written a similar book.[45]

By contrast, in criticizing Speaker Newt Gingrich's book deal on the grounds that he was "cashing in from public office," William Safire urged that "[p]ublic officials should not compete with private citizens as providers of media content."[46] In Safire's view the media content Gingrich offered was sufficiently generic that it embraced the possibility of competing private suppliers. The advantages Gingrich brought as Speaker in conceiving and promoting his book on American civilization gave him a competitive advantage over other private citizens whose tax dollars and civic exertions enabled the Speaker's effort, but who might also want to remuneratively express their own views on American politics. Hence, Gingrich reaped accusations of "using his high position to generate book sales" or "exploiting [his] office for personal gain."[47] But where the Speaker may be offering a generic product others might also provide, the memoirist is not.[48] The market for at least certain kinds of memoirs is segmented precisely because the product is so personal, and no part of the official's principal is harmed.

Contemporary public debate is rich in the ambiguous, paradoxical discourse that surrounds private gain from public office. Where it exists, private gain from public office must abide in a realm sufficiently unofficial for the act in question to comprise genuinely private gain—not a part of the official's public responsibilities—but it must also be sufficiently proximate to official terrain for it to redound to public office, not to the official's personal qualities or attributes. Yet what stands to establish the one claim could undermine the other, an internal tension that afflicts the arguments of both agency and official alike. And if these conceptual issues were not sufficiently bewildering, the normative issues would more than make up. When the fiduciary concept is applied to government, it is the public as a whole, not the immediate client, that is more aptly thought of as the principal, the entity to which the official owes his or her role-moral obligations. For officials (in contrast to lawyers, doctors, and managers), both inter-principal *and* intra-principal interest-conflicts thus unavoidably and pervasively complicate the exercise of fiduciary responsibilities. With any given case of private gain from public office, the interests of the principal—the public itself—will be more or less harmed, more or less helped, depending on the circumstances—hence the perplexities that surround the normative issues of private gain from public office.

8

The Revolving Door: I

Critics from all quarters—political and judicial, journalistic and academic—unremittingly attack the postemployment laws for embracing neither reason nor rhyme.[1] Certainly, concerning any given one of the hundreds of postemployment laws operative in the United States, the charge might stick. Rare is the individual statute or regulation, at either the federal or the state level, that displays a readily discernible policy rationale, or whose convoluted legal terminology has any mnemonic appeal for those who must abide by it.

For anyone who harbors hope that the federal postemployment laws might yet reveal some underlying principles, Steven Kelman offers the following three as natural candidates:[2] first, the need to prevent "ingratiation" or "going soft"; in other words, the possibility that an official could favor a future private employer "while in office in order to reap personal gain afterward." Second, inhibiting the "influence which could naturally be exercised by a man of capacity upon people with whom he had been associated"; in other words, the possibility that the official, now out of office, would be favored by her former colleagues when she makes representations to government on behalf of her new private employer. And, finally, the need to prohibit "profiting from public service," regardless of whether the official has engaged in ingratiation or influence.

Since, in his view, the federal postemployment laws are ill-crafted if they are meant to embody either of the first two principles, Kelman argues that they are best understood as reflecting a deep-seated concern with "profiteering"—profiting from office once one leaves it. Kelman's attempt to explain a raft of law by reference to one unifying principle is heroic and illuminating. But we should reflect on the fact that each of the three postemployment principles Kelman identifies—against ingratiation, influence, and profiteering—replicates, by extending it into the postemployment domain, the principles animating three of the major categories of conflict: abuse of office, undue influence, and private gain from public office.

Recall that abuse of office arises when an official, while still in office, does out-of-role business with—or is hired by—a private interest whose fortunes he can affect in-role. For its part, revolving-door "ingratiation" arises when an official *in the future*—that is, after he leaves office—does business with, or is hired by, a private interest whose fortunes he was able to affect while in-role.[3] Undue influence, of the sort prohibited by the conflict-of-interest provisions in 18 U.S.C. §203 and 205, arises when an incumbent official, acting out-of-role, influences his current colleagues to favor certain interests with which he is affiliated in a private capacity. For its part, "revolving-door influence" arises when an official, once having left office altogether, influences his former official colleagues to favorably affect interests with which he is now privately affiliated. And if one kind of private gain from public office arises when an official, while in office, draws on knowledge or stature derived from his public role to profit financially—consider the EPA official who offers a marine biology course at the local college—the kind of postemployment profiteering that concerns Kelman arises when an official, once having left office, does the same: the memoir-writing secretary of state. The three leading candidates for "animating spirit of the revolving-door laws"—ingratiation, influence, and profiteering—are simply the postemployment equivalents of three of the five major conflict-of-interest denominations: abuse of office, undue influence, and private gain from public office.

Postemployment versions of the other two principal conflict-of-interest categories, "self-dealing" and "private payment for public acts," do not exist. Indeed they are hard even to imagine. Why? Because in self-dealing and private payment for public acts, the *officeholder's* only actions take place in-role. In self-dealing, the officeholder uses her official role to favor her own interests; in private payment for public acts, she performs official acts that are privately underwritten by others. Neither are possible once she leaves office—she is no longer in any position either to officially affect her own interests or to perform official acts—and hence neither self-dealing nor private payment for public acts have any real postemployment analogues.[4]

By contrast, in each of the other three cases—undue influence, abuse of office, and private gain from public office—the official herself performs key acts that all take place out-of-role. In undue influence, the out-of-role official influences another official. In abuse of office, she performs out-of-role private services for another private interest. And in private gain from public office, she reaps some form of benefit out-of-role. These are all things that former as well as incumbent officeholders, acting out-of-role, can do; hence, the three map onto the postemployment analogues of influence, ingratiation, and profiteering.

There is, then, strong *prima facie* reason not to dismiss any one of the three as a possible prime mover behind the postemployment laws. And, in fact, not only do all three principles resound in the last many decades of postemployment debate, but they are joined by yet a fourth: Something objectionable arguably happens whenever an ex-official exhibits "disloyalty" or "switches sides," leaving government and then acting against U.S. interests—even if her doing so involves no prior ingratiation with her new private employer, no subsequent attempts to influence former official colleagues, and no profitable use of government-derived knowledge or stature.[5]

The four concerns—with ingratiation, influence, profiteering, and disloyalty—bear a set of symmetrical relationships one to another, displaying rhyme as well as reason. The problem with the first two, influence and ingratiation, is that they each involve the possible impairment of official judgment. When influence has been exercised, the judgment of the ex-official's former colleagues might be impaired—impaired by the favor with which they naturally greet her importunings on behalf of a new private employer. When ingratiation occurs, it is the official's own in-role judgment that gets encumbered by her willingness to curry favor with someone she knows might be able to hire her once she leaves office.[6]

Profiteering and switching sides, by contrast, can still bother us even in circumstances where there is no possibility that anyone's official judgment has been impaired. Recall the New York Bar Association's pronouncement that it is "possible to imagine an official who acts impartially, does not play favorites, and is a model of public decorum," but who nevertheless violates the stricture against "the use of public office for private gain."[7] Similarly, as the editors of the *Harvard Law Review* once put it, "[t]he fundamental impropriety of switching sides does not involve [any] substantial concern that the fairness and impartiality of the government decision-making process would be compromised."[8] The side-switching officeholder need not help her future private employer while in government, entreat her former colleagues once outside, or even make private use of any of her government-derived expertise or prestige. As long as she is acting against a party—the United States—whose partisan she once was, the pure element of treachery remains. Hence, while ingratiation and influence impair the in-role performance of at least some officials, profiteering and disloyalty, arising as they do in a penumbra realm outside-of-role, need not.

John Sununu's former aide Ed Rogers offers an illustration of the difference. On leaving the White House in 1991, Rogers immediately received a $600,000 contract from Sheik Kamal Adham; Rogers' job was to counsel the Sheik as he resisted Justice Department attempts to bring him before a grand jury in the BCCI (Bank of Credit and Commerce International) affair. Rogers had not been in any position to affect the Sheik's interests while in the White House nor, upon his departure, did he make any contact with his former colleagues on the Sheik's behalf. Hence he was in no position either to ingratiate himself with Kamal before leaving office, or to exercise influence on his behalf afterward. Rogers did, however, switch sides—immediately turning against the government on his departure from office—and in so doing he profited from his governmentally derived skills and stature (he had had no legal experience upon entering the White House). To end the ensuing controversy, Rogers returned the $600,000.[9]

A further distinction cross-cuts this one, having to do with whether pecuniary interest is necessarily implicated. On the one hand, both ingratiation and profiteering by definition entail the ex-official's reaping some form of postemployment financial benefit. It is unlikely that an official would ever use her role to ingratiate herself with a private party, whether a business or an individual, for any reason other than future pecuniary gain. Nor is it easy to imagine how an official might profit in a nonpecuniary sense from government service, at least in a way that might provoke criticism.[10]

Neither postemployment influence nor postemployment side-switching, by contrast, require an ex-official to have any pecuniary interest at stake. An ex-official can exercise influence on former colleagues without being remunerated for it. And she can, as well, switch sides for nonpecuniary reasons. One can importune the government, and one can desert its cause, for a host of motivations beyond the merely financial. The words themselves—*influence* and *disloyalty*—betoken more politically charged, less pecuniarily tinged evils than either ingratiation or profiteering (see Table 2). Not surprisingly, laws that seem pretty clearly aimed at either influence or side-switching often apply *regardless* of whether the official is being paid or has any other kind of financial interest at stake.

The four principles are related, both positively and inversely, in yet other ways. There is a sense, for example, in which influence becomes a greater problem to the extent that side-switching becomes a lesser one. Former officials who represent an array of clients before their old agencies may, in any given situation, pursue a particular client's adversarial interests with a deliberately diminished zeal in order to preserve a better long-run relationship with the agency. In other words, in order to be better able to exert continued influence, the ex-official might have to be less acute in his side-switching, his

Table 2

	Official judgment impaired	Official judgment not impaired
Pecuniary interest involved	Ingratiation	Profiteering
Pecuniary interest not necessarily involved	Influence	Side-switching/disloyalty

disloyalty, than he might otherwise have been in any given case. As Edward O. Laumann and his colleagues have discovered, "loyalty to [his private-sector] client" may be "inconsistent" with the former official's "maintenance of cordial continuing relationships with government officials," the kind of relationships that make for influence.[11] Some of the Washington lawyers Laumann and his colleagues discuss, in fact, seem to have stronger ongoing relationships with their governmental adversaries than with their private clients.

Similarly, the very kinds of insider knowledge that enable postemployment profiteering might also diminish postemployment side-switching. "After retiring to a private role, the former government official may retain some of the attitudes and insights acquired while in government," Thomas Morgan writes—attitudes and insights from which he might profit, certainly, but which might also dispose (for example) a "former Justice Department or Securities and Exchange lawyer [to] set a tougher compliance program for his client than a non-alumnus of those agencies."[12] On this argument, the information and skills one takes from one's government role, although lucrative, come accompanied by dispositions and habits that will incline one to maintain a certain loyalty to one's former agency and its interests.

Consider, also, that weak postemployment laws make for rapid turnover. Rapid turnover, certainly, entails increased possibilities for both ingratiation and disloyalty, since it implies that officials are seeking private-sector opportunities and then deserting the government at an ever-quickening pace. But a rapidly spinning revolving door also diminishes the capacities for influence and profiteering. The stereotypical political appointee—who leaves government for a more attractive private-sector position after a short tenure in office—is for that very reason less likely to have developed the kind of internal governmental contacts and knowledge that allow for postemployment influence and profit. As John P. Heinz *et al* put it, "contacts with officials are useful only as long as the officials remain in office, and we know that the turnover rate among officials, with respect to top appointees, is high."[13] Paradoxically, low postemployment barriers may have a homeostatic quality. If they are minimal enough—allowing for profuse and frictionless egress from government—then they erode at least some of the reason for raising them, namely, the concerns with profiteering and influence. In sum, the four evils stalking the world of postemployment may in complicated ways palliate one another, perhaps even mitigating the need for certain types of regulation.

Rhyme and Reason

Assuming that there are four discernible principles that any revolving-door legal regime could conceivably reflect, how coherently do the much-derided federal postemployment laws express these principles? The answer is: Whether intentionally or not, individual federal statutes display more focus, and the law as a whole a far greater logic, than critics would allow. To see this, it is necessary to wade a bit into the legal language, bearing in mind all the while Robert Reich's reminder that "[c]omplicated codes of laws and regulations lack the emotional charge of mythic struggle, but they are where the action is."[14]

Begin with the pair of federal postemployment statutes that seem most clearly to embody one or another of the four principles. The first, 18 U.S.C. §207(c), is crafted to express a concern only with postemployment influence, not ingratiation, nor profiteering, nor side-switching. It bars senior ex-officials (for one year after leaving office) from making representations to their former agencies "with the intent to influence" their old colleagues. Because this statute prohibits attempts to influence even in situations where the U.S. may have no stake—where the ex-official may be importuning her former colleagues on matters exclusively of interest to contending private parties—it bespeaks no concern with switching sides against the government, only with "blow[ing] official decisionmaking off course."[15] Because the statute applies even if the new private employer—on whose behalf she exercises influence—is not one she could possibly have affected while in office, it exhibits no concern with ingratiation.

Nor, finally, does 18 U.S.C. §207(c) seem especially concerned with profiteering (postemployment private gain from public office). Postemployment statutes signal a preoccupation with profiteering when they focus on the former official's involvement, in her new private capacity, in *particular* matters involving *specific* parties with which she had been *personally* and *substantially* involved while in government. The less a matter is particularistic and specific in its import—the more it takes the form of a broad political or regulatory question—the greater the chances that her knowledge or insights concerning it could have materialized as easily from out-of-role as from in-role expertise and experience.[16] And the less the official was personally and substantially involved in a matter—the more formal or distant her involvement—the less likely she is to have gleaned any special knowledge or insight from which she might profit.[17] But because 18 U.S.C. §207(c) prohibits the official from making postemployment representations on any matters now pending before her former agency—regardless of how broad and general, and regardless of whether she had had any personal or substantial involvement with them—it betokens no particular concern with profiting from office. Instead, its concern is with influence: After all, a former senior official can twist the arm of her old bureaucratic subordinates on any kind of matter, no matter how generic, even if she had had nothing to do with it while in office.

In a similar way, the postemployment provisions in 18 U.S.C. §208 reveal a fairly straightforward concern with pure and simple ingratiation. They explicitly prohibit officials from negotiating for postemployment positions with firms whose interests they are able to affect in office, regardless of whether U.S. interests would be at stake in their future work (no need for disloyalty), regardless of whether the matters on which they might labor for their future employer are specific issues with which they had previously been personally involved (no need that they profit from office), and regardless of whether they would be contacting their former colleagues (no concern with influence).

When critics hurl salvos at the federal revolving-door laws, their targets usually center on a clutch of three remaining statutory provisions—18 U.S.C. §207(a)(1), (a)(2), and (b).[18] Although they vary in important ways, each can most economically be understood as a hybrid prohibition against switching sides and profiteering. Indeed, since the other two principles, against influence and ingratiation, already find near-pure expression in 18 U.S.C. §207(c) (in the case of influence) and 18 U.S.C. §208 (in the case of ingratiation), such an understanding of the remaining three laws has an initial attractiveness.

To make the point, let me explicate only the first of the three, 18 U.S.C. §207(a)(1). This statute confines itself to regulating the ex-official's involvement in particular matters involving specific parties with which the ex-official had been personally and substantially involved, thereby signaling a concern with profiteering from officially derived knowledge of a file. But the matters also must be ones in which the U.S. continues to have an interest, and in this way the statute also suggests a concern with postemployment side-switching.[19]

There is a certain embodied wisdom in mixing the principles against switching sides and profiteering, in diluting one with the other, when placing them in legal form. Both principles operate in the penumbra zone, implicating postemployment issues that arise (unlike ingratiation and influence) above and beyond the central concern of impaired official judgment. Consequently, a criminal statute that prohibited switching sides in pure form, or that prohibited postemployment profiteering in pure form, would be especially draconian. A pure "switching sides" statute, for example, would prohibit any action against U.S. interests, on any matter notwithstanding how general and public it may be, and notwithstanding that the ex-official's involvement with it may have been neither personal nor substantial.[20] A pure postemployment profiteering law, by contrast—while confining itself to situations where the official's involvement was personal and substantial and the matter itself particular and specific—would not be restricted to situations where the U.S. remained a party or maintained an interest. But in combining the particular narrowing approaches suitable to both a law against side-switching and one against profiteering, the statute circumscribes that area within the "penumbra realm" to which it applies. It penalizes neither profiting nor disloyalty but, in effect, profiting *from* disloyalty. The law comports with the sentiment Congressman Barney Frank expressed in a 1988 hearing, when he declared that it would not "be my intention to bring out a bill that would say to a former executive or legislative official, you may not sit in an office and strategize, you may not share your information." Instead, Frank concluded, the law "should deal with the problem of people switching sides where they have gained particular information about a particular issue."[21]

The only dissonant note here is that 18 U.S.C. §207(a)(1) confines itself to postemployment representational activities, which is required neither by a concern with profiteering nor one with side-switching. A former officeholder can profit from his personal and substantial involvement in a specific matter in many ways other than by contacting ex-colleagues. And if an ex-official finds herself working against the U.S. interest, it would still be a case of switching sides even if the former official's actions against the U.S. involved no representational activities. But perhaps that is why the most popular kind of amendment 18 U.S.C. §207(a)(1) provokes—in efforts that recur over decades—would broaden its applicability to include all manner of postemployment work affecting U.S. interests on particular matters with which the official had been personally involved, and not simply representations made on those matters to the government.[22]

Advising, Informing and Influencing: A Complication

Although they bar representations meant to influence former government colleagues, all three statutes do allow ex-officials to convey purely factual material to their old agencies as long as no attempt to persuade accompanies it. Providing that the communication has the effect of transferring hard objective information, in other words, and does not become a more subjective attempt to advise a course of action, it is permitted.[23] As an old set of National Science Foundation ethics regulations put it, "you must not couple the information you supply with any attempt to influence the decision on the proposal other than what inheres in the provision of the information itself."[24] The surrounding debate, consequently, centers on whether such an objective/subjective distinction is meaningful: "How," a 1979 House report asks, "can the preparer of a tax return"—say a former Internal Revenue Service (IRS) employee—"communicate information to the IRS about the manner in which he prepared the return without influencing the ultimate question of whether the return is proper?"[25]

When it comes to concerns with postemployment profiteering, by way of interesting parallel, some have tried to draw just the opposite distinction. It is less permissible for an ex-official to impart to a new employer hard, objective information he may have derived from his previous official role and more acceptable for him to offer that employer subjective advice or counsel loosely based on such information. Here, the overt, unvarnished transfer of factual material is prohibited, whereas using such material to influence one's employer in her course of action enters a gray area—presumably because it is filtered through the official's own psychology and does not derive directly and undilutedly from his role. Others, however, question the meaningfulness of this distinction. "Current laws forbid former employees from disclosing classified and confidential information," a 1987 House report observed; "[n]o law, however, bars a former employee from giving a client advice based on confidential information acquired during governmental service. This poses the risk that prohibitions on disclosure of sensitive information can be defeated by former officials who scrupulously avoid disobeying the law, but nonetheless advise a client to pursue a strategy suggested by the former employee's knowledge."[26]

One can, in short, more permissibly inform than influence government on behalf of a private interest, but more permissibly influence than inform a private employer based on knowledge one derived from working in government. The burden of the offense in both influencing and profiteering, then, hinges in part on a distinction between objective and subjective communications.

9

The Revolving Door: II

The federal postemployment laws, carping to the contrary, display both rhyme and reason.[1] The four principles each assume notably faithful legal incarnations; each one seems completely or at least substantially to inspirit a particular law or set of laws in ways that largely make sense. But this is not the end of the story. Though the term *revolving door* commonly signifies the postemployment issue, it could be taken to apply to a number of other situations where individuals traverse the space between the public and the private sectors. Major government consultants, for example, might find themselves in several revolving doors simultaneously; presidential transition-team members only once and briefly at that. Those who served in the military while in government, or who subsequently go to work for foreign entities upon leaving it, labor under (or are continually threatened with the possibility of) particularly acute postemployment strictures. Finally, former government attorneys and their private partners operate under a distinctive set of rules. Yet despite the sprawling regulatory complexities provoked by these additional revolving-door categories, the four principles provide a parsimonious way of understanding them, too. For in each of these supplementary situations, a particular pair out of the four concerns—whether ingratiation, influence, profiteering, or side-switching—looms larger than the other pair, and it is a different pair in nearly every case.

Consultants

When it comes to consultants' conflicts of interest, concerns with ingratiation and profiteering bulk largest, while issues of side-switching and influence recede into the background. Most major consultants, whether firms or individuals, do not inhabit particular official roles in the way full-time officeholders do but rather range across an array of them—writing speeches for legislators, drafting policy for commissions, preparing congressional testimony for agency heads, designing specifications for military procurements, and so forth.[2] Consultants not only operate across a gamut of official roles but, in addition, they may have entire stables of private-sector clients, perhaps running into the thousands. Because consultants (unlike most officials) have the capacity, whether they are advising or in effect deciding policy, to range across numerous governmental roles—and because unlike most businesspeople they link, through their clientele, with any number of private interests—the possibilities for "ingratiation," for using a (quasi) official role to benefit private clients current and prospective, is uniquely protracted.[3] Similarly, because consultants are privy to official information across an array of agencies, departments, functions, and roles—and because the range of private-sector opportunities they may possess is so comparatively unbounded—the risks of their profiting privately from their public activities, of gaining an unfair advantage for their clients, also ramify.[4] Consultants, too, might find themselves with the capacity to use government-owned plant, equipment, and materiel for their "commercial nongovernment ventures."[5] It makes sense, then, that even though they are at most "part-time" officials, consultants enjoy no exemption under 18 U.S.C. §208, the statute that prohibits self-dealing and ingratiation with a future employer. And, reasonably enough, they are equally subject to the nonstatutory injunctions against profiteering.

While the possibilities for ingratiation and profiteering loom especially large to consultants, the remaining two postemployment concerns—influence and disloyalty—apply to consultants with no more (and perhaps even less) force than they do to former full-time officeholders. Influence varies not according to the breadth but rather the depth of one's professional and personal relationships with in-role officials. While the consultant's range of official contacts might be *broader* than the average officeholder's—after all, she does business with a wide compass of departments and agencies—precisely for that reason they are not (as a general statement) as *deep*. Consultants are not in a position to become professional superiors to the officials with whom they work, engendering the kinds of deference that allow for the possibility of future postemployment influence. Nor (because their relationships with officials assume a project-by-project form) are consultants as likely to grow whatever *professional* relationships they develop with officials into *personal* ones, of a kind that may blossom within a bureau of full-time officeholders who continuously collaborate across many projects.[6] In her book on the early years of the Clinton presidency, for example, Elizabeth Drew dwells on the gulf between officials and consultants that can erupt even at the highest levels: "One White House official," Drew writes, "said, 'There's general frustration with the consultants coming in and at the last minute blowing things up. People here say, "Fine. Take these hours, take this salary."'"[7]

This kind of official-consultant divide would explain why 18 U.S.C. §203 and 205—which bar full-time officials, acting outside of their roles, from influencing any governmental entity on behalf of a private-sector client—apply in only a limited way to consultants and special government employees.[8] And as for the concern with pure side-switching, it simply does not emerge in discourse over consultants, who are expected to have a variety of private-sector clients and who, after all, are not government officials.[9]

In sum, because the government consultant operates in closer proximity to the private sector than does the full-time official—because, in archetypal form, she possesses a stable of private-sector clients to an extent no full-time official could replicate—her capacities for ingratiation and profiteering both ramify. But precisely to the extent that the government consultant operates at a greater distance from government than the full-time official, her capacities for influence and side-switching are more circumscribed. Not for nothing did four consultants to the Clinton White House—James Carville, Paul Begala, Mandy Grunwald, and Stanley Greenberg—publish an op-ed in the *Washington Post* denying that their roles involved any side-switching or the exertion of influence: "We do not represent foreign governments. We do not represent outside interests before government." And not for nothing did the *Post* itself publish a duelling editorial the same day, accusing the four of offering a diversionary defense, when the real problems with their activities involve ingratiation and profiteering: "Our own view is that they understate to the point of distortion their own roles inside the White House,"—"they help not just to dress up policy but to make it"—"as well as understate their various connections in the outside world."[10]

Transition-Team Members

The four principles configure themselves slightly differently in the case of transition-team members, those private individuals who restructure agencies or recommend personnel for executive offices in the months prior to the inauguration of a new administration. Here, concerns about influence and profiteering dominate. Because new administration incumbents will owe their jobs and working conditions to particular transition-team members, those members—once having returned to the private sector—will command a greater capacity to exercise influence than other kinds of ex-officials or officials acting out-of-role.[11] Similarly, profiteering—the capacity to turn government-derived insights or stature to private account—is very much a live possibility for transition-team workers, who serve on premises and have access to agency files and records.[12] And, as it happens, heightened concerns with influence and profiteering offer a robust way of explaining the evolution of transition-team conflict-of-interest strictures. Former transition-team members are barred from making representations before relevant agencies for a set period, a stipulation that reflects a concern with influence. And they are prohibited, for a period, from working on particular matters with which they may have been personally involved while on the team, a stricture that bespeaks a focus on profiteering.[13]

But transition-team members avoid the two remaining revolving-door concerns, ingratiation and disloyalty. Because the administration has not yet entered office, transition workers are in no position to affect official actions, hence in no position to ingratiate themselves with future private employers. Transition workers, as Philip J. Harter puts it, "have ambiguous authority and no power to make decisions."[14] True, transition-team operatives for a particular agency could configure it to be more industry-friendly than it might otherwise have been. But the capacity to do anything fine-grained for a potential employer in the three-month period before the president's inauguration, especially by comparison with those who will then become full-time administration officials, bulks less prominently.[15] And because transition workers report to the president-elect, not the president—because they have never been on the government "side" *per se*—disloyalty, or switching sides, is not a charge to which they are vulnerable.[16]

Defense Officials

Over and above the postemployment laws that apply to all officials, employees of the U.S. Department of Defense labor under their own (oft-repealed or amended) special statutory and regulatory revolving-door strictures. What distinguishes former Defense officials—justifying, if anything does, the extra burdens—is their greater capacity to exercise influence over former official colleagues once out of office, and to ingratiate themselves with future private employers while still in-role. The military's hierarchical organization, arguably, amplifies the feelings of deference and subordination, or paternalism and sponsorship, that undoubtedly exist elsewhere in government. Certain kinds of ex-military officers, accordingly, might find their capacities to exercise influence over former colleagues magnified, at least by comparison with other former officials.[17] For many defense suppliers the Pentagon is a monopsony, which additionally raises the stakes whenever ex-Defense officials, whether military or civilian, are able to exercise influence in marketing, negotiation, and renegotiation with their former bureaus. Both the hierarchical and the monopsonistic faces of the Defense establishment heighten the capacities and the incentives for postemployment influence, which helps explain why former military personnel, in particular, have been subject to special strictures on postemployment contacts with their former colleagues.[18]

As far as ingratiation goes, the military's "up or out" system means that a large proportion of military personnel, at any given time, will be thinking of their private-sector futures in a particularly searching way. Also, civilian Defense Department procurement officials—like Nuclear Regulatory Commission inspectors, who are also intensely regulated—can find themselves living on-site, for a period of years, with departmental contractors, working out of private instead of government offices in overseeing a procurement.[19] Both the increased level of official turnover and the close-quartered longevity of the procurement relationship with private businesses mean that Defense officials—since many already have one foot out of the door, either mentally or physically—may be particularly vulnerable to ingratiation. And this deepened concern with ingratiation accounts for the extra array of (often redundant and ill-crafted) postemployment strictures under which Defense procurement officials have labored.[20]

On the other hand, whatever postemployment burdens fall on Defense officials, they cannot be explained by any heightened concern with either profiteering or disloyalty. Indeed, the Army recruits personnel precisely on the promise that military office *will* lead to personal gain. And while a kind of loyalty is obviously integral to the military credo, it is not the kind that applies (at least with any greater force than for non-Defense officials) to the sorts of switching-sides problems that result from the revolving door. In sum, what distinguishes Defense officials from non-Defense officials has to do with characteristics of their official role and department. Hence, it is ingratiation and influence—the two postemployment concerns that implicate in-role behavior and performance—that assume greater prominence.[21]

The "Foreign Revolving Door"

Yet another strand of debate surrounds this question: Should ex-officials who go to work for foreign entities be subject to restrictions greater than those visited on former officeholders working for domestic concerns? Here, the distinguishing feature is not the official role the ex-officeholder may have held but the kind of private-sector clients he subsequently serves. Consequently, it is the two postemployment concerns that do *not* necessarily implicate in-role official performance—the concerns with profiteering and disloyalty—that loom larger in debate over the "foreign revolving door."

Consider first the situation in which the ex-official's foreign client is a state (or a political party), as distinct from a company or a firm. When the entities on either side of the revolving door are both governments—when the official's future employer is not a private firm but a foreign state or other political entity—concerns with disloyalty assume a transcendent form, going beyond official side-switching to take on some of the characteristics of a betrayal of country.[22] Similarly, when an ex-official finds herself working for a foreign state (as distinct, say, from a domestic firm), it is less easy for her to argue that there are at least some among her principal—namely, the American public—who are being helped by her profiteering even though others may be hurt. More of those to whom the ex-official owes a fiduciary obligation—U.S. citizens and taxpayers—are likely to be disadvantaged in instances where she goes to work for a foreign government.[23]

But while the fiduciary-based objections to profiteering and the concern with disloyalty should be more highly activated where the ex-official works for a foreign government, concerns with ingratiation and influence—notwithstanding some confusion on this score—need not be.[24] As far as ingratiation is concerned, there is no reason why an official would skew her in-role performance any more highly in anticipation of a job with a foreign government than she would in contemplation of a position with a domestic firm.[25] Nor is there any reason why an ex-official lobbying on behalf of a foreign government would have any greater—or any less—power to influence the decisions of her former colleagues than one who lobbies on behalf of a domestic interest. The capacity to influence has to do with the nature of her official contacts, not her private clients.

Debate over the "foreign revolving door" becomes more contested when it concerns ex-officials who go to work for foreign firms. Certainly, there are those who believe that former officials working for foreign firms should be treated no differently than those in the employ of domestic companies. After all, the private interests of a foreign-owned firm—especially if it employs American workers—in fact may be more consonant with the U.S. national interest as a whole than those of a competing American-owned firm, especially if the American firm employs a largely foreign work force. There is no reason, on this argument, why an ex-official who goes to work for Toyota in a trade action against Ford is engaging in a more egregious kind of side-switching, or is profiteering in violation of fiduciary obligations any more profoundly, than one who goes to work for General Motors.[26] Notably, those who would place especially heavy strictures on ex-officials who work for foreign firms feel compelled, as does Pat Choate most prominently, to liken foreign firms more to foreign governments than to domestic firms. Much of Choate's argument rests on the claim that foreign firms are generally more quasi-governmental in their organization than their domestic American competitors, having recourse to greater financial resources from, and structural links to, their own states. On this argument (and perhaps only on this argument) would ex-officials in the employ of a large foreign firm, quasi-governmental as it is, show an unequivocally keener degree of disloyalty, and a more undiluted form of the fiduciary betrayal embodied in profiteering, than do ex-officials who lobby for domestic firms.[27]

Former Government Attorneys

Yet another set of distinctive postemployment concerns centers on the activities of former government attorneys, who are governed by state licensing rules along with the federal postemployment statutes and regulations. Here, the question is not whether the former government attorney should be subject to strictures greater than those applying to other former officials. Rather, it is whether an attorney formerly employed by the government should be subject to any greater restrictions in her subsequent professional activities, simply because she used to work for the government, than one whose former clients are all private individuals or organizations. Are any of the four postemployment principles likely to come into greater play for the former government attorney than for the "ordinary" private-sector attorney?

To begin with, consider that the capacity for ingratiation is uniquely bound up with official role, with the official's ability to use her office to favor (or disfavor) a potential private employer. In the case of the government attorney, capacities such as these generally center on the power to commence or terminate legal action involving a prospective private client, in hopes that the client might ultimately retain her. An attorney working for one private client is simply far less likely to be able to use that representation to create an opportunity for herself with another prospective private client.[28]

If the capacities for ingratiation are greater when the attorney formerly acted for government, so are the possibilities for influence. One of the distinguishing characteristics of government as a client is that, unlike a private-sector client, it also often constitutes the forum in which disputes are played out, not just a party to them. And this creates possibilities for undue influence where they could not possibly exist for an attorney whose previous client was a private entity. An attorney will never find herself pleading for the opposing party *before* a former private client.[29]

While the possibilities for both ingratiation and influence loom larger when the attorney's former employer is the government, the possibilities for side-switching/disloyalty and profiteering offer more ambiguous cases. Indeed, in some ways they are even less troubling for the former government attorney. "[U]nlike the private lawyer, who can identify a duty of loyalty to an individual client, the government lawyer works for an abstraction, the identity of which is so diffused that the duty of loyalty is . . . hard to identify."[30] Indeed, loyalty itself assumes a new meaning when the client is not only an abstraction but a chameleon, capable of reversing its own positions on legal issues as administrations change.[31] Finally, "even more than a private attorney, the government lawyer has a duty to seek justice rather than the result desired by his [governmental] client."[32] In other words, the government lawyer, as fiduciary for the public, may have a conflict of loyalties even within her role. She bears a fiduciary obligation to the government's partisan position, certainly, but also to broader legal and constitutional principles that may require her to temper her partisan zeal and observe obligations to those on the other side.[33] Hence government lawyers command unusual latitude—official discretion—when acting for their "clients" by comparison with the discretion available to private lawyers. In fact, government lawyers, as various commentators have observed, often make decisions as a client, not just a lawyer.[34] All of these observations tend to diminish the scope of disloyalty for a former government attorney. Or, at least, they suggest several kinds of circumstances in which, for the former government attorney as compared to her private-sector counterpart, the treachery of switching sides attenuates.

As for profiteering, the former government attorney may well acquire an adversarial advantage, on behalf of a private client, from knowledge or skills she derived from her governmental role. The question, however, is whether this capacity is any greater—any more troubling—than whatever capacity a private attorney possesses to exploit the confidences or information imparted by a previous private client in aid of a subsequent one. Here again (all other things being equal), the public quality of the ex-government attorney's former employer comes into play. Relatively more (if certainly not all) of the information a government attorney receives from her client is arguably publicly accessible, whereas none of the information an attorney receives from a private-sector client will fall into that category: A "government attorney does not have an obligation of confidentiality to the degree that a private attorney does because of the government's duty to deal openly with its citizens."[35]

Partners

While the statutory postemployment provisions explicitly do not apply to partners of former government attorneys, professional rules prohibit an attorney's partners from doing anything forbidden the attorney herself. In effect, the Bar will take the behavior and circumstances of a single lawyer and impute them to each of her partners, meaning that in most cases, whatever prohibitions apply to the lawyer herself will automatically blanket her entire firm. The problem for the former government attorney, however, is that she will become a "Typhoid Mary"—unemployable—if the statutory prohibitions under which she labors automatically extend to any firm that might hire her. Much litigation and internal Bar Association energy has gone to debating whether, or to what extent, the rules' imputation provisions should extend to partners of former government attorneys.[36] Here, I simply want to note which of the four postemployment concerns principally counsel in favor of imputation and which against.

Clearly, a former government attorney has the capacity to share officially derived knowledge, and hence her ability to profit from office, with her partners.[37] Likewise, the former government attorney's ex-official colleagues, cognizant of her association with a firm and its financial interests in a particular case, may be disposed to treat even her partners' representations favorably.[38] That a former government attorney's capacities for profiteering and influence can travel to other members of her firm is not much in dispute. Instead, disagreement arises over whether different kinds of intra-firm "screens" or "Chinese walls"—organizational structures that segregate the former government attorney from the rest of her firm for certain purposes—adequately address these two problems. Some argue, specifically, that when a firm handles a case for which the former government attorney's exclusive government-derived knowledge might be helpful, a screen that severs any information-flows from the former attorney to her partners should foreclose any imputation of profiteering. Others urge that screening the flow of fees *from* her partners *to* the former attorney should, in most cases, deal with the issue of influence. If her former official colleagues know that the ex-official is not receiving any fees in a particular case, they will not feel the pressure of her desires or wishes.[39] Opinion, however, is far from unanimous on either point.[40]

By contrast, a former government attorney's compromised loyalty or capacities for ingratiation are not as readily imputed to partners. An attorney's new private colleagues, themselves never having served in government, cannot easily carry whatever pure taint of switching sides might attach to the former government attorney herself.[41] And since it is her partners *with whom* she would have ingratiated herself while in government, they cannot by imputation become ingratiators themselves. Disloyalty and ingratiation cannot be imputed, and screening is irrelevant to such concerns.[42] Table 3 outlines the various possibilities.

Public discourse over the revolving door is, first and foremost, an ongoing attempt to make sense of the law—to determine what bothers us about of-

Table 3 Special revolving-door situations—principles particularly implicated

	Ingratiation	Influence	Profiteering	Disloyalty
Consultants	Yes	No	Yes	No
Transition teams	No	Yes	Yes	No
Defense officials	Yes	Yes	No	No
Foreign revolving door	No	No	Yes	Yes
Former government attorney	Yes	Yes	No	No
Legal partners	No	Yes	Yes	No

ficials' postemployment activities and to codify those concerns in statutes and regulations. And what I am suggesting is that the federal revolving-door laws display far greater rhyme and reason—they come closer to capturing those concerns—than is often allowed. Certainly there have been some regulatory excesses. But much more often, the four principles—against ingratiation, influence, profiteering, and switching sides—provide a parsimonious means of explaining the revolving-door regime's major contours. And, in pairs, they also fan out to sensibly structure the regimes that apply to specialized revolving-door situations—consultants, transition workers, defense officials, foreign-interest lobbyists, and former government attorneys and their partners.

Summary

Part I presented a topography of conflict, a map that delineates its major realms—self-dealing, undue influence, abuse of office, private payment for public acts, and private gain from public office. It explored the boundaries between these realms, traced the features that dominate their terrains, and charted their respective postemployment annexes. This topography is meant to present a big picture—to pick up the major normative hills and valleys without sinking too far into the brack and brine of regulatory underbrush and focus on what is more likely to remain permanent than ephemeral about the landscape.

And if we were now to imagine ourselves viewing this terrain while receding into space, until only one feature remained discernible, what would it be? It would be the prophylactic quality of our approach to conflict, or, to use the language that invariably crops up, the law's focus on "objective standards that are easy to administer" instead of "subjective assessment[s] of . . . states of mind"—its having "substituted an objective, generally applicable test for a subjective, individualized judgment of [mental states]."[1] Whether in self-dealing, undue influence, abuse of office, or private payment for public acts, what we prohibit are objectively ascertainable factual situations or acts: an official being in a position to affect her own interests, being importuned by another, engaging in private business with someone whose interests she can affect, receiving a public-salary subvention even from someone whose interests she cannot affect. And we prohibit these more-or-less objectively cognizable situations and acts in order to prevent the possibility of unknowably impaired subjective mental states, where in any given case the official may—but may not (who can say?)—succumb to the encumbrances posed by her own pecuniary out-of-role interests, professional in-role interests, private producer rent-earning possibilities, or public-service psychic income.

Only at the outer edges of the realm of conflict, where conflict in effect disappears—and I am referring to private gain from public office, where there need be no encumbered official mental state—does the prophylactic approach recede. Here, in determining whether an instance of private gain from public office has occurred, we must (if crudely) parse the psychologies of officials, asking ourselves whether their knowledge, expertise, and stature have inner origins—whether they constitute the person herself—or whether instead they are attributable to her official role. And the answers we give invariably arrive in inexact, subjective language; they "have an amorphous quality about them."[2] But generally, when it comes to conflict, we have moved from the subjective to the objective, the inner to the outer, the mental to the observable. And yet, as I will show, when it comes to *interest*, we have headed in just the opposite direction.

II

INTEREST

10

Interest, Bias,
and Ideology

If an official has a conflict of interest, then her judgment is encumbered. The word *conflict* pertains to judgment—as in "conflicted judgment"—while the word *interest* pertains to encumbrance, as in "encumbering interest." Having explored various conflicts that befall official judgment, I now examine different interests that could conceivably constitute encumbrances. And what quickly becomes apparent is that interests—at least if we mean "pecuniary" interests—are by no means the only entities that pose encumbrances. Just as our concerns in the realm of conflict have moved beyond self-dealing to embrace more controversial categories such as "abuse of office" and "private gain from public office," so our concerns in the realm of interest, or encumbrance, have moved beyond the pecuniary to encompass the ideological, the associational, and the psychological. "Influences," "loyalties," "concerns," "emotions," "predispositions," "prejudgments," "animuses," "biases," "affiliations," "experiences," "relationships," "attachments," "moral constraints," "ideological agendas"—all of these, at one time or another, have been viewed as every bit as encumbering of official judgment as pecuniary interest itself.[1] Hubert Humphrey's remark to agriculture secretary-designate Earl Butz— "you can put [your stocks and bonds] in escrow but I don't think you can put your philosophy in escrow"—offers but one illustration. Or consider Peter Strauss's rumination over the relative merits of a government agency hiring a former private businessman, as opposed to someone whose previous career had been in public-interest advocacy: "Texaco employees are likely to perceive [their] employment . . . more in economic than in ideologic terms; for employees of the Environmental Defense Fund the opposite may be true. If one assumes a permanent severance of prior employment ties on coming to a government job, the EDF employee seems if anything more likely than the Texaco employee to experience a carry-over of his former loyalties."[2]

When it comes to interest, debate quickly bleeds into—indeed, it comes down to—the question of where, in the sprawling psychological realm beyond the merely pecuniary, to draw the line separating the encumbering from the nonencumbering. And, in so doing, it opens up onto a host of contemporary American political conundrums.

Politicians, judges, and commentators use a familiar terminology to capture the distinction between pecuniary encumbrances and these other, more psychological, impairments. Pecuniary interests are "objective"—hard, measurable, external, and visible to the naked eye—whereas ideologies, associations, loyalties, and predispositions are "subjective," less fathomable, less visible because more internal.[3] Viewed this way, our understanding of interest has, in broadening from the pecuniary to the psychological, headed in a direction opposite to that taken by conflict. In the realm of conflict, the law has abandoned inner subjective inquiries for external, objective standards; no matter how unclouded the official's actual subjective mental state might be, if the closest objective indicators available suggest a conflict, there's a conflict. But in our understanding of interest, we have moved from objective to subjective. No matter how completely the official may have divested his externally cognizable pecuniary interests, we may still be willing to contemplate an almost unbounded set of inner psychological states as "encumbrances." We have, in essence, moved from a world where we are prepared to say that a particular official—say a Charles Wilson—is the type to subjectively surmount any conflict caused by his objective pecuniary interests, to one where we assume even subjective encumbrances—attitudes, beliefs—place an official, a John Tower, in objective conflict.

Of course, to move from objective pecuniary-monetary toward subjective psychological-ideological understandings of encumbrance is to enter a realm of intense disagreement. For every Humphrey who views a Butz's philosophical leanings as an encumbrance on judgment, there will be a Butz to deny this, insisting instead that such philosophical leanings, far from encumbering his judgment, actually constitute his very capacity to exercise it—part of the mental apparatus that he appropriately brings to bear when making official decisions. Even if we are able to tell which of an official's particular beliefs, commitments, or interests accounts for his position on a particular issue—itself no easy task—we will thus often strenuously disagree whether those particular features constitute, or else impair, his capacity to make official decisions. It is precisely because this kind of disagreement is so irresolvable that some political thinkers, Judith N. Shklar most prominently, have suggested that we abandon our preoccupation with the sincerity or hypocrisy of public figures. We are, Shklar says, far too fixated on whether an official's policy pronouncements originate in a sincere attempt on his part to judge the public interest, or in a hypocritical effort to advance some kind of self-serving encumbrance on judgment. We should just insist on good decisions in accord with external, even objective norms: "social rules" or conceptions of "the general good."[4]

Shklar's argument here is imbued with the liberal temperament her work as a whole embodies. Yet contemporary American democratic discourse would seem to stand it on its head. Precisely because we are so often unable to measure official behavior against an *objective* standard of the "general good"—precisely because the "public interest" remains contested over so many policy domains—we find ourselves, by default, gauging whether officials' judgments accord with their own genuine *subjective* conceptions of the public good, as opposed to originating in some kind of selfish encumbrance on their judgment. Accusations of hypocrisy and protestations of sincerity of the sort Shklar criticizes in fact permeate American public discourse.[5] For Shklar, it is the impossibility of ever defining the boundaries of someone else's subjective "conscience" that requires us to measure officials against objective or social notions of "the general good." But in fact, as Daniel Callahan has observed, it is our frequent failure to "develop a consensus of what the public interest is" that forces us to inquire into the "conscientious beliefs" of individual officials and citizens.[6]

Of course, our failure to develop an objective notion of "what the public interest is"—the absence of any kind of independent criterion for gauging correct outcomes in many policy areas—does not stop each of us from using his or her own individual views of the public interest to measure official decisions. Whenever an official falls short of my subjective conception of the public interest in a certain area, I engage her in policy disagreement. But when there is no overarching consensus on where the public interest lies, another prominent strategy is to show how an official's policy stance conflicts not with one's own view of the public interest, but with that held by the official herself. It is not just that we disagree with the policy on the merits; we suspect the official, herself, disagrees with it on the merits. As Meg Greenfield pointedly notes, instead of "[g]ood, frontal, rough political debate," we try to suggest that "the other guy . . . doesn't believe [what he's saying] himself."[7] Or as Amy Gutmann and Dennis Thompson put it, in assessing "citizens and officials [when they] espouse their moral positions," we cannot avoid looking "for sign[s] of political sincerity [which] indicate that a person holds the position" genuinely.[8]

But in determining whether an official's position flows from her own sincere, genuine consideration of the merits, we are ceaselessly borne back to Humphrey-Butz–style disputes. We continually find ourselves, in effect, arguing over which of an official's beliefs, attachments, and interests constitute her "subject," a term philosophers use to describe the "motives that identify [an individual] as the moral agent she is [or] constitute her moral being."[9] And we must determine which of her beliefs, attachments, and interests seem merely *selfish*, in that although they are part of the self, they remain extrinsic to the subject, to those parts of the official on which she properly calls in making judgments. As Govert den Hartogh puts it, because officials cannot make their "decision[s] within an objective framework, [t]here are only individual subjects . . . deciding . . . within the framework of their own religious, scientific and moral views."[10] Our daily democratic dialogue, to use den Hartogh's terms, thus requires us to identify and limn each others' subjective frameworks. It requires us, as Harry Frankfurt puts it, to "constru[e] some of a person's desires as integral to him in a way in which others are not"; it necessitates our distinguishing those of an individual's "volitional elements that are integrated" into the subject from "those that remain in some relevant sense external to [it]."[11] And the "individuals" in question, I should emphasize, are principally politicians, appointed officials, and senior civil servants. Largely absent from discussion here are ministerial officials engaged in pure procedural activities with little capacity for exercising judgment—and judges, for whom (at least in certain kinds of cases) there is "an independent [that is, objective] criterion for the correct outcome."[12] On the other hand, citizens exercise political judgment too; and although they do not fall under the embrace of the conflict laws discussed in Part I, they very much fall victim to the kinds of encumbrances discussed here.

A "disinterested person," David Bromwich says in his "Genealogy of Disinterestedness," is one who will "be affected by nothing but what he sees, hears and feels to be the merits of the case."[13] Not what *are* the objective merits of the case—that may remain inveterately controversial—but what *he* sees, hears, and feels to be the merits of the case, which necessarily embarks us on a search for a definition of "he" or "she," the boundaries of the subject. In this way, too, our discussion in the realm of "interest" has relinquished the objective for the subjective. While the term "subject" nowhere appears in democratic discourse, the concept, as I shall show, is everywhere.

In the rest of Part II, I gather together and explore a number of strands in American public discourse, interpreting them as attempts to draw the boundaries of the genuine subject in just this way. The chapter that immediately follows, "Limousine Liberals, Country-Club Conservatives," examines some of our most vexing debates over official sincerity and hypocrisy. These exchanges, I suggest, invariably hinge on whether one or another of an official's personal features—characteristics, beliefs, commitments, projects, purposes, traits—is better understood as integral to her capacity to exercise judgment or else encumbering of it, constitutive of the subject or else external to it. Hypocrisy is not the same thing as inconsistency, nor is sincerity consistency. Limousine liberals—those whose political positions seem inconsistent with certain personal interests and traits—are alternatively praised for the self-transcendent conviction of their political stance and criticized for its inauthenticity. Country-club conservatives—wealthy businessmen who take compatibly conservative political positions—are alternatively criticized for the "self-servingness" of their political utterances and praised for their wholeness and authenticity. And in both cases what is at issue is how best to interpret the personal feature (for example, the wealth) in question: as a selfish interest encumbering the capacity for political judgment, or as betokening a subjectively harbored commitment constitutive of the individual's moral-political worldview.

The subsequent chapter, "On Character in American Politics", explores our contemporary preoccupation with the character of public figures. In looking at the case of Bill Clinton in particular, I suggest that much of the controversy he has provoked comes down to whether—and to what extent—the pursuit and occupancy of office itself is better understood as a low selfish interest or as the embodiment of an official's highest subjective commitments.

I then turn from encumbrances posed by the personal features of officials to those created by their relationships with others, beginning with the crucial realm of *quid pro quo*. Much of our debate over *quid pro quo*—unlike our discourse over self-dealing, abuse of office, and the other conflict categories discussed in Part I—takes place in a realm beyond law, in media and political forums where we speculate freely and directly as to whether (say) a legislator's receipt of a campaign contribution actually did encumber her official performance on a particular file. And because we here operate in a realm beyond law, we necessarily also operate in a realm beyond prophylaxis. Our discourse over *quid pro quo*—rough-hewn, speculative, and unstructured as media and political exchanges can be—thus does attempt to assess, or pretend to peer, directly into the state of mind of the official concerned. We pronounce our views, as citizens, politicians, and journalists, on whether the official indeed experienced a *malum in se* encumbered mental state itself, not on whether he simply committed some kind of anterior *malum prohibitum*.

The chapter on *quid pro quo* explores the framework within which we conduct these kinds of debates. I argue that we stamp cases of *quid pro quo* as legitimate or illegitimate—according to certain principles I extract from discourse—depending on whether they seem to flow from the subjects of the officials and citizens concerned or else from self-serving features extrinsic to those subjects. Frequently, of course, we reach no consensus. In the two following chapters, on spousal conflicts of interest and combinations of roles/*ex parte* contacts, I turn to situations where it remains unclear whether a particular belief or interest constitutes or else encumbers an official's judgment *because* it is unclear whether it flows from within the official personally or is intruded on her by someone else.

After having looked at whether various subjective ideologies, prejudices, or relationships with others encumber or else constitute the official's judgment, I return to the more confined, objective realm of pecuniary interests—encumbrances on judgment that are objective in the hard, quantifiable sense—and ask whether they remain encumbrances for officials whose roles are not judgmental but advocatory. Specifically, in a chapter called "Hold the Interest, Vary the Role," I examine the oft-made argument that by sharing pecuniary interests with constituents, a legislator can represent them in a more effective way, even if doing so encumbers her capacity to judge the public interest as a whole. Finally, a chapter on *de minimis* explores debate over whether a pecuniary interest can become so insignificant or trivial that it ceases to pose an encumbrance on judgment at all.

11

Limousine Liberals,
Country-Club Conservatives

During the 1990 congressional campaign in Arkansas' second district, Republican Jim Keet attacked Democrat Ray Thornton for being a limousine liberal. Thornton's strong pro-welfare views were "ironic," Keet declared, given that Thornton was a "member of one of the wealthiest families in the state."[1] During the Massachusetts senatorial contest of the same year, Senator John Kerry accused his Republican opponent, Jim Rappaport, of being a "welfare conservative." Rappaport's strong opposition to government subsidies was more than a little "hypocritical," Kerry said, given that Rappaport was accepting such subsidies to run his family's dairy farm.[2] Although substantively the inverse of limousine liberalism, welfare conservatism displays the same moral structure. Both are instances where an individual's public utterances—her expressed belief as to what lies in the public interest—are inconsistent with one of her personal interests.

It is by no means immediately evident, however, why Thornton's limousine liberalism should be seen as "ironic" or Rappaport's welfare conservatism deemed "hypocritical." After all, someone who adopts particular political positions, even though they fly in the face of certain features of her identity, can just as easily seem courageous and sincere. More precisely, she will seem courageous and sincere to the extent that the inconsistent features in question—the love of limousines, the attraction to subsidies—are better interpreted, in the way pecuniary projects or ambitions often are, as self-serving encumbrances on the subject's capacity for political judgment, not as constitutive of it. That the limousine liberal's public utterance, namely her support for redistributionist liberalism, runs counter to her own selfish interests will then suggest, to some at least, that she is genuinely committed to that liberalism on its own terms. It will suggest that we locate her professed liberalism further into her own genuine subject, because it is so obviously *not* located in a prominent selfish "volitional element external" to it. As E. J. Dionne puts this point, "[t]he most powerful form of moral witness is when people speak out against what are perceived to be their own interests."[3]

125

So, for example, in discussing the plight of contemporary liberalism in New York City, the urbanologist Ester Fuchs recently remarked, they "have their self interests, big . . . deal . . . I'd like to bring back the limousine liberals. At least those people had compassion; at least they cared."[4] One could lend "welfare conservatism" a precisely analogous interpretation: Jim Rappaport must genuinely have opposed subsidies on the merits, must truly have deemed their abolition to lie in the public interest, since their termination would have hurt his own selfish interests. "Early in 1994," the journalist James Fallows reports along similar lines, "ABC's *Prime Time Live,* cohosted by Sam Donaldson, ran a feature on an insurance-lobbying association that took congressmen on junkets to resorts. One week later the show had to run a brief disclaimer, saying that Donaldson himself had spoken, for pay, to the same group the previous year . . . 'You can look at this as hypocrisy,' [Donaldson's colleague] Jeff Greenfield said of the Donaldson episode, 'Or you can say it shows he took the money and then [criticized] them anyway.'"[5]

Indeed, if limousine liberals are praised for being "moral witnesses" or "compassionate and caring"—for the genuine, self-abnegating commitment they harbor to their liberalism—they are also attacked for "hypocrisy" and "irony," for being insincere in their liberal commitments. One of two mirror-image interpretive moves underlies most attempts to depict such inconsistency as hypocrisy.

The first derogates what the limousine liberal claims is her genuine subjectively rooted belief in liberalism by reinterpreting that belief as, itself, a judgment-encumbering interest—or, at least, as a means of realizing a set of encumbering interests. Although an individual's liberalism may reassuringly conflict with her self-serving *pecuniary* interests, critics will nevertheless call attention to any coherence her liberalism displays with other kinds of self-serving interests, social or political, the individual may possess: interests in being fashionable, popular, and so forth. Any such coherence will pull her liberalism back up from the depths of genuine subjectivity, implanting it instead in the realm of features that impair the personal capacity for judgment on the merits. In the midst of his famous attack on limousine liberals, Tom Wolfe took pains to exempt from his criticism those wealthy individuals who supported the NAACP (National Association for the Advancement of Colored People) and CORE (Congress of Racial Equality) during the 1960s, on grounds that "they must have been sincere about it because these organizations never had much social cachet."[6]

Take another example: In 1986, a Canadian senator staged a hunger strike to protest the termination of Katimavik, a federally supported youth program he had politically sponsored some years previously. On the twenty-first day of the strike, the senator, through representatives, successfully extracted a compromise from the government—at which point he off-handedly remarked, to a reporter, that he regularly goes without food for up to ten days at a time as part of a health regimen. This revelation was not well taken. It seemed somehow to discount by one-half the moral force of what he had done (in fact, the senator may have become the only politician in recent memory to appear hypocritical by revealing that he had been doing exactly the *same thing* privately as he had been doing publicly).

But why, exactly? In staging the hunger strike, the senator himself would seem to have wanted this interpretation placed on it: The strike was a political act, a statement about the public interest which, in running so directly and self-evidently athwart a self-serving personal interest—the interest in not starving to death—obviously embodied and demonstrated genuine subjective commitment to Katimavik on the merits. Yet when it was revealed that the strike, far from running athwart the senator's personal interest in not starving to death, actually served (what, for the purposes of a political judgment about youth policy) was an "external," judgment-encumbering interest in fasting, the amount of commitment embodied in the act seemed disvalued and was discounted.[7] The reverse strategy, it should be noted, also sometimes crops up. That is, when someone is accused of advancing a political belief simply because it will help serve certain judgment-encumbering selfish interests, the "accused" might cast as a judgment-encumbering selfish interest another personal feature with which that political belief is reassuringly inconsistent. There "can be no doubting [J. P. Morgan's] sincerity," the historian David Loth commented, "when, accused of driving the nation into [World War I] for the protection of his bank and clients, [Morgan] cried, 'Do you suppose I wanted to get my own son into the war? He went, though.'"[8]

The second critique of limousine liberalism inverts the first one. Instead of demoting an official's or citizen's erstwhile subjective commitment to liberalism to the status of a self-serving interest, it elevates the individual's interest in limousines to the status of a subjective commitment. On this interpretation, what others might see as the selfish interest in limousine-possession—external to and encumbering of the subject's capacity for political judgment—in fact bespeaks a set of subjectively constitutive commitments to the legitimacy of acquisition and the illegitimacy of redistribution—subjective commitments inconsistent with a public utterance on behalf of redistributive liberalism.

Pecuniary pursuits that might on some interpretations be deemed selfish, judgment-encumbering interests can be reinterpreted thusly to imply beliefs or commitments resident in the subject, through a variety of symbolic, logical, or psychological arguments and assumptions. An individual who possesses limousines knows, and therefore accepts, that others will attribute to her—and hence her love of limousines will come to symbolize—the subjectively harbored belief that a considerable amount of inequality is permissible or proper. Perhaps the very possession of limousines predicates certain views concerning the worth and legitimacy of acquisition which, in owning limousines, the individual must logically embrace as part of her own subjective constitution. Perhaps the possession of limousines can never remain just a pure "external" encumbrance without in some way entering into and affecting the individual's deepest subjective dispositions, without turning her away, psychologically, from the commitment to mutual aid embodied in the liberalism she espouses. Riding in limousines, on this argument, withers whatever subjectively rooted capacity one might have possessed for empathizing with the experiences of less-privileged others.

If the pecuniarily acquisitive trait realized in limousine possession is elevated along any of these lines—if it is necessarily attended by subjectively constitutive commitments to the legitimacy of inequality, the limits of mutual aid, and the worthiness of material accumulation—then it entails an incompatibility with the individual's publicly expressed liberalism that seems troubling. For on any of these interpretations, it is no longer a mere judgment-encumbering personal interest with which the individual's public support for redistribution seems reassuringly to conflict. Rather, it is a set of subjective commitments and practices, a way of life, with which her publicly uttered liberalism seems disturbingly ill at ease. To the extent that such beliefs, commitments, and practices firmly take up residence in the subject, they necessarily displace the individual's inconsistent liberalism. Certainly, they make that liberalism sit less comfortably there. As Harry Frankfurt puts it, "a person who decides what to believe," whether through intellection or practice (in this case, a belief in the legitimacy of acquisition and the limits of mutual aid), "provides himself with a criterion for other beliefs: namely, they must be coherent with the belief upon which he has decided."[9]

What all of this means is evident in the typical rhetorical strategy employed by former Interior Secretary Manuel Lujan, who attacked the "local newspaper that runs passionate editorials about recycling, but then refuses to use recycled newsprint to publish that editorial."[10] In Lujan's view, the newspaper's desire to purchase nonrecycled newsprint was not a judgment-encumbering selfish interest the paper bravely flouts each time it publishes a pro-recycling editorial, thereby giving reason to believe in its genuine commitment to conservation. Rather, Lujan saw in the newspaper's desire to use nonrecycled newsprint an implied belief, commitment, or acknowledgement, rooted in the editorialist's subject, that recycling has its discontents. To then advocate it is inconsistent, and we have license to question the paper's genuine commitment to its publicly espoused conservationism.

During Senator Bob Kerrey's 1992 campaign for the Democratic presidential nomination, the *New York Times* and the *Washington Post* revealed that although Kerrey was advocating universal employer-mandated health coverage as a candidate, as a businessman he had refused to provide insurance for the part-time workers employed in his Nebraska restaurant chain because of the cost. The *Times* saw "inconsistency" and "hypocrisy" in Kerrey's situation; the *Post* saw "irony." But to be able to criticize Kerrey's inconsistency in this situation, one would have to interpret his business practices, specifically his avoidance of health-coverage for his part-time employees, so as to imply a set of subjectively harbored beliefs incompatible with his professed liberalism. And, indeed, some of his critics did just that. Jenny Brown, vice-president of the local Hotel and Restaurant Employees Union, said that Kerrey's business decision to forgo health-coverage for his part-time workers shows that, contrary to the "impression" he gave when campaigning, he is not "for the blue-collar worker." For Brown, Kerrey's pecuniary interest in avoiding premium payments for his part-time workers had weaved itself into his subjectivity, there evoking, signifying, or surrounding itself with certain implied commitments and beliefs about the relatively low priority of workers' rights. It is on this kind of interpretation that Kerrey's combination of expressed political liberalism and established business practices would bode forth in hypocrisy or irony.

Kerrey, in his own defense, never denied that his advocacy of universal health care was inconsistent with his business practices. But, he argued, those business practices—his avoidance of premium payments—did not signify a subjectively harbored commitment to *laissez faire*, which, in supporting universal health coverage, he disingenuously contradicted. Rather, they signified an encumbering financial interest which, in supporting universal health coverage, he courageously surmounted. Observing that he was in the very small minority of business owners who had come out in favor of employer-mandated universal coverage, Kerrey invited others to conclude that he must have arrived at that position in an unencumbered way, that he believed in it genuinely and on the merits.[11]

Perhaps a more evocative example is the case of a politician cool to gay rights who himself happens to be gay. Such a politician is rarely, if ever, praised for courageously expressing certain beliefs as to what lies in the public interest, even though they run athwart the pursuit of his judgment-encumbering personal interests. Instead, on the more governing interpretation, he is criticized for inauthentically advocating views as to what lies in the public interest inconsistent with other subjective beliefs and commitments he has (or must have) developed as a result of his personal life.

It may, in some circumstances, appear not only as if such a politician is acting against his own subjective commitments—that is, against characteristics that constitute him as a moral agent—but that he is doing so to serve certain other judgment-encumbering interests such as political popularity or electoral success (he may be concerned about the political consequences of being thought pro-gay or known to be gay). Such an interpretation would further remove his political stance against gay rights from the realm of the genuine. But the reverse possibility is also available. For example, politicians who change issue positions—thereby arguably betraying their own subjective commitments—can point to the electoral consequences of the switch as evidence that they would not have undergone them had they not genuinely changed their minds. For example, when her government abandoned an election commitment to abolish Canada's Goods and Services Tax (GST), Deputy Prime Minister Sheila Copps, according to her supporters, "actually showed integrity in voting for a budget that did not abolish the GST even though she knew there would be consequences for her."[12]

To sum up: In neither of their two lines of attack do critics of limousine liberalism challenge the notion that something reassuring attaches to an individual whenever her publicly expressed political beliefs run against—are manifestly not subservient to—her selfish interests. Instead, critics either demote the belief in liberalism itself to the status of a judgment-encumbering interest or, conversely, they elevate her pecuniary interest in limousines to the status of a set of subjectively harbored beliefs and commitments. Some critics, in other words, will recontextualize what appear to be the individual's subjectively constitutive liberal beliefs about the public interest, accounting for them through other encumbering interests the individual may have in being chic, powerful, and so forth. And others will reinterpret what seems to be an encumbering interest in limousines—endowing it with the significance of a subjectively housed commitment to material possession, property, or accumulation—on the assumption that while public utterances that run athwart one's encumbering interests reassure us of their genuineness, public utterances that run athwart one's beliefs and commitments do not.

Inconsistency: Some Complications

The limousine liberal claims sincerity to the extent that her liberalism is inconsistent with—works against, defeats, impedes, thwarts, flouts—a feature of her identity better understood as a judgment-encumbering selfish interest, not as a subjectively harbored commitment. In two further kinds of cases, however, this strategy is unavailable to the limousine liberal. First, her liberalism may in fact fail to defeat or impede her selfish interests because, although her advocacy may well help give that liberalism real effect, she will somehow be able to exclude her own individual interests from being affected by it. Consider a parent who aggressively campaigns to bring busing to her school district while sending her own child to private school. Or, to move beyond limousine liberalism, consider the legislator who opposes laws to improve the quality of tap water while drinking bottled water at the office.[13] A variant would be the extremely wealthy liberal who would not even notice the effect of the redistributionist policy she advocates, although its burdens would be felt by many who (although comfortable by some standards) are less well off than she.

Second, the limousine liberal's expressed liberalism may in fact fail to defeat or impede her selfish interests because, although standing to have her interests adversely affected by the liberal program she advocates, she knows that in advocating it she will have no real effect on bringing it about. Consider the parent who, although sending her own child to public school, advocates busing only because she knows enough others will oppose it, or the professor who proposes that academic and custodial staff periodically swap their jobs, knowing "it could never happen in a million years."[14] In both cases of complicated inconsistency, even if we interpret the personal feature in question—not wanting one's child bused, not wanting to drink unsafe water, not wanting to do custodial work—as a judgment-perverting personal interest, we are still not likely to regard the individual's inconsistent public utterances as courageous or as endowing her with the quality of a "moral witness speaking out against her own interests."

But why not, exactly? In the first case—of the pro-busing parent who sends her child to private school, or the deregulator of tap water who consumes the bottled variety—in the absence of any redeemingly and adversely affected selfish interests, all that remains is a disturbing conflict between a subjectively harbored personal belief and a publicly uttered political commitment. On the one hand is the subjectively harbored belief in the harmfulness of busing or unregulated tap water implied in her private activity; on the other, the political commitment to their utility averred in her public expressions. The critique here is that "[o]ne cannot maintain one's integrity," as Lynne McFall puts it, "if one has [subjective] commitments that conflict."[15]

In the second case—of the parent who sends her child to public school while advocating busing in a deliberately ineffective way, or the professor who does not really want to clean sinks but who promotes a job-swap knowing it will never happen—all that remains, in the absence of any seriously realizable political position, is a disturbing coalescence between various self-serving interests. In her advocacy of busing or job-swapping, the individual is able to pursue certain judgment-encumbering selfish interests—in identifying herself with popular or apparently altruistic pro-busing or pro-equity political views—while, because of her advocacy's actual ineffectiveness, in no way impinging upon other judgment-encumbering selfish interests: the interest in not having her child bused, the interest in not having to clean windows. She can be faulted for "trying to have it all."

Discourse abounds over both kinds of "complicated inconsistency." Both, too, attract charges of hypocrisy. Members of Congress, to take another set of examples, have been accused of hypocrisy on either score—for effecting policies that would go against their interests *were* they to be affected by them, or for ineffectively advocating policies that would adversely affect them. Congressmen who passed equal-opportunity employment legislation—legislation affecting all firms and institutions except Congress itself—attracted charges of hypocrisy. And so did those who recently advocated politically popular campaign-finance reforms counter to their own electoral interests, knowing full well that their colleagues were going to vote against such measures in sufficient numbers to ensure their defeat.[16]

Yet those charged with these dual forms of hypocrisy have recourse to certain defenses. For example, the perceived sincerity of an individual's expressed policy views can sometimes be preserved, even in the face of personal features that signal contrary commitments, precisely because she is able to exclude herself from among those the policy would actually affect. Consider the case of Bill Clinton, who as a student had sought to be exempted from going to war, but—when he became commander-in-chief—was in a position to order others into battle. Numerous critics have assailed Clinton for "hypocrisy" on this score, by which they mean that he was in a situation of "incompatible commitments." Clinton's evident lack of personal commitment to military service, they say, put in question the genuineness of his own stated political commitment to, hence his capacity for, executing vigorous defense initiatives.

But one could readily imagine a response, to the effect that Clinton is exactly the kind of commander we would want to lead us into war, just because his own inconsistent subjective commitments will helpfully leaven and season his prosecution of military policy.[17] As Bernard Williams has put this point, "[t]he consideration that [officials] should not order something unless they were prepared to do it themselves"—a consideration rooted in concerns about hypocrisy—"should be counterweighted with the consideration that if they were prepared to do it themselves, they might be far too willing to order it."[18] Or perhaps the very person we want promulgating a busing policy is someone who would not bus her own children: Precisely because such an official's implementation of the busing policy would be modulated by a belief that busing has certain ill consequences for bused children, she would be appropriately self-questioning, self-tempering, and so forth.

It is noteworthy, though, that Williams's defense of such salutary internal conflicts becomes available precisely to the extent that, while the political actor in question may be in a position to effect the policy concerned, she will herself remain wholly unaffected by it. To see this, reconceive the Clinton case. Suppose now that the war were being fought by a citizen militia of which the president is necessarily a member, so that he is now not just an effector of, but is also among those affected by, his military policy. While whatever subjective reticence he harbors about war might still usefully modulate him as an effector of policy, if he were also among those affected he would possess a live personal interest that might well encumber his judgment, leading us to question his commitment to the war effort.

Take a different example. When the antipornography circuit attorney for St. Louis, George Peach, was arrested for soliciting a prostitute, his response was as follows: "I'm Mr. Tough Guy to some people . . . [But] I have feelings for anyone charged with a crime . . . I tell my people, it's the state versus a human being . . . I'm not a person without feelings when it comes to a person charged with a crime." The tempering of prosecutorial zeal by a conflicting subjective commitment to humane treatment may be reassuring, but when that subjective commitment is tied to a personal judgment-encumbering interest in leniency—when Peach is among the affected, not just the effectors, of the prosecution policy he espouses—we may then question the subjective sincerity with which he holds to it.[19]

As these cases illustrate, we may sometimes be prepared to accept an individual's pursuit of a particular policy as sincere, notwithstanding that she seems to harbor inconsistent subjective beliefs, precisely if there is then no possibility of her own interests being affected by it. The pro-busing parent who sends her children to private school, for example, can be read in two different ways. By one interpretation, her unwillingness to send her children to public school signals a subjective reservation about busing troublingly inconsistent with her public support for it. And it also deprives her of any personal stake—any manifest willingness to allow a selfish interest to be adversely affected—that might reassure us of her genuine commitment to busing on the merits.[20] By another interpretation, she harbors a subjective reservation about busing that reassuringly temporizes her public support for it. And she additionally remains bereft of any adversely affected personal interest that might otherwise compromise her aggressive pursuit of a pro-busing policy.

When a subjectively-harbored commitment inconsistent with a public position can be a salutary temporizer—the pacifist commander-in-chief, the humane district attorney—we do not then want that subjective commitment to come attached with, or seem more plausibly interpretable as, an encumbering interest (avoiding the draft or going to prison). That is why officials who avail themselves of this "salubrious moral conflicts" interpretation should not then occupy the role of citizen—of one who is affected by the policies they seek to effect.

Of course, officials are precisely those most likely to avail themselves of a "moral conflicts" interpretation in the first place. Because they have a mandate-derived obligation to pursue their policy views full-tilt, any potentially adversely affected personal interest constitutes an unacceptable friction, a drag on their capacity to fulfill their official functions. Ordinary citizens, by contrast, are under no obligation to advocate, let alone pursue, any particular policy program. That a citizen may nevertheless choose even to utter a policy position that could adversely affect her selfish interests is, therefore, more likely to seem courageous; we are more likely to interpret that inconsistent interest as providing reassuring traction, a fixed point from which any policy distance seems reassuring.

Turn, now, to the second type of "complicated inconsistency," where someone stands accused of "trying to have it all." Consider the case of the journalist Sam Donaldson, who was recently charged with "hypocrisy" for accepting federal mohair subsidies for his hobby ranch while vocally attacking the federal subsidy program as contrary to the public interest. Donaldson, his critics said, was trying to have it both ways. He was hoping to enjoy whatever notoriety he could derive from adopting an appealingly "hard-charging" antisubsidy stance as a commentator—all the while reaping the pecuniary rewards that come from taking subsidies as a rancher—because he knew that his opposition to subsidies was unlikely to have any real effect, given the tremendous political forces arrayed in their favor. But where Donaldson's critics thought he was exploiting a disturbing consistency between his two encumbering interests in provocative journalism and remunerative ranching, Donaldson himself claimed to be displaying a reassuring consistency between two subjectively rooted beliefs.

Specifically, Donaldson argued, his expressed political belief—that it is wrong to have a subsidy program—can be regarded as eminently consistent with a personal feature of subsidy-taking, if the latter simply signifies the subjective belief that *until* subsidies are eliminated, it would not be wrong to take them. Donaldson's is a recognizable "collective-action" defense: Precisely because he is incapable of overcoming the intransigence of others, so as to realize his first-order policy views, Donaldson has had to develop a set of second-order beliefs, equally genuine and rooted in the subject, about how best to operate in the meantime. As the *Washington Post*'s Howard Kurtz reported: "Donaldson denounced agricultural subsidies from his pundit's chair on *This Week With David Brinkley*. But since sheep subsidies prop up the market price . . . he says he'd be crazy to pass up the money. 'I'm operating this ranch as a business,' he says . . . 'I don't think I should be required to say that I will forgo what every other rancher participates in.'"

"I believe," Donaldson added by way of analogy, "that taxes on high-wage earners should be raised but [do] not feel compelled to send in more money from my bank account until they are raised. While I drive the speed limit of sixty-five, I believe it should be lowered to fifty-five."[21]

One could read the job-swap–proposing professor in the same light: He sincerely believes the university should adopt a policy requiring job swaps. But unless or until he is able to persuade the administration to take such a course, he also believes—in an equally subjectively rooted way—that it would be wrong for anyone to expect him to suffer the social, psychological, and financial indignities associated with being the only one to relinquish his lectern for a mop and pail.

But when those with some meaningful capacity to put their policy views into effect cite the problem of collective inaction to explain otherwise inconsistent behavior, it often rings hollow. To see this, consider George Bush's and Dan Quayle's experience during the 1992 presidential campaign when each, although a strict "pro-lifer," acknowledged that he would "support" his granddaughter (in the case of Bush) or daughter (Quayle) were she to choose to have an abortion. Both were widely accused of hypocrisy and both—along with their supporters—attempted a collective-action defense. "Quayle didn't say he thinks his daughter should have the legally sanctioned 'freedom to choose,' he merely acknowledged that the law gives her that prerogative"; "the vice-president's statements were consistent with his pro-life views . . . and the reality that abortion is legal."[22] According to Bush's spokesman, "his public position is completely consistent with his private beliefs," for in offering to support his granddaughter, "he was not making a *political* statement about choice or saying that abortion is solely a woman's decision" but was instead making a statement within the context of abortion's existing legality.[23]

These collective-action defenses sat uneasily with some of Bush's and Quayle's critics precisely because, as powerful officials, the two were in a position to *orchestrate* collective action. They did not simply have to take abortion law as given but—to a greater extent than almost any others who might have held the same combination of political and personal commitments—Bush and Quayle were in a position to effect real changes to abortion law in accordance with their views. For their critics, then, the more appropriate question was not whether Bush's and Quayle's willingness to countenance an offspring's abortion was consistent with "the reality that abortion is legal," but whether it was consistent with their persistent and powerful campaign to drive "reality" away from the point where "abortion is legal." Bush and

Quayle themselves behaved as if they faced not an unmovable wall of legal reality—in everything they did politically, they signaled a refusal to take liberal abortion law as a given—but rather a domain of protean legal mutability, a realm in which the governing law was in fact scarcely recognized to exist. In voicing their subjective commitments to their (grand)daughters, they were thus naturally measured as law-makers, not law-takers. As one editorial put it, Bush obviously

> would not want . . . limited choice . . . available to his own granddaughter, so it is puzzling that he is trying diligently to restrict the choices available to other American women . . . He has appointed many anti-abortion judges. He proudly touts his record of seven anti-abortion vetoes in the last four years. Along with Quayle, he has advocated the addition of the anti-abortion amendment to the U.S. Constitution. He has, in short, done everything possible to make sure that his granddaughter and her peers never have the option of a safe and legal abortion.[24]

It is for those with a relatively negligible capacity to effect their first-order policy views, then, that a collective-action argument to explain otherwise inconsistent behavior rings most true. The job-swap–proposing professor, for example, can be read in two different ways. In one interpretation, his insincere advocacy of job-swapping—artfully calculated as it is to free-ride off the opposition of others—allows him to reap the political credit that comes from mouthing an attractive political view, without in any real way threatening his own interests in staying at the lectern. But there is another interpretation available: Precisely because his sincerely meant job-swapping policy views are incapable of being realized anytime soon, he has had to develop a set of subjectively rooted beliefs about how best to operate in the meantime (namely, stay at the lectern).

On the first and more critical interpretation, what would seem to be fixed—central to his identity—is the professor's encumbering interest in staying at the lectern. His job-swapping policy views, by contrast, are merely contingent, held and expressed only because, and just to the extent that, he cannot have any real effect on making them happen. On the second and more sympathetic interpretation, however, it is the professor's job-swapping views that are portrayed as fixed, genuine, fundamental to his identity. It is his staying at the lectern, by contrast, that is depicted as contingent, something he is doing only because, and just to the extent that, he cannot make his policy views come to pass. What for the professor's critics is an insincere exercise in free-riding off the opposition of others, for the professor becomes a sincere response to the collective inaction of others. But those who offer collective-action explanations for personal behavior inconsistent with their public utterances—usually, ordinary citizens—should not then seek to occupy the role of official, or, more generally, of anyone who is in a position to surmount collective-action problems and put their policy views into effect.

Consider, just to tie up a loose end, the situation of Jim Rappaport, who like Sam Donaldson accepted subsidies personally while opposing them politically but, unlike Donaldson, sought election to be among the effectors, not just the affected, of an antisubsidy policy. In Rappaport's case, it would not have gone over well had he depicted his subsidy-taking as signifying a subjective belief in the legitimacy of drawing subsidies as long as the law permits. After all, he was seeking a mandate to effect changes in that law, and his taking subsidies arguably put in question his commitment to making those changes. On the other hand, Rappaport might more plausibly have depicted his inconsistent subsidy-taking as a self-serving interest, because he could then have made the claim—given the real efficacy of a senatorial candidate's public utterances—to have been courageously pursuing a particular policy path notwithstanding his own contrary selfish interests.

Consistency

Consider, now, the flip side of limousine liberalism: the situation of the "country-club conservative," or, more generally, anyone whose public utterances are thoroughly consistent with central features of her identity.[25] During the 1990 congressional campaign, Democrat Ray Thornton observed that Republican Jim Keet's views as to what lies in the public interest—namely "supply-side economics" which "reward[s] those who are wealthy in hopes that some of it may trickle down"—completely coincided with (that is, if enacted would serve, abet, and promote) one of Keet's most prominent personal features: his endeavors as a wealthy businessman.[26] Others echoed Thornton's opinion, attacking Keet for being "a rich . . . tunnel-visioned Republican."[27]

If Keet's business ambitions are best interpreted as self-serving encumbrances on his capacity for political judgment, then were he to have made public utterances *in*consistent with them, we might have credited those utterances as genuine. However, since Keet's public utterances cohere rather closely with those business ambitions, interpreting those ambitions as self-serving encumbrances on judgment—as his critics did—would lead us to question the extent to which his policy views are rooted in the genuine subject. Thornton's attack is of a piece with the more generic critique of "corporate leaders," advanced by the Canadian columnist Jeffrey Simpson, who propound "ideas . . . evidently self-serving—taxes are too high, government is too intrusive," and so on. "I long," Simpson adds, "for some plutocrat who might say something original."[28]

Similarly, presidential candidate Steve Forbes, a holder of great wealth, found himself attacked for proposing a flat tax from which he would have personally benefited. Yet the fact that he was also placing much of that wealth at stake in his campaigning—by spending vast sums on television advertising—suggested to some (such as a "homemaker" from Nashua, New Hampshire) that "he's sincere in what he says."[29] And on yet another interpretation, "when Steve Forbes pushes his flat-tax proposal, charges that he, more than almost any other American, will personally benefit from it fail to stick. No, he is a man acting out of pure principle. He is not trying to get rich; he already is rich."[30] Just as a limousine liberal can be so rich that the antiwealth public positions she takes fail to attain "virtuous" inconsistency, so (apparently) a country-club conservative can attain such wealth that any public position consistent with it fails to trouble us.

There are, however, two defensive strategies available to the country-club conservative. First, he can endeavor to elevate his business activity, itself, from its more readily perceived status of an encumbering interest to the perhaps less obvious class of a commitment constitutive of the subject's capacity to make judgments. On such an interpretation, Keet's business ambitions would constitute not simply "volitional elements external" to the subject but a personal feature necessarily enveloped in, significant of, and committing him to, a set of beliefs, experiences, and principles, housed in the subject, part of who he is. For Keet, the proper construction would be that he possesses not a naked encumbering interest in his pecuniary activity but an attendant set of subjectively rooted beliefs and experiences in the virtues of the market and capitalism, and it is with these beliefs and experiences, not his encumbering interest in profits, that his supply-side views (reassuringly) cohere. Analogously, when Canadian physician William Hughes—leader of a coalition opposing caps on physicians' salaries—was revealed to be the province of Ontario's "highest biller," he argued, according to newspaper reports, that "it is possible to see his high billings as proof that he believes in the message he is trying to spread."[31]

In a different context Denis Donoghue, in favorably reviewing a recent book supportive of political and civic rights for homosexuals in America, declares, "I am not, in my own person, directly caught up in [the issue]. But I should declare an interest. My youngest daughter . . . is a lesbian."[32] Donoghue then goes on, however, to describe his relationship with his daughter in terms that leave no doubt about his genuine love for and commitment to her. His discussion, in other words, certainly allows for the conclusion that the relationship is part of what constitutes his subjectivity, who he is as a critic, and whatever genuine capacity he brings to judging a work on its merits—notwithstanding that he felt compelled to declare the relationship as a possible encumbering interest.

The reconceptualization of what might be taken to be a selfish interest—so that it instead appears to be a subjective commitment—characterizes Michael Kinsley's defense of a nuclear-power lobbyist who, without revealing his industry links, writes a pro-nuclear opinion piece for a newspaper. Kinsley concludes that no disclosure is required. Such a view makes sense, however, only if the lobbyist's industry ties, the personal feature with which his editorial opinions about the public interest are so snugly consistent, are better interpreted not as an encumbering interest but as significant of a set of beliefs that go to the heart of who the lobbyist is as a subject. And, indeed, this is what Kinsley believes. The fact that the lobbyist's opinion piece "comport[s] with . . . a past commitment to a particular set of beliefs" in the nuclear industry, Kinsley writes, is "reassuring, not objectionable."[33] Reassuring, because it suggests a consistent wholeness; it suggests that the lobbyist's public utterances are genuine, not self-serving. If, however, the term "commitment to a particular set of beliefs" in the nuclear industry were replaced with "certain ties to and interests in the nuclear industry," as it well could be, then we would be less reassured. Neither interpretation denies the presence of internal consistency; the question is, "consistency between expressed pro-industry views and what?"—a judgment-encumbering interest or a subjectively constitutive commitment? While a view's consistency with subjective commitments and beliefs locates it in the subject, its consistency with what may be described as an encumbering interest places it outside.

This first defense of country-club conservatism—where the personal feature denoted by the term "country-club" is interpreted as a subjectively constitutive commitment and not an encumbering interest—is a universal strategy, equally available to defensive "welfare liberals." Hillary Clinton told a 1996 campaign audience that, as the "parent of a child who will go off to college next year, I particularly like my husband's proposal that we allow any family to deduct up to ten thousand dollars a year for education expenses."[34] And liberal "Republicans . . . innoculat[ed] themselves on Medicare, sometimes by displaying their own Medicare-dependent parents, in a kind of video validation of their sincerity on the subject."[35] As go country-club conservatives, so go welfare liberals: In both cases, politicians who arrive at their political views on the basis of those views' correspondence with what could easily be understood as judgment-encumbering selfish interests—the interest in reduced-cost education or public health insurance—implicitly cast those personal traits as constitutive of the subject and their views therefore as genuine.

Assume now, though, that the business pursuits that incontestably cohere with, and sustain, a country-club conservative's supply-side beliefs *are* better characterized simply as judgment-encumbering interests and not just as constitutive of his subjective commitments and principles. Still, the country-club conservative has available a second line of defense. He might show that while his pro-business policy views concededly comport with an encumbering interest he happens to possess, they also cohere with a number of other subjectively-constitutive beliefs he demonstrably has. Here, the suggestion is that the remainder of his subjectivity (other mutually sustaining conservative beliefs, for example) explains his belief in supply-side economics far more profoundly than does his encumbering pecuniary interest. And, indeed, Jim Keet's defenders made just such an argument.[36]

In both defenses of country-club conservatism, the "accused" accepts that one's public utterances raise questions to the extent that they cohere with one's judgment-encumbering selfish interests. In one, however, she reinterprets her pecuniary aspiration not as a judgment-encumbering interest but as rooted in, or significant of, a subjective belief in the free market consistent with her belief about what would serve the public interest (supply-side economics). On the other, she recontextualizes her belief about the public interest—the virtues of supply-side economics—embedding it in a number of other cohering, sustaining (conservative) subjective beliefs. Both tacks attempt to take back and redraw the boundaries around the subject, so that the subject accounts for the belief (in supply-side economics), instead of abandoning it to the realm of selfish, judgment-encumbering interests. Both accept that while public utterances that cohere with judgment-encumbering interests are suspect, public utterances that cohere with subjectively constitutive beliefs and commitments are not. Discourse over instances of consistency, of the country-club conservative variety, thus complements discourse over inconsistency, of the limousine-liberal variety. There, public utterances that conflict with subjective beliefs and commitments are suspect, while public utterances that conflict with what are interpreted to be encumbering selfish interests are reassuring.

Braided together, charges of hypocrisy and counter-avowals of sincerity compose a central and enduring strand in American democratic discourse. The question we address time and again is not whether the judgment expressed by an official conforms to some ineffable objective notion of the public interest. Rather, it is whether those of his beliefs or interests with which his judgment accords (or conflicts) are better understood as constitutive of his own subjective judgment or as self-serving encumbrances on it. What is so striking is the pervasive polarity of disagreement on this question. In any given case, what features some interpret as encumbering interests, others will characterize as subjectively harbored beliefs and commitments. What some see as beliefs and commitments, others will resolve into certain encumbering interests they may serve. As Archibald Cox once said, "of course people come [to politics] with their relationships and their attitudes," but they should not put "money or personal advantage . . . over the sincere pursuit of the public interest."[37] Yet in any given case, "money and personal advantage" could—or so some will claim—betoken or be linked to experiential constituents and commitments of the subject. Conversely, "relationships and attitudes" could be deemed to encumber the subject's capacity to make judgments on the merits. On the structure of such disagreement will hinge the all-important question as to whether, as Cox puts it, that official's "pursuit of the public interest" is "sincere."

12

On Character in
American Politics

Vast tracts of contemporary public discourse, it turns out, dissolve into the question of whether a particular personal feature falls into the class of subjective commitment or selfish encumbrance. But we also engage in the same debate over official role itself; we alternatively classify the pursuit and holding of office as a selfish, vainglorious interest, and as a paramount means of realizing one's deepest subjective commitments. And *this* particular disagreement, I claim, goes to the heart of the intense debates over the character of public officials with which we have become familiar.

Bill Clinton is the inevitable example. My interest here lies at a sublegal level. Assuming the president did not break any laws, to what extent were the various "character" allegations leveled against him relevant to his public performance? After all, as those who would dismiss our preoccupation with the private lives of officials point out, Clinton had already amassed a twenty-year official record. Why, even assuming their accuracy, should any of the stories circulating about his private behavior have anything to do with our assessment of him?[1] "The same juices that drive [politicians] to horse around . . . may drive them to start wars," Michael Kinsley has written by way of explaining the public pertinence of a politician's private life.[2] For a novice candidate with no previous political record, a history of his horsing around may be the only thing we have available for evaluating him. But in Clinton's case, we had an established record of him not starting any wars. So of what "proxy" value was the information that he horses around?

A preliminary distinction: Although they are often confused, Clinton's situation differs from that of both John Kennedy and Gary Hart. The problem with Kennedy, according to his critics, was that he saw himself as a privileged figure, someone to whom the ordinary moral legislation of mankind simply did not apply. Hart may not have scorned our moral norms themselves, but—when he was accused of conducting an extramarital affair—he did question their application in his particular case. Denying any misconduct, he claimed to have been misjudged. Clinton, by contrast, came across as neither "above the law" nor "falsely judged" but as someone trying to avoid arrest. He sought not to transcend the legislative aspects of our moral norms, nor to deny the judgment visited on him, but instead merely to elude its execution and enforcement. Where Kennedy may have been something of a moral outlaw (with all the allure that entails) and where Hart in effect pled temporary insanity (or, as he called it, "bad judgment"), Clinton was taxed for being slick. Of course, if it ever definitely transpires that Clinton broke any laws in the way he handled his private financial and sexual activities, then those activities would become relevant to our assessment of him as a public official. But it is a matter of debate as to whether he did, and in any even it is the "horsing around" that compels our attention. The question is: Should it?

Such information, I argue, is of value, although not as proxy for the substance of an official's beliefs but as an indicator of his commitment to them. Americans ultimately admire (even if they do not always immediately reward) politicians who, in the words of John Tyler, "regard as nothing any position or office which must be attained or held at the sacrifice" of their principles.[3] But office is not only a vessel of self-serving perks, pleasures, and ambitions which politicians should be expected to sacrifice in the name of higher personal principles. It is also an instrument through which politicians seek the realization of their highest principles and, consequently, it is also something for which they should be expected to sacrifice certain personal pleasures, perks, and indulgences. The pursuit of office, in other words, can be interpreted as an encumbering personal interest—a self-serving ambition, a hunger for power, a desire for notoriety—which a politician should be prepared to sacrifice in the name of his subjectively-constitutive beliefs and commitments. But it can also be interpreted as the vehicle through which officials can most effectively pursue those ideas to which—on the merits—they are most genuinely committed, and for which they should be expected to sacrifice more selfish personal interests, pursuits and distractions.

Bill Clinton himself spoke of "elected office as a high calling," and when for a brief moment he entertained the possibility of risking his life by going to Vietnam, it was for what he saw, at the time, as the higher purpose of "maintaining [his] political viability within the system," a viability that ultimately allowed him to pursue his most constitutive political purposes. Intriguingly, Clinton was reviled for this remark. To his critics, it may have been "amazingly sincere" but it was also "utterly cynical."[4] It suggested not that Clinton was willing to risk his very self in return for preserving the chance to realize his most cherished subjective commitments. Rather, it showed that Clinton was prepared to sacrifice his subjectively harbored anti-war commitment for the sake of the self-glorifying, judgment-encumbering pursuit of office.

My purpose here is not to criticize Clinton but rather to justify a way of talking about all officials, Clinton included. Suppose, as Clinton's critics believe, that notwithstanding his professed veneration of office—and the opportunity public service provides to realize one's most important subjective commitments—Clinton was continually willing to put the offices he held at risk for purely selfish pursuits, testing the boundaries of sexual, financial, and personal misbehavior. Clinton, on the account of his former aide Betsey Wright, was perpetually "terrified" that his indiscretions could mean his losing elections, even as he continued to engage in them.[5] If we believe someone is unwilling to sacrifice or pay any kind of conventionally expected price for a particular opportunity, then we are entitled to question his commitment to it and the larger possibilities it affords. As revelations mounted in the 1992 presidential campaign—and notwithstanding whatever personal hurt they may have caused her—what putatively troubled Hillary Clinton was the possibility that they would "now cost the Clintons the chance for which she had worked so hard and sacrificed so much."[6] Having sacrificed so much for her husband's presidency—and the chance it offered to realize her deepest commitments—Hillary Clinton, on this account, was disturbed that Bill Clinton had not done the same. An official's private (mis)behavior becomes publicly relevant because it places in question his seriousness of purpose, his sense of priority, and his commitment to the project to which he has ostensibly dedicated his life.

The theme of sacrifice—sacrifice of office, sacrifice for office—figures centrally in our judgments of politicians. The best politicians will treat the pursuit of office, by turns and where appropriate, as a selfish interest that they are prepared to sacrifice *and* a subjective commitment for which they are prepared to sacrifice, lending it just the right priority in each circumstance. True, it is not always easy for either historical or contemporary figures to hit the exact note. Daniel Webster showed no interest in sacrificing selfish indulgences for the sake of office (Webster was "on the take" in an impressive number of ways) but, quite admirably, displayed no tendency to sacrifice subjectively harbored principle for office either: Webster supported the Compromise of 1850 at the cost of his long-nurtured presidential aspirations. Others, such as Michael Dukakis, seem to subordinate nearly all selfish indulgences to the pursuit of office (Dukakis, one reporter said, "never goes off the record"[7]) but, arguably, nearly all visibly deep commitments too: hence Dukakis's famously misguided pledge to abandon "ideology" and instead bring "competence" to the presidency.[8]

The reason why Clinton's character became so talismanic is that, to his critics, he appeared unprepared to risk his office for higher principle but evidently all too willing to risk it for a variety of lower pursuits. The president was attacked for simultaneously being a cautious husbander of political capital—even when he was twenty points ahead he "abandon[ed] his own previously stated principle by signing a [popular] Republican-initiated welfare reform bill"[9]—and a reckless gambler of political coin, hazarding his office with every personal indiscretion. As the legal scholar William Van Alstyne put it, "in the president's manner of handling [the Lewinsky matter] he has probably spent almost fatal political capital."[10] Such a judgment was only reinforced when his friends heroically overstated what personal sacrifices the president had made at various points in his life, praising him for reining in his youthful desire to indulge in drugs because his "political future" was just too important: "It wasn't because he couldn't or didn't want to get high," one of them earnestly told Clinton biographer Roger Morris.[11]

The metaphor of "political capital" is instructive. According to the critique it sustains, the president holds a certain amount of political capital in trust—in the manner of a fiduciary reposed with someone's financial capital—to be used for principled political purposes, not expended on his own personal interests. When the president signed the Welfare Reform Act of 1996, those who resigned from his administration in protest might well have asked themselves, "What is the purpose of the president's political capital if not to be spent defending a welfare bill more consonant with his beliefs? What is the president saving it for?" Now, they know. Or, as David Broder observed, "When Republicans offered to help [Clinton] regain the vital trade negotiation authority all other recent presidents have enjoyed, he spurned them because he did not want to risk alienating Democrats who might [have] save[d] him from impeachment."[12]

It is in this way that the president's personal behavior becomes relevant to an assessment of his public life: as a constructive measure of the intensity, not a proxy for the content, of his political commitments. Thus, the *New York Times*' Michael Oreskes was apt to remark that while "Clinton was a reckless man" when it came to the Monica Lewinsky affair, he was a "highly cautious and conservative president, to the repeated frustration of the Democratic Party's traditional base"; Oreskes was wrong, however, to conclude that therefore Clinton's "private behavior tells us little of his public life."[13] If a politician's private life were supposed to reveal the substance of his public life, then Oreskes would be right: there seems, in Clinton's case, to be no connection, and on that score it's irrelevant. But if a politician's private behavior instead signals the level of commitment he bears to his public life, then there's an obvious pattern—and it becomes relevant.

"I care more about the president's agenda than he does," lamented one former aide; "I never believed," said another, "that Bill Clinton would actually risk his presidency—a job he had studied, dreamed about, and prepared for since he was a kid—for something so frivolous, so reckless, so small."[14] And notably, those who chastised the president for his inability to sacrifice his personal desires to the exigencies of his office, then attacked him for his inability to sacrifice his office for an even higher good. "A president more concerned with the national interest than his own self-preservation," the *Atlanta Journal-Constitution* editorialized in wake of the Lewinsky matter, "would realize that resignation is his only option. Sadly, Bill Clinton has shown himself incapable of such sacrifice."[15]

It is not surprising that Bob Dole's presidential campaign took on the theme of sacrifice, emphasizing in particular Dole's war record but extending it as well to more controversial arenas, such as Dole's decision in April 1996 to resign from the Senate to run for president. Some of Dole's critics, predictably, denied that in resigning he had in any way "reinforc[ed] his reputation for sacrifice," arguing instead that what Dole had given up was not the "prestige and power" and "comfort of a Senate seat" but rather the "baggage" of a supremely unpopular Congress.[16] A more interesting attack came from those who sought not to deflate but to inflate the sacrifice he made, suggesting that in relinquishing his Senate seat of thirty years Dole had given up not mere "perks and prestige" but "his very identity," all for the sake of his petty presidential ambitions.[17] The attack had sufficient salience that Dole felt compelled to respond: "Some may find [my resignation] surprising given that Congress has been my life," he said, "but that is not true. With all due respect to Congress, America has been my life."[18] Yet when Senator John McCain praised Dole for making his "country the love of his life," one began to wonder: what (with all due respect to the country) about Elizabeth Dole?[19]

If the theme of sacrifice—of office and for office—has become central to American public discourse, it is because it offers perhaps the most powerful external evidence available for gauging the depth of a politician's commitment, the extent to which his priorities are well placed. Certainly, if Michael Kinsley is right and a politician's personal behavior attains relevance only as an indicator of his likely public behavior, then it loses its relevance the longer that politician has actually been pursuing or holding office. But if a politician's personal behavior signifies the level of his commitment to his public enterprise, then that behavior gains relevance precisely to the extent that he has spent his life pursuing or holding office. We might forgive a novice candidate his past indiscretions—after all, he has been a private citizen up until now—but a career politician who has all the while been carrying on gives us pause.

The problem we now face, however, is not just that the facts about a politician's character are contestable; increasingly, so are the values Americans use to assess it. Minutes before Dole's acceptance speech to the 1996 Republican National Convention, his former aide Sheila Burke commended Dole as a man who had "sacrific[ed] his family life for public service." Yet on the heels of Colin Powell's speech to the same convention three days earlier, party spokesmen hailed the general as a man who had "sacrificed" an almost certain opportunity to serve as president of the United States in order to preserve his capacity to lead a decent family life. As the nation's consensus on the central values of both public service and private life continue to erode—as there continues to be less and less agreement as to what in life is worth sacrificing for what—debate over character in politics may be reaching its outer limits. As long as the pursuit of office remains double-edged—at once venal and noble, an encumbering interest and the very embodiment of commitment[20]—we will use it to gauge a politician's character, but we will do so in ever-more contested ways. We will continually seek evidence that he is willing to sacrifice the pursuit of office, understood as a self-serving interest, for his subjectively constitutive principles, and that he is prepared to sacrifice his selfish interests or indulgences for office, understood as an outlet for the official's most subjectively harbored beliefs or commitments. But as to what constitutes such evidence, we will, it seems, ever more profoundly disagree.

As a final note, consider a possible explanation for a phenomenon that continues to frustrate some supporters of President Clinton. Ronald Reagan was able to speak convincingly about family values even though he had divorced his first wife and enjoyed poor relations with his children. But Bill Clinton was no longer able to do so, in light of his marital infidelity.[21] There would indeed be a double standard here, if what we generally do is read the *content* of an official's public pronouncements against the backdrop of his personal behavior. After all, at this level both Reagan and Clinton display a similar inconsistency. The fact that Reagan was able to talk about family values, while Clinton no longer credibly could, must therefore mean that for most people an official's personal behavior signifies something else. What we actually do, I would argue, is use the backdrop of an official's personal life to gauge the *commitment* with which he holds his public positions. Viewed through this lens, the two situations are quite different. Clinton, on this reading, risked sacrificing the aims and goals embodied in his pursuit of office in order to indulge his wanderings from family life. By contrast, Reagan—like Dole—was prepared to sacrifice the redoubt of family life, neglecting his children, for his single-minded pursuit of the principles and goals embodied in his campaigns for office. Clinton jeopardized his political causes in order to flout the exigencies of family life; Reagan neglected the exigencies of family life in order to advance his political causes. One might think that both Reagan and Clinton got their priorities wrong and yet still believe that Clinton's behavior revealed far less commitment to the high aims of office than did Reagan's. What else could explain the difference in treatment?

13

Self-Generated versus Other-Imposed Encumbrances on Judgment

Thus far, I have examined mainly "internal" encumbrances on official judgment. Internal encumbrances originate within the official, flowing not only from her own pecuniary holdings but also from her own psychology and history, beliefs and commitments, projects and characteristics. An even more troubling set of encumbrances, however, finds its source outside the official, in the financial holds and political pressures exerted by others. American public discourse, in fact, is rife with explicit comparisons between self-originated and other-imposed encumbrances on official judgment, and it is invariably the other-imposed that emerge the worse for the juxtaposition. Not only a sharp, but an invidious, distinction between the two pervades debate. Encumbrances placed on officials by others, whether financial or psychological, are simply seen to be more judgment-perverting than similar encumbrances, whether pecuniary or ideological, when self-originated by the official.

On the financial plane, consider Lloyd Cutler's view that "getting a one-thousand-dollar honorarium from General Motors will corrupt an official more than owning two-hundred and fifty thousand dollars worth of stock."[1] Or Harold Ickes, Sr.'s pithy observation, "I have never known a public official to corrupt himself."[2] Or Senator Richard L. Neuberger's claim that "the native integrity of the average human being is most jeopardized by favors he has accepted from somebody else rather than because of any holdings that have long-since been his own"—presumably because the former more likely represent a deflection from, while the latter are more likely integral to, his subjectivity.[3]

Or consider the tendency for wealthy political candidates to point to their own personal riches as an argument for their political incorruptibility, their capacity to withstand the financial blandishments of others. What they offer, in essence, is a formidable set of internal encumbrances—their prodigious personal interests—as a reassuring bulwark against anything that might be externally imposed, and they rely on a perceived differential between the two to reap political benefit. "People are 'looking to plutocrats,'" one reporter concluded in an analysis of Steve Forbes, "because of the perception that they cannot be bought off with a campaign contribution."[4] "[T]hanks to Perot," another declared two years earlier, "millionaire candidates are touting their wealth as a signal that they're untainted by PACs"; businessman Charles Woods, for example, bankrolled his own campaign for a Nevada Senate seat because, according to his campaign coordinator, "he doesn't want to be beholden to anyone."[5] There is, of course, a flip side: "Most people assume [Nelson] Rockefeller already has so much money he wouldn't have tried to get a little more," the commentators William Greider and Thomas O'Toole observed, but the "problem really is the other way around: what impact would that great economic power have on government and politics if it were marshalled in attendance with presidential power?"[6] Greider and O'Toole's concern, though, is very much a minoritarian strand. Rich candidates would not persist in touting their wealth were there not a perceived differential, were personal holdings not considered—all other things being equal—less encumbering, more proximate to the subjectively-constitutive, than external holds.

As with financial, so with psychological encumbrances. What could qualify as a genuinely subjective belief or commitment when generated internally— an official's partiality to a particular industry or ideology, for example— might, in common perception, take the form of an encumbrance when its proximate cause lies without, in the importunings of a litigant, the ministrations of a lobbyist or the pressure of a campaign contributor. Jeffrey Abramson makes this point about jurors, when he describes as an overly "demanding notion of impartiality" the idea that we must "requir[e] jurors to be independent not only of the dictates of others but also of their own opinions and biases."[7] The phrase "dictates of others" evokes an outside force diverting a juror from what would otherwise be her own subjectively plotted course of action; an inner "bias or opinion," by contrast, suggests either a far more tempered encumbrance ("bias") or even a trait constitutive of subjective judgment itself ("opinion"). The same applies to judges: "[C]ourts discussing judicial disqualification express no concern for the presence or strength of a judge's inner conviction" as the trial develops, "*absent* evidence of disqualifying sources of information." That which passes muster as a genuine "conviction" as long as it flows from the judge's own internal subjective thought processes can, if instigated by another, become an encumbrance.[8]

An identical differential exists at the other end of the (quasi-)judicial- (quasi-)legislative spectrum, in the realm of rule-making. Rule-making entails the "right to [a] hearing and [the] opportunity for cross-examination or rebuttal"—in other words, the right to counter the external pressures placed on decision-makers by one's opponents in a rule-making proceeding—but not the right to a decision-maker free of internal "bias."[9] Encumbrances imposed on rule-makers by others, such as *ex parte* contacts, have always been viewed as more serious impairments on official judgment than any but the most flagrant internally germinated biases—even if the result is the same. For "unlike bias, prejudice from improper contacts results solely from extrinsic factors."[10]

There is, then, a deep sense in which political and judicial discourse treats an official's "own opinions and biases" or "inner conviction" as more readily consignable to the realm of the subject, as less encumbering, than "extrinsically" imposed interventions or the "dictates of others." And this distinction emerges across domains, judicial, quasi-judicial, and quasi-legislative. On the psychological as well as the pecuniary plane, outer-sourced encumbrances are more poised than those inwardly sourced to compromise official judgment.

Now, consider an intriguing legislative case: Some defend the practice of allowing legislators to retain significant personal interests in oil, telecommunications, steel, and so forth, on the grounds that actively interested legislators render unnecessary the more dangerous role of the outsider professional lobbyist. "If you do not allow legislators to hold interests," one congressman urged along these lines, "what you are saying is that it's alright for interests to be represented by lobbyists and you want the expertise on the outside of Congress looking in but you do not want any of the expertise in Congress itself. I don't think that fits with my understanding of representative democracy."[11] Better that the interests, even the advocacy for those interests, be internal to officials than external—precisely because an internal interest is less likely than its external equivalent to divert the legislator from (what we understand to be) his subjectively chosen course. Senator Malcolm Wallop derisively but accurately characterized this argument as "an accusation that . . . lobbyists are able to pull our reason away from any manner of self-control."[12] While externally offered expertise is more likely to take the form of a velvet glove covering a lobbyist's extrinsic pressure, internally generated expertise (that is, the legislator's own) is more likely to constitute—to have taken root in—the genuine subject of the official concerned. Here, a relatively draconian view of lobbying regulation is coupled with a relatively lax view of official conflict of interest, especially self-dealing.

In fact, what holds for officials holds for citizens. Following the 1994 congressional elections, the *New Yorker* did a short piece on Scott Sanders, an actor who provided the voice-over for many of the campaign's most successful negative televison ads. "The basic idea behind Sanders' approach," the magazine reported, "is that the voice of outrage, which is the essential voice of the negative commercial, is not the voice of some angry street-corner man ranting at you, but the voice of *you* ranting at you. 'It's not the way people talk—

it's the way they think,' [Sanders] says. 'It's the voice that is in your own mind speaking to you . . . What I try to do is take that voice and put it into what I say, so that when you hear the commercial you hear in it this voice that is in your mind already.'"[13] Sanders would not make such an argument were he not aware that we regard the external imposition of bias as more troubling than the same views (rants) if germinated within.

Public discourse thus discloses a tendency to treat encumbrances imposed on officials from without, whether financial or ideological, as more troubling than those evolved from within. Or, rather, to treat the former as encumbrances where the latter might yet be understood as subjectively harbored beliefs and commitments. This, as with other interpretive characterizations of discourse, is best thought of as a tendency—a kind of burden or incidence of discourse—not an absolute rule. And it reaches its greatest pitch in public discourse over *quid pro quo,* where others place both financial or political holds—whether through personal gifts or campaign support—on officials who have the capacity to affect their interests.

14

Quid Pro Quo and Campaign Finance

Bribery law, as numerous commentators have pointed out, is limited in scope.[1] Bribery is a nonprophylactic offense, meaning that we require a showing that the accused official took something *"in return for being influenced* in his performance of an official act," that his judgment, in other words, was actually encumbered. But as a factual matter, bribery is often impossible to prove because of the opacity of the briber's and bribee's mental states. And as a normative matter, bribery quickly shades into a gray area, where the actual practice of democratic politics—its requirements that citizens and groups be allowed to express their preferences in a variety of ways, and its expectation that officials show their responsiveness in a variety of ways—makes it difficult to isolate any evil involved. But it is precisely in this area of factual opacity and normative *chiaroscuro,* an area beyond the law, where the kinds of *quid pro quo* that dominate democratic discourse usually arise.[2]

I define *quid pro quo* as an exchange of value between an officeholder and a citizen (or group), an exchange which, for either factual or normative reasons, fails to rise to the level of bribery, but in which the transfer made by one to the other is prompted by the transfer—whether already-made or yet-to-be made—from the other to the one. The value that a citizen or group transfers to an official, the *quid,* typically takes the form of a pecuniary offering of some sort, including hospitality, entertainment, transportation, or a material object, or else a campaign contribution. But within the class of *quid* I also include verbal interventions such as lobbying—pressing an official to take a particular position[3]—and endorsement of or opposition to his candidacy, both of which, depending on the circumstances, can impose non-material encumbrances on an official's judgment. The value the officeholder provides in return, the *quo,* takes the form of some kind of official action benefiting the citizen's or group's interests, from support for a bill or an intervention before an executive agency to the granting of access or the subtle shifting of a congressional committee's agenda.

Extortion, Gifts, and Gratuities

A few preliminary distinctions are necessary. Even the ambiguous notion of *quid pro quo* examined below—the kind that for factual or normative reasons falls short of criminal bribery—notoriously blurs into several other transgressions, principally extortion by officials, inappropriate gifts given to them, and gratuities received by them. Each of the three varies the theme of *quid pro quo,* and they relate to one another in a discernible structure.

First, consider the border between bribery/*quid pro quo* and gratuity. In archetypal situations of illegal gratuity, no one contests the existence of the *quid* and the *quo.* It is the *pro* that seems attenuated in some fashion. As the D.C. Circuit Court recently put it, "in contrast to bribery, the gratuity and the official act"—the *quid* and the *quo*—"need not each motivate the other." In other words, there need be no full-fledged *pro.* All that the gratuity statute, 18 U.S.C. §201(c)(1)(A), requires is a "unidirectional relationship." The private party must pay the gratuity "for or because of" an official act, but the official need not have executed the act because of the gratuity.[4] Hence "an explicit *quid pro quo* . . . need not exist if only an illegal gratuity is involved . . . the official act for which the gratuity is given might have been done without the gratuity, although the gratuity was produced because of the official act."[5]

Now hold that in mind and then ask: What if it is not the *pro,* but the *quo,* that becomes the object of controversy, bleeding into the realm of the speculative? Consider the position Donald Smaltz adopted when, as independent counsel, he brought former Agriculture Secretary Mike Espy to trial for accepting meals, luggage, and tickets to sporting events from major American food producers. For the purposes of criminal prosecution under 18 U.S.C. §201(c)(1)(A), Smaltz argued, it didn't matter whether the *quid*s that Tyson Foods and Sun-Diamond Growers gave to Espy prompted no identifiable act—a *quo*—in return. Although the law literally requires that a "thing of value" be given to an official "for or because of [an] official act," Smaltz claimed that the statutory definition "reaches gifts to federal officials motivated by matters that may not yet be pending before those officials . . . or perhaps even which may never actually be pending."[6] In effect, for Smaltz, all that was required was that the gifts have been given to Espy for or because of his "official position," and not because of any identifiable act.[7]

Lawyers for Espy, Sun-Diamond, and Tyson all vigorously objected that such a construal, for all intents and purposes, winnowed the *quo* into meaninglessness and couldn't constitute an offense.[8] Debate accordingly hovered over the question of where, as we move along the spectrum from "given for or because of a specific act" to "given for or because of the office as a whole" the notion of *quo* peters out, with Judge Patricia Wald opining that the distinction "between gifts motivated by an official's 'position' and gifts motivated by an official's 'acts' eludes me altogether . . . inherent in an official's 'position' is his capacity to perform regulatory acts which will affect the gift-giver."[9]

There is indeed a gray area here. But this much can be said: Just as an attenuated *pro* takes us from the realm of *quid pro quo* toward the domain of gratuities, an attenuated *quo* takes us from the realm of *quid pro quo* toward the domain of gifts. The federal gift regulations already prohibit an official from taking a gift, a *quid*, from anyone whose interests he can affect or otherwise given because of his "official position."[10] No need to inquire about the actual *quo*; it matters not whether the gift motivated an official act or more broadly encumbered official judgment. Who could ever know for sure? The gift regulations take a prophylactic approach to *quid pro quo*, and Espy violated them. But they are also noncriminal, and it is only as we rise to the level of criminality—bribery or illegal gratuity—that pressure to interpret the statutes nonprophylactically mounts, as defense and prosecution tussle over how much evidence of an affected official act, a *quo*, there need be. Ultimately, in the *Sun-Diamond* case, the Supreme Court held that there had to be more evidence than the prosecution supplied.[11]

Finally, *quid pro quo* overlaps with extortion, and in particular with the famously contested Hobbs Act offense on which an official "obtain[s] property from another . . . under color of official right."[12] As a first cut, we can locate extortion on a spectrum between "abuse of office" and "bribery." Recall that in abuse of office, officials "coerce other persons to provide . . . financial benefits to themselves, their families, or their business connections."[13] This is why the abused private party—the one transferring value to the official—is never charged; only the abusing official is culpable. Likewise, extortion embodies a coercive element which, however implicit, suffices to implicate the official but not the paying private party. As in abuse-of-office cases, the extorted individual is never indicted. Instead, he is deemed to have been preyed upon by the "color of official right,"[14] concerned that if he fails to give the official something of value he will suffer either a private-market loss—he won't get a contract, his shipment will be held up at customs—or else a public penalty, if the official has falsely claimed entitlement by law to a fee for his official services.[15] Unlike abuse of office, however, and like bribery, the extorting official performs no private-market act in recompense for the *quid*, leaving himself beholden to square the account by executing an official act.[16] Extortion, then, borrows the coercive element from abuse of office and the absence of private-market recompense from bribery. It is the most serious form of *quid pro quo* offense.

But there is something more. In bribery, generally, the *quo* the official gives in return for the *quid* is something to which the private party is not entitled. A bidder won't get a contract on the merits, so he bribes the official to let it to him anyway. In extortion, the *quo* is far more likely to be something to which the private party *is* entitled on the merits—whether a clearance through customs or a clean bill of health in a plant inspection—and the official refuses to grant it unless the private party disgorges the *quid*. In bribery, the official is paid to do something he shouldn't otherwise do. In extortion, he extracts payment for something he should do anyway.[17]

But this distinction between extortion and bribery—which is fairly well-established—also implies something significant about the difference between extortion and gratuity. If the official who falls afoul of the Hobbs Act's extortion strictures accepts a *quid* for doing what he *should* have done anyway, the official who runs athwart the gratuity statutes (recall that gratuities do not motivate or influence but simply reward official acts) accepts a *quid* for doing what he *would* have done anyway.[18] Thus extortion is most readily evident in situations where officials execute quasi-judicial or certain kinds of procurement functions, that is, situations where there may be an independently discernible "right answer" or "entitlement" or "merit score" that lets us know what the official should have done. Where (as is more typically the case) there are no clear standards as to what the official should have done, extortion blurs into bribery and an official could be charged with either. As James Lindgren puts it, "bribery and extortion overlap. In most payoff situations, we won't clearly know who actually deserved to get a public contract . . . If the bidder doesn't pay, he gets less than fair treatment (coercive extortion). If he pays, he gets more than fair treatment (bribery)."[19]

Analogously, gratuity is most readily evident where officials fill ministerial roles where they enjoy no discretion or where they could not have executed any official act other than the one they did. In such cases, the *quid* is less likely to have motivated the *quo* and more likely to have been a reward or a tip for what the official would have done anyway. Consequently, where there are no tight bounds on what an official could have done, debate arises over whether a particular offense was a gratuity or a bribe. Where an official commands discretion, the question of whether the *quid* motivated or simply reciprocated for the *quo* is more likely to be unanswerable; here, the distinction between gratuity and bribery "breaks down."[20]

The kinds of *quid pro quo* addressed shortly, however, fail to rise to the level of criminal bribery (much less extortion), although do they blur into the realms of gratuities (whenever the *pro* is sufficiently contestable) and gifts (whenever the existence of the *quo* is open to dispute). My interest here lies with the kinds of *quid*s, *quo*s, and *pro*s that occupy everyday democratic discourse, the sorts that arise when a politician takes a campaign contribution or some form of hospitality from a private party, and then grants that party special access or votes for legislation that benefits its interests—and we must ask ourselves what to make of it. Just because the facts that would establish any given *quid pro quo* are opaque, and beyond ultimate legal cognition as bribery, does not in any way mean that the public at large does not spend a huge amount of time debating whether a *quid pro quo* has actually taken place. And precisely because the norms governing democratically appropriate *quid pro quos* are so ill-established, they have unleashed a flood of discourse weighing whether various kinds of *quids*, *pros* and *quos* are more or less in conformity with good democratic practice. What I do here is look first at factual and then at normative debates over *quid pro quo* in the vast realm beyond legalistically defined bribery, critically examining some of the principles that protagonists—politicians, lawyers, commentators, ethics officials, citizens—bring to bear. For the most part, the factual questions arise when *quid pro quo* involves both elected *and* career officials; the normative issues adhere largely to elected officials alone.

Factual Matters

Whenever citizens, journalists, or politicians entertain the possibility that a *quid pro quo* might have occurred, they find themselves straying considerably afield from the evidentiary confines granted to the courts. Indeed, much public discourse over *quid pro quo* is itself a debate over which evidentiary standards to impose in determining whether an exchange, a *quid pro quo,* has taken place in situations short of out-and-out bribery. Here, I approach the factual issues of *quid pro quo* from (so to speak) the other direction, from the perspective not of bribery law, which governs illegal exchanges, but of contract law, which governs legal exchanges. After all, both contracts and *quid pro quos* are exchanges of a sort. And in remarkable ways, discourse over whether a *quid pro quo* has in fact occurred in any particular case resembles (while in some respects reconfiguring) venerable debates in contract jurisprudence over how to ascertain whether an agreement, a contractual bargain, has taken place in controversial factual circumstances.[21]

Contract jurisprudence pits "classical" or "traditional" against "critical" or "revisionist" theorists.[22] Two issues are key. First, on the classical or traditional approach to contract law, a contract is said to exist when A and B concurrently exchange promises or performances. "Contract recognizes obligation only in the event of present exchange," classical scholars believe; it consists in "contemporaneous agreement."[23] Where judicial controversy begins to arise—where factual situations begin to enter the realm of the quasi or noncontractual—is when this contemporaneousness, this propinquity, begins to dissolve and there emerges a "time lag between performance [by A] and promise [by B]."[24] No past commitment or performance of an act by A for B, no matter how generous, suffices to contractually oblige any subsequent commitment or performance made by B for A. Successive discrete promises or transfers of value back and forth do not constitute a contract on the strict classical approach, and classical contract jurisprudence will not impute contractual intent to the parties in such circumstances. "[T]he general English rule is that past consideration or benefit [from A to B] is not sufficient to make a [subsequent] promise [from B to A] legally binding"; a "commitment made in recognition of a previously received benefit [is not] enforceable."[25]

For classical contract law, the distinction between propinquity and nonpropinquity—between contemporaneous exchanges and those separated in time—signals a vital difference in motivation of the involved parties. A contemporaneous exchange suggests that "each party views the performance that he undertakes as the price of the performance taken by the other"[26]— that each "act[s] in anticipation of compensation"[27]—and that they both therefore operate out of the self-interest that lies at the heart of contract.[28] A "transaction which fails to meet the requirement of an agreement for a present exchange," by contrast, "is the practical equivalent of an undertaking to give something for nothing."[29] Where "a promise [from A to B] is separated in time from beneficial acts [done by B for A]," all that classical contract jurisprudence will see is a series of gifts, motivated unilaterally, beneficently, or altruistically, not a contract predicated on mutuality, reciprocity, or self-interest.[30]

For there to be a contract, there must be some propinquity between the items exchanged, but there need not be proportionality. Hence, a second characteristic of "classical" contract law is its willingess to include within the category of "valid contract" exchanges involving items not even remotely equivalent to one another in value. Any consideration at all, as long as it is offered by both sides, suffices to constitute a contract. "[A]lthough consideration is required for a binding contract," Michael Bayles has written, "the adequacy of consideration is supposedly not examined by courts . . . for courts to say otherwise is an interference with freedom . . . courts will not inquire whether the goods are worth one hundred dollars even if no one else would pay seventy-five dollars for them."[31] Or, as another commentator has put it, "the principle of the classical school is that courts will not review the adequacy of consideration that strangers make in the market."[32]

According to the "classical" school of contract, then, a series of nonpropinquitous value-transfers back and forth between parties does not constitute a contract, while a set of disproportionate value-transfers does not exclude the possibility of contract. One could express these twin points in a slightly different way by using the distinction between objective and subjective jurisprudential approaches employed in Part I, in which a legal principle "lies at the objective end of [the] spectrum if its application depends on a directly observable state of the world, and at the subjective end if its application depends on a mental state."[33] So: On the one hand classical contract law takes what is clearly an objective approach to the issue of nonpropinquitous value-transfers back and forth over time between two parties. No matter what the subjective intent of either party might be, no contract exists in such circumstances. It matters not whether A's mental state, in unilaterally transferring value to B at some particular point, is such that he anticipates, expects, hopes, or even knows that—at some future point—B will transfer value back to him in return. Nor does it matter whether B views any future transfer to A as reciprocation, repayment, or compensation to A. All that the law sees, all that is objectively visible, is a sequence of unilateral acts. The law cannot cognize any subjective links that might actually operate to transform it into a mutual agreement, that is, a contract.

On the other hand, while taking this largely "objective" approach to the question of whether nonpropinquitous value-transfers constitute a contract, "classical" law allows an entirely subjective approach to prevail on whether disproportionate value-transfers constitute a contract. That is, courts will enforce whatever individual parties to a contract have themselves deemed to be reasonable consideration, regardless of whether their understanding fails to comport with social standards of equity. Such an approach is subjective because it "depends on . . . the parties' mental states"; and it is certainly not objective, if "objective" means an approach that refers to external, societal notions of proportionality.[34]

This twofold "classical" judicial approach narrows what constitutes a contract beyond the point that many contemporary critics deem reasonable (perhaps some nonpropinquitous exchanges of gifts or commitments do constitute meaningful exchanges between the parties) but broadens it unreasonably in other ways (perhaps even some contemporaneous exchanges are so inequitable as to rule out the possibility of a meeting of the minds). And, indeed, both of these "classical" approaches to the factual determination of contract—the rigid, objective, exclusionary tack taken toward nonpropinquitous exchanges, and the expansive subjective latitude accorded disproportionate exchanges—have come under fire from contemporary jurisprudential critics.

On the question of nonpropinquitous exchanges of commitments or benefits, Michael Bayles writes, "the old rule that a past benefit conferred does not make a [subsequent] promise enforceable is being replaced by the individualized principle that such a promise [may be] enforceable."[35] Bayles describes this newer approach as "individualized"—in other words, subjective—in that it would require courts to parse the psychological intent of the parties in particular cases. Specifically, it would require courts to recognize that "most unilateral promises are made from a mixture of selfishness and altruism, or reciprocity and benevolence."[36] And to the extent that elements of selfishness, reciprocity, or anticipated return form part of the psychological impetus for a succession of promises made or benefits extended between two parties, then no matter how nonpropinquitous or otherwise seemingly unrelated they may appear on "objective" criteria, an agreement—a contract—should be found.[37]

While they advocate an expansive, subjective approach to the question of whether nonpropinquitous transfers of value can ever constitute an exchange, critics of the classical school advocate a more exclusionary objective approach—less individualized or case-specific, more uniform—to the question of whether disproportionate exchanges are capable of constituting a contract. Specifically, critics ask that courts apply social standards of fair exchange in order to void gross inequities of the sort that might, nevertheless, have constituted fair consideration in the subjective view of "strangers in the market."[38] As Melvin Aron Eisenberg puts it, "[t]he idea of reviewing a bargain for fairness . . . implies that an *objective* value can be placed on a bargained-for performance."[39]

Judicial discourse over private contracts is pertinent to public discourse over official *quid pro quo* because it distinguishes, in an instructively fleshed-out way, objective and subjective approaches to the factual question of whether an exchange has taken place between two parties. On a subjective approach, an exchange or agreement has occurred whenever the parties think it has, no matter how nonpropinquitous or disproportionate the value-transfers. On an objective approach, an exchange or agreement has occurred only when it meets uniform, cognizable standards—standards of propinquity and proportionality. As we have seen, "classicists" in contract law take an objective, exclusionary approach to nonpropinquitous performances or promises but allow a more subjective, expansionary approach to prevail when it comes to the question of disproportionality. Critics of "classical" contract law would adopt a more subjective, expansionary approach to successive or nonpropinquitous performances or promises, but an objective, exclusionary approach to disproportionate or inequitable agreements.

Yet in public discourse over *quid pro quo,* while one can readily discern analogous objective and subjective approaches, there is no "mixing and matching." That is, the faultlines of debate divide those who would take a wholly objective, exclusionary approach to both questions—to both nonpropinquitous and disproportionate exchanges, denying the status of each as *quid pro quo*—from those who, insisting on an expansive subjective approach, remain open to the possibility that substantially nonpropinquitous and disproportionate mutual transfers of value may still constitute *quid pro quo*. On the first side (the exclusionary, objective side) one invariably finds accused officials, and on the second (the expansive, subjective side), their critics. Public discourse over *quid pro quo* does not parallel so much as it "perpendiculars" judicial discourse over contracts—although it deals with very much the same set of issues.

Take the first question, the question of whether successive, nonpropinquitous promises or performances back-and-forth between parties constitute *quid pro quo*. Here, accused officials take an exclusionary, objective approach. Any value-transfer from citizen to official (say a campaign contribution) and then from the official back to the citizen (say a particular legislative initiative) must—in the absence of any "contemporaneous agreement," that is, in the absence of bribery—be deemed to have been performed only on its own isolated merits. Each would have occurred anyway, unilaterally. Neither took place in light of the other. Nonpropinquity means there was no *quid pro quo*. Hence that prominent strand in democratic discourse, according to which the passage of a "decent interval" between value-transfers—a "temporal buffer" between official "favor and request" for funds—means that the two could not possibly be linked.[40]

Along these lines, one rhetorical strategy accused legislators have available is to point to a "prior" disposition or predilection on their part to perform the particular *quo* in question (say voting for a bill favorable to the interests of a contributor). Any such predisposition to perform the *quo*—and especially any actual performance of the *quo* that antedates the *quid* (the campaign contribution to the legislator)—suggests that the motivation for performing the *quo* was internal or unilateral; that it was not generated by the "other," by the citizen, or in anticipation of the *quid*. "Votes don't follow money," as Congressman Barney Frank puts it, "money follows votes."[41] "PACs [political action committees] are not buying anyone," on this argument, "they're rewarding."[42] So if legally cognizable bribery bleeds into legally cognizable gratuity as the link between *quid* and *quo* attenuates into a one-way motivational transaction, then sub-legal *quid pro quo*, likewise, bleeds into something deemed even more innocuous: everyday democratic "reward." A considerable body of political-science literature buttresses this idea. "PAC contributions," John R. Wright notes, "are often rewards for past support rather than inducements for future support." "Voting record attracts contributions," Kevin B. Grier and Michael C. Munger argue along similar lines, "rather than contributions determining voting record."[43]

For her part, however, the citizen who offers the campaign contribution—the *quid*—will often make the same argument. She will point either to a predisposition on her part to perform the *quid* (make the campaign contribution) or else to its actual performance some time prior to the *quo* (the legislator's vote) as evidence that the *quid* was unilaterally motivated, in no way meant to oblige a subsequent *quo*. "Any contribution . . . by someone the legislator has helped," on this argument, is "not . . . a *quid pro quo* but rather a wholly voluntary offering based upon a belief in the effectiveness of the legislator as sharpened by experience."[44]

Notably, while officials in *quid pro quo* situations emphasize their predisposition to commit the act—voting in a certain way, for example—and their imperviousness to influence, once the *quid pro quo* rises to the level of bribery, the "entrapment defense" encourages them to emphasize their vulnerability to influence and their lack of any kind of predisposition to commit the act. Consider a major difference between the Abscam (1980) and Keating Five (1989) scandals. In Abscam, federal legislators were charged with bribery for promising to use their offices—for promising to help Arab businessmen gain U.S. residency or procure government grants and licenses—in return for payments from undercover FBI agents. Several defended themselves by insisting that they were not in any way "predisposed" to perform these acts; that in fact they would not have done so absent the FBI's relentless and high-pressure inducements, wheedlings, and cajolings.[45] According to the entrapment defense to bribery, if the official can show that he was strenuously influenced to commit the act, then by definition he was not predisposed to do it—and because he was not predisposed to do it, he should be exonerated.

In the noncriminal *quid pro quo* situation of the Keating Five, by contrast, each of the accused senators availed himself of just the opposite line of argument. If he could show that he was predisposed to commit the act anyway—assisting Charles Keating in his battles with regulators—then by definition he wasn't influenced. And if he wasn't influenced, he should be exonerated. Usually the other party is moved to deny influence in bribery cases and magnify it in *quid pro quo* cases. Thus, at trial, the Abscam FBI agents insisted that they had not influenced the legislators,[46] while Charles Keating notoriously declared, "One recent question, among many others raised in recent weeks, had to do with whether my financial support in any way influenced several political figures to take up my cause. I want to say in the most forceful way I can: I certainly hope so."[47]

The objective stance toward nonpropinquitous value-transfers between officials and citizens thus mirrors the classical approach in contract law, on which A's commitment or performance of an act for B—if it takes place measurably "prior" to B's commitment or performance of an act for A—argues for classifying them both as "unilateral" rather than "reciprocal." To take just one of innumerable examples, in 1982 the lobbyist Robert Gray helped Nancy Thurmond, wife of Senator Strom Thurmond, to stage a charity ball; some time later, Senator Thurmond was able to assist Gray with "an important bill before [his] Judiciary Committee."[48] Gray insisted that he would have helped Mrs. Thurmond anyway out of support for the charity; Thurmond insisted that he would have promoted the bill anyway because he supported its principles. The two were unrelated incidents, unilateral acts. And if indeed they were unilateral acts, that would preclude the possibility that they were motivated out of mutuality, in anticipation of one another.[49] Such a stance is purely objective because it refers only to the series of external acts themselves and, seeing no explicit link between them, refuses to inquire or speculate further as to whether they are conjoined within the inner, subjective mental states of the participants. In 1987, a House committee declined to censure Representative Fernand St. Germain for intervening with the Federal Home Loan Bank Board on behalf of a bank that had provided him stock options. Taking very much an objective stance, the committee concluded that "speculation about motive is not evidence [and] it would be inappropriate to attribute improper action to an individual based solely on inferences and speculation."[50]

Those who accuse or criticize officials, for their part, urge a more complicated subjective view of what, on simplistic objective terms, could be characterized as nothing but a series of discrete, unilateral transfers of value back and forth between an official and others. Critics refuse to exclude the possible inner psychological coexistence of a predisposition to perform an act on its own terms *and* a desire for reciprocity in performing it, of benefits conferred in the past *and* anticipated return, of unilateralism *and* mutuality—in short, of a succession of objectively unrelated value transfers *and* subjective *quid pro quo*—in the minds of legislators and contributors.[51] Critics of officials thus reject, as do critics of classical contract law, the notion that "subjective states of mind are nonexistent or that because they are unobservable they are unknowable."[52] Like critics of classical contract jurisprudence, critics of officials are unwilling to exclude the possibility that the "promise to give money without anything in return," or "the promise [of an official act] without anything in return," may yet constitute *quid pro quo:* "The test . . . is motivation."[53]

When we move from the issue of nonpropinquitous promises or performances to the issue of disproportionate promises or performances, accused officials once again take an exclusionary objective view. Specifically, they calibrate exquisitely the commitments or acts involved in a given putative exchange, using any sign of inequity as an indication that no *quid pro quo*—no exchange—has in fact occurred. Officials' critics, on the other hand, are moved to take a subjective, expansionary view of what constitutes *quid pro quo*. Critics will endeavor wherever possible to insist that an exchange *has* taken place, in the minds of the participants, despite any objective disproportionality between *quid* and *quo*.

To elaborate: For accused officials, "the relative size" of the promises or performances exchanged becomes "an important criterion for the classification of the relationship."[54] If a gift, contribution, or other value-transfer—from a contributor, let us say, to a legislator—is either too small or else too large in proportion to the "favor" the official grants to the contributor, the official (and the contributor) will argue that the transfer was motivated by friendship, not *quid pro quo*. A small gift, on the one hand, could not possibly motivate official action. "No Congressman," as Senator Mitch McConnell has put it, "would ever sell his office or introduce a bill in exchange for a meal or a ticket to a football game." Transfers of value so trivial are better accounted for as "tokens of friendship, not attempts to leverage official acts."[55] On the other hand, a gift so large that an official act could not possibly recompense it will, as well, be classified (by the beneficiary official *and* the benefactor citizen) as a gesture of friendship, not the instigator of an official act.

So, for example, in the 1972 Poulson affair in England, John Poulson defended himself from charges of bribing local officials—including George Pottinger, a civil servant to whom Poulson at one point gave a house—by arguing that "I am innocent of corruption . . . I never tried to bribe anybody . . . What I have done is been generous on a ridiculous scale." Pottinger, for his part, insisted that the case was "about two people, about a human relationship, the friendship of one man for another."[56] Concerning the connection between Bill Clinton and James Riady, the *New York Times* mused: "Why would someone who is not an American citizen and has no major interests here contribute huge sums to be involved in our political process? From the Democrats' corner, the answer is: Friendship. James Riady is said to really like Bill Clinton."[57]

If a transfer of value to an official is either sufficiently small or else sufficiently large in proportion to the official act in question, then it could not—so the officials in question thus argue—have been meant to prompt or recompense that act. Friends continuously bestow disproportionate or "asymmetrical" favors on one another; it is precisely such asymmetry that explodes any notion that they are motivated by the expectation of return. Indeed, asymmetry precludes the possibility of pointing to any particular *quo* that is meant to recompense the *quid*. If an erstwhile case of criminal bribery bleeds into a lesser violation of the prophylactic gift rules as an identifiable *quo* moves beyond view, then in similar fashion, the *quid pro quo*s we popularly debate descend into tokens of affection and regard as the *quo*s begin to fluctuate wildly in value. If there exists any kind of inequity between *quid* and *quo,* then—on this line of argument—the expansive category of "friendship" emerges to account for it, siphoning the situation away from the class of objectionable *quid pro quo.* The claim officials here make—that for a *quid* to have a *quo* there must be some equivalency between the two—draws theoretical sustenance from the objective, exclusionary approach that critics of classical contract law apply to disproportionate exchanges. According to Jane Baron's wide-ranging critique of contemporary gift and contract law, it is "the return of [an] exact equivalent" that makes an exchange an "economic" as opposed to a "social" one. Or, in more pertinent terms, a contract—a *quid pro quo*—as opposed to a "token of friendship."[58]

Critics of officials, for their part, are far more insistent on including even substantially disproportionate *quid*s and *quo*s within the purview of cognizable, censurable *quid pro quo.* For them, a precise calibration is unnecessary. Much more of what officials classify as social acts (acts of friendship) are for critics economic acts, acts of exchange. Critics, for example, claim that "lobbyists often form relationships with legislators that give the appearance of normal social relationships but are in fact relations of mutual convenience," and that gifts initially prompted by friendship may conclude as purchases.[59] While by objective social standards any significant disproportion between *quid* and *quo* may bring into question the existence of a *quid pro quo,* critics of officials are unwilling to abandon the subjective possibility that, in the minds of the particular individuals in question, some impetus toward reciprocity may have coexisted with a friendship or relational motivation.[60] Along the lines of *classicists* in contract law, these critics are prepared to recognize as a *quid pro quo* a set of acts far broader than an objective account, straitened by notions of proportionality, would allow. Hence, they attack officials, on the one hand, for the pettiness (let alone the betrayal of trust) involved in taking trivial sums in return for official acts and, on the other hand, for the greed (let alone the betrayal of trust) involved in taking large sums.[61]

When it comes to factual discourse over *quid pro quo*—to debate over the fact of its existence in any given case—contract jurisprudence provides a richer model than bribery jurisprudence. Not that *quid pro quo*s are legitimate in the way contracts are—that is a normative issue. But on the factual issue, discourse participants approach *quid pro quo* in terms far broader than the "narrow scope" allowed in bribery jurisprudence, with its highly straitened criminal standards of proof. Instead, officials and their critics opt for an array of approaches remarkably similar to those wielded by classical and critical contract theorists determining whether, in controversial cases, two parties have as a matter of fact reached an agreement.[62]

There is, however, another (and perhaps more fundamental) way of conceiving factual discourse over *quid pro quo*. What officials and their critics disagree over is how to draw lines within the self—the selves of officials, principally, but also those of citizens—dividing those attributes and relationships that constitute the subject, the political and moral actor, from those that encumber it. Officials who deny the existence of *quid pro quo* in any given situation generally banish from the realm of mutual self-interest any transactions with citizens that are remotely nonpropinquitous or disproportionate. In doing so, they expand the domain of official action motivated by genuine, subjectively constitutive personal conviction or personal relationships. Any lack of propinquity means that both the official and the citizen acted out of subjectively constitutive principle and predisposition, not *quid pro quo* or self-interested reciprocity. Any lack of proportionality means they acted out of subjectively constitutive friendship and feeling, not *quid pro quo* or self-interested reciprocity. Although this approach is in one sense (a jurisprudential sense) "objective," in another it allows for a notably expansive moral-political subject—one in which genuine conviction and genuine consanguinity occupy a large space.

For officials' critics, by contrast, even nonpropinquitous or disproportionate exchanges can result from motivations of reciprocal self-interest. In so saying, critics take what I have described as a jurisprudentially "subjective" approach, subjective in that it refuses to "accept conventional objective signs [of nonpropinquity and disproportionality] as tokens of . . . interior mental states," but instead countenances speculative incursions into those mental states.[63] Yet these critics do so to the end of drastically narrowing the class of acts that presumptively flow from the official's genuine moral-political subject—from genuine principle and genuine friendship—and broadening the class that is encumbered by mutual self-interest. At the most fundamental level, the divide in "factual" discourse over *quid pro quo* is over where to draw (or, more exactly, over how to approach drawing) the boundaries between the genuine and the encumbering; over whether, once we have left the realm of evidence that meets high criminal standards, we use objective versus subjective approaches to come at the question of whether a *quid pro quo* exists.

That discourse over *quid pro quo* so mirrors jurisprudential debate in the realm of contract suggests that these stances, the objective and the subjective, are fundamental in any noncriminally constrained attempt to determine whether encumbering self-interest—or else something more genuine—has motivated a value-transfer between two individuals. Self-interest is the active ingredient in both contract (legitimate exchange) and *quid pro quo* (a more questionable kind of exchange). And in both arenas the same principles, and debates, have emerged to direct our search for it.

Quid pro quo and Strict Liability

When it comes to most of the conflicts discussed in Part I—self-dealing, abuse of office, and the like—the "objective" approach mandated by prophylactic law, which prohibits various combinations of externally cognizable roles and interests, criminalizes many more relations between officials and interests than would a subjective approach, which allowed us to speculate about who would and who would not mentally rise above her encumbrances. It is when we move to a nonprophylactic setting—the setting in which we debate the *quid pro quo*s that daily beset democratic discourse—that an objective approach involves a far narrower sweep than a subjective one. To require objective evidence of propinquity and proportionality will bring far fewer situations within the ambit of *quid pro quo* than will an approach that allows us to speculate more expansively about subjective motivation.

But another difference emerges between the prophylactic conflict-of-interest laws and our popularly mooted approaches to *quid pro quo*. Recall that as prophylactics, most conflict-of-interest laws make it an offense merely to be in situations that *might* lead to the *malum in se,* a tainted state-of-mind, which is the real evil to be expunged. Because conflict-of-interest law so removes the offense from the actual harm in itself, offenders are not usually deemed strictly liable. Nor is it even sufficient that they display mere general intent. Rather, they must have had some heightened knowledge or understanding—some specific intent—concerning various elements of the offense.

Just the opposite is the case with the kinds of *quid pro quo*s that so engross us in daily democratic discourse. Here, in a political realm beyond the reach of law and hence any kind of prophylactic prohibition, the competing objective and subjective approaches I have detailed both claim to tell us directly about mental states themselves. The objective approach confines itself to outward signs, while the subjective approach is prepared to plunge right in, but both are means of descrying—of passing popular judgment—on the extent to which the official's judgment was actually encumbered.

And it is precisely because *quid pro quo* (as we debate it in political and media forums) fixes on the *malum in se* of an encumbered state-of-mind itself that it has, in effect, become a strict liability affair. Since the offense itself is defined by a certain mental state, once having satisfied ourselves that it exists—whether we use cautious objective or bold subjective criteria—we then need make no separate inquiry to determine whether the official had the mental state necessary to be a knowing or intending offender.[64] It is hard to imagine an official taking a campaign contribution *in return* for an official act, and yet not doing so knowingly or even intentionally. Whenever the *actus reus* that constitutes the offense centers on a particular mental state, it will be unnecessary to then further establish that the offender had some kind of requisite *mens rea*. By establishing the offensive act we have established the offending actor and have, in effect, moved into the realm of strict liability.

One could make the same observation about bribery itself, which is simply *quid pro quo* that does meet certain stringent legal standards of factual proof and normative egregiousness. True, bribery is not technically a strict liability crime. To be guilty of bribery, an official must have had a corrupt intent. Yet many commentators have critiqued bribery law on precisely this score. "The distinction of a . . . culpable intent under the bribery subsection breaks down," Daniel Lowenstein has written, "because it is difficult to conceptualize a public official accepting a thing of value for or because of his official acts and at the same time not doing it corruptly."[65] In effect, Lowenstein and others are saying that to prove the mental state necessary for the act of bribery itself is to prove the mental state—the *mens rea*—necessary for there to be a corrupt, intending, knowing bribee. Hence the legal offense of bribery, like the more politically colloquial offense of *quid pro quo*, should be understood as a strict liability affair in this sense: Once I am satisfied that the act which constitutes the offense occurred, I will hold the official strictly liable as an offender without further inquiries.

Since bribery/*quid pro quo* involves two parties, however, questions do arise as to whether—assuming only *the one* has the mental state necessary to commit the offense—we should nevertheless hold *the other*, as well, strictly liable as an offender. Consider the gift rule as it covers contributions to officials' legal defense funds. For there to be an offense, Kathleen Clark points out, the contributor must have intended to give because of the officeholder's position. But to be an offender, the official need not knowingly accept a gift so motivated (much less actually be influenced in the performance of his duties); he is strictly liable if indeed that was the contributor's intent. In other *quid pro quo* situations, while not strictly liable if the contributor gives intending to influence an official act, the official (a senator, say) *is* liable "if a reasonable man were to conclude that the gifts were intended to influence [his] vote," even if the actual senator himself had no idea.[66]

My point here is meant to be relative, not absolute. Certainly, one can imagine a campaign contribution influencing an official's decision-making without her realizing it.[67] And one can imagine an official *not* being influenced in her decisions while knowing a gift was intended to influence her. Nevertheless, suffice to say that in our public discussions of *quid pro quo*, by comparison with the other conflict-of-interest domains, we enter more directly into the realm of mental state in determining the offensive act, and therefore come closer to strict liability in designating someone an offending actor. In most other terrains of conflict, we assume a prophylactic approach to the offensive acts and, therefore, shy away from adopting a strictly liable approach to offending actors.

Normative Issues: The *Pro*

By no means are all exchanges between contributors and politicians—no matter how propinquitous and proportional—illegitimate in democratic politics. Having just examined "gray area" debate over the factual issues of *quid pro quo*, I now explore discourse over its normative issues, over the place of *quid pro quo* in the workings of the American polity. I look first at some central normative issues surrounding *pro*—norms that divide good from bad exchanges whatever is being exchanged—and then at normative arguments surrounding specific *quid*s and *quo*s themselves.

First, the normative issues of *pro*. Consider two hypotheticals. In one, a Republican businessman who favors a tax cut contributes to a Democratic senator who opposes a tax cut; in light of the contribution, the Democratic senator then votes in favor of the tax cut. In the other instance, a Republican businessman who desires a defense contract for his firm contributes to a Democratic senator who opposes granting it, but who then—in light of the contribution—supports the bid. The divergence in their party affiliation is meant to suggest that the businessman's contribution could not have been meant for any purpose other than influencing the official on the specific issue of the tax cut or the contract bid. Let us further assume, just to avoid irrelevant complications, that the businessman's contribution is decisive in electing the senator in either case, and that the senator's action is instrumental to the delivery of the tax cut in the first instance, and to the award of the contract in the second.

I am assuming that both cases fall beyond the realm of bribery, in that while the facts as I have stated them may be available through the application of various objective or subjective lenses—of the sort described earlier—they would not be established in a criminal court. Both cases, in other words, fall within the realm of the legal. Nevertheless, as a general statement we would view the first kind of case as normatively less troubling than the second. And the question is: why?

The answer, I would suggest, is that in the first case we can identify at least some vestige of democratically salubrious deliberativeness of a sort absent in the second. Because the Republican businessman in the first instance will see the tax cut promulgated, the rest of the Democratic program, which he abets by contributing to the senator, may actually seem less objectionable to him, genuinely, on the merits. The rest of the Democratic program (in particular, its redistributive social-policy planks) might strike his genuine subjective judgment in a more benign light *precisely to the extent* that what he may see as its initiative-dampening effects are mitigated by the Republican tax cut. Likewise, in reverse, for the senator: The tax cut—which, let us assume, will disproportionately benefit the wealthy—may seem genuinely less objectionable to her, on the merits, because reaping the contribution enables her to pursue an offsetting Democratic social program. Because tax cuts and social programs have some logical or coaxial links, so that a change in the status of one can reasonably alter one's view of the other, a *quid pro quo* of this sort could at least be construed as embodying some element of genuine, rational compromise, as making sense to each party from the viewpoint of their respective subjective beliefs. The tax cut may make the Democratic social program seem (even if marginally) more acceptable on the merits to the Republican contributor. And her heightened capacity to enact redistributionist Democratic social policy may make the tax cuts genuinely less troubling, on the merits, to the Democratic senator.

One could not, however, so readily make the same argument in the second case, where the senator delivers not a tax cut but a government contract. True, by making the contribution to get the contract for his firm, the businessman may find himself better able to weather financially what he regards as the storm of a Democratic social program. And by helping let the contract to get the contribution, the politician may be in a stronger political position to advance the Democratic program she believes in. But these are reasons external to the relationship of *quid* and *quo,* not internal to it. Getting the contract, in and of itself, does not make the Democratic social program any less troubling, on the merits, to the businessman, as a tax cut would. Nor is the senator's strengthened capacity to pursue a Democratic program likely to make the contract less obnoxious to her, again on the merits, in the way her capacity to pursue a Democratic social program might make a tax cut seem less objectionable on public-policy grounds. In the contract-for-contribution case there is no normative connection between *quid* and *quo.*

To see this from a slightly different angle, imagine that in the "contract-for-contribution" case the Republican businessman intends to devote any profits he realizes to charity, not slip them into his own pocket. Even so, the Democratic program he abets by contributing to the senator's campaign will not—simply by virtue of his getting the contract—become any more acceptable to him on the merits. Or imagine that, in the eyes of the Democratic senator, her election is simply an instrument for bringing about needed social change, not a means of self-aggrandizement. Even so, the contract she eases through in order to get elected will make no more sense to her on the merits; her political judgment—in supporting it—will still have been encumbered.[68]

What matters, in other words, is not the extent to which the *quid*s and *quo*s each party seeks for himself or herself—the businessman seeking his contract, the senator seeking her reelection—are motivated by genuine subjective commitments and not encumbering selfish interests. What matters is whether the *quid* and *quo* each is willing to *grant* the other—the businessman contributing to the senator's re-election, the senator assisting the businessman's contract—has any roots whatsoever in their respective subjects. After all, these are the political acts that each must execute. And any such exchange begins to pass muster as a legitimate deliberative compromise only if the entire *quid pro quo*—and not just part of it—displays at least some roots in the genuine subjects of both parties.

This is by definition a gray area. Hence, we remain somewhat uneasy even with the case where the Republican businessman, seeking a tax cut, contributes to the anti–tax-cut Democratic senator, causing a change in the senator's stance. It would be implausible to think that such a tax cut would become entirely acceptable on the merits to the Democratic senator, given her subjective commitments, even if she *is* now able to bring in a redeeming Democratic social program. Nor is it plausible to think that a fiscally expensive Democratic social program would be wholly acceptable to the Republican businessman, now that he has a mitigating tax cut. Nevertheless, there is some rational connection between the two, and getting a tax cut in exchange for supporting the senator's campaign falls relatively more in conformity with the deliberative nature of democratic interaction—democratically functional compromise—than does the contract-for-contribution case where each party does something in which he or she is less likely to believe.

Consider, in this light, the disagreement between Judges David Bazelon and George MacKinnon in 1971's *D.C. Federation of Civic Associations* v. *Volpe*. In his opinion for the court, Bazelon prohibited Transportation Secretary John Volpe from approving construction of a bridge through District of Columbia park land in return for a congressman's willingness to vote funds for the construction of the D.C. subway system. In dissent, MacKinnon argued that the bridge and subway were logically linked, so that to get the one would have made it more genuinely easy to accept the other: "It is obvious," MacKinnon wrote, that "if the subway program were to proceed without the necessary highway construction, that the modes of transportation being built would not be efficient or effective."[69] The judges' disagreement, in other words, was over whether Volpe, in getting the subway approved, could more genuinely have favored the bridge. Or, put another way, they disagreed over whether Volpe's desire for subway funds encumbered his decision concerning the bridge, or whether it constituted part of the legitimate judgment he brought to bear in considering it on the merits. But the very nature of the Bazelon-MacKinnon debate bears out the main point: The more the *quid* and *quo* seem connected on ideological or logical grounds, the less likely we are to view an exchange as mutually encumbering, and the more likely we are to give it at least some credit for being genuine.

Normative Issues: *Quids* and *Quos*

Now turn from the different *pros* connecting *quid* and *quo* to a normative assessment of various types of quids and quo's themselves. Let me begin with four kinds of *quids* citizens provide for (elected) officials. Specifically, citizens can offer various types of gifts to an official or else contribute to her campaign, and they can lobby an official or else contribute volunteer services (or endorsements) to her campaign. The former pair (personal gifts, campaign contributions) generally involves money, while the latter (lobbying, volunteer work) constitutes "speech," understood as direct democratic participation. The money-speech distinction, loose as it may be in some contexts, at least explains why personal gifts and campaign contributions are more heavily regulated than lobbying and volunteer work.

But I am interested in drawing another, cross-cutting kind of distinction. Within each "couplet"—monetary gifts and campaign contributions, verbal lobbying and volunteering/endorsement—a further difference can be identified. Gifts to officials are far more heavily regulated, or at least circumscribed, than contributions to their campaigns. Lobbying remains the perennial object of ever-more stringent regulatory initiatives in a way in which volunteering/endorsing never would be. And the difference in our approach to these four *quids*, I argue, can be explained by our sense of how each of them might perturb official judgment and lead an official to perform an act in which she does not subjectively believe.

Giving an official a gift differs from contributing to her campaign along exactly the same lines that lobbying distinguishes itself from volunteer work/ endorsement, even though the first set of activities is monetary and the second is "speech." The difference between a gift and a campaign contribution is this: We prohibit a gift—assuming it falls into none of the various exemptions for gifts from friends and family, commercial discounts, or awards—because we fear it must be meant to induce an officeholder to perform a particular official act or set of acts (and, of course, if the facts meet certain strict criminal-legal requirements, any such gift becomes a bribe). A campaign contribution, by contrast, is meant to support the official herself—to abet the ideology, the platform, the *totality* of acts the official is pledged to perform.

Conceptually, this distinction is clear. In practice, campaign contributions are often meant not so much to support the election of a candidate as to impel him or her to perform a particular official act. And as a normative proposition, any such contributions are indistinguishable from gifts.[70] The fact that the contribution may go the candidate's campaign while a gift might go to the candidate personally is not a material difference.[71] Discourse instead makes a strong normative demarcation between—on the one hand—gifts *plus* campaign contributions meant to prompt the official's performance of a specific (legislative) act and—on the other hand—campaign contributions meant to promote the official's election whole-cloth. In other words, we draw a line between what Daniel Lowenstein and Joseph Weeks have separately called a "legislative strategy" and an "electoral strategy" for contributions. One way to understand this distinction would be as follows: When an external intervention—a monetary transfer from a citizen or group to an official—is meant to advance that citizen's or group's position on a particular single issue, it runs a relative risk of pushing the official off her own subjectively plotted course. But when the monetary transfer is meant to support the entire panoply of positions an official takes, then such external intervention is confluent with the official's own subjectively plotted course.[72]

There are actually two considerations at work here. It is not just that the gift addresses a specific act or issue that may concern the official, whereas the contribution is diffused over the entire array. It is not just, in other words, that the gift is particularistic while the contribution is holistic. It is that the gift is meant to *move* the official, to instigate her to do something she would not otherwise; whereas the contribution is meant to reinforce the official, to support her in doing that which she would do anyway on the basis of her own subjective deliberations. Of course, it is more than conceivable that a monetary intervention might remain particularistic—addressed only to a specific act or issue—and yet not be meant to move the official's position on that issue but rather reinforce it. In legal forums, such *reinforcing* particularistic monetary interventions are often demoted from full-scale bribery to the lesser offense of gratuity. In political forums, they are often demoted from the more malign circumstance where (as Barney Frank puts it) the vote follows the money, to the more benign situation where the money follows the vote. Hence monetary interventions centered on particular issues—while troubling in either case—are nevertheless accorded greater latitude to the extent that they are meant to reinforce the official's position on a particular issue rather than alter it.

But to return to the main distinction: Whereas a gift, where troubling, is meant to *move* an official on a *particular* issue-position, a contribution is meant to *reinforce* the official's *entire array* of issue-positions. A contribution, as the Supreme Court held in *Buckley* v. *Valeo,* is an inarticulate gesture of support, not a more nuanced communication that could in any way shape the candidate's platform.[73] Contributions, which support an official's own subjectively chosen positions across the board, thus provoke less political and judicial controversy than gifts, which run the risk of wrenching the official out of position on one particular issue.

The same kind of distinction applies to citizens' nonmonetary interventions with officials. The acts of lobbying a legislator and volunteering-for/endorsing her campaign both fall under the class of largely protected (verbal) political speech or participation. Yet within this class, lobbying is less protected than volunteer-work/endorsement. As a general statement, we feel greater discomfiture at the notion of an individual or group verbally (or through other modes of direct participation) swaying an official on a particular issue than we do at the prospect of their verbally (or through other modes of direct participation) supporting or opposing her total campaign. Lobbying stands a greater chance of wrenching an official's stance on a particular issue out of the subjective web of beliefs and commitments that support it. Volunteer work or endorsement, in which a citizen supports an official's views across a range of issues, stands a greater chance of respecting the integrity of the official's subject.

Here, too, it is not just that lobbying addresses a specific act or issue the official may handle (whereas volunteer work is diffused over the entire array). It is that lobbying is meant to move the official, to instigate her to do something she would not otherwise do. To see this, consider that a verbal intervention meant to reinforce the official to do what she would have done anyway—even on a particular issue—is treated relatively benignly in discourse. For example, several recent empirical studies downplay the extent to which lobbying should, in fact, be understood as the endeavor to influence or move officials from what would otherwise be their subjectively rooted approaches to a particular issue. Instead, on this view, lobbying more often attempts to "mobilize the bias"[74] or "strengthen the commitment members have to an already established position" on a given question.[75] Lobbying, in other words, is meant to reinforce, not impose upon, the subjectivity of members. Although they are often not explicit about it, those people offering these findings, however empirically intended and well-founded, are making a normative point as well. Lobbying is a less nefarious activity than is often portrayed if, indeed, it is meant to work with, not against, genuinely subjective legislative judgment. On this view, lobbying is not meant to move legislators on a particular question so much as to bolster their already germinated subjective approach to it.[76]

In the class of monetary political activity, we thus prefer contributions to gifts. And in the nonmonetary class, we prefer volunteer work to lobbying.

No matter how articulate or inarticulate the political activity in question happens to be, we are more sanguine when citizens enable officials to pursue or expound their own subjective beliefs and commitments—their own philosophies, ideologies, platforms—than when they intervene to move officials off their subjectively plotted courses. Discourse reveals a preference, evident across both monetary and nonmonetary classes, for holistic and supportive rather than particularate and instigative interaction. If "constituents do not agree with a representative," as Heinz Eulau and John D. Sprague have put this point, "they should throw him out—it is not up to the representative to change."[77] None of this is to suggest that we live in an antideliberative polity, where open-mindedness among officials is disvalued and citizens are to be discouraged from attempting to persuade those who govern them. Verbal engagements as a class—whether holistic or particularistic, whether meant to reinforce or change the official's views—are still considered more democratically salubrious than most monetary engagements. That is, we are much less inclined to regulate citizen-official interaction the more verbal-deliberative, and the less mute-monetary, it becomes. Hence the more particularized and instigative verbal activity—lobbying—is still less regulated than the more holistic and reinforcing monetary activity of making a campaign contribution. Nevertheless, within each class, and whether monetary or verbal, incursions by different citizens and groups into the arc of an official's subjective trajectory are treated with greater concern than those that sustain it *in toto*.

This preference runs deep in discourse but also wide. Along similar lines, for example, the House ethics rules permit citizens and groups to give a congressman something of value—an award—for what they deem to be good official performance *in toto* but not for performing a particular official act.[78] Tax-exempt single-interest groups run the risk of losing their tax status unless, in their advocacy communications, they "point out the limitation of judging the qualifications of an incumbent on the basis of a few selected votes."[79] Cut from the same cloth is the public disfavor accorded political contributions made through single-interest PACs or bundling, instead of made directly in the contributor's own name.[80] If we were to prohibit individuals from making contributions through PACs or bundling, so politicians and commentators have argued for twenty years, we would in effect submerge any particularistic intent a contributor may have beneath a gesture of support for the candidate *in toto*.[81]

All of this reveals a deep, pervasive preference for external interventions, *quid*s, that stand a better chance of abetting officials' own subjective convictions than of encumbering them. I do not mean to suggest that there is nothing else going on here—that discourse fails to disclose other reasons for opposing PAC contributions, for example, or that views about bias-mobilizing lobbying are unmixed. Nevertheless, a consistent faultline distinguishes between totalistic support and particularistic attempts at moving officials. For good or ill, part of what we are continuously concerned to do in structuring democratic practice is to protect—provide a measure of insulation for—the official's capacity to engage in her own processes of genuine subjective judgment, shielded from what are deemed encumbering external intrusions. If parsimoniousness is a virtue in political interpretation as well as social science, then this one principle recommends itself as able to account for large portions of contemporary democratic discourse.[82]

These four *quids*—contributions, gifts, voluntarism, or lobbying—exhaust the major ways citizens intervene with officials. As encumbrances that extrinsic "others" impose on the decision-maker, they naturally attract the lion's share of attention in our discourse over *quid pro quo*. Still, a less prominent and often more academic strain of commentary focuses on the *quo*s officeholders execute in return, implicitly rating the differing degrees to which they, too, bespeak encumbrances on official judgment.

The *quo*s that legislators have to offer likewise fall into four broad classes: voting on a piece of legislation that benefits the *quid*-giver; intervening with an executive agency on behalf of the *quid*-giver; granting the *quid*-giver special access to hear her side of a controversy—"money," as former Congressman Thomas Downey puts it, may not "buy . . . a position, [b]ut it will definitely buy you some access so you can make your case"[83]—and shaping the legislative agenda so that the *quid*-giver's pet issue gets on the docket. Despite their substantive differences, the four can be redescribed as different points on a common spectrum. To vote for or against a piece of legislation is to pronounce finally on a controversy. To intervene before an executive agency is to propound one side of a controversy. To grant special access to a particular party is to *consider* one side of a controversy. And to frame the agenda is to open up a controversy for consideration in the first place. In other words, the spectrum of *quo* goes from closing a question (by voting on it) to endeavoring to close it part way (by intervening with an executive agency) to being open to it part way (by granting access to a privileged side of the story) to opening it up fully in the first place (by intervening with legislative colleagues to get it on the agenda).[84]

We can, all other things being equal, graduate the seriousness we attach to any given *quid pro quo* as the *quo* moves through these four categories. Statutes and rules prohibit the first two—legislative votes and legislative interventions with executive agencies—from ever being the *quo*s in a *quid pro quo*. Officials may not sell their legislative votes or influence with the executive in return for *quid*s, whether gifts or campaign contributions. No regimes, by contrast, govern the latter couplet: granting access and shaping agendas. Legislators talk freely about granting access in return for various *quid*s; the shaping of agendas, for its part, is usually too murky an undertaking even to constitute a cognizable *quo*.[85] And if our overall concern lies with unimpaired judgment, all of this would make some sense. A mind that closes a question wholly or in part is more shuttered than one that opens a question, whether in part or wholly.

Now consider each "couplet" separately: First, legislators who accept *quid*s in return for voting a particular way are generally treated more harshly, both legally (if it rises to that) and politically, than those who accept *quid*s for intervening with an executive agency.[86] Selling one's vote is considered (if sometimes only marginally) a greater crime than selling one's services as an advocate.[87] There is an embodied logic here. In the first case, the legislator herself is the final decision-maker whom the *quid*-giver seeks to reach, which makes any encumbrance she harbors more significant. In the second, she intervenes with others—executive officials—and it is they who are the decision-makers, diluting and possibly checking whatever impairment the legislator herself carries.

Turn now to the second couplet: access-granting and agenda-manipulation. Legislators who accept *quid*s for granting access attract greater criticism, or at least profile, than those who accept *quid*s in return for subtly shaping a legislative or committee agenda.[88] And, again, there is an implicit rationality here. Access-granters are themselves the decision-makers in whose minds any clouding of judgment takes place. Agenda-manipulators must intervene with others—legislative colleagues—who are equally the decision-makers, capable of palliating or even countering whatever impairment preys upon the legislator herself. The typology of *quo*s thus takes the form shown in Table 4.

The Rules of *Quid Pro Quo*

Public discourse over *quid pro quo* displays the following structure. First, and as a factual matter, we recognize that some gray-area situations of value-transfer between citizens and officials do not constitute troubling *quid pro*

Table 4 *Quo*s

	The legislator acts principally as the final decision-maker	The legislator acts principally as an intervenor with others
Opening the mind	Partially: access-granting	Fully: agenda-shaping
Closing the mind	Fully: legislative voting	Partially: executive branch intervention

quo, but rather issue genuinely from the subjects of those involved. They are likely to represent gestures of principle or friendship that we regard as subjectively constitutive. Other kinds of value-transfers, though, are likely to display the mutual self-interest that is definitive of *quid pro quo,* just as it is definitive of contract or any other kind of exchange. Debate arises precisely because of the competing interpretive principles, objective and subjective, officials and their critics seek to marshall in determining whether any given situation falls into one or the other category.

Second—and assuming the factual existence of a *quid pro quo*—we nevertheless distinguish some types as normatively more troubling, as more inconsonant with democratic norms than others. When we make such distinctions, what we are again doing is determining which *quid pro quo*s are likely to be more, and which less, encumbering of the subjects of the officials and citizens involved. Certain kinds of *pros*—links between *quid* and *quo*—will do less violence to subjective genuineness than others. Wherever a logical or ideological connection exists between *quid* and *quo,* the very fact of getting the *quid* could bring having to perform the *quo* more into conformity with one's subjectively constitutive beliefs. In the next place, certain kinds of *quids* or *quos* themselves will also seem to do less violence than others to the subjects of the officials involved. In the realm of *quids*—interventions citizens make with officials—we favor holistic contributions and campaign volunteer work over particularistic gifts and lobbying. And we prefer gifts and lobbying meant to reinforce officials' positions—gratuities or "bias-mobilizing" lobbying—over those meant to alter officials' positions. When it comes to *quos,* the acts officials perform for citizens, we favor those that involve the official opening up an issue to other minds or keeping her own at least partially open (agenda-shaping, access-granting) to those that involve an official partially closing other minds or completely closing her own (intervening with the executive, voting on the floor).

In both our rhetoric and the implicit rules we have established, we show a remarkable solicitousness for preserving and protecting officials' and citizens' capacities to exercise genuine political judgment. Or, more exactly, for ensuring that the political acts they perform are in conformity with beliefs and commitments that constitute rather than encumber their subjects. Certainly this is not the only thing going on in these strands of discourse, but it is a recurrent impulse evident across a range of disparate topics—from campaign contributions to lobbying, from PACs to access-granting, from volunteer work to bribery, from gifts to agenda-manipulation. Democratic discourse over official conduct reveals a definite protectiveness of genuine, subjectively rooted judgment—not a total sealing-off, but certainly a pronounced guardedness.

15

Spousal Interests

Other-imposed encumbrances troubles us more than the self-generated type. That is why criminal bribery is more serious than criminal conflict of interest, why externally sourced lobbying generally troubles us more than internally sourced biases and opinions, why politicians and commentators make observations like "the native integrity of the average human being is most jeopardized by favors he has accepted from somebody else, rather than because of any holdings that have long since been his own."[1] But the border between self and other blurs, and discourse reveals at least two sets of circumstances where we disagree over whether an official's encumbrance originates in another or in the official herself, and where our entire normative assessment hangs on which side we take.

The first is the longstanding debate over the encumbrances that spouses, who may have their own financial interests and business activities, impose on their official mates. A spouse is not part of the official himself, but neither is she a wholly separate other. The ambiguities in their relationship, played out against a backdrop where other-imposed encumbrances are more worrisome than self-generated, shape our debate over spousal conflicts of interest. The second debate, which plays out more in judicial than political forums, surrounds the meaning of unencumbered agency decision-making. An office-holder might find herself combining more than one official role—deciding a case she earlier prosecuted—or, although occupying only a decision-making role, might find herself in close contact with other officials occupying prosecuting or partisan roles. The first situation, commonly called "combination of roles or functions," arises when an official internalizes two or more incompatible roles in ways that encumber official judgment. The second, *ex parte* contacts, occurs when officials occupying distinct roles interact externally in ways that bias decision-making. But the boundaries between the two blur, and in that blur reside longstanding conundrums over the meaning of unencumbered official judgment. The following two sections look first at spousal conflicts of interest and then at combination-of-roles and *ex parte* contacts.

The much-debated question of spousal conflicts of interest goes directly to the shadowy line between self- and other-engendered encumbrances. Two seemingly contradictory strictures, found in most conflict-of-interest regimes, frame the issue (and everything that can be said of spouses applies, depending on the particular conflict-of-interest regime, to minor children and perhaps other close relatives).

First, most jurisdictions require officials to disclose creditors' identities and the amounts owed on the grounds that financial beholdenness to others constitutes an encumbrance on official judgment. Only one kind of creditor is ever exempt from this requirement: spouses. Virtually no regime requires officials to disclose debts to their husbands or wives. On the other hand, virtually all jurisdictions require officials to disclose *assets* held by spouses—including spouses' financial portfolios, jobs, gifts, and other sources of remuneration—on the grounds that spousal assets can constitute encumbrances on an official's judgment. No other class of asset-holder, no matter how closely linked to the official, faces such a requirement; few regimes require the disclosure of assets held by anyone else, such as a friend or partner, with whom the official may have a financial association.[2]

When it comes to an official's debts, spouses are the only "others" excluded from conflict-of-interest regimes, the only others to whom indebtedness is not thought to constitute an encumbrance. When it comes to an official's assets, however, spouses are the only "others" included; they are the only others whose holdings *are* thought to constitute an encumbrance. These two characteristics of spousal treatment are staples of American conflict-of-interest regimes.[3]

Why do we not think that debts to spouses make officials beholden, in the way that debts to other "others"—such as business partners—might? There could be only one reason: A spouse is better understood as "part" of the official himself, as constitutive of his own subjectivity and not as an extrinsic "other" capable, through her financial hold, of diverting the official away from his subjectively plotted course. Any financial debt an official might bear toward his spouse, on this view, would be canceled by the spouse's affective feelings for the official, and supererogatory to whatever affective obligations the official feels toward his spouse in any case. By comparison with most other relatives, and with all friends and associates, the spouse is less an "other" and more a resident of the official's own subject, part of the official's subjective ties, commitments, and allegiances. The only discussion I have been able to find where a wife (as the spouse was in this case) is portrayed as exercising encumbering influence over her husband's official judgment—as not constituting but rather diverting him from his subjectively plotted political course—arises precisely where, in the realm of affective relations, the two became sundered. In her profile of Hillary Clinton, the journalist Connie Bruck writes: "Bill's indebtedness to Hillary increases with each new allegation of sexual impropriety," and suggests that as a result, the president might have pursued policies at the First Lady's behest that went against his better judgment. An official's financial "indebtedness" to a spouse is not generally thought to constitute an encumbrance—because the emotional tie overwhelms it—but emotional indebtedness may well constitute an encumbrance.[4]

Why, on the other hand, do we feel spousal assets place the official in conflict, in a way that the assets of additional kinds of "others," such as business associates, do not? Because, again, the official's own self is better conceived as extending to incorporate the spouse, so that the spouse's interests are folded into the official's interests, thus encumbering his judgment.[5] Official and spouse are "one individual" for these purposes; "what's mine is yours" governs.[6] If—when it comes to indebtedness—the spouse blurs into the official so that his debts to her are no longer extrinsically imposed encumbrances, then when it comes to the spouse's assets, the official blurs into the spouse so that her assets *do* become part of his internal encumbrances. One and the same view of the official-spouse relationship, then, accounts for what may seem to be contrary treatments of debts to and assets of spouses—the unique exclusion of the one, and the unique inclusion of the other, in American conflict-of-interest regimes. In the official-spouse relationship, the spouse is an exceptionally weak "other," the official an exceptionally expansive self. That his spouse is an exceptionally weak "other" with respect to the official means that no one ever charges a spouse and official with engaging in a *quid pro quo*. That the official is an exceptionally expansive "self" with respect to the spouse means that the space enlarges within which officials, because they benefit from both their own and their spouses' assets, might find themselves accused of self-dealing.

Debate over spousal conflicts highlights certain tensions between long-sought gender-equality goals. Thirty years ago, as Mr. Justice W. D. Parker pointed out in a milestone Canadian conflict-of-interest inquiry, an official's spouse—generally a wife—was relatively more dependent financially on her official mate because her own financial wherewithal came nowhere near equal to his. While this relative degree of dependence blurred any financial distinction between the two and strengthened the "what's mine is yours" argument for spousal disclosure, the relative inequality (often triviality) of the spouse's assets sustained a *de minimis* objection against spousal disclosure.[7]

By contrast, today the "trend is toward greater independence of each marital partner and greater equality in marriage."[8] Spouses' relative independence has come to argue—in the minds of some feminist critics of spousal disclosure—for exempting spouses, for regarding them essentially as "others" whose interests are their own, thereby posing no encumbrance on the official.[9] On the other hand, it is spouses' financial (near) equality that argues, more and more, for the substantial weight spousal interests may carry with the official and consequently for their disclosure.[10] Thirty years ago, spousal financial dependency argued for disclosure while spousal inequality of assets argued against it. Today, spousal independence argues against disclosure while spousal equality argues for it.

Just as it enlarges the capacity for self-dealing, the spousal relationship also increases the possibilities for private gain from public office. If the spouse's financial interests have the capacity to encumber the official's public-role judgment, then surely the official's public aura extends over the spouse in her private financial affairs.[11] A spouse's private profit from an official's office generally takes one of two forms: Either the spouse may herself assume a public position—as when wives of prominent legislators are appointed to executive or legislative office—or the spouse might profit on the private market, as when spouses of legislators become lobbyists.

Ironically, the penumbra of the official's role seems to extend more elastically when the spouse seeks a private as opposed to a public career. In 1993, Hillary Clinton sought legal status as a public official in order to keep secret the meetings of the President's Task Force on National Health Care Reform, a committee composed of herself as chair and several high-level officials. The Federal Advisory Committee Act requires such committee meetings to be conducted openly if even one member is a private citizen, on the grounds that extra-governmental sources of advice to the president need closer scrutiny than intra-governmental sources. In claiming to be an official, Mrs. Clinton argued that her husband's public role had so imbued her, and the work she had done to assist it was so prodigious, that she had become a public official in her own right. She wore the mantle of public office so completely, Hillary Clinton claimed, that she ceased being a private individual merely tinged or advantaged by an association with an official; instead, she had come to cohabit the president's official role with him. She was, as the court itself put it in recapping her argument, a "virtual extension of her husband."[12] The plaintiff, the Association of American Physicians and Surgeons, rejected this position. As close as she was to the president personally, they urged, she remained outside the ambit of his role officially—an argument with which the court agreed, although it ruled in Hillary Clinton's favor on other grounds.[13]

Along similar lines, during her campaign for a New York Senate seat, Hillary Clinton reaped criticism for exploiting her husband's official role—including the high-profile access it provided her to domestic and foreign leaders—on the grounds that her doing so constituted a kind of unfair private gain from public office. Benefiting from an "aura that lets [her] tower over mere politicians," the journalist Peter Beinart wrote, Hillary Clinton began "her New York campaign under the guise of performing the duties of the First Ladyship."[14] No incumbent official, however—say a vice president or a senator running for president—ever incurs the same kind of criticism; for them, occupying one public office (and thus enjoying a certain amount of access and profile) and seeking another is all part of the same public role. Mrs. Clinton's more attenuated relationship to public office, however, made her vulnerable to the charge of gaining privately from it.

Even in the legislative realm, wives (it is thus far always women) who attempt to succeed their husbands in Congress occasionally find the coattails, the penumbra of role, rudely cut short. Notwithstanding whatever substantial contribution a wife may have made to her husband's political career—notwithstanding that she may have cohabited the role with her office-holding mate—he might nevertheless take his official aura with him. True, this doesn't often happen. The vast majority are victorious. But when Peggy Begich, widow of Congressman Nick Begich, unsuccessfully sought to succeed him in Congress, one local party operator said her problem was that "[t]he party people . . . could not relate to her as part of Nick."[15] Even Representative Mary Bono, whose critics argued would never have been elected to Congress had she not been advantaged by her late husband's public notice, believed that very little of his public profile adhered to her. "We worked as a team," she has said, "but I deliberately chose to stay out of view, and now they say I've never done anything."[16]

When the spouse herself seeks the mantle of her officeholding mate's official role, then, that mantle often retreats from her. Conversely, when she seeks to escape the mantle of her officeholding mate's official role—when she seeks not a public but a private career—she often cannot escape it. "Ellen Proxmire wanted to do something on her own," the journalist Donna Fenn wrote. "Ironically, striking out on her own [as a convention organizer] meant becoming more identified with her husband," Senator William Proxmire. For to no small degree it was her clients' awareness and her own subtle use of her husband's office that brought in business.[17] Although "striking out on her own" in the private market, Ellen Proxmire nevertheless courted accusations of private gain from public office.[18]

In private gain from public office situations, spouses thus face a conundrum much like the one that confronts officials themselves, who must claim either to be acting wholly in-role—hence not gaining privately—or acting so far out-of-role that there is no possibility that public office was involved.

Where spouses seek to cohabit and operate wholly within their mate's official role, as did Peggy Begich, they have a tough row to hoe. And where they seek no part of that role, preferring to operate wholly within the private realm—as did Ellen Proxmire—they also have a tough row to hoe. Instead, they end up mostly in the middle, in the realm where they are seen to be gaining privately from their spouse's official role.

Or else they might find themselves moving from public role to private life in complex ways. So, for example, when the personal relationship eroded between the actor/TV journalist Donna Hanover and her husband, New York Mayor Rudolph Giuliani, Hanover ceased participating as frequently or as closely as she had previously in the mayor's official life. The result: Hanover was criticized, in essence, for private gain from public office, first for living at Gracie Mansion and enjoying the services of a four-person staff while performing little in the way of official work in return, and then for "using City Hall staff and connections to foster her postdivorce career." Hanover's argument that she was winnowing her official and political activities so as to "avoid any perceived conflict of interest in my profession"—in her private-sector career as a reporter—did not win over critics. "There is every reason to believe," Jenet Conant wrote in *Vanity Fair,* "that Hanover's detachment from her husband and from his campaign is motivated not so much by professional propriety as by personal necessity."[19]

American conflict-of-interest regimes, then, extend a characteristic treatment to spousal debts, assets, and private business activities, the best reading of which would suggest a fusion of the spouse into the official so that the spouse is less "other" and more "self." True, as *Physicians* v. *Clinton* and the experiences of spouse-candidates suggest, the spouse is not always so much a part of the official that she fully co-occupies his role—at least not in the eyes of courts and the public—but she comes close. In spousal conflict-of-interest situations, both the official's subjectivity and his encumbrances expand to incorporate those of his mate; the official becomes both self and other.

16

Combination of Roles and *Ex Parte* Contacts

I want to look, briefly, at two important areas of administrative law—areas that bear very much on the question of unencumbered official judgment—through an unusual lens. The first has to do with "combination of roles" (or "combination of functions," as it is generally termed juridically) and the second with "*ex parte* contacts"; the lens is the self/other distinction set forth previously. That distinction explains something of a puzzle these two legal doctrines collectively generate.

Consider the case of *Ward* v. *Village of Monroeville,* in which the mayor of Monroeville, Ohio—responsible for the town's budget—also judged disputes over municipally imposed fines, thus, according to the Supreme Court, improperly occupying both a "partisan" and an "adjudicative" role.[1] What worries us about combination-of-roles is the consequences for judgment that may follow when, concerning any given issue, a single person embraces more than one official function—investigative, prosecutorial, negotiational, advisory, decisional—playing them off internally within her own mind. The very same kinds of combinations-of-role are far less troubling, we have come to believe, when it is not a single official but an entire agency that combines these different functions, apportioning them among various officeholders—some of them advocates and others decision-makers—who work with one another. As the court said in *Pangburn* v. *Civil Aeronautics Board,* "the provision of [the Administrative Procedure Act] which prohibits the same person from investigating and rendering a decision in the same matter expressly excludes from its operation the agency [itself]," so that some agency officials can occupy investigative roles while others assume prosecutorial and still others decision-making responsibilities.[2] "The fact that independent minds perform the different functions," the legal scholar John R. Allison has written, "may be quite meaningful despite a structural relationship between them."[3]

It was not always thus: "Early in the administrative era," Allison writes, "some observers took a monolithic view of agencies as decision-makers, a view necessarily leading to the conclusion that the same decision-making agent is performing all functions."[4] This view, however, did not prevail, which is just as well. Ameliorating it would have required a wholesale reorganization of government of the sort proposed by the President's Commission on Administrative Management in 1937, which recommended a splitting of each agency into two, one "to investigate and prosecute and a wholly separate one to adjudicate."[5] Agencies may thus combine investigative, advocatory, and decision-making roles in ways that individual officials may not.

There is a crucial gray area here. Some kinds of "structural relationships" within an agency between individual advocates and individual decision-makers can become so intimate, so non-arm's length, that they grow tantamount to a combination of those functions *within* the minds of the officials concerned. They may amount to situations where the decision-making official in effect is doing her own investigating and advocacy. "Although not constituting actual functional combinations, [such] relationships among those performing different roles in a decision-making process [also display a] close association to true combinations."[6] But the fundamental principle of combination-of-roles remains: Certain kinds of deliberations that may not occur within the mind of a single decision-making official may far more readily occur between different officials.[7]

There is a sense in which discourse over *ex parte* contacts tacks in just the opposite direction. *Ex parte* contacts are communications on the merits of a particular case or cause, made to a decision-making official, without proper notice to other parties or inclusion in the public record. Often (and what is of interest here) the kind of *ex parte* contacts that draw legal sanction are made by other officeholders, such as when an FTC official occupying a prosecutorial role talks over a case with one of the decision-making commissioners.[8]

Yet the very exchanges and deliberations that *ex parte* doctrine forbids *between* officials—between decision-makers and advocates, between impartial and partial officeholders—*can* take place within the mind of a single official. As a proceeding unfolds, agency decision-makers are necessarily allowed to commence the internal process of reaching their own conclusions. Indeed, they are expected to develop their own partialist perspectives, opinions, and even biases and prejudices in the course of coming to judgment: Recall Peter Strauss's observation that judges need not disqualify themselves simply because they develop a strong "inner conviction" as a trial progresses, "absent disqualifying [external] sources of information."[9]

The distinction between acceptable self-generated "convictions" and unacceptable other-imposed information, I must emphasize, applies only once a process of decision-making has begun. Prior to the beginning of in-role judgment formation, it is actually the other way around: A judge or agency commissioner who comes to a decision-making process with internal biases or personal prejudgments formed out of role generally risks disqualification. But an official who comes to a decision-making process having simply been exposed to others who may have developed partialist perspectives or opinions on a future case is not disqualified. After all, the law cannot prevent a decision-making official's professional, social or business encounters with those who might, at one point, become parties before him.[10]

Courts, then, have repeatedly distinguished between personal "bias and prejudice external [as opposed to] internal to the proceeding" in its origins. If the decision-maker "comes into the proceeding with an open mind, then any other subjective bias is part of the normal course of proceedings; otherwise it is a predisposition."[11] By contrast, *ex parte* contacts extrinsically imposed by others who might bear *identical* biases or prejudices, including those imposed by other officials, *are* forbidden once a decision-making proceeding has commenced, but are permissible beforehand.

Once a particular process of judgment has begun, then, a decision-maker's *ex parte* contacts—unchallenged exchanges with partisans in a case or controversy—are more troubling than any unchallenged partiality she might develop internally. But here, too, is an important gray area. Certain kinds of exchanges between agency decision-makers and agency advocates are so intimate, so closely held, that they begin to resemble an activity taking place within the mind of the decision-making official herself. They are more akin to situations where the decision-making official is drawing her own conclusions, developing her own partialities, or engaging in her own internal processes of judgment formation than exchanges in which others are assaulting her thought processes with their own views. *Ex parte* law accords leeway to both judges and agency commissioners, should they wish to consult other officials—whether their own research counsel or colleagues—while in the process of coming to a decision.[12]

Under certain circumstances, a decision-maker may even consult those who are doing the advocacy and investigating in the case at hand, if doing so is somehow necessary to fill in the blanks of her own internal deliberative process, but not if it resembles an external intervention.[13] Such *ex parte* contacts between a decision-making official and others, courts and commentators have said, are tantamount to nothing more than the decision-maker reading newspaper editorials or law review articles on the topic, and in such cases, courts have refused to require the record to contain "every informational input"—every exchange with an agency adviser or expert—"that may have entered into the decision-maker's deliberative process."[14] There exists a long-recognized distinction between decision-makers "us[ing] their expert staffs" on the one hand, and "the evils of *ex parte* contacts" on the other.[15] The former is constitutive of the official's working-out of his own inner judgment, the latter of an externally imposed encumbrance.

Indeed, some courts have recently expanded this approach to define the entire agency itself, and not simply the ultimate judging official, as the decision-making unit. This expansion allows them to treat *all* contacts between judging and advisory/investigatory officials as part of the agency's natural, permissible, internal processes of subjective reflection and not as unlawfully *ex parte*. By contrast (as I noted above), whenever courts trying *combination-of-roles* cases have viewed the entire agency, and not just the ultimate judging official, as the decision-making entity, then the agency's having combined diverse functions within itself—even though it might have distributed them across various agency personnel—was still troubling.[16] In sum, when an *ex parte* situation bleeds into (or can be more readily classified as) a single decision-making official seeking out, receiving, and assimilating information from others, according to her own inner lights, our concerns diminish. It is only when *ex parte* contacts seem to involve communication between distinct individuals occupying separate roles—when they are more aptly depicted as other minds deliberately engaging and moving the decision-maker's—that they pose a problem.

It would seem, then, that there is an important if singular sense in which combination-of-roles and *ex parte* discourse pull in opposite directions. Combination-of-roles courts become relatively more exercised when one official, within the confines of her own mind, does both the decision-making and the investigating or advocating in a particular case. They are less disturbed when an official wholly concerned with decision-making is engaged from without by other officials occupying advocatory and advice-giving roles within the agency. *Ex parte* courts, by contrast, grow more troubled when a decision-maker seems to have been engaged from without by others, including other officials occupying advocatory and advice-giving roles. They are less concerned, however, whenever they interpret such contacts as instances where decision-making officials engage in their own investigative or advice-seeking activities. On such an understanding, any exchanges made with others are really extensions of a decision-maker's own internal process of forming judgment.

The distinction I draw between combination-of-roles and *ex parte* concerns may seem counterintuitive to administrative-law scholars, since combination-of-roles and *ex parte* issues are often jurisprudentially linked. They are linked because there exists a large middle ground—and it is this middle ground that interests most legal scholars—where exchanges between the decision-maker and other agency officials are sufficiently constructable as extensions of her own mental processes to avoid the charge of *ex parte*, but sufficiently extrinsic to her own mental processes that she is able to avoid the charge of combination of roles.[17] This middle-ground, though, has obscured the deeper tension between the two that interests me here.[18] For situations can arise where an official's involvement with others is such an extension of her own mental processes that it banishes *ex parte* concerns but begins to raise combination-of-roles anxieties. Conversely, circumstances can emerge where the involvement between an official and others is sufficiently arms-length to erode combination-of-roles but raise *ex parte* issues.

This is, however, a tension that can be resolved—or at least explained—at a deeper level. Consider two evocative statements made by leading scholars, both of which, by their different linguistic turns, point to a means of reconciliation. The first describes the harm that can arise when a single official combines roles. Those who have participated in a particular proceeding as investigators or prosecutors, Nathaniel L. Nathanson writes, "are likely to have convinced themselves in advance of the correctness of their position . . . and are thus unlikely to be useful" in participating in "disinterested" decision-making.[19] The reflexive phrase "convince themselves" is worthy of attention. It suggests that in combining roles—say advocatory and decision-making functions—an official in essence subdivides into two selves, one of which prevails or exerts influence upon ("convinces") the other. An official who combines roles is best understood, by this interpretation, not as an unencumbered subject coming to judgment. Rather, hers is a situation in which, metaphorically if not literally, an external "other" influences the decision-making subject—even though both "other" and "decision-making subject" reside in the same person, the same official. It is as if the official's former incarnation—her former role as investigator—is not part of her subject but rather an external force encumbering it, pushing it off a genuine course. Physically she may be one official, but metaphysically she is two.

Now turn to *ex parte* and consider Steven Lubet's observation that *ex parte* rules do not preclude a judge from consulting other judges or court personnel whose function it is to aid the judge in carrying out her adjudicative responsibilities, because such personnel essentially comprise an "arm of the court."[20] Lubet's focus is on the judiciary, but if *ex parte* contacts of this sort are allowed for judges they must necessarily be permissible for most other officials, and he explains why. Beyond a certain point, the others making *ex parte* contacts are better understood not as "other" people but as limbs of the decision-maker herself. Here, metaphorically if not literally, the subject of the official expands to incorporate both herself and the others with whom she communicates, so that the dialogue between them becomes internal to the workings of her own genuine subjectivity. Physically, there are two officials; metaphysically there is one.

On a *physical* plane, then, combination-of-roles doctrine grows uneasy as a particular kind of deliberation takes place within the mind of a single official, while *ex parte* prohibitions kick in as it becomes an exchange between two or more. But metaphysically, the two can be reconciled. Combination-of-roles discourse grows perturbed only where it reckons that an "other" is preying upon the subjective judgment of the decision-maker—albeit an "other" who operates in intimate internal proximity—such that there really are two officials, the one encumbering the other, at work. *Ex parte* discourse is unperturbed, by contrast, where the "other" is essentially an extension of the decision-maker's subjective judgment, where there really is one subject spread across two people. We divide "good" *ex parte* contacts from "bad" *ex parte* contacts—just as we divide tolerable combinations of role from intolerable combinations of role—not by where we physically draw the line between the decision-making official and others (on this plane, the two discourses are in tension) but by where we constructively draw the line. Once again, other-imposed encumbrances are more troubling than those self-generated, but what falls into which category is very much a matter of dispute.

17

Hold the Interest,
Vary the Role

"I represent the oil business in Oklahoma, because it is Oklahoma's second-largest business and because I am in the oil business . . . They don't want to send a man here who has no community of interest with them, because he wouldn't be worth a plugged nickel to them." Senator Robert Kerr's 1962 comment[1] is perhaps the most famous statement of a doctrine that resounds throughout American political history: A legislator who shares pecuniary interests with those she represents fortifies her capacity to advocate for those interests. Often, the same kind of claim gets made on behalf of executive officials, usually in the form of a response to the "regulatory capture" critique. What we want in an auto-industry advisory committee member is precisely someone who *does* hold stock in General Motors; a commerce secretary *should* have broad business links.[2] The "Kerr argument" shifts our focus—from whether nonpecuniary ideologies, biases, and relationships encumber officials in their judging roles to whether pecuniary interests can actually assist officials, and legislators in particular, in their advocacy roles.

Although Kerr's line of argument is deeply ingrained in American public discourse, its complexities have not been explored.[3] Most of those who dispute the Kerr argument head-on point out that the legislator must not only advocate for constituency interests, she must judge the public interest, and that while the possession of certain kinds of pecuniary interests might assist her in the first capacity, it hinders her in the second. "I think," Harold Ickes, Sr. once said, "that it is not expecting too much of a senator or a representative who has a financial stake in silver or gold or iron or coal, or especially in natural gas or oil, to stand aside . . . when he is called upon to vote on legislation affecting his private . . . interest . . . What owner of natural gas or oil would want to stand before a judge who had an adverse interest with respect to oil or natural gas and let him pass upon the merits of a case involving his ownership?"[4] Others make the same argument about executive officials, whether they are members of cabinet or advisory committees.[5]

But what I want to suggest here—by placing the Kerr debate in a larger context—is that both Kerr and those who take the contrary view share a mistaken presumption. What they share is the presumption that at-stake pecuniary interests assist the legislator in carrying out her advocacy functions, even if they impair the legislator in performing her judging tasks. Where they disagree, of course, is simply over whether it is the legislator's advocacy role or her judging role—her obligations to her constituents or to the public at large—that is paramount. But the more we explore American legislative debate and practice, the more likely we are to question this shared presumption. We will, in fact, discover that a legislator's capacity to advocate for the interests she is supposed to represent is usually *hampered* if she shares some of them. And her capacity to judge the public interest and the worthiness of the legislative proposals before her may actually not, in most circumstances, find itself particularly encumbered by her possession of affected interests. The reason? The standard of *partiality* we require of any advocate—whether in political, legal, managerial, or other spheres—is more difficult for her to achieve as the interests she is supposed to represent proliferate and pluralize. By contrast, the standard of *impartiality* we require of a judge—in whatever realm: political, legal, or otherwise—is easier to achieve as the interests she is supposed to weigh proliferate and pluralize.

Advocacy

To see this, begin by comparing advocacy in the judicial and the legislative realms. In the judicial domain the lawyer fills the advocacy role. The client on whose behalf the lawyer advocates may, depending on one's perspective, be better conceived as an individual or as an interest. If the client is understood to be an individual (whether a person or a corporation), it will possess an array of interests only one (or perhaps a few) of which the lawyer represents in any given case. If the client is an interest, it is possible—as in class-action situations—for it to be harbored by a range of individuals, only one (or perhaps a few) of whom retained the lawyer in any given case. In neither instance, certainly in its pure form, is the entity for which the lawyer advocates especially pluralized or complicated. Where the lawyer represents an individual in respect of a few particular interests, or an interest in respect of a defined class of individuals, then her sharing in the client's stake as an advocate, whether through a corporate board membership or a contingency fee, is considered less than worrisome. In fact, many consider it a spur to zealous advocacy.

Of course, there can arise circumstances where faithful legal advocacy becomes more difficult to execute because the client itself, whether individual or interest, becomes relevantly pluralized and manifold. A client who is an individual, for example, may well possess numerous interests, all of which he engages the lawyer to represent. Usually, though, this kind of client takes corporate form: a business firm, an association, a nonprofit organization. A lawyer acting for such a client might find herself in a situation where her pecuniary interests—say the stock she holds in the corporation—aligns her with some of the interests possessed by her corporate client but not others, even though she is supposed to represent the client across all the implicated interests. For example, legal counsel who happens to hold shares in a client corporation, or sit on the board, might—because of her view as to how best to improve her stake—prefer a risky approach to a choice the company faces. Other shareholders or board members, by contrast—lending a higher priority to different corporate interests in good community relations, long-term market share, and industrial peace—might deem it in the corporation's overall interest to pursue a more conservative course. Here, where the interests counsel is obligated to represent conflict within the client, her sharing some but not all of those interests may well impair her capacity to represent a chosen path.[6]

Conversely, clients that take the form of interest-classes—say the class of all those harmed by a particular product or service—may embrace individuals other than the ones who have engaged the lawyer. In class-action suits, a few individuals harboring the interest in question—say in suing a company for a defective product—might retain the lawyer, aligning her interests with theirs through a contingency-fee arrangement. The lawyer, though, remains obligated to represent all individuals who share the interest, not just those few who retained her, and many of those others may conceive the interest far differently and seek an alternative resolution to the suit. Indeed, this is the stuff of class-action conflicts of interest.

A lawyer who shares client interests, then, will find her capacity for faithful advocacy compromised if (a) the individual she represents harbors conflicting interests which she is also compelled to represent or (b) the interest-class she represents is harbored by conflicting individuals whom she is also compelled to represent. But assuming neither possibility arises—assuming the lawyer represents an individual in respect of (at most) a small number of particular interests, or an interest in respect of a defined class of individuals—then her sharing in the interest in question, as an advocate, is considered less than worrisome. For lawyers-as-advocates, the possibility that their sharing interests with the represented entity will not encumber but actually assist them increases, as the represented entity narrows to one individual (and one of her interests) or to one interest (shared by a few individuals).

Using this framework—on which the capacity for faithful advocacy grows more difficult as the individuals or interests to be represented proliferate—what are we to make of the capacity of the legislator to act as a faithful advocate for her constituency? A constituency is neither a single individual (with a range of interests) nor a single interest (harbored across a range of individuals) but an aggregate of individuals and their interests. A legislator, as advocate, is charged with representing a huge cross-section of individuals, although whether she represents all individuals in her constituency or only some is a question for mandate theorists. And the legislator is charged with representing a wide range of the interests such individuals possess, although whether she represents all of their interests or only some is a question for agenda theorists. Any pecuniary interest the legislator might possess, even if shared by many of the individuals she represents, is thus unlikely to be shared by all. And even those individuals who do share it are likely to harbor other interests that conflict with it, and to which they may assign a far higher priority. Any pecuniary interests the legislator possesses, then, would seem fraught with peril, certain to skew the faithful performance of the role of legislative advocate. So what are we to make of the Kerr argument?

According to the Kerr argument, his oil holdings would not only fail to hinder an Oklahoma senator, they would actually help him carry out his official role. At least, they would assist him in that part of his job that requires him to advocate the interests of Oklahomans. But Kerr's claim faces a twofold challenge. First, for many individual constituents, conflicts will arise between their interest in a healthy oil industry and various other interests they may harbor and that he is obligated to represent. Notwithstanding oil's importance to Oklahomans whether or not they work in the industry, there will always be those who rank other interests they may have—in energy consumption, say, or environmental protection—ahead of oil profits. Second, within the functional interest-class of the oil industry, conflicts may arise between the various individuals who harbor it. The way in which big oil understands the oil interest may clash with the understanding of small producers; the way in which engineer-managers conceive the oil interest may conflict with the views of rig workers; individual oil firms will always be rivals at one level. If the legislative constituency is indeed variegated in these ways, then a senator's oil holdings would seem to compromise his capacity to act as its advocate. His particular oil holdings would skew his capacity to represent individual constituents across all the interests (including those that conflict with the oil interest) that they may harbor.[7] And his particular oil holdings would skew his capacity to represent the oil interest itself as shared by all individual constituents (big oil producers and small, petroleum executives and rig workers) who harbor it.[8]

We can, however, make a couple of further distinctions here—distinctions that partially, but by no means completely, resurrect the interested legislator's capacity to advocate for her constituency. First, within the class of those individuals who harbor the functional interest in a prospering oil industry, internal conflicts are most likely to evaporate as the issue at hand becomes more generic and broad-ranging. During Senator Kerr's time, an increase in the oil depletion allowance may well have benefited the entire class of those who harbored the oil interest: big firms and small firms, management and labor. Hence his holding shares in a particular petroleum company would not, in this case, have impaired his capacity to speak for all individuals who held the oil interest. But as the issue in question becomes more fine-grained and narrow, conflicts between the individuals who hold the oil interest are more likely to emerge. If an individual oil company were to have sought Senator Kerr's advocacy in securing a contract with the government, for example, then his holding shares in a competing firm could well have impaired his capacity to speak for this one. An oil-holding legislator can represent the oil interest *per se*, then, provided he does so on extremely general issues in which the individuals harboring it do not come into conflict. The more fine-grained the issue, the more likely it is to hit individuals who possess the oil interest differentially. And the greater will be the risk that the particular form in which the legislator possesses that interest will put him in conflict with other individuals who possess it, but whom he might be required to represent.

Conversely, there also exist circumstances where an oil-holding legislator would not be incapacitated in representing an individual constituent *even where* that individual accords a higher priority to interests she possesses other than her interest in a healthy oil industry, such as the interest in environmental protection or a prosperous farm sector. Suppose that an Oklahoma environmentalist urged Senator Kerr to support a tax on energy consumption, or a farmer asked him to advocate a looser monetary policy. If it is in the interests of a healthy oil sector that energy not be taxed (as it almost certainly is), or that money remain tight (as it would be if oil companies have a lot of cash reserves), then the fact that the senator holds interests in the oil industry *would* pose an impairment on his capacity to represent his environmentalist or farmer constituents in a faithful way. On the other hand, a more specific or narrow version of the environmental or agricultural interest—an environmental interest in taxing clear-cut logging, or an agricultural interest in farm loan guarantees—would not have touched on, hence conflicted with, the oil interest. Even less would an environmental group's interest in securing federal funding touch on the oil interest, or a particular farmer's interest in obtaining a subsidy adjustment. In these cases, Kerr's oil holdings would have posed no (or certainly less) impairment on his capacity to advocate. By and large, then, as the (non-oil) interests harbored by individual constituents expand from the narrow to the "polycentric," their capacity to come into conflict with the (oil) interests held by the legislator increases. And, consequently, his capacity to advocate for them faithfully diminishes.[9]

To sum up: The entity for which the legislator advocates, the constituency, is generally more heterogeneous than the entity for which the lawyer advocates, the legal client whether conceived as individual or as interest. It is difficult enough for an *unencumbered* legislator to faithfully represent an interest when the individuals harboring it conceive it in conflicting ways, or when the individuals she represents hold interests that conflict with it in various ways. An *encumbered* legislator will have an even more difficult time of it. Where the advocacy role requires the representation of *many* interests held by *many* individuals, as does the legislator's, then her possession of any one of those interests could pose an encumbrance on zealous representation.

In fact, as an advocate for her constituency, the interested legislator remains unimpaired only under two "ideal type" circumstances. She can represent individual constituents, who also hold the (oil) interest in question, provided the particular issue at hand is general enough so that no conflict arises between them and the legislator over how to realize it. And she can represent other (environmental, agricultural) interests individuals may hold, provided that the issue at hand is specific enough that no conflict arises between those interests and the one the legislator holds. Pure functional representation (of the oil interest) at the most general level, and pure client representation (of environmental and agricultural interests) at the most fine-grained, are thus the two forms least incompatible with the interested legislator-as-advocate. But once the functional representation descends into a fine-grained level of economic competition or conflict, the interested legislator can no longer represent the (oil) interest as shared by many individual constituents. And once client representation ascends to the level of a polycentric political cause, the interested legislator can no longer represent those individuals whose (environmental, agricultural) interests might conflict with the oil interest. In neither case can the legislator dodge the possibility that her interest will become an impairment on legislative advocacy, on her capacity to represent the interests of her constituents.

Judging

If an advocate represents only one clearly defined interest, as a lawyer often does on any given file, then her sharing in that interest may be necessary and even desirable. By contrast, to the extent that an advocate's obligation is to represent a plurality of interests—as it is for a legislator—then her sharing in any one of them risks skewing her capacity for faithful advocacy. When it comes to judging, however, the reverse is the case. On the one hand, if her obligation is to judge between two sharply opposed claimants in an adversarial setting—as it is for the courtroom judge—then her sharing at-stake interests with only one of those parties is likely to constitute a major encumbrance, a noticeable thumb on the scale. On the other hand, to the extent that the judging function requires reconciling plural interests in a deliberative setting—as it does in the legislative case—then sharing in any one of them is less likely to pose a significant encumbrance. So while the standard of unencumbered *advocacy* (as we have seen) is in fact higher in the legislative than in the judicial setting, the standard of unencumbered judgment is lower.

That impartial legislative judgment is less vulnerable than the judicial variant to interested participants is well known, if not often explicated. What remains wholly unexplored is the extent to which this claim is inconsistent with both the Kerr argument and its critique, each of which relies on the notion that interested legislative judgment is more troubling than interested legislative advocacy. To begin with, consider that in the judicial setting, a judge whose personal holdings incline him toward party A does a disservice exclusively to party B, who bears its full force. There is little chance that the judge's ruling—although adverse to party B in respect of the particular interest B has at stake in the case—will help B in virtue of other interests B holds outside of those at stake in the case. Nor—unless the judge's ruling is one of general application—is there much chance that large numbers of individuals other than party A (or those who directly share A's particular interests, such as the judge) will be helped by his ruling. B experiences only losses; only A experiences the gains.

In both these ways, the kind of judgment legislators exercise reaches far more broadly. Yes, a legislator who owns a small business will benefit from a budget resolution that reduces the employer's contribution to employee health plans. But that particular interest is one he shares with countless other individuals, namely, other employers. As for those individuals who harbor competing interests—namely, employees—they may see some of their *other* interests advanced by the budget resolution, say by its provisions for family leave.

When congressmen and commentators minimize the judgment-perverting impact of a legislator's personal holdings, as they often do, it is generally along one or another of these two lines. As one legal scholar has put it, "policymaking of a general character may well have a significant but hard to anticipate effect on private interests."[10] While any given law supported by an interested legislator may be prejudicial to some interests an individual citizen possesses, it might well help the very same individual in others.[11] And, as another legal scholar has put it, "since legislative bodies must be constituted from the general public, it is inevitable that . . . the legislator's interests [will be] common to many persons." While any given legislative act may well benefit an interest the legislator possesses, it will also benefit a great many other individuals who also happen to share that interest. In such circumstances, the "potential for adverse effects from such conflicts is quite low."[12]

Of course one may question these assumptions in particular cases. Most jurisdictions excuse the interested legislator from voting—and some require recusal—to the extent that the legislative act in question affects few interests other than her own or few individuals other than herself, in other words, to the extent that the legislative act in question takes on a quasi-judicial character.[13] Many legislative acts, however, assume a form either sufficiently omnibus across interests, or sufficiently universal across individuals, that the legislator's interest becomes a relatively light thumb on the scale. Democratic discourse and practice allow the interested legislator a good deal more latitude in exercising her judging function than they allow the interested courtroom judge.

Advocacy, Judging, and Interest

A legislator, Ronald M. Levin writes, must be both advocate and judge.[14] According to the Kerr argument (and its critique), her sharing interests with those she represents will make the legislator a more faithful advocate, even if it may make her a less impartial judge. This model may work well for the judicial realm. But in the legislative realm, the entity requiring advocacy—the constituency—is pluralized and polyglot; the entity requiring judging—the public interest—even more so. Consequently (and certainly by comparison with the judicial realm), the possession of a pecuniary interest is more likely to divert the legislator from faithful advocacy than impair her capacity for unencumbered judgment.

Discourse bears this out in many ways. Some of the sharpest criticisms recently directed against legislators, for example, are those that constituents have leveled against congressmen whose pecuniary interests have interfered with their capacity for faithful advocacy—often before the executive, sometimes before their legislative colleagues. So in 1991, Washington Congressman John Miller—at the behest of a Seattle-based fishing company, also a campaign-contributor—pressed for lower safety standards for one of the company's vessels, which then capsized, killing nine men. "The congressman," the *Wall Street Journal* reported, "defended his intervention by saying he was helping a constituent." "Our brother was one of your constituents, too," replied a sister of one of the sailors, "and he's dead now."[15] But while legislators whose interests may have been at stake in their advocacy for constituents draw especially bitter criticism, legislators whose interests may have been at stake in their judgments of the public interest enjoy, among the public at large, considerable tolerance—certainly by comparison with interested judges and most interested executive officials.[16] Despite its prominence, the Kerr argument is overwhelmed by other presumptions or arguments embedded in democratic practice and discourse. Legislators are not officially acting as lawyers; neither do they wear judicial robes. Interest-holding legislators risk impairing their advocacy role long before they corrupt their judging activities.

Sympathy, Courage, and Interest

Apart from the Kerr doctrine, one other prominent argument justifies suspending the conflict-of-interest strictures in the name of representative efficacy. "I still go home every weekend for a hurried gaze at the people of my state, masquerading in the guise of a man trying to find out what's going on," Senator Howard Baker once mused, but "who in the world can find out what's going on in other people's minds?" Instead of the hopeless travail of trying to enter the minds of his constituents, Baker said, he himself maintained an outside business activity, a law practice, so that he could derive the experiences of a citizen personally, "first hand." Doing so "makes me more responsive to what is really going on in the public rather than relying on somebody else telling me these things or reading about them in newspapers and books." Hence, Baker urged, legislators—in the name of becoming better constituency representatives—should engage themselves in outside business activities.[17]

Certainly not everyone shares Baker's views. For his senate interlocutor, William Proxmire, legislative representation *is* "a matter of going home to see your constituents, talk[ing] to your constituents, understand[ing] your constituents, not working as a lawyer [or] teacher, but working full time representing your people." It is within her role as a representative, not outside of it as a citizen or businessperson, that the legislator comes to the better understanding of her constituents. Indeed, once one occupies a legislative role, in Proxmire's view, then one really can *never* know what it is like to live as a citizen. "[I]t is impossible for us to view things through the eyes of our constituents," Proxmire urged; "we can talk to them, yes, but . . . we no longer really live in the community with them, work at jobs in the economy. We cannot see things through their eyes."[18] For Proxmire, the role penetrates the official—making it impossible for her ever to have the experiences of a citizen while in office—but the official can penetrate the minds of other citizens. For

Baker, the minds of others are less accessible and the role of office more escapable than for Proxmire.

What are we to make of Baker's defense of legislators who earn outside income, of his argument that only those representatives actively engaged in businesses—or professions—will embody their constituents' wishes and aspirations? It is certainly a recurring theme. Earning outside income, one congressman told his colleagues in a 1981 debate, will enable "us to live more like our constituents."[19] But in weighing this claim, consider that there are others who, although just as supportive of outside income-earning activities for legislators, advance precisely the opposite reasoning. Out-of-role business or professional activity, they say, will keep members healthily *independent* of their constituents' wishes and aspirations. With access to external sources of income, legislators (indeed, all officials) will be less fearful of putting their offices at risk by taking unpopular stands in which they believe. Outside business activity, Senator Ted Stevens declared in a 1979 debate, will allow "us to take a position which keeps our independence [and] in the national interest, to vote against the wishes of our constituents."[20] "One of the things I have noticed about this House," another congressman said during the 1981 colloquy, is that "members who . . . have the most attractive alternatives to serving in it are the ones who seem to maintain their independence," and cited as an example a colleague whose ongoing medical practice brought in four times his congressional salary.[21]

In other words, radically conflicting "delegate" and "trustee" understandings of representation underlie a common defense of outside earned income for legislators. On a pure delegate view, a legislator is obligated to implement her constituents' wishes and demands, even if, on her best judgment, those wishes and demands contravene the public interest. On the trustee view, she must follow her own judgments as to what lies in the public interest, even if her constituents disagree.[22] Indeed, one periodically finds proponents of external income sources for legislators simultaneously making both arguments, urging that outside business activities will lead legislators to more closely reflect constituent opinion *and* free them from a too-tight bond to constituents' wishes. During the 1979 debate, Congressman Ed Derwinski declared that "when Congress a few years ago removed themselves from being part of the people, by requiring arbitrary economic severance from their family businesses, they created a body economically isolated from many of the problems of the people" but also a body "dependent to an unhealthy degree on their U.S. governmental pay [and therefore] unable to vote against the wishes of our constituents."[23] Another congressman asked his colleagues "to allow us in our professions and in our businesses and in our trades to be able to remain citizen politicians," but in the same breath extolled outside business activities because otherwise "every vote we cast [will be] based on the premise of will we or will we not be re-elected . . . because we have no job to go back to, no profession."[24]

Howard Baker might defend outside business activities on the grounds that they bring representatives into tight alignment with constituents. But his own political allies—those who defend outside business activities because they allow representatives to operate with some independence from constituents—are his worst philosophical enemies.

18

De Minimis

The landscape of discourse is littered with claims about how entities beyond pecuniary interests—ideologies, biases, attachments, or relationships—can encumber official judgment. It is also rife with the suggestion that pecuniary interests themselves might in fact *not* be encumbering for officials in advocatory, as opposed to judging, roles. Having explored the surrounding debates, I now turn, suitably briefly, to one final strand of "interest discourse."

Just as "conflict" can fade out of the picture as we enter the realm of pure "private gain from public office," so "interest" can fade out of the picture as we enter the realm of *de minimis.* The *de minimis* question is simply this: Assuming that whatever level of interest is deemed encumbering to the least psychologically resistant official must be prohibited to all (an assumption explored in Part I), then how do we go about determining what that level is?

There have been two principal contenders for a suitable approach to *de minimis.* First, any conflict-of-interest regime could exempt an interest, asset, gift, salary, or fee from the category of encumbrance provided it falls below a certain percentage of the official's total holdings or remuneration, no matter how wealthy the official happens to be.[1] The governing assumption would be that even the least psychologically resistant official won't be swayed by a matter affecting only a certain small percentage of her total income or wealth. Such an approach, as Roswell Perkins noted, does "not depend on the financial interest being insubstantial in any absolute sense, or as applied against a standard of the average government official. The test is individualized and personal to the particular official."[2]

Yet although this percentage test still gets advanced, it also elicits an ultimately decisive democratic criticism. It would allow richer officials higher *de minimis* exemptions, based not on our estimation of their particular psychology or integrity—their subjective capacity to resist conflict—but on our measure of their objectively knowable interest holdings. Better to apply the same absolute—and necessarily low—set of dollar figures to all officials.[3] "[R]equiring disclosure [above] a specified dollar amount treats all . . .

equally"; as well, it is far "easier to administer and investigate than a percentage test."[4] Although a percentage test is in a sense an objective one—hard, measurable, ascertainable—an absolute test is even more so.

It is worth noting that when it comes to interest above the *de minimis* level, ethics committees and courts have occasionally taken the subjective approach to encumbrance—the one that brings within its sweep ideologies, beliefs, and relationships—and extended it even to pecuniary interests. Thus, in discussing Senator Harrison Williams's claim—made during the Abscam affair—that no "objective" value attached to the personal mining interests afforded him by a phony Arab sheikh seeking to immigrate to the United States, Senator Howell Heflin said, "The standard for judging a thing of value is subjective; that is, the test is not just whether the thing received has actual value in the commercial world, but whether Senator Williams believed it had value."[5] But at the attenuated tail end of pecuniary-interest-as-encumbrance—the realm of *de minimis*—a ruthlessly objective approach to interest prevails, one which aims "at a precise certainty of application, drawing clear categorical lines at a point of approximation arbitrarily chosen."[6]

Summary

Much of "interest" discourse, I suggested at the beginning of Part II, is dominated and even determined by an absence: the absence of any objective conception of the public interest. Because we cannot know objectively where the public interest lies in any given instance, we want to know where officials, genuinely and subjectively, believe it lies. The various debates explored in Part II—over how to determine which official judgments originate in the genuine subject and which in self-serving encumbrances—have become pivotal, but also enormously controversial, in American public discourse. Whenever our concern lies with charting the bounds of another individual's genuine faculty of judgment, as it increasingly does in discourse, we are compelled to move beyond the external layer of objective pecuniary interests and begin to explore encumbrances of a more inner, subjective nature.

Obviously, I mean to suggest a parallel between the theme argued in Part I on "conflict"—where we have moved from the subjective to the objective—and the one just set out here on "interest," where we have moved from the objective to the subjective. In the realm of conflict, we refuse to invade officials' minds to hazard individualized subjective guesses as to whether they actually have succumbed to (or else surmounted) their encumbrances—guesses, that is, as to whether they are in inner conflict. Rather, we prefer to base our conclusion on whether an objectively ascertainable factual situation *could* place an official in conflict. Instead of subjectively rating each individual official "on the scale of imperviousness to motives of personal gain,"[1] we objectively hold that if a particular encumbrance "is to be allowed to disqualify in any case it must in all, and it is impossible by any scale to measure the different effects it may have on different minds."[2] But then, in looking to the kinds of entities that could count as such encumbrances—that is, in the realm of "interest"—we have moved well beyond the objective and the pecuniary to embrace a huge range of subjective and psychological traits.

Only at the outer edges do these tendencies abate. In the far conflict realm of private gain from public office—where conflict fades out of existence—we abandon objective prophylaxis. Instead, we attempt to determine—in an unavoidably crude if subjective and individualized way—which aspects of a given official's gain originate in her own knowledge, skills, and stature and which in her role. In the outer interest realm of *de minimis,* conversely, we are no longer in the domain of subjective and amorphous psychological encumbrances. Instead, we adopt a ruthlessly objective approach.

Our twofold approach to conflict and interest may seem paradoxical. But any paradox disappears when we consider that legal liberalism requires that we take an objective approach to conflict, and political liberalism necessitates our adopting a subjective approach to interest.

Legal liberalism prohibits the sanctioning of states of mind. It prohibits, in other words, our penalizing the purely subjective; the most we can do is regulate its objective proxies and manifestations. Political liberalism precludes our elevating one conception of the public interest above all others as "objective." Instead, it compels us to determine whether the particular beliefs, projects, and purposes that underlie another's view of the public interest constitute her genuine capacity for subjective judgment, or instead are more aptly characterized as encumbrances on it. In displaying the structure it does, discourse over conflict of interest simply fulfills the logics of legal and political liberalism at the crossroads where they meet in public debate. As long as we abide in a liberal polity, with legal inhibitions against invading the subjective, and political inhibitions against availing the objective, then debate over conflict of interest will remain front and center in American public life.

III

APPEARANCES

19

The Meaning of "The Appearance of Official Impropriety"

In *Wild* v. *U.S.* (1982), a U.S. Court of Appeals upheld the dismissal of Lawrence A. Wild, a Chicago employee of the U.S. Department of Housing and Urban Development, on the grounds that Wild had violated the department's code prohibiting appearances of official impropriety. Wild's offense was to allow private rental units he owned, in the words of the court, "to deteriorate so badly that it . . . did not escape newspaper comment." In his defense, Wild argued that as a *matter of fact,* the newspaper's impressions were inaccurate: he had either demolished or rehabilitated the vast majority of the units in question, and he had plans to do the same with the remainder. And in any case, Wild urged, as a *normative proposition* the appearance standard is "so vague as to fail to provide adequate notice" regarding what kind of "off-duty conduct places [an official's] job on the line"—indeed, the point and effect of the appearance standard, as the court itself had acknowledged, is "to make conduct that is not necessarily forbidden by any express regulation a ground for separation." In writing for the court, however, Judge Richard Posner held that under the appearance standard, "the question is not whether the employee had [in fact] engaged in the alleged misconduct," but whether he could be perceived as having done so. Judge Posner also held that the appearance norm itself, despite its necessarily "sloppy use of the English language, [nevertheless] adequately conveys its concern that an employee not conduct himself in a way likely to bring public obloquy on HUD"—and that in this case, the "irony of a professional employee of HUD" moonlighting as a "slumlord" could "reasonably have been construed," by Wild, "to undermine public confidence in . . . the agency."[1]

Wild exemplifies the central moral problem raised by almost all cases of the appearance of official impropriety, whether they involve political figures or civil servants. According to its critics, the appearance standard contravenes two fundamental principles of legal justice: the principle against prejudgment of the facts and the principle against retroactive law. According to its defenders, the appearance rule serves a fundamental political purpose: the preservation of public confidence in government.

Both the realm of apparent conflict of interest—which embraces the appearance of self-dealing, the appearance of private payment for public acts, the appearance of private gain from public office and the like—and the more general forms of the appearance of official impropriety (that occur, for example, when an official appears to embezzle agency funds or even commit murder[2]) are all covered by the same appearance standard. Each such case invariably provokes the same tension between legal principles and political ends. Hence, my discussion here operates on a more general level. I refer to the appearance of official impropriety as a whole, although most of the examples are instances of the appearance of one kind of conflict of interest or another.

For "the appearance of official impropriety" to have any meaning, it must in the first instance be distinguished from "real official impropriety." "Real official impropriety" occurs whenever an official (i) *commits an act* which (ii) is *prohibited by law,* specifically, by one of the laws governing official impropriety in general and conflict of interest in particular. The appearance of official impropriety, then, takes place when officials "create the *appearance* that they are violating the law or ethical standards"[3]—which means it may arise in one of two cases. It may emerge in situations in which the act in question is clearly prohibited by the ethics laws or is otherwise uncontroversially classifiable as "official impropriety," but in which the official did not in fact commit the act—even though the public, to a greater or lesser extent, believes that he did. The appearance of official impropriety may also arise in situations in which the official uncontroversially committed the act in question, but in which no ethics law prohibits, and no overwhelming moral consensus condemns, that particular act—even though, to a greater or lesser extent, some part of the public believes that there should have been such a law, or else that the conduct in question ought to qualify as "official impropriety." The appearance of official impropriety, in other words, can take either a factual or a normative cast (or often both). Either (a) it *looks* like the official did something wrong, or (b) the official did something that *looks* wrong.

Consider Office of Government Ethics Letter 85X19, which concerned a case of the *appearance* of "private payment for public acts." A group of private, nongovernmental contributors had given anonymously to a defense fund for an official facing litigation arising from his government work. This was not a case where private parties actually underwrote an official's salary—and hence official acts *per se*—in violation of the "real" conflict-of-interest statute, 18 U.S.C. §209. Yet it might have appeared so to the broader public.

After all, a reasonable person, informed partially if not totally, could have cognized just those facts that rise to a real offense—private parties giving money to an official who provided no private-market consideration in return—without perceiving those facts that deflate any quality of actual violation, namely, their having given anonymously and that the payments underwrote something *related* to official acts, not official acts *per se*. To the public, it would *look* as if the officeholder had done something wrong. Or, alternatively, having cognized all the facts, at least some members of the public might have concluded that while a literal violation of the law did not occur, a spiritual violation of the law's prophylactic norm did. If *non*anonymous private payments for *official acts* themselves are to be prohibited—in the fashion of 18 U.S.C. §209—then why not, with an abundance of prophylactic caution, prohibit even anonymous private payments for official-related defense funds? After all, anonymity is far from airtight. And officials, or payors, might care as much about the outcome of litigation surrounding official acts as about those acts themselves. To them, the officeholder will have done something that *looks* wrong. Others, however, will dismiss these concerns, arguing that they carry the principle of prophylaxis way too far. For them, no norm will appear to have been violated.

Opinion 85X19 and the *Wild* case exemplify the dual objection that officeholders invariably level against the appearance standard: that its enforcement violates two central tenets of legal justice. In the first place, they urge, the appearance standard involves an element of *factual prejudgment*. To apply it is to penalize an officeholder regardless of any legal determination as to whether he committed an act of official impropriety, and in advance of a complete exploration of the (often mitigating) facts of the situation. This is what it means to say that under the appearance standard, officials can be punished if it merely *looks* as if they did something wrong.

In the second place, the appearance standard is said to involve a significant element of *legal retroactivity*. By definition, appearance violations consist of acts other than those captured by any established ethics law or widespread normative consensus. The substance of what the standard prohibits can be known only after the act has occurred, depending as it does on whether an improper appearance has registered in the mind of (some sufficient segment of) the public. This is what it means to say that the appearance standard countenances sanctioning an official for doing something that merely *looks* wrong.

In contrast to the appearance standard, principles of legal fairness generally hold that an individual be sanctioned only after the fact; that is, after the actuality of a crime has been determined at law. Legal principles also require that the substance of an offense be defined before the fact, so that an individual may know in advance whether a contemplated act is legally prohibited. Or, as Judith N. Shklar has described it, "[t]he principle of legality" holds "that there shall be no punishment without crime . . . and no crime without law."[4]

Before scrutinizing these claims, it is worth querying whether such legalistic objections are not misplaced, whether they have even a *prima facie* bearing on the appearance question. Appearance proceedings, unlike many *real* conflict-of-interest or other official-impropriety prosecutions, are not criminal but administrative affairs—the most severe penalty is usually removal from office—and, in administrative settings, less stringent standards of proof and the retroactive imposition of rules often obtain. Indeed, some appearance proceedings are essentially political affairs, involving political figures whose claims to office we would not want to protect with any legal safeguards, criminal or administrative. Is it not, then, an illegitimate overreach for critics of the appearance standard to demand protections against factual prejudgment and legal retroactivity appropriate to criminal proceedings? And if such "legalistic" claims *are* misplaced outside of criminal settings, does the appearance standard really pose any kind of moral dilemma at all?

Any presumption that "criminal" procedural safeguards are required only in formally criminal proceedings is, however, out of keeping with both evolving constitutional law and much contemporary legal theory.[5] If the essense of the criminal-style sanction—and the reason why those subject to it need heightened procedural safeguards—is that it is morally "stigmatizing," "censuring," and "condemnatory";[6] and if the "stigmatic effects" of a sanction center on "impaired reputation," "diminished employment prospects," "social ostracism," and "damaged self-image,"[7] then a citation for "the appearance of official impropriety" plainly possesses the character of a criminal sanction.[8] If the "fundamental principles of due process require a positive correlation between severity of sanction on the one hand and stringency of procedural protections on the other"—if it is the possibility of moral stigma which ought to trigger criminal-procedural protections—then appearance defendants ought *prima facie* to have available appropriate legal-procedural safeguards.[9] Because appearance proceedings typically risk violating due-process rights against factual prejudgment and legal retroactivity, any heightened safeguards should focus on them.[10]

Neither contemporary legal theory nor constitutional law would thus reject *prima facie*—on the grounds that appearance proceedings are not formally criminal affairs—appearance-defendants' claims not to be factually prejudged, nor be made subject to retroactive norms. But more important, the *prima facie* dismissal of such legalistic concerns is foreign to appearance "jurisprudence" itself. Of course, no one proposes to hamstring the presidential appointment power with legalistic procedures. But even in the case of officials removable at will by the president (and not simply those removable for cause through administrative proceedings), if the appearance-defendant is thought to have been subjected to substantial prejudgment on the facts, or to substantially retroactive norms, his case is unlikely to be uncontroversial or regarded as wholly unproblematic.[11] It is not just that those *defending* an alleged appearance-transgressor regularly appeal to legal norms or common-moral sensibilities in objecting to his punishment in the face of less than fully-explored factual situations, or in the face of retroactively-imposed norms. It is that no one filling the *prosecutorial* role in appearance proceedings, either, has ever dismissed the *prima facie* legitimacy of defendants' claims against factual prejudgment or retroactive law, on the grounds that such claims apply only in formally criminal cases. Indeed, because appearance tribunals and "prosecutors" emphasize the moral seriousness—the near-criminal nature—of appearance violations and penalties, it would be inconsistent for prosecutors to dismiss them.

While appearance-standard proponents never dismiss legalistic principles *prima facie,* they do argue that those principles are trumped by an overriding political end. As the federal appearance rule itself originally stated, the standard is required to preserve public confidence in government. Three conjoined claims are actually at work here.[12] First, mere *appearances* or *perceptions* of official impropriety erode public confidence and trust in the individual officials concerned;[13] indeed, they are among the principal causes of such erosion.[14] Second, the erosion of confidence or trust in particular officials has a tendency to reflect not just on those officials as individuals but to "metastasize" into an erosion of confidence or trust in government as a whole.[15] And finally, beyond a *de minimis* point, the erosion of confidence in government will begin seriously to impair the workings of liberal-democratic regimes.[16] By seeking to sanction individual cases of apparent official impropriety, the appearance standard, it is said, plays a central role in protecting the health of the polity through the preservation of public confidence in government. Of course, only if an apparent impropriety takes place in the absence of any real underlying impropriety does it make sense to speak of the ensuing loss of public confidence as a vanished civic good, rather than as a lost public delusion.[17] Indeed, only in the absence of any real impropriety does it necessarily make sense to describe lost "public confidence" as the leading victim of an apparent impropriety; otherwise, it may be more reasonable to speak of actual damage to the "public weal" or some comparable entity.

In its fundamentals, then, the appearance standard's central moral tension displays the following two poles: On the one hand, there are those who believe in the insuperable applicability of two fundamental legal principles that preclude "punishment without crime" and "crime without law," factual pre-judgment and legal retroactivity. On the other hand, there are those who be-lieve that in the case of public officials, these principles can and should be "trumped" by a particular political imperative: the need to preserve public confidence in government. In the next chapter, I assess the legal arguments against and then, in the subsequent chapter, the political argument in favor of the appearance standard.

20

The Legalistic Attack on the
Appearance Standard

Factual Prejudgment

How does the appearance standard entail an element of antilegalistic, factual prejudgment? In appearance cases, the facts are prejudged because no trier of fact weighs all the evidence, exculpating and mitigating as well as incriminating, against a legal standard-of-proof, in order to establish that an act of official impropriety has been committed. Instead, the task for the entity disciplining the official in appearance cases—whether administrative board, congressional committee, president, or court—is to estimate the (more or less incomplete) level of the public's factual knowledge of the case, and the (more or less) prejudiced inferences the public will draw from that knowledge. If the public so imagined would believe that an act of official impropriety has occurred, the disciplining entity must conclude that a violation of the appearance standard has taken place. The disciplining entity may then impose sanctions. Hence, viewed legalistically, appearance proceedings entail "punishment without a crime."

Structurally, the factual prejudgment that the appearance standard may be said to entail consists of three elements: (a) an officeholder who did not commit a real official impropriety; (b) a public which, to a greater or lesser extent, believes that the officeholder did commit that impropriety; and (c) a disciplining entity which (i) has no knowledge—that is, no legally sufficient basis to conclude—that a real official impropriety has in fact been committed, but (ii) does have reason to conclude that the public, to a greater or lesser extent, believes a real official impropriety has been committed, and (iii) on these bases punishes the officeholder for committing an appearance violation. It will be helpful to examine (a), (b), and (c) in turn.

The assumption that the officeholder is innocent of any real official impropriety, as stipulated in (a), is central to the moral issue. In practice, of course, the appearance standard may well be applied in "gray area" cases where an officeholder's innocence of real official impropriety is borderline, technical, or uncertain. It has almost certainly been used in situations when an office-holder committed a real official impropriety (or, at least, the disciplining entity so believed), but the disciplining entity did not think it had the evidence necessary to mount a winning case.[1] Here, instead of belying a hidden reality of propriety, the appearance of impropriety indicates the unprovable reality of impropriety. In these cases, a public convinced (on the basis of appearances) of the officeholder's guilt would still be prejudging him in a formal legal sense—by "prejudge," I mean coming to a judgment in the absence of all the pertinent facts—but it would not be *mis*judging him in any deeper, more substantive moral or political fashion, that is, coming to a wrong judgment. And when, in such a situation, the disciplining entity finds the officeholder guilty of an appearance violation, it is best understood to be convicting him of a lesser legal offense, not performing a political act designed to restore the lost good of public confidence. When the appearance standard is used to punish a real violator, it involves no morally problematic prejudgment on the part of the public, nor does it represent an attempt, on the part of the disciplining entity, to restore lost but merited confidence. To preserve, for purposes of analysis, the appearance standard's central moral tension between legal norms and political ends, I henceforth assume that the standard is applied only when no real official impropriety has been committed.

Consider (b)—the stipulation that the public has prejudged the case, that is, judged, on the basis of an incomplete assessment of the facts, that the officeholder committed a real official impropriety. We can distinguish this type of prejudgment from instances in which the public, seized with the incompleteness of the facts at hand (or at least sensitive to the possibility that those facts may be incomplete) suspends judgment—as, for example, when "polls indicate[d] that many people [were] withholding judgment about White-water because they know too little about it."[2] To the extent that the public's judgment remains tentative or inconclusive in the face of an incomplete factual record, a full prejudgment has not taken place. Alternatively, we might imagine situations in which the public amasses all the facts of a case but then still concludes—erroneously but honestly—that the official committed an impropriety when in fact he did not. When a mistaken judgment is made in the face of a complete factual record, it is a form of misjudgment—not prejudgment.

As a matter of practice, situations of suspended judgment and situations of misjudgment are much less common than the one in which the public forms a (more or less) conclusive judgment on the basis of a (more or less) incomplete set of facts. As a matter of definitional principle, neither situation gives rise to the problem I am calling "the appearance of official impropriety." For an appearance of official impropriety to arise, the public must prejudge the issue. It must come to a *judgment*—a mistaken judgment—that the innocent officeholder committed an official impropriety, and it must do so *pre-* (that is, prior to) an acquisition of all the facts, in other words, on the basis of appearances. More exactly, the disciplining entity must conclude that the public has done so. The disciplining entity's judgment that an appearance of official impropriety has occurred thus necessitates its imputing to the public, and then giving legal effect to, a measure of prejudgment.

Let us now turn to a consideration of (c), a disciplining entity which, having no legally sufficient basis to conclude that the officeholder committed a real official impropriety, but judging that the public nevertheless believes he did, determines that an appearance violation has occurred. Described this way, the disciplining entity itself engages in no prejudgment. The disciplining entity itself does not judge, in the absence of all of the facts, that a real impropriety occurred. Rather, it judges that an appearance of impropriety arose in the public mind, and it does so on the basis of a different set of facts than those required to establish the real crime. From its own perspective, the disciplining entity does not punish officials because they *appeared* to it to commit the crime of real official impropriety. Rather, it punishes them because they *really* committed something called "the appearance of official impropriety." If the disciplining entity properly judges that an appearance of official impropriety did occur, and forbears from concluding that the *reality* occurred, it engages in no prejudgment. The disciplining entity would, however, not be punishing the official in the first place unless the public *had* prejudged him on the question of real official impropriety.

On what basis might the disciplining entity determine that an appearance violation has taken place? Its task is to ascertain the extent of the public's prejudgment of the case, which means it must come to some determination as to the conclusiveness of the public's judgment and the completeness of the factual knowledge on which it is based. Such a task is contoured by the following premises: First, the more tentative or withheld the public's judgment remains in any given case, the less likely it is that any appearance of impropriety will settle in, or that any full-blown loss of confidence will ensue. Second, assuming—as I have been—that appearance transgressions take place in the absence of any real official impropriety, the more familiar the disciplining entity can assume the public is with all the facts of a case—the more aware the public becomes of their mitigating complexity—the less likely it is that any incriminating appearance will materialize, or that any loss of confidence will result. "The need to avoid . . . the appearance of impropriety," one observer has written, "requires persons to think about and understand how certain conduct they know to be innocent will look to others" at a distance; another speaks of the "superficial appearance of evil, which a knowledge of the facts will dissipate."[3]

The opposite, of course, is usually the case when the impropriety is real:

With real impropriety, the less the public knows of the facts (or the more obscured its understanding of them), the less likely it will appear as if the official did something wrong. Conversely, the more that comes out, the more it will seem as if the official did something wrong until, at last, with all the facts on the table, the reality of his guilt is established. Thus it is that we simultaneously require officeholders to conduct themselves to both pass muster even under the gaze of the most "casual observer" and bear "the closest scrutiny."[4] There is no contradiction or even tension here: The first criterion deals with apparent impropriety, the second with real impropriety.

Given the impossibility of determining definitively and empirically, in any given case, the extent of the public's factual knowledge, and the firmness of the judgment it has made on the basis of that knowledge, the issue for the disciplining entity then becomes: What measure of prejudgment should be imputed to the public as a general rule? No disciplining entity, it should be emphasized, ever establishes that the public has actually taken notice of the facts or formed the judgments that comprise the appearance. In the *Wild* case, for example, the level of "the public's awareness of Wild's affiliation with the agency was presumed by the court; . . . HUD offered no *evidence* that Wild's activities were known by the general public."[5] The appearance is always imputed, never proved, and the question then is: What standard should the tribunal use? Here, a spectrum exists, from a reasonable, well-informed public to a cynical ill-informed public.

The one pole is represented in the position taken by the U.S. Office of Government Ethics and by the Senate counsel in the Keating Five Inquiry. According to it, the disciplining entity should consider whether an appearance of official impropriety would register in the mind of a "reasonable, well-informed observer."[6] Since relatively few innocent officials are likely to appear to commit improprieties to a public that assimilates a large preponderance of the facts while remaining careful not to leap to judgments, a "reasonable, well-informed public" constitutes a high threshold. At the opposite pole, consequently, are those who object that while assuming such a public might approach legal fairness, it also runs the risk of collapsing the entire distinction between appearances and realities.[7] For them, "appearance exists [precisely] where we do not know what went on," and the disciplining entity should therefore consider whether an appearance of impropriety would register in the minds of "[c]itizens [who] have no way of finding out what the reality is" and who are "ethically justified" in "assum[ing] the worst."[8] Here, the standard might be an "unknowing and disrespectful public" or the "most suspicious and cynical members of society."[9] Such an approach would impose on officeholders the obligation "to avoid any circumstances that could be misunderstood or misconstrued in any way"; to not "allow misperceptions, however ill-founded, to arise," and to "guard against even marginally credible allegations."[10]

My interest here lies not in resolving this dispute but simply in schematizing what is at stake in it. Specifically, it is only as we move down the spectrum of ever-more limited factual knowledge and increasingly conclusive judgment on the part of the public that "appearance" itself—as a distinct category—emerges and then grows. And, in lockstep, so do both the political arguments for, and the legalistic objections to, invoking the appearance standard. The political argument for the standard—that it is needed to deal with and deter blows to public confidence—has its greatest force when citizens come to conclusive judgments about officials in the face of incomplete information. The legal argument against the standard—that its imposition involves the disciplining entity's giving legal force to a public prejudgment of crime—equally increases as the public "trier of fact" is presumed to be less informed and more judgmental.[11] To the extent that it is geared toward preserving confidence in the eyes not just of reasonable well-informed citizens, but of those who are ill-informed and judgmental, the appearance standard will both do the greatest amount of political good and represent the greatest violation of legal justice.

Legal Retroactivity

What does it mean to say that the appearance standard entails antilegalistic, retroactive law-making? Appearance proceedings often retroactively make offenses of the acts they prosecute because no law governing official impropriety, either in letter or in spirit, prohibited those acts when they were committed. Had there been such a law, the charge in question would have been brought under *it,* and not under the appearance standard. Insofar as the appearance standard is itself an existing law, its application is not *literally* retroactive. But since it enjoins officials from "creat[ing] an appearance that they are violating an [ethics] law or [other ethics] standards," to transgress the appearance rule, it would seem, is explicitly to do something other than break any existing laws governing official impropriety, including the conflict-of-interest laws. If the appearance rule *is* a law, it is a uniquely "out-of-law" law, conceived not as part but rather as something exclusive of the extant body of relevant statutes and standards.[12] Whatever acts it might prohibit are expressly not acts that the polity has seen fit, through the legislative and rulemaking organs of government, to make the subject of any existing ethics law.[13]

The reason is that the appearance standard, in its "normative" cast, explicitly concerns acts about whose moral status there is simply insufficient social agreement for legislation or regulation: All that can be said is that they *look* wrong. To say that an official did something that *looks* wrong is to enter a realm of normative uncertainty in which citizens more or less disagree—whether within or between themselves, whether contemporaneously or over time—whether a given act is or should be deemed "official impropriety." Notwithstanding the formal existence of the appearance rule, then, the term "appearance of official impropriety" is arguably so vague that the rule's application, in a given situation, is nothing the officeholder could have anticipated. The standard thus becomes retroactive for all intents and purposes.[14] A law "so vague that [people] of common intelligence must necessarily guess at its meaning and differ as to its application [may begin to] violate the first essential of due process."[15]

Many laws—those governing obscenity, for example—are inscribed with vague terms and hence are potentially retroactive in effect. But such other vague laws differ from the appearance standard in at least two respects. First, obscenity laws cover categories of acts that, whatever their precise borders might be in practice, the legislature has shown itself willing to bring under the law and to stamp as criminal. With the appearance standard, by contrast, the legislature has explicitly not seen fit to bring the acts in question under the laws governing official impropriety, nor otherwise to stamp them as real crimes. In the second place, when the courts determine whether a given act falls into the class of obscenity, the law assumes a community consensus or norm to which judges and juries can refer. Obscene acts, for instance, might have to be deemed "exceptionally morally repugnant by persons of ordinary sensibilities."[16] When it comes to adjudication under the appearance standard, by contrast, we are by definition dealing with acts about whose normative status the community—persons of "ordinary sensibilities"—are likely to disagree, perhaps deeply. For "a court . . . to adopt . . . values that are not generally shared by the community and that have not been approved by the community's representative institutions [is to] undermine the possibility of rendering decisions that will be perceived as fair."[17] It is this kind of legal injustice, an amalgam of legal retroactivity and vagueness, that its critics see in the appearance standard.

Certainly, concerning the normative status of any given act of apparent impropriety there may be more or less social disagreement, and so the complaint of retroactivity and vagueness can have more or less credibility. At one end of the spectrum, there may be situations where an act—although not yet prohibited in the letter nor even the spirit of the law—is nevertheless deemed an "official impropriety" by a preponderance of the public. To the extent that such a sentiment is clear and widely held, an officeholder who commits the act cannot credibly claim that the appearance standard is being applied against her wholly *ex post facto*.[18] And, to the extent that public disapproval is substantial in this way, those disciplining the officeholder can plausibly charge that her conduct has done considerable injury to public confidence. Where there is substantial—if not complete—normative agreement that a particular act constitutes official impropriety, any moral tension involved in imposing the standard will thus be lopsided: there will be little retroactivity, but a considerable gain to public confidence. So in the case of Office of Government Ethics Letter 85X19, where an official—within the letter of the law—took anonymous contributions for his legal defense fund, if a substantial majority viewed this as a violation of the conflict-of-interest law's prophylactic spirit, then punishing him retroactively would involve less injustice, and a greater restorative to public confidence, than if the public were divided on the question.

As we then move out along the spectrum toward a class of acts subject to greater normative disagreement, however, the more plausible will be the claim that the appearance standard is being interpreted in a way the putative transgressor could not have anticipated, and the less plausible the claim that the conduct in question will substantially erode public confidence. "[W]hen public attitudes toward sexual conduct are shifting," for example, "there is usually little reason to believe the disclosure of the conduct will cause much political damage" in the way of "undermin[ing] confidence."[19] Finally, if we were to move to a point at which very few people saw the conduct in question as official impropriety, then "retroactivity" arguments against criminalizing it through the appearance standard would carry great weight, while the gains in public confidence would be negligible—or even negative. All of this suggests that in "normative" appearance trials, the greatest tensions between (a) the legal stricture against retroactive law and (b) the political benefit that derives from shoring up public confidence will arise where the polity is deeply and evenly divided, whether between or within individual citizens, on the normative issue.[20]

Finally, as public discourse suggests, the type of normative disagreement that allows for the very possibility of "the appearance of official impropriety" is often contoured around two distinct issues: what it means for an act to be "official" and what it means for an act to be "improper."[21] There will be little normative disagreement on either score when, for example, a customs employee uses smuggled narcotics—little disagreement, if not absolutely none.[22] Here the officeholder is engaging in conduct widely regarded as both *improper* and as possessed of an *official* "nexus"[23]—official, in that it impedes, contradicts, or defeats the purposes for which the official is working in public life. Frequently, however, we find ourselves in situations in which there is more argument and controversy on the one score and less on the other. For example, in his "personal" life an official may be committing acts that are unarguably or uncontroversially immoral but that also can only *arguably* or *controversially* be said to defeat or contradict the purposes for which he is working in public life—that is, they can only arguably or controversially be said to have an "official nexus." Falling into this category would be the case of a Securities and Exchange Commission (SEC) officeholder who commits acts of domestic violence.[24] Here, the official import of the unambiguously improper conduct falls into a kind of penumbra zone, turning as it does on questions such as, "To what extent are the particular responsibilities of his office associated with law enforcement broadly understood?" or "To what extent has the administration made family violence a policy priority?" These are issues that may invite disagreement or ambiguity. Nevertheless, the official is at the very least obligated to admit to, correct for, and pay the price of his improper behavior—even if he continues to assert that, by his own lights, he has done nothing that could appear to be *official* impropriety, or that renders him unfit for his particular public office.

A converse set of cases arises where, in his personal life, an official may be committing acts that are only arguably or controversially morally unacceptable, but that *un*arguably or *un*controversially defeat or contradict the purposes for which he has chosen to work in public life. Consider, for example, the attorney general who belongs to an all-white or all-male club. Such an official can at the very least be expected to apologize for having allowed his personal conduct to undermine his capacities as a public official, and to correct for and alter his behavior. He can be expected to do so even if, by his own lights, he is unprepared to say that the conduct in question was improper, that it violated any moral norms—associative norms of "private" life—as he, along with a good section of the public, had always understood them.

Legal Norms and the Appearance Standard: A Summary

The legalistic attack on the appearance standard rests on a certain view of the domain in which legalistic arguments and considerations are apt. It is an expansive, substantive view—one consonant with much contemporary jurisprudence and deeply implanted in the moral problem as participants in appearance discourse conceive it. Of course, on a more strictly circumscribed or formalistic understanding, norms against prejudgment and retroactivity might be deemed inapplicable in appearance proceedings, or indeed in any domain outside of the criminal. But current legal theory, constitutional law, public discourse, and a common-moral attentiveness to "humane interests" have all lent those norms a central place in administrative and political terrain—such as the appearance proceeding—that lies far beyond the formally criminal.

In the same strictly formal way, the appearance standard itself, as an extant law, is not retroactive. Nor, in determining whether an official committed an appearance violation *per se,* need the disciplining entity itself prejudge the pertinent facts. But for participants in appearance discourse, what matters are the moral questions that arise not when the standard is viewed abstractly and formally but when it is read against the political and legal context in which it is embedded. What matters is how appearance cases map onto—what they mean in terms of—the realm of whatever society deems to be real crime and real law. And here critics see the appearance standard as involving punishment without any (real) crime, or crime without any (real) law. It involves punishment without a judge, jury, or other body having found a real crime, but it gives legal—that is, punitive—effect precisely to a public prejudgment of the facts of the case. And it creates crime without a legislature having passed a law so stipulating—indeed, without a widespread public consensus having so invested the law—but rather precisely on the basis of the retroactive instantiation of norms controversial within the public.

Appearances and *Quid Pro Quo:* A Loose End

One question lurks here. Is *quid pro quo*—the kind that dominates daily democratic discourse—better understood as a real or an apparent impropriety? Answer: It has characteristics of both. In one sense, *quid pro quo* can be construed as the appearance of bribery. Quid pro quo betokens a set of situations that—either because we are uncertain factually or disagree normatively—do not rise to the level of a legally actionable bribe. A congressman, say, takes a campaign contribution from the insurance industry and later votes against the Clinton health-care package. Factually, in such a case, we cannot establish any connection between contribution and vote in a way that meets criminal standards. Normatively we cannot say, with sufficient consensus, that such a connection—unless it did rise to the level of bribery—would be transgressive of democratic principles. All that remains is an appearance—an appearance of bribery. And yet, *quid pro quo*-committing officials are rarely cited under the appearance standard for allowing an appearance of bribery to arise. The *quid pro quo*s that so engross us go largely unpunished, whether under the appearance standard or any other law.

The reason is that *quid pro quo,* like bribery—but unlike most of the other conflict-of-interest categories—is a nonprophylactic offense. To conclude that either a bribe *or* a *quid pro quo* has occurred we must be satisfied that a particular mental event, a *malum in se* itself, has actually taken place; we must be satisfied that the official actually was motivated, influenced, or incited to perform an official act because of some sort of private favor. For bribery, we require a high level of factual certainty and normative clarity about that mental event, a level sufficient to bring a legal case. For *quid pro quo* we require a lower level of factual certainty and normative clarity, a level sufficient only to start a political discussion. And yet, because both *quid pro quo* and bribery subsist in the mental states of officials, and although *quid pro quo* might constitute the appearance of bribery, it is rarely corrigible in the way most appearances of impropriety are. It is *relatively* easy to determine whether what appears to be a federal bank regulator holding a federal bank loan is, in reality, a federal bank regulator holding a state bank loan. It is far less easy to say whether a *quid pro quo* is really a bribe. To do the former we need more facts about the external world; to do the latter we need more facts about the official's inner state.

This is why *quid pro quo* rarely dissolves into either innocence or guilt. *Quid pro quo*s just sit there in a nether world, albeit a nether world at the center of democratic political debate. True, they fail to rise to the level of legally established bribery and so are properly called "appearances" of some sort. Yet they come much closer to the actual *malum in se* than do most real conflict-of-interest offenses, having already pierced the prophylactic veil and crossed the frontier of mental state. No wonder, then, that we remain skittish about pursuing most kinds of *quid pro quo* under the appearance standard. After all, doing so would require a disciplining entity to divine the public's state of mind not about a set of external facts surrounding the officeholder, but about the officeholder's own state of mind.

What results instead is the kind of polarization on display in the Senate's 1991 censure of Senator Alan Cranston, whose official efforts on behalf of Charles Keating and requests that Keating contribute to Cranston's voter-registration organizations were made—repeatedly—in close proximity of one another. On the one hand, Senator Howell Heflin emphasized that this proximity was *so* great that it was Cranston's actual "improper conduct, and not the appearance of impropriety, that caused the [ethics] committee's reprimand." On the other hand, Senator Warren Rudman—in countering Cranston's claim that *any* senator who helps a campaign contributor creates the appearance of impropriety—retorted that "the committee unequivocally rejects that [notion]."[25] When it comes to cases of *quid pro quo,* officials are more comfortable parsing them into the categories of real impropriety or real propriety; to open the door here to the appearance standard would be to grab a tiger by the tail.

21

The Political Justification for the Appearance Standard

Formalistic circumspection about wielding legal norms has played no role in appearance discourse, where legalistic concerns are not only accorded *prima-facie* validity but form one pole of the debate. But what of the other pole? Are there democratic principles on which the standard's political purpose— requiring officials to preserve confidence in government—can justify the kind and degree of prejudgment and retroactivity often involved? The appearance standard calls upon officials to do something above and beyond simply not committing any real official improprieties. Of what does this extra layer of commitment consist? Is it a reasonable one to impose on democratic officeholders?

To pursue this question, it will prove helpful to explore certain features shared by appearance proceedings on the one hand and some of the major political trials of the century on the other—the Moscow Trials of the 1930s and the war crimes trials at Nuremberg. Just to be explicit about the obvious, I am not suggesting that the crimes punished at Nuremberg can be placed on the same scale as an appearance of official impropriety. Nor am I suggesting that the penalties inflicted by the legal system itself at Moscow are commensurate with the sanctions to which appearance violators are subject. The use of analogy requires that there be "some shared characteristics" between the analogized cases, but this "does not mean that all characteristics are shared."[1] The major political trial and the appearance proceeding do display some shared characteristics, because each subverts legal norms for the sake of political ends—albeit ends with vast differences in moral character—and each is concerned preponderantly with officials, not citizens. In any case, an analogy such as this, as Cass R. Sunstein points out, is useful not to the extent that Moscow and Nuremberg are *proximately similar* to the appearance proceeding, but rather to the extent that they are *plausibly relevant* to it: the use of "analogy depends on the fact that there are both plausibly relevant differences and plausibly relevant similarities between" the two classes or cases in question.[2] Both similarities and differences, in other words, can be illuminating as long as they are "relevant" to the analytical purpose at hand.

The Political Trial

"What the principle of legality demands," Judith N. Shklar writes, "is a law, and also an act made criminal by law. In political [trials] either one or the other or both may be lacking."[3] The "first possibility," Shklar continues—the situation in which "there is law, but no criminal act"—was exemplified at Moscow. The "second possibility—that there is no law which designates the actual acts performed as criminal"—characterized Nuremberg.[4]

At Moscow, defendants were tried under established revolutionary law not for acts they had already committed but rather for "future, potential, as yet uncontemplated acts."[5] Or, to the extent that they were tried for acts they had actually committed, it was "for the unintended, as yet unrealized, future consequences of those acts."[6] However "subjectively" innocent the Moscow defendant might have been, Shklar says, the "objective" laws of history made it possible to impute crime to him before the fact—before the fact of a guilty state-of-mind let alone an offensive act. In this sense, the Moscow trials were what Shklar, quoting Merleau-Ponty, calls "drama[s] of historical responsibility, of subjective innocence and objective treason."[7]

Here, of course, Shklar's use of the terms "objective" and "subjective" do not refer—as they did in my discussions of "conflict" and "interest"—to the different approaches we might take in plumbing the mental state of officeholders as they judge the public issues before them. Rather, the terms refer to different ways of characterizing the mental state of the public—or, more exactly, to the kinds of institutions and instruments the public might bring to bear—in judging officeholders. "Objectivity," as John Calvin Jeffries notes, refers to legal findings that issue from an "official, authoritative, judicial process," while "subjectivity" characterizes the factual reality as it would appear from a "lay, non-authoritative" perspective.[8] It was from the prevailing "official, authoritative, judicial" perspective—in other words, from an "objective" standpoint—that the Moscow defendants were guilty. But from any lay, non-authoritative, perspective—in the world, that is, as it would have appeared to most people subjectively—there was absolutely no evidence of guilt.[9]

"Whatever the motives of the accused and the actual character of their acts at the time of commission," Shklar concludes in discussing Moscow,

> if these acts had an effect harmful to the progress of revolution, [then the accused] were responsible and indeed guilty on the basis of revolu-

tionary justice. [At Moscow] error was crime. The point is, of course, that even the erroneous character of the "criminal" action remain[ed] to be revealed in the future and [was] still a matter of conjecture at the time of the trial . . . [10]

For all practical purposes, then, the Moscow defendant was convicted of "err[ing] in his predictions," of showing a lack of "total prescience."[11] In that they presented factual prejudgment—punishment without crime—on a grand scale, the Moscow trials were essentially "trials of the remote future."[12]

The situation with Nuremberg was the reverse: There, monstrous acts had demonstrably been committed, but no law yet existed by which they could have been judged illegal. The idea of "a charge that had never even been heard of before the trial"—crimes against humanity—however defensible on any moral argument, nevertheless remains "foreign to legal traditions."[13] Indeed, in the case of Nuremberg, not only did the violated law not exist at the time of the acts in question, neither did the presiding trial court nor even the relevant judicial system.[14] Nuremberg, as Shklar puts it, was an endeavor in "trying the past"; it presented legal retroactivity—crime without law—on a grand scale.[15]

Moscow and Nuremberg each suborned legal norms to political purposes. Of course, there are crucial moral differences between Moscow and Nuremberg, which consist largely in the political ends served in each case. Because Nuremberg was meant to teach a supreme political lesson—that high public officials must place the dictates of individual conscience rightly informed above those of prevailing social mores—the trial was justified. Because the Moscow trials placed spuriously politicized notions of historical guilt above personal innocence, they were not. "As in all political trials," Shklar concludes, "it is not the trial itself that is important, but the political values involved. The question is always, 'What politics?'"[16] It now remains to examine further the structure of the (a) factual prejudgment and (b) legal retroactivity entailed in appearance proceedings, and to do so in light of the major political trials. From such an examination will emerge a more exact answer, in the case of appearance proceedings, to the question that Shklar says must be asked of all political trials: What are the political ends to be served, and can they justify the violation of legal norms involved?

Political Trials, the Appearance Standard, and Factual Prejudgment

First, consider the structural resemblances and differences between the type of factual prejudgment exhibited at Moscow and that entailed in appearance proceedings. At Moscow, as Shklar notes, the defendants could have been found guilty only in an "objective" sense. It was a set of "objective" laws—the only objective laws operative at the time were those pertaining to "historical truth"—that were used to attribute criminal acts to the defendants. The use of the term "objectivity" here by Shklar, of course, runs along the lines Owen Fiss suggests: "An objective interpretation is not necessarily a correct one . . . Objectivity speaks to the constraining force of the rules and whether the act of judging is constrained; correctness speaks to the content of the rules."[17] In appearance cases, by contrast, it is precisely in an "objective" sense that the defendants are innocent. For in appearance cases, the only relevant "objective law"—the objective legal standards pertaining to fact and evidence—is not invoked to attribute criminal acts to the accused. Indeed, the conduct in question raises an appearance issue precisely because, on objective legal standards of fact determination, no official impropriety has been committed.

On the other hand, as Shklar says, at Moscow the defendants were "subjectively innocent"—innocent, that is, from the perspective of the vast majority of human subjects. From no known "subjective" or "human" perspective, using the five senses available to human beings, could one conceivably have come to the factual conclusion reached by the reigning "objective" law. If appearance-defendants are guilty of a crime, by contrast, it is *only* in a subjective sense. Much of the public perceives them to have done something wrong: One thinks here of the frequent use of the term "smell test" in appearance-discourse and proceedings, and the typical use of the term "subjective" to describe appearance-situation judgments of fact.[18] The Moscow defendants were "subjectively" innocent even if somehow "objectively" guilty. At appearance proceedings, the defendants are "objectively" innocent even if in some sense "subjectively" guilty.

When they are described in this way, one important "plausibly relevant" similarity and one important "plausibly relevant" difference emerge between the type of factual prejudgment characteristic of a major political trial on the one hand and that symptomatic of appearance cases on the other. The two are similar, in that a significant element of antilegalistic unfairness results—in either case—from a divergence between objective and subjective determinations of fact. Unfairness results, in other words, from a willingness to validate and act upon factual conclusions that are based on only one of the two criteria, subjective or objective, even when the other does not lend its support. To judge the facts on the basis of an objective historical algorithm in advance of any subjective confirmation from the five senses, or else to judge the facts on a subjective, perceptual basis in advance of any objective, procedural confirmation, is—in either case—to *pre*-judge.

The two situations are dissimilar, however, in that the peculiar failure of the defendant differs in each case. As Shklar notes, the fact that, at Moscow, subjectively innocent defendants were found objectively guilty means that they were convicted of making errors in "prediction." They were guilty not of a legitimately adjudged crime but of a political ineptitude—the inability to place themselves in the position of a vanguard and to see the facts by the lights of "history." In many appearance situations, by contrast, the fact that objectively innocent officials are nevertheless "subjectively" guilty means that—to employ the vernacular frequently used by both principals and commentators—they are guilty of an error in "perception."[19] They failed to realize how things would look, how they would be perceived. Such officials are guilty not of a crime but of a political incapacity—the inability to place themselves in the position of the public and to see the facts by the lights of the polity. An error of perception is not the same thing as an error of prediction. Penalizing the latter is a good deal more troubling than penalizing the former. Nevertheless, both are more readily classifiable as political errors than as legal crimes. Perhaps this is why, in both political trials and appearance proceedings, a notable proportion of those deemed to have committed the act in question are either made to confess (in the case of political trials), or else choose to confess (as is the case with appearance proceedings), to "mistakes" and not to "misfeasance."[20]

Political Trials, the Appearance Standard, and Legal Retroactivity

Consider, now, the structural resemblances and differences between the type of retroactive law imposed at Nuremberg and that entailed in appearance cases. Nuremberg defendants argued that neither prevailing law nor prevailing social mores criminalized the acts in question at the time they were committed. To such an argument, the principal response has always been that regardless of the prevailing norms, the defendants' personal consciences should have rebelled at the prospect of committing such acts. Legally criminalizing them *ex post facto* was far from indefensible.

Officials who complain about the *ex post facto* character of the appearance standard, by contrast, argue—with no small degree of plausibility—that their consciences are clear. They claim to see nothing officially improper in what they did, and they contend that they therefore could not have been expected to anticipate the "criminalization" of their actions. The obvious and typical response is that whatever his conscience may in fact have been telling the officeholder at the time, social-political mores in at least some part of the polity had already begun condemning the acts in question. Punishing those acts *ex post facto*—legally validating *ex post facto* what a sensitivity to social-moral developments might have told the officeholder at the time—is far from indefensible.

Thus officeholders miss the mark when—as they often do—they defend themselves from appearance charges by insisting that their consciences are clear, and that they are being judged against social norms that have not been embodied in law. In the final days of the Jim Wright affair, the *New York Times'* Michael Oreskes showcased a peculiar line of argument employed by the Speaker and some of his defenders. The Speaker, it was being said in his defense, was "sticking to his guns," displaying "guts," standing up for what he knew to be right even though the bulk of society saw it differently, and so on.[21] "Integrity," the Speaker himself had written, "is not merely a matter of financial honesty or moral behavior . . . [it is] the state or quality of being complete, undivided or unbroken . . . [i]ntegrity, then, is first and foremost the condition of being oneself."[22] One of Wright's congressional defenders, Oreskes further reported, had described the Speaker as being "'totally out of sync with the times,'" "meaning it," Oreskes went on to note, "very much as a compliment." The idea of being deliberately "out of sync" with the times, of pitting one's conscience against an evolving set of social mores, would— had it been available to any of them—have been an exonerating argument for a Nuremberg defendant. But Wright's situation was exactly the reverse. In his case, what was wanted was not a display of personal conscience but rather— to use the term most frequently employed—a show of "sensitivity" to social norms.[23] Or, as the *New York Times* editorialized, Speaker Wright's actions "from all appearances . . . violated *common* conscience."[24] "The essence of [Edwin] Meese's brief," the columnist Michael Kinsley wrote along similar lines, "is that by his own standards he has not merely done nothing illegal— he has done nothing wrong. Now that we know his standards, we can judge him by our own."[25]

Political Judgment and the Appearance Standard

On further exploration, then, both the political trial and the appearance proceeding hold officials to account for displaying particular sets of political incapacities. According to the reigning Stalinist fiction, the Moscow trials raised no insurmountable problem of factual prejudgment because the political figures in question ought to have exercised prescience. They should have been able to predict the historical consequences of their acts (or, in some cases, the acts themselves) by referring to revolutionary doctrine. And Nuremberg raised no insurmountable problem of legal retroactivity because the major political figures in question ought to have exercised their own consciences. Along similar lines, appearance proceedings—it is said—raise no morally fatal problem of factual prejudgment because the implicated officeholders ought to have been able to "perceive" their own acts in the same (before-the-established-fact) way others would. And appearance proceedings raise no morally fatal problem of legal retroactivity because implicated officeholders ought to have been "sensitive" to the (after-the-fact) interpretation that could be placed on the term "appearance of official impropriety" by others.

As political capacities go, there are of course important differences between prescience and conscience on the one hand, and the lower-grade faculties of perception and sensitivity on the other. The latter pair of qualities calls neither for impossible farsightedness nor extraordinary courage, and we may be less bothered by the "antilegalism" involved in ensuring their regular use by officeholders. Even so, to the extent that legalism is a handmaiden of liberalism, as Shklar claims it is, the appearance standard can be said to impose an illiberal regime on officeholders.[26] It does so to the end of penalizing those officeholders who—as many do in defending their actions—equate the lack of an objective, legal determination of guilt with the absence of any subjectively perceived wrongdoing, and who equate a clean conscience with a satisfactory sensitivity to public norms. The major political trials, notably, punished officials who did just the reverse. Nuremberg punished officials who equated a sensitivity to public norms with a clean conscience. And Moscow punished those who made the mistake of equating the lack of any subjectively perceivable wrongdoing with the absence of any possibility of an objective, legal determination of guilt. The appearance standard, then, places a set of illiberal constraints on officeholders in order to heighten their democratic representativeness—in order to ensure that officials perceive reality the way the public does and are sensitive to norms that the public harbors. This, in the case of the appearance standard, is the answer to the question that must be asked of all political trials, namely: What are the political ends served?

The Appearance Standard and Strict Liability

Let me turn briefly from the nature of the offensive acts to the status of the offending actor in appearance discourse. Assuming the appearance standard is politically justified, does it make sense to hold appearance offenders strictly liable? Or ought some form of fault—some intent to violate the standard, some knowledge that one was violating the standard—have to be shown?

As a matter of practice, those who fall afoul of the appearance standard are held strictly liable. This may seem strange, since in many cases of *actual* conflict of interest, strict liability and even general intent has been abandoned. But its abandonment has had to do with the peculiar nature of "actual" conflict-of-interest law. Recall that if conflict-of-interest law were ever to try directly prohibiting the moral harm in question—an impaired mental state—it would be intolerably vague (conflict-of-interest law thus operates at considerable prophylactic remove from the harm in question), but law so denuded of moral content relinquishes its capacity to hold offenders anything near strictly liable. The appearance standard, by contrast, does not operate at any such remove from the moral harm *it* seeks to prevent: the erosion of confidence in government. Indeed, it has the vague wording—"employees shall endeavor to avoid any actions creating the appearance that they are violating the law or the ethical standards"—to show for it. Strict liability, in one sense, becomes more justifiable the more tightly a law's language cleaves to the particular harm it seeks to regulate. And in any case, the more vague the law the more difficult it is to prove intent and knowledge.[27]

But suppose we *were* to abandon strict liability in appearance cases. Then, once an appearance of impropriety materialized in the public's mind, we might find ourselves holding the official concerned to a different level of perception and sensitivity, a different kind of mental state, than we attribute to the public. Yes, we would have to say of any given appearance case, perhaps the public's factual perceptions or normative sensitivities were tweaked—hence an offensive act was committed. But the official herself, because of her own factual or normative obtuseness, had neither knowledge of nor intent to commit an appearance violation. Hence she is not an offending actor. This kind of an approach, however, would defeat the very purpose of appearance law, which is to ensure an alignment between the perceptions and sensitivities of the official and the public. In appearance jurisprudence, then, to prove an offensive act *is* necessarily to prove an offending actor. And if to prove the offense is to prove the offender, then the offender is strictly liable.

Thus it is that the language of ordinary crime is less pertinent to appearance cases than is the language of political crime. Ordinary criminal jurisprudence concerns *acts* about whose moral status the legislature—and the public generally—have reached a consensus embodied in law. Where normative disagreement principally arises is over the moral responsibility of criminal *actors*, over the appropriate degree of fault or liability to be assigned in any given case. Political crime, by contrast, arises in a realm where there is a greater degree of controversy over the normative status of the acts in question, but where there is less controversy over the moral responsibility of the (official) actor.[28]

A Possible Communitarian Query

One might accept that maintaining the appearance of official propriety—and thus retaining public confidence in government—is of paramount importance and yet still query whether officeholders should bear sole (or even preponderant) responsibility under the standard. If citizens were more participatory and civic-minded—if they paid more reasoned attention to the facts, details, and nuances of public life—we would run into fewer factual appearance problems *per se*. And, when we did, the "prejudgment" objection to punishing the officials concerned would be weaker. Similarly, if citizens were to coalesce (more than they have done) around common political and moral norms, we would also run into fewer normative appearance problems, and, when we did, the *ex post facto* objection to punishing the officials concerned would be weaker. When appearances of official impropriety arise, in other words, the reason may not be that officeholders are lacking in the requisite representative-democratic capacities of perception and sensitivity. It may be that in their political lives, citizens are displaying traditionally "liberal"—thin, inadequate—civic capacities of engaged factual awareness and consensual norm formation. Appearance problems would abate, on this argument, as the citizenry evinced some of the participatory habits and concordant values advocated by contemporary communitarian political theorists.

What should we make of this "communitarian query?" Should we expect citizens to be better informed about the facts of public life, and more in accord about the norms of public life, than they currently are? The debate over the particular civic virtues liberal citizens should be expected to display is, of course, a central one in contemporary political philosophy. Its different participants impute specific sets of virtues to the ideal liberal citizen which vary dramatically on the spectrum from thin to thick, from less to more accommodative of the communitarian critique.[29] And, as might be expected, to the extent that the tranche of virtues in question is thinner and less accommodative of communitarian concerns, the writer in question—though not averse to the notion of liberal citizens displaying civic virtues *per se*—is nevertheless unlikely to require of citizens virtues sufficient to shoulder responsibility for ameliorating the appearance of official impropriety. Bruce Ackerman, for example, writes that "an ongoing commitment to informed citizenship may unduly deflect our energies from the struggles of everyday life."[30] George Kateb includes among the positive virtues of liberal citizenship "a pervasive skepticism" towards officials; one need not quarrel with the utility of such a virtue in order to believe that it predisposes citizens toward seeing the appearance of impropriety.[31] But even those liberals who go a significant way toward accommodating the communitarian critique stop short of including, among their suggested citizen virtues, those specifically necessary to ease appearances of official impropriety.[32]

Thus far, then, the weight of the discussion suggests that liberal citizens cannot, by and large, be expected to share a significant, ongoing responsibility for most appearances of official impropriety that may arise. The more important point, however, is that to the extent that we locate our polity on the liberal "end of the spectrum," then we will—and should—hold officeholders, not citizens, responsible for appearances of impropriety and for maintaining citizen confidence in government generally. At the deepest level, the appearance standard is thus a problem for liberal polities. The tension it raises—between the need to impose on officeholders the responsibility for promoting a fundamental political good and the need to extend to officeholders two fundamental norms of legalism—surfaces only to the extent that (thin) liberal conceptions of civic virtue and (substantive) liberal conceptions of legalistic justice reign.

Conclusion

In his study of Aristotle and Kant on political judgment, Ronald Beiner writes that the exercise of political judgment—on the part of political actors—must be premised on an awareness that "a situation without pre-judgments . . . would not be a human situation" and must involve an "understanding [of] the emotions, character and moral purpose of one's [public audience], as well as [an] anticipation of the emotions, character and moral purpose that they . . . will tend to ascribe to you."[33] A capacity to take into account the public's factual prejudgments, as well as an ability to anticipate the public's changing normative purposes—its political perception and political sensitivity—are traits central to a traditional western philosophical understanding of the nature of political judgment. If there is a political justification for the appearance standard, it is that it affords us a tool with which to elicit precisely this type of judgment from our public officials.

IV

REMEDIES

22

Recusal, Divestiture, Balance, and Disclosure

Conflict-of-interest law, as prophylactic law, both punishes and prevents. Most laws claim this twofold goal, of course. But in the case of *non*prophylactic law, the punishment itself becomes the preventive; it is the prospect of punishment *ex post* that affords the preventive *ex ante*. For prophylactic law, by contrast—and certainly for conflict-of-interest law—the mode of punishment and the mode of prevention differ. Conflict-of-interest law comes with both penalties *and* remedies.[1]

In its punitive mode, conflict-of-interest law for years provoked a debate centering on the relative appropriateness of criminal versus civil/administrative penalties. At the most practical level, the 1989 Ethics Reform Act resolved this disagreement by introducing, into the criminal statutes, a range of civil penalties which those prosecuting *and* those accused had demanded for decades, and whose impact was briefly discussed in Part I. On a more philosophical plane, the debate over punishment resolves itself into prior questions having to do with the very possibility of distinguishing criminal from civil or administrative sanctions of the sort pursued in Part III. Most conflict-of-interest law, though, contemplates the need not only to punish but prevent violators. And here, debate opens up onto a unique set of political and jurisprudential issues surrounding "remedy."

Conflict of interest lends itself to four remedies: recusal, divestiture/blind-trust, balance of interests, and public disclosure. Recusal, which removes the interested officeholder from any conflicting official roles, emerges from the practice of the judiciary. Divestiture/blind-trust, which removes any conflicting interests from the in-role officeholder, originates in the concept of the fiduciary. Of the four, recusal and divestiture/blind trust are the more venerable. No matter what level of American government one canvasses, the two constitute the only statutory or regulatory remedies to be found up until the 1960s.

Public disclosure and balance of interests, by contrast, are of more recent vintage. Although not unheard-of previously, they became serious possibilities for the first time in the 1960s. And, without in any way eclipsing recusal or divestiture-blind trust, they each attained widespread statutory or regulatory status in the 1970s. Whereas recusal and divestiture are distinctly legalistic in their cast, both public disclosure and balance of interests constitute more frankly political remedial approaches, resting not in conceptions of judicial rectitude or fiduciary trusteeship but in notions of democratic accountability (disclosure) and representative pluralism (balance).

Each of the political approaches represents a challenge to one of the two more longstanding legally derived remedies. Public disclosure, to begin with, inverts the principles that govern divestiture/blind-trust. Proponents of public disclosure argue that officeholders may legitimately remain in possession—and aware—of their financial interests as long as those interests are made visible to the public as well. Advocates of divestiture/blind-trust, by contrast, argue that as long as the public is going to remain *un*aware of an officeholder's private interests, then those interests should be made invisible or irrelevant to officials themselves. Divestiture's roots lie in "fiduciary" or "trustee" understandings of public office, understandings that impute to the principal (the public) a minimal capacity to understand and control the professional's (the official's) activities. Public disclosure, by contrast, exhibits affinities with "delegate" or "agency" understandings of public office, understandings that assume a maximal capacity for such knowledge and control.

In similar fashion, the newer political remedy of "balance of interests" upends the older law-based remedy of recusal. Balance rests on the idea that strongly interested officeholders are precisely what we want in certain situations. Provided the interests they represent are pluralized and strategically balanced, interest will counter interest, issuing forth in the public good: conflict*s* of interest as remedy for conflict of interest. Balance thus prevails as the remedy of choice when commissions and committees engage in collective policy-making for a defined, if pluralized, constituency. A task force setting microbiological criteria for food should, arguably, seat representatives from industry, consumer, health, and scientific organizations. And senators have been known to take into account balance within a department or agency when confirming appointees.[2]

Balance assumes an exact counterpoise of roles and a uniqueness of personnel across a particular range. If General Motors is represented on an automobile industry advisory committee, so should Ford be. Precisely because of the interests she represents or embodies, no official—that is, no member of such a decision-making body—can replace or be replaced by any other. Balance thus works most effectively when the decision process assumes a legislative or quasi-legislative form, and where a reliance on recusal would disenfranchise those for whom no other representative is available.[3] Or, as the legal scholar

Peter Strauss has written, "the wide range of officials who may participate in any given rule-making is itself some assurance of objectivity," and in such situations "recusal may, by changing [say, a] commission's balance," defeat "the considerations of diversity . . . that led to the selection of a multimember format" in the first place."[4]

Recusal, then, presumes precisely what balance must deny: an interchangeability of personnel, or a fungibility of role, at least across a particular range. It assumes that another official within the decision-making body can be found to replace the recusing one, and that "undelegable responsibilities within the federal executive establishment are comparatively rare."[5] Recusal is thus far more suited to a (quasi-) judicial than a (quasi-) legislative process, where one judge or decision-maker can easily substitute for another, and where the reliance on a pluralistic clash of interested officials would be particularly inapt.[6]

Remedies Intragovernmental and Extragovernmental

There is yet another (and cross-cutting) way of understanding the four remedies. Recusal and balance, although at odds in important respects, are mutual alternatives precisely because they both are "intragovernmental" remedies. To make them work, government bureaus must organize themselves in particular ways. Recusal's feasibility relies on government's capacity to find substitutes for the recused official—namely, other officeholders without similarly affected interests—and on its ability to structure itself so that the issue in contention is kept away from the disqualified decision-maker. Balance's workability, by contrast, depends on government's capacity to find complements for the interested official—namely, others whose equally affected interests will balance hers—and to structure itself so that issues *not in contention* are kept away from the balanced decision-making unit. This bears further explanation. Consider a government advisory committee composed entirely of representatives from auto companies. Such a committee will remain (more) balanced as long as its mandate is confined to intraindustry matters such as supplier management, but not if its deliberations expand to embrace broader social issues such as pollution control—in which case, the absence of an "environmental" representative will render the committee unbalanced and potentially biased in its judgment.

In order for either recusal or balance to take effect, then, the official herself remains staid and intact. What springs into action, all around her, is a series of intragovernmental processes that find substitutes or complements for the interested officeholder. By contrast, divestiture and disclosure form their own "marriage of contraries" precisely because they share the opposite characteristic. Both are *extra*governmental remedies, relying on changes the official herself undergoes, on acts she must execute.

Indeed, because both disclosure and divestiture are "extragovernmental" remedies—remedies that work changes on officeholders personally instead of on government organizations—they each operate free from a certain kind of constraint. So, for example, there may be good reason for us to ask an officeholder to disclose *all* of her interests and not just those which she can affect in her official role: While a few courts "have required that the disclosed interest have some relationship with or bearing on official duties," most, "because of the difficulty of defining duties and the fact that officials are continually changing roles, have said they need not be related."[7] Likewise, there may be situations where we would want an officeholder to divest *all* of her interests—either converting them into liquid assets or placing them in a blind trust—and not only those which she can affect in her official role. So, for example, within several of the Department of the Interior's major subdivisions, each official—no matter how junior and confined her role—must divest herself of anything her bureau as a whole might affect, even if she herself in no way touches it.[8]

Such overbreadth, by contrast, would be nonsensical in the case of either recusal or balance, the two intragovernmental remedies. It would serve no purpose (at least, no remedial conflict-of-interest purpose) for an official to recuse herself in situations where her role will not affect any of her interests. We would not, for instance, remove an Agriculture Department official, whose assets resided in high-tech funds, from making a decision affecting cattle feed. Similarly, nothing remedial would be accomplished by appointing an official to balance a committee, when her role on it would *not* lead her to affect any of her interests. We would not, for example, judge an official's capacity to balance an Automobile Industry Committee on the basis of her real-estate holdings.

Not surprisingly, then, disclosure and divestiture draw their fiercest criticism from officeholders themselves. Recusal and balance, by contrast, meet their stiffest opposition from groups concerned with good government—recusal because it hands decision-making over to an often imperfect substitute instead of encouraging the officeholder herself to shed her personal interests, balance because it reduces the public interest to a clash of biased decision-makers instead of encouraging individual officeholders to embody the public interest.[9]

Remedies, Conflicts, and Interests

Notwithstanding the tendency for officials, commentators, and others to express across-the-board preferences for one or another of the four remedies, a more fine-grained look reveals that each, in fact, is suited to only some but not all of the different types of conflict. Self-dealing, to begin with, lends it-self to each remedial approach. For self-dealing to occur, an official must oc-cupy an intragovermental role—one potentially remediable through recusal or balance—and she must possess an extragovernmental interest, one she can either divest or disclose. Which remedy is most suitable in any given circum-stance will depend on the nature of the office as well as on the issues of gov-ernmental and personal cost noted previously. But when it comes to the array of conflict possibilities beyond self-dealing—undue influence, abuse of office, private payment for public acts, private gain from public office—as well as sit-uations where interests deepen into biases, predispositions, and ideologies, some remedies become more fitting than others.

Undue influence and private gain from public office are committed by of-ficials acting wholly *out-of-role,* whether by privately importuning their of-ficial colleagues or privately earning remuneration based in part on officially derived knowledge or stature. The two are, consequently, not amenable to any of the four remedies, which work *ex ante;* instead, they lend themselves only to *ex post* penalty. Undue influence is punished legally, through the pen-alties provided under 18 U.S.C. §203 and 205. And private gain from public office is punished politically, such as when officials reap criticism for cashing in on governmentally derived experience or reputation.

The two remaining prophylactic conflict categories, abuse of office and pri-vate payment for public acts, also require some out-of-role, nonofficial acts in order to occur: In abuse of office, the official must perform private-market services; in private payment for public acts, a private party must pay his of-ficial salary. But "abuse" and "private payments" also, in part, implicate the *in-role* official. In abuse, the official must have the in-role capacity to affect the interests of the private party with whom he does business. In private pay-ment for public acts, the official must perform public acts for which he re-ceives a privately sourced salary subvention. Because each involves the in-role official in some fashion, both abuse of office and private payment for public acts are remediable, but in complex ways.

In abuse of office, the officeholder has the official capacity to affect not her *own* business interests but rather the interests of others who are in a position to engage her business interests. Hence, neither recusal—which could re-quire a great many disqualifications, one for each affected customer or cli-ent—nor balance—which would require a melange of different counter-vailing forces, one for each affected customer or client—are particularly promising. Abuse implicates far too many ever-shifting private interests for government to perpetually be reorganizing itself, whether through recusal or balance, in order to neutralize the encumbrances it poses. Instead, disclosure of client or customer lists sometimes suggests itself as a remedy for abuse of office.[10] More obvious is straightforward divestiture. In Air Force Secretary Harold Talbott's case, had he divested himself of his interests in a consulting practice that various Air Force contractors had retained, he would have been done with it.

A more interesting possibility is a form of blindness, where the officeholder is made unaware of her firm's clients *and* the clients are made unaware of the officeholder's connection to the firm.[11] Judges, for example, are forbidden to be "officers, managers and employees . . . involved in income-seeking on a day-to-day basis," for the reason that their constant contact with customers would give them knowledge of who "is and who is not a customer," paving the way for "influence," "pressure," "intimidation," and "coercion."[12] Conversely, in order to minimize the possibility that potential clients might know that an officeholder—especially one who could affect their interests—is connected to a particular business, federal executive officials are enjoined from using their titles or referring to their offices in their outside enterprises.[13] Or to look at a legislative case, it was insufficient that the book deal between Newt Gingrich and HarperCollins—owned by Rupert Murdoch, whose business interests the Speaker could have affected—was ultimately confined to customary market terms. To avoid a charge of abuse, as Gingrich's spokesman Tony Blankley recognized in explaining a 1994 meeting between Gingrich and Murdoch, it was also necessary for him to assert that "Gingrich didn't know Murdoch owned the publishing company in question, and Murdoch didn't know of the book deal."[14]

In abuse situations, the official may find herself with the in-role capacity to affect any number of interests that have transferred value to her, but to which she is not beholden, having provided private-market consideration in return. In situations of private payment for public acts, by contrast, the official *does* become beholden to a private entity, receiving value from it which she does not recompense, but it is an entity whose interests she has *no* ability to affect in-role. Here, since the official cannot affect the interests to which she is beholden, neither recusing her from her role nor balancing her execution of it—the two intragovernmental remedies—would have any impact. Unlike in abuse of office, where the two remedies seem impractical because the official's role affects too many pertinent interests, here they are futile because the role affects none. Both divestiture and disclosure—the two extragovernmental remedies—would, however, have some effect. Officials entering government can be required to divest themselves of overgenerous pension plans or termination settlements—funds and settlements that seem designed to top up the officeholder's official salary—and they can certainly be made to disclose them. A form of blind trust would also seem appropriate in some cases of private payment for public acts. This explains the effort to ensure that the contributors to Bill Clinton's defense fund were kept "secret not only from the public, but from Clinton himself. If he doesn't know to whom he's beholden," as one Clinton aide put it, "he won't act as if he is."[15]

It would seem, then, that recusal and balance—the two intragovernmental remedies—fade as plausible candidates, and the twin extragovernmental remedies of divestiture and disclosure come to the fore, as the conflict in question becomes more attenuated, as it blurs from self-dealing into abuse of office or private payment for public acts. Precisely the opposite happens, though, as the *interest* in question becomes more attenuated, as it blurs from the pecuniary into bias, ideology, prejudice, and predisposition. Here, intragovernmental recusal and balance become more robust, while extragovernmental disclosure and divestiture recede in prominence.

Bias, ideology, prejudice, and predisposition occupy a realm more personal, more internal, more arguably integrated into the subject than does "mere" pecuniary interest. Hence, remedies that rely on altering or revealing the person of the offending official—such as divestiture and disclosure—are unlikely to suffice. One cannot divest oneself of one's biases or prejudgments because they are so integral; one cannot easily disclose them because they are so internal. True, disclosing one's biases or prejudices is not unheard-of, although obviously no paper form is available for doing so adequately. But any such disclosure usually does not suffice as a remedy in and of itself. Rather, it allows for a diagnosis that then paves the way for recusal in quasi-judicial situations and balance in quasi-legislative or peer-review circumstances. Compared with disclosing a pecuniary interest, which serves a remedial purpose, disclosing a psychological bias comes far closer to admitting an irremediable incapacity to make an unencumbered decision. Irremediable, that is, through anything that can be done to or by the decision-maker herself.

Divesting a psychological bias—or even monitoring its effects through disclosure—is thus simply less easily accomplished than divesting a pecuniary interest or monitoring its effects through disclosure.[16] Recusal, by contrast, remains a plausible option for decision-makers, especially judicial or quasi-judicial decision-makers, who are seized with bias or animus.[17] And where a quasi-legislative or collective decision-making process involves biased or predisposed officials, and where those officials are so integral to the process as to be unrecusable, the only possible alternative is balance—either through collaborating colleagues or supervising superiors.

Because balance and disclosure burst forth on the scene far more recently than the older-vintage remedies of recusal and divestiture (and because each exhibits a more broadly political, less narrowly legalistic cast), they have produced the richest contemporary debates in the realm of remedy. And this is so notwithstanding that balance, at any rate, may be the least commonly used of the four. For along with disclosure, balance has provoked by far the greatest number of major judicial and political controversies. Balance discourse opens up unique questions having to do with the meaning of "fair representation" in a realm uncharted by political theory—the realm of the "quasi-legislative," a domain populated largely by executive branch committees, commissions, and task forces located between the legislative and the judicial realms, both of whose representational issues have been far more extensively explored. Debate over disclosure, for its part, uniquely configures issues of privacy, political rights and identity, adding its own twists and dimensions to several questions of longstanding centrality to democratic politics. I turn to balance first.

23

What Is a
Balanced Committee?

Whenever a collective body participates in making a government decision—and in particular, a decision that affects a confined range of interests, each of which ought to have some say in making it—balance affords the most suitable remedy for encumbered judgment. Balance is most apt, in other words, when the task is quasi-legislative in character, where "quasi" implies that the decision-making body has the capacity to influence but neither ultimately make nor simply rubber-stamp government decisions, and "legislative" signifies a concern with law-, rule- or policy-making.[1]

In practice, the greatest debates over balance arise in litigation between the government and interest groups over the composition of "federal advisory committees," bodies comprising citizens representing various interests, such as the White House Conference on Aging, the National Industrial Pollution Council, or the Grace Commission on Cost Control in Government. Here, more than in any other strand of American public discourse, one finds parties and courts grappling with the meaning of unbiased *group* decision-making and focusing in particular on two questions: First, given that any kind of commission or committee or task force will implicate only a circumscribed set of issues, how should we approach the question of placing bounds on its mandate? Should a governmental cost-control committee, for example, be understood to affect the interests of the poor, and should the poor therefore have representation on it? Put another way, given its mandate, would the committee show bias if the poor weren't represented? And second, how should we select members to represent (those who hold) the various affected interests? Suppose a cost-control committee is understood to affect the interests of the poor. That still fails to settle the question of who should be selected to represent them in order to cure any bias. These problems arise neither in the legislative realm, where constitutions set the mandates of legislative bodies and electoral mechanisms exist for choosing representatives, nor in the judicial sphere, where an already-made statute sets the bounds for a judicial proceeding and standing criteria exist for choosing representatives.

Balance cases get litigated under the provision of the Federal Advisory Committee Act (FACA) that each such quasi-legislative body be "fairly balanced," meaning that all the interests it affects must be represented on it. Only if a committee is balanced in this way will its decision-making be unimpaired, remedied of any significant bias. After all, a committee whose decision-making is weighted disproportionately in favor of only some of the interests it affects is, all other things being equal, as encumbered as an individual official whose decision-making is weighted inappropriately in favor of certain interests she affects.[2] The typical FACA balance case involves litigation commenced by a public-interest group seeking representation on a given committee—a committee which, the group invariably alleges, is "seriously imbalanced," lacking members truly representative of all the interests it affects and therefore biased. According to the defendant U.S. government, which struck the committee's mandate and appointed its members, the challenged committee is invariably well-balanced—appropriately representative of all affected interests—and hence unbiased. But there is a discernible structure that almost all balance cases follow.

The government's first move, typically, is to characterize the decision-making body's mandate as a narrow one, touching on issues that affect only the particular interests of those, usually members of the private sector, who are already represented. A privatization commission, the government will argue, was struck only to determine which government programs are "more appropriately part of the private sector," and "*not* to determine whether or not privatization in general is a good or desirable public policy."[3] A cost-control task force composed of 150 private-sector representatives, the government will claim, was struck only to advise on "narrow" management issues and not to wander into "broader policy questions"; any "imbalances" alleged by plaintiff will thus be "irrelevant to the ability of the [commission] to perform its function fairly and impartially."[4] Plaintiff groups invariably respond that however narrow a committee's mandate might originally have been, it will by its very nature broaden and expand to affect the excluded interest. "[C]ommittees in government seldom operate wholly within their charter," a public-service union argued when attempting to secure representation on President Reagan's Privatization Commission, "and hence the original representation usually turns out not to be balanced."[5] "[T]he committee has departed from its narrow mandate," an antihunger group claimed in seeking representation on the Grace cost-control commission, "and is [now] considering substantive changes in federal programs."[6]

Obviously, any court settling this kind of dispute would have to refer to the facts of the particular case. My interest here lies in juxtaposing this recurrent argument with a second habitual strand of debate over balanced group decision-making. Conceding that the body will affect the excluded interest fails to settle the question of who should represent it, the government invariably notes. The quasi-legislative realm has available neither the electoral mechanism for choosing representatives that characterizes the legislative domain, nor the standing criteria that prevail in the judicial sphere. Why should the National Treasury Employees' Union represent those who may be harmed by privatization? On what grounds can the National Anti-Hunger Coalition claim to represent the interests of the poor on a government cost-control body? Why wouldn't someone the government selects to represent that interest do just as well?

In pressing this claim, the government argues that plaintiff groups, such as the National Treasury Employees Union or the Anti-Hunger Coalition, are incapable of representing the pure public interests in question—the interests of program beneficiaries, the interests of the poor—because they inevitably develop their own "private" interests in ideological positioning and organizational longevity. Such groups invariably adopt shrill or extreme positions more consistent with their private interests in organizational notoriety than with the public interest which they should full-throatedly be representing. Judge Lawrence Silberman, for example, denied a consumer organization's claim to represent the (concededly affected) consumer interest on an FDA Food Safety Committee on the grounds that such an "organization . . . would have an economic interest in the work of the Committee—not shared by the public—and therefore a special interest."[7] According to plaintiff groups seeking representation on advisory committees, however, "these arguments are silly on their face."[8] On the contrary, public-interest groups insist, "their [claims] ought to be . . . accorded higher priority" precisely "because they . . . do not have ordinary 'special interest' attachments" and they therefore *can* represent, in a pure and undiluted way, the (public) interests for which they claim to speak.[9]

In describing committees, then, the government claims that they admirably confine themselves to their putative "private-interest" mandates and so do not affect the excluded interest. When characterizing plaintiff groups, however, the government claims that they *never* confine themselves to their putative public-interest purposes, and so ought not be selected to represent the excluded interest. Plaintiff groups themselves take just the opposite tack. According to the typical plaintiff, the sociology of committees is such that committee concerns inevitably move beyond those of narrow or private interest toward those of broad and public interest; hence it is a good bet that the committee will affect the excluded interest. But the sociology of groups, according to plaintiff groups themselves, is such that their concerns rarely move from those of broad and public interest toward those of narrow or private interest. Hence, the group can be counted upon to faithfully represent the excluded interest.

I am not suggesting that there is anything necessarily paradoxical about either government or group doctrine in general, although one could raise that question in particular cases. But together they give a flavor of the contestation that surrounds the concept of a balanced, hence unbiased decision-making body—a type of broad controversy over the sociology of entities, such as committees or groups, that simply does not arise in disputes over recusal, divestiture, or disclosure (which is controversial in its own ways). And in fact this is only half of the story. Two other arguments invariably braid themselves into balance litigation.

The government, as I have noted, typically argues that committee mandates are too narrow to affect whatever the excluded interests happen to be, that techniques of privatization and cost-control, for example, are sharply focused topics capable of being segregated, and discussed separate and apart, from the broader social questions of government's role that affect various public interests. True, at some sufficiently broad level of generality or attenuation, anything can be said to affect anything else. But then if we *are* going to argue at such broad levels of attenuated connection, the government claims, not only the plaintiff interest, but an "infinite" number of other interests, might be deemed equally affected by any given committee's work. "If the court were to follow the logic of plaintiff's argument," urged the government brief in the *Anti-Hunger Coalition* case, then "virtually every special interest . . . in the United States [could] claim that it might be affected" by the Grace Commission on Cost Control; the "churches [would] have a right [to be represented]. The hospitals [would] have a right. The schoolteachers [would] have a right . . . And you can go on and on."[10] If the court were to conclude that a technical committee on microbiological criteria for food affects the excluded consumer interest, Judge Silberman declared, then the similarly relevant interests "to be considered by [the] advisory committee are virtually infinite . . . I can conceive of no principled basis . . . to determine which . . . deserve representation on particular advisory committees." The line between those with "'direct interests' and those with 'tangential interests'" would turn into a "hopelessly manipulable" one, the judge added, so manipulable that courts and agencies "would be obliged to make an arbitrary decision as to how attenuated an interest must be before it should be classified as 'indirect'" and hence excludable.[11]

Plaintiff groups, for their part, deny that the interest universe is so bereft of organizing and segmenting principles.[12] In support of its brief for membership on the Grace Commission on Cost Control, for example, the Anti-Hunger Coalition claimed to be "unique in the entire universe of possible interest," possessing an "extremely specific, definable disproportionate interest . . . in [the Commission's] activities." "If you were to take [a] sharp focus," the Coalition's lawyers urged, "you would really dismiss tremendous numbers of groups which would claim some type of theoretical, hypothetical interest in what is going on, and really be left with a relatively small number such as plaintiffs . . . who have a direct stake."[13]

Again, what makes this particular dispute interesting is its resonance with one last strand of discourse that wends its way through balance debate. Assume that the government concedes one of the points mentioned above and allows that groups do have the capacity to represent particular public interests—whether the consumer interest, the health interest, or the environmental interest—in an unalloyed way, at least without being distracted by their own private organizational interests. That still doesn't mean that any given group actually speaks for any real live individuals. As Jeremy Rabkin argues, groups can claim to

> represent interests instead of directly representing the people assumed to hold those interests. But just to that extent, they do not really represent anyone . . . for it is notorious that people are not always interested in their interests . . . Thus near majorities of union members have ignored the counsel of their union officials in successive presidential elections over the past two decades. And the reason, in all likelihood, was not that they disagreed with union officials about their interests *as* union members but that they did not see this interest as predominant.[14]

A "steelworker, for example, may like clean air as much as the next person but still prefer to put up with a bit more air pollution rather than see the closing of the plant in which he works." Hence an "environmental group" will not speak for him.[15] Individuals, government briefs assume or argue, possess interest hierarchies in which some interests are always "predominant" or "preferred" to the ones groups represent.[16]

Plaintiff groups, for their part, deny that individuals are the entities which such group decision-making bodies ought to represent in the first place. When faced with the government's claim that they can never represent individuals—only at best disembodied interests—plaintiff groups essentially argue that after a point, there *are* only interests. Individuals do not exist, if individuals are conceived as rank-orderings of multiple interests, orderings that may well give predominance to interests other than the one the plaintiff group represents. Here, too, theory is available to stiffen argument. The legal theorist Joseph Vining denies that "[w]e are each one person; [that] we rank our values and order our loves; [that] we each resolve the conflicts within us and speak with a single voice"; instead "there is no objective necessity ordering an individual's interests [and t]here may indeed be no ultimate structure of our wants."[17] Or, as the political theorist John Burnheim puts it, "I may well have conflicting interests as a producer and a consumer, [but it] is not desirable that I settle in advance for some one balance between these conflicting interests. [Better that] my diverse interests each have its own representative. Each representative [would] do the best for a specific interest in the circumstances."[18]

Although Vining deconstructs the individual in order to critique quasi-judicial standing criteria (criteria which traditionally require the represented to be real individuals), and Burnheim does so in order to critique pure-legislative electoral criteria (which traditionally require the same), it is actually quasi-legislative plaintiff groups that have most extensively, and perhaps most appropriately, adopted this vocabulary.[19] Noting that FACA's legislative authors quite explicitly conceived of committees as forums for the representation of "competing interests," not of individuals,[20] they reify disembodied interests—converting them into the represented—by stipulating that committee members should be "representatives of conservation, environment, clean water," and so forth. Sympathetic courts have done so as well: In the *Anti-Hunger Coalition* case, for example, Judge Gerhard Gesell wrote of the need to represent "the interests of hunger [and] the interests of the environment" in a way that would jar in either a legislative or judicial setting.[21]

There is, again, an interesting parallel between these latter two disputes. The first asks: Assuming a link *is* going to be posited between the committee's mandate and the excluded interest, would it have to be one of such generality that it would then be impossible to exclude—as less than directly affected—representatives of innumerable other interests? According to the government, interests within the public realm of the democratic polity are simply incapable of being ranked and ordered in a sufficiently definitive way that a committee's mandate can be said to directly affect some—and in particular the litigating interest—but not the great "myriad" beyond. According to groups, however, drawing such rankings and orderings is far from impossible. The other dispute asks: Even assuming the committee's mandate does directly affect the excluded interest, how can the plaintiff group possibly show that it speaks for any real individuals who happen to hold that interest? According to the government, interests within the private realm of the individual citizen are ranked and ordered in sufficiently definitive ways such that any given single-interest group cannot possibly represent any real individuals. According to groups, however, such rankings and orderings simply do not exist.

According to the government, in other words, the external universe of interests discloses no ordering or priorizing principles, such that it would be possible to say, of any given interest, that it is more directly affected by a committee's mandate than others. But the individual's internal world of interests *is* eminently well-ordered and priorized, such that it is impossible to say of any group, concerned as it must be with one or two isolated interests at most, that it can meaningfully represent any real individuals. After all, individuals may well lend priority to interests other than the one for which the group claims to speak.

On both scores the plaintiff group's position is precisely the reverse: Within the external political arena, interests *are* capable of being intersubjectively ranked or priorized, at least in such a way that any given committee mandate can be said to directly affect some and only indirectly others. Within individuals' inner preference orderings, by contrast, interests are rarely intrasubjectively ranked and priorized; therefore, groups representing individuals' separate interests do not misrepresent individuals themselves.

Debate over balanced, unbiased committees reveals a suggestive structure that goes directly to questions at the heart of democratic theory. The issues hinge on the extent to which different kinds of interests assume primacy within committees and within groups, along with the extent to which different interests assume relationships of priority within the polity and within individuals. Litigation, while hotly contested, discloses a pattern sufficiently robust that balance can be a meaningful remedy, depending on our capacity to answer these questions in any given case. As a byproduct, balance discourse is *the* only fount of thought that bears on a paramount question in democratic politics, the question of fair quasi-legislative representation.

24

Disclosure and
Its Discontents

Public disclosure, balance's partner in the realm of "political" remedies, has spun its own quite knotty strands of debate. According to its most ardent advocates, disclosure precludes not only the need for any other remedy, but the need for any conflict-of-interest law at all.[1] With full disclosure, on this argument, the public can come to its own unaided judgment as to whether any given official is in conflict. Knowing this, officials will comport themselves properly.

Of course, disclosure *need* not operate in the absence of other established remedies or enforcement mechanisms. Often it is used simply as a backstop, a means of checking whether an official has indeed divested conflicting interests, or should be recusing herself in a particular case, or is in fact making an unalloyed contribution to a balanced decision-making process.[2] Nor need public disclosure operate in the absence of law or regulation, such as rules about gifts or outside income, that would aid the public in determining what is and is not a conflict. Nevertheless, advocates of disclosure often say that disclosure is *all* we require, that it supplants the need not only for other remedies or modes of enforcement but for legislation and rules themselves. Their line of argument, and the set of countervailing concerns it provokes, offers the best way to engage the political issues of public disclosure.

Here is the argument for pure public disclosure restated: Public disclosure works by "revealing the possibility of . . . conflict," as Senator Philip Hart once put it, "leaving it to the voter to decide whether the conflict has influenced the official acts of the congressman or senator," and to the congressman or senator to "imagine the [public] reaction"—on the assumption that "if he doubted he could justify it to the public, the requirement of disclosure" would lead him to recuse or divest.[3] A couple of things are noteworthy here. First, pure public disclosure places the viewing citizen in the role of lawmaker and judge. And second, it places the "accused" themselves— that is, the putatively wrongdoing officials—in the role of law-enforcers or policemen.

When various disclosure-proponents argue that disclosure "does not attempt to define the rights and wrongs of the situation" but simply gives the "people . . . the facts by which to make their judgment"[4]—or that it "avoids difficult questions of right and wrong" and instead "sharpens [the public's] judgment of right and wrong"[5]—the vocabulary is revealing.[6] Pure disclosure, it would seem, casts the public in the role of both legislator and adjudicator. Give them the facts, the raw data of a disclosure form, and the citizenry themselves will evolve and then apply the appropriate norms to them. "Disclosure talk," moreover, is just as revealing when it comes to the self-policing, self-enforcing role in which it casts officials: "[D]isclosure is self-policing," Senator Hart urged, "in that it would at least make an official stop and consider the implications of a particular course of action."[7] *We* do not need to require recusal or divestiture of officials because, given public disclosure, they will exact these remedies of themselves.

Not surprisingly, what makes critics of public disclosure uneasy is precisely this twofold notion, namely, that citizens themselves are capable of acting as lawmakers—as legal arbiters of right and wrong—and that the potential transgressors can act as their own policemen. Far better, say critics of disclosure, for officials to assume their rightful role as lawmakers, passing various kinds of substantive ethics regulation which citizens, the media, and tribunals can then use as guidelines for executing a policing function. "Disclosure means nothing unless there are standards against which to measure the facts disclosed"; the "public needs a yardstick," as one prominent theologian put it, "as to what is and what is not proper conduct."[8] Likewise, officials need—indeed, they often ask—others to handle the matters of enforcing and policing. As debate over appearance problems shows so well, an accused official herself may not be in the best position to judge public opinion. Nor are officials particularly willing to confront public accusations absent the shield provided by some kind of independent validating body, such as the Office of Government Ethics or a legislative ethics committee. Judicial conflict of interest provides a lesson here: From an approach that allowed an individual judge to decide for herself whether her interests could be perceived to encumber her judgment in any given case—and hence whether to recuse or divest—the rules evolved to impose a common enforcement mechanism on all federal judges.[9]

Put another way, disclosure—according to its critics—both attenuates and exaggerates the prophylactic nature of conflict-of-interest regulation. On the one hand, as Senator Hart's statement implies, disclosure—of the pure form we are discussing here—does not go so far as to prophylactically prevent even the *possibility* that an official's interests may encumber her judgment, as do recusal and divestiture. Rather, it allows the official to remain in-role *and* in possession of her affected interests, and instead invites the public to determine whether in any given case "the conflict has influenced the official act." In other words (to harken back to earlier discussion), pure disclosure does not necessarily prevent a *malum prohibitum;* rather, in requiring us to hazard a guess as to whether any actual influence *did* occur, it mandates the public to determine whether a *malum in se,* an actual tainted state of mind, does in fact exist in any given case.

But if public disclosure pierces the prophylactic veil in this sense, thereby placing an enormous judging burden on the public, in another it extends it, and in so doing places a difficult self-policing onus on officials. Most conflict-of-interest laws are prophylactic in that (for example) they make it a crime for officials to possess interests which they can affect in-role, regardless of whether those interests actually impair their judgment. But most disclosure regimes generally go beyond this, not only requiring the disclosure of personal interests even if the official cannot affect them in role, but then converting the *failure* to disclose such *non*conflicting interests into an offense. In other words, they erect a second *malum prohibitum* around the first. "[D]isclosure imposes [a] sanction not on inherently discreditable conduct but on a failure to report financial status and transaction, irrespective of fault";[10] it creates "a whole new layer of technical, not substantive requirements for which it makes officials strictly liable."[11] For officials, the self-policing element of disclosure can thus be as fraught as the legislative-adjudicative role is for the public.

Disclosure, Precommitment, and Prejudice

One of the ironies of disclosure is that by going public about a personal interest, an official might actually *create* an encumbrance on judgment where none previously existed. Recall that in his debunking of contemporary conflict-of-interest fixations, Michael Kinsley argues that a nuclear-power lobbyist writing a pro-nuclear op-ed need not disclose his industry ties, since his bias will be made plain in his writing. But Kinsley also argues, conversely, that journalists who support particular politicians *should* disclose their biases, dropping the pretense of neutrality through an outright endorsement. Kinsley notes, for example, that during the 1972 presidential election the Newspaper Guild strongly supported George McGovern but, apparently after some internal debate, decided against endorsing him publicly. Kinsley asks whether in fact the guild should not have made explicit what presumably would have been implicit in its members' journalism anyway, namely a pro-McGovern bias, so that their readers—with this disclosure in mind—could have made an informed judgment of their reporting.[12]

Kinsley's argument—that the nuclear lobbyist need not disclose—works, as noted in Part II, only if the lobbyist's industry links are viewed as constitutive of his subjective capacity for political judgment, not as an encumbrance on it. Kinsley's claim that an ostensibly objective journalist should drop the pretense and admit to a genuine subjective perspective, for its part, works only if the very act of disclosure will not convert that subjective commitment into an encumbrance. In fact, though, it may very well do just that. By transforming a private belief into a public declaration, the journalist binds herself. She creates a tether or drag on her ability to adjust her views in an agile fashion purely on the merits. Should a McGovern fail her in some fashion, she might well—as a result of having gone public—be more reluctant to critique him; alternatively, she might be more vitriolic in her anger than she would otherwise have been. For the guild to have explicitly endorsed McGovern would have tied it to his positions, giving it an added vested interest in their—and his—success, notwithstanding the ever-present possibility that guild members might become disenchanted with them on the merits. If, as Kinsley argues concerning the nuclear lobbyist, simply to vent a bias (say, by writing an op-ed) is to disclose it, then certainly disclosure, in that it creates a public commitment, can sometimes generate added bias.

Now return from the realm of journalists to that of officials. An official who no longer holds to a certain set of beliefs to which he once genuinely subscribed might, nevertheless, develop an encumbering interest—not necessarily pecuniary, but political, reputational, or psychological (an "intellectual vested interest" or "ego involvement")—in maintaining and advancing them.[13] And it is the fact of an official's having taken a *public* position on an issue—even if at a time when she subjectively held to it on the merits—that gives her a continuing interest in perpetuating it. Once a judge "takes a stand in a book or article on a question before the court, the public may wonder whether his public commitment to [that] position will make him insensitive to the arguments of counsel and render him unwilling to admit he was wrong."[14] Adjudicatory officials, as well, have found themselves disqualified in cases where they publicly articulated a stance on a material issue:[15] "Conduct such as this," the court declared in *Cinderella Career Schools* v. *FTC,* "may have the effect of entrenching a Commissioner in a position which he has publicly stated, making it difficult, if not impossible, for him to reach a different conclusion in the event he deems it necessary to do so after consideration of the record."[16] Even a rule-making official, in the eyes of some, must take care lest his "vigorous and consistent advocacy" of a particular viewpoint have the effect of "commit[ting] himself in the public mind."[17] At neither end of the judicial-legislative spectrum is the problem the holding of the position *per se;* that is, the fact that the official may have harbored a strong subjective commitment in and of itself.[18] Rather it is the expressing of it that can create a vested interest. The issue is not private adherence but public identification.

There is, however, something perverse about the idea that publicity can create an encumbrance on judgment, since publicity is typically considered a remedy, a solvent, a "disinfectant" for encumbrances on official judgment. According to disclosure advocates, if an official harbors a previously formulated point of view on an issue before her, then even if she has subjectively embraced it—in fact precisely because it is genuine—the public ought to be apprised of it. Some scholars, in this vein, have gone so far as to criticize injunctions *against* judicial speech-making. Such injunctions are supposed to prevent judges from developing vested interests in upholding particular judicial doctrines. But while it may be encumbrance-creating for a judge to declare publicly his privately held beliefs, it can also be encumbrance-eroding. As Steven Lubet points out, "not only is it undesirable to isolate a judge from opinion-shaping forces, it is undesirable to give the impression that this has been accomplished; and in the absence of nonjudicial activities that reflect the tenor of a judge's ideas, the public and the bar will have no way of knowing his proclivities. A ban on nonjudicial activities will not erase bias, it will simply hide it."[19]

In sum: Disclosure may "corrode" or "disinfect" encumbrances on official judgment (hence some argue that even judges should hold forth on their biases) but it may also create them, which suggests to some that even quasi–legislators should keep quiet about their commitments.

If one of public disclosure's discontents is its occasional tendency to bring an element of encumbrance to official judgment, another is its capacity to bring an added measure of prejudgment to the public. While its defenders urge that "disclosure [will] give the people more confidence in their public officials in light of all the rumors and innuendoes . . . being circulated"—that it "will relieve officeholders of the suspicion that so often surround[s] their public acts"[20]—its critics object that disclosure will in fact "arouse rather than allay suspicions."[21] Why would disclosure exacerbate our suspicions? For the same reason that privacy can sometimes dissipate them. "Privacy," Ruth Gavison writes, "allows ignorance to mitigate our prejudice"; in fact even "gossip usually concerns people who are already known in their other facets, and thus partial truths are less misleading. In contrast, there is no way that most readers of newspapers can correct for the one-dimensional images they receive through print."[22]

And no way, similarly, they can correct for the images they receive through public disclosure. Precisely because the public is ill-equipped to assess its contents, disclosure will not alleviate suspicion but, to the contrary, "will make things look worse than they are."[23] Disclosure, Senator Carl Levin notes, "hasn't prevented [public] institutions from being held up to public scorn."[24] In this way, disclosure can undermine the very public confidence it is supposed to shore up, just as it can encumber the official judgment it is supposed to purify.

Disclosure, Excuses, and Justifications

Public disclosure, it would thus seem, is no mere window passively displaying encumbrances on official judgment. Often disclosure becomes part of the picture itself, a drag or skew on judgment of its own. Consider another couplet of popular arguments. On the one hand, an official will use the very fact of his having disclosed a questionable act as evidence that he harbored no wrongful intent in committing it. Thus, when charged with evading honorarium limits by means that the Senate Ethics Committee ultimately found unacceptable, Senator David Durenberger noted that he never tried to hide the payments in question, reporting them on his disclosure forms and describing them to other senators. As the committee itself observed, "[t]he Senator's counsel argued that he would not have done so had he believed that the arrangement was in any way unethical or improper."[25] Durenberger claimed, in other words, that although he had done something wrong, the surrounding transparency guaranteed that he acted from a sincere belief that he was conducting himself properly, not from a questionable desire to advance his own interests.

But there is a flip side: "When it was first revealed in the press that [former Agriculture Secretary Mike] Espy had taken free gratuities," the journalist David Grann noted, "he sent reimbursements through the mail. Rather than regard this as exculpatory evidence, [independent counsel Donald] Smaltz used this to charge him with . . . Mail Fraud."[26] According to Espy's critics, the fact that he did the right thing by paying for the gifts only *after* they were disclosed was not exculpating but inculpating. It was precisely because "Espy paid for several gifts after his conduct came under investigation," according to the *Washington Post*, that the independent counsel "said he did so in a last-ditch effort to save his job and gloss over his misdeeds."[27] Here, transparency suggested that Espy acted not out of a sincere desire to do good, but out of a less than edifying need to protect his own interests; likewise with Al Gore's campaign aide Tony Coelho, who "made the government liable for a $300,000 personal loan—a loan that was not repaid until after its embarrassing disclosure."[28]

If an official is going to do something wrong along the lines of Durenberger, it would seem that he will reap more credit—his judgment will be deemed less encumbered—if he does it *with* disclosure. But if he is going to do the right thing, as did Espy and Coelho, he will reap more credit—his judgment, again, will seem less impaired—if he does it *without* disclosure. Disclosure, or its absence, not only reveals but itself affects the extent of an official's impairment.

Now consider the case of President Clinton's national security aide, Sandy Berger, against whom the Justice Department brought a 1997 complaint under 18 U.S.C. §208, the self-dealing statute. Berger participated in matters that may have had a direct and predictable effect on his family's holdings in Amoco Corporation, even though the White House counsel had earlier advised Berger to divest. In his answer to the complaint, which he settled by making a payment to the U.S. Treasury, Berger offered two defenses. First, he claimed not to have realized that he had failed to sell the stock in question; the White House's direction to divest had simply slipped his mind. Second, Berger noted, he had never tried to hide the Amoco holdings. Indeed, he signed two annual financial disclosure forms, one on May 15, 1994, and another on May 15, 1995, that correctly noted his family's continued ownership of the stock.[29]

Prominent as they are in conflict-of-interest discourse, these two arguments—"I didn't realize it" and "I didn't try to hide it"—do not hang together well. To disavow one's own knowledge about something—say, one's failure to divest—is to offer an *excuse*: although your conduct may have been wrong, you are saying, you cannot be held responsible for it. To insist on everyone else's knowledge of something—to claim you never tried to hide it—is to offer a *justification*: You are saying that the act in question was not wrong, as far as you knew, at least according to common practice. The two arguments can work if they are offered separately. But an official who, perhaps out of an abundance of exculpatory caution, makes them contemporaneously risks appearing as if he alone didn't know what was going on *while* everyone else did. Consider the case of former British Columbia premier Mike Harcourt, whose New Democratic Party (NDP) government was accused of maintaining links with the Nanaimo Commonwealth Holding Society (NCHS), a nonprofit organization charged with mishandling gambling revenues. "I'm not sure who [runs] the Commonwealth Society and whether they are New Democrats or not," Harcourt said at one point in an excusing vein, while later insisting, in a justificatory voice, that "[o]f course the relationship between the NDP and the NCHS has been known for many decades."[30]

Officials' Political Rights

Public disclosure raises two further questions. Does it egregiously burden officials' and would-be officials' political rights, by providing a deterrent to office-seeking and officeholding? And does it pose any kind of threat to officials' privacy rights?

One way of addressing the first question—one way of measuring disclosure's heft as a deterrent to would-be officeholders—is to compare it with other such putative obstacles. Requiring an official to disclose her financial interests and associations is, on most accounts, less constitutionally burdensome than requiring an individual to produce a certain amount of financial resources—by way of a property qualification or a filing fee—before being allowed to run for office.[31] Conversely, requiring an official (or anyone for that matter) to disclose that she possesses certain *political* interests and associations—requiring her to disclose her membership in various political causes—would generally be considered more burdensome than requiring a would-be officeholder to come up with a certain number of political supporters, by way of names on a petition, before being certified as a candidate for office.[32] The disclosure of financial links is *less* troubling than the establishment of financial hurdles as a condition for office, while the disclosure of political links is *more* troubling than the establishment of political hurdles as a condition for office.

But this surface contrariety lends itself to resolution at a deeper level. Financial disclosure shares with political hurdles (signatures) the capacity for ensuring a measure of official fidelity to democratic will. With financial disclosure, citizens can more effectively judge official decisions; with political hurdles, there is some assurance that a candidate's views enjoy popular support. On the other hand, political disclosure shares with financial hurdles (filing fees, property qualifications) the character of inhibiting political participation without any redeeming democratically ameliorative characteristic. Viewed in this setting, then, financial disclosure falls into a distinctly secondary class of burdens on officials' participative rights, as indeed courts have recognized for decades.

Voyeurism

It is also settled that whatever privacy rights officials have, they are insufficient to prevent at least some form of public financial disclosure. Consequently, the privacy-based assault on disclosure has evolved into two further critiques, one rather pointed and the other very broad.

The pointed critique surrounds this question: Should we require officials to disclose only the *sources* of their outside income (stocks, contracts, fees)? Or ought we insist that they also disclose *amounts*, even within certain broad bands? Here, strange argumentative bedfellows reveal themselves. Those who remain sympathetic to officials' privacy needs, as one would expect, deny the public's need to know amounts as well as sources. The flip-side, though, is that they often find themselves arguing that a trivial amount can pose just as great a conflict of interest as a large one. Former OGE Director David Martin, who acquired a reputation as an in-house critic of much conflict-of-interest regulation, argued at a 1988 conference that most officials should be exempt from having to disclose the amounts of outside income they derive from various sources. Identifying the sources themselves, Martin said, should suffice; others joined him in criticizing those who seek to know precise figures as "voyeur[s]."[33] Yet to shore up his case—to deny that amounts are relevant to public consideration—Martin felt compelled to acknowledge the possibility of conflict even in situations well below what many would consider *de minimis.* It is because one dollar is the same as five thousand dollars, Martin argued, that there is no need to disclose amounts. Those who do not want to impose the most drastic disclosure regime on officials—those who downplay the need for the public to know amounts—thus, ironically, are compelled to take a more draconian view of the offense itself: "if you're an inch off the cliff, you're a foot."[34] Or, as Thomas D. Morgan puts it, "once a conflict-creating interest exists, the conflict is not technically of greater or lesser magnitude depending on the size of the interest. All that is left [to justify amount disclosure] is a general curiosity about the extent of a public personality's wealth."[35]

Conversely, as it would follow, those who take a more radical view of the disclosure remedy—requiring the disclosure not just of sources but exact amounts as well—must dilute their stance by adopting a more gradualist view of the offense itself. Common Cause, the leading advocate of amount-not-just-source disclosure, justifies its absolutist approach to disclosure by adopting a relativistic approach to conflict. "The legislative history of the Ethics Act," Archibald Cox told a 1988 hearing, "underscores the need for a sufficient number of categories of value to reflect the magnitude of the holding and thus the potential magnitude of the conflict of interest."[36] Or, as the executive director of the Florida Ethics Commission said before a 1980 federal hearing, "I think there is a big difference between $1,000 and $10,000"—a claim which prompted the anti-amount-disclosure Senator Malcolm Wallop to dissent: "No, they're all conflicts of interest."[37]

Identity

Yet disclosure—not simply of personal pecuniary interests, but of all the kinds of personal traits and qualities that could conceivably encumber official judgment—raises an issue that goes far beyond privacy, although the two are often confused. Our current preoccupation with public figures who may have hidden details of their private lives from the public—that is, our current joust with issues of privacy—in fact masks the advent of the opposite but unremarked phenomenon: the official whose public knows more about his private life than he does himself. What emerges from recent discourse is not so much a threat to officials' privacy as to their very identity.

Consider: Some of the most dramatic moments in our recent politics, it would seem, involve public figures who failed to disclose details of their private lives to an unknowing public. But on closer examination, many such incidents appear to have become controversial for just the opposite reason: The public had become apprised of information concerning the lives of public figures when—for that moment and, in some cases, for some time beyond—such information remained unknown, forgotten, or doubted, by the public figures themselves.

Take as an example Senator Joe Biden's attempt—three days before he dropped out of the race for the Democratic presidential nomination in the early fall of 1987—to contact his old law professors to confirm for himself what millions of Americans already had come to know: that, as a law student, he had plagiarized a course assignment. In the ensuing hours, Biden hastened to learn further information about his own past—his other law-school records, for example—before the press did, a spectacle that was repeated almost exactly eleven months later by Dan Quayle. Biden's predicament was widely treated as just another case of a public figure concealing an incriminating detail about his past, keeping it always in mind so as to guard against it ever slipping into the public domain. But it might as easily have been understood as the plight of a public figure altogether banishing from memory an incriminating detail from long ago, only to discover it surfacing at the very forefront of public consciousness. And then there was Biden's "borrowed" rhetoric during a candidate's debate in the same campaign. At the time, a Biden adviser explained, "He's under a huge amount of pressure. He didn't even know what he said. He was on automatic pilot." In other words, through layers of consciousness crowded with the details of briefing notes, scheduling problems, and the names of local party stalwarts, Biden half-recalled a piece of boilerplate he had heard who-knows-where and inserted it unthinkingly into a speech recited by rote—only to have the media unearth the true author, British Labour leader Neil Kinnock, and publicize the discovery to millions of Americans. This was not, so Biden's aides argued, a case of Biden's doing something wrong, and knowing it while we didn't. Rather, it was one where Biden unknowingly did something wrong, and others came to realize it before he did.[38]

Evasions such as Biden's—he initially refused to acknowledge both instances of plagiarism—could be interpreted as an attempt by a duplicitous public figure to slow the passage of embarrassing truths from private darkness to public light. But they might as easily have been interpreted as efforts by a

disoriented public figure to unearth details from the penumbra of his life—
his unconscious, his memory, his paper flow—and, purely reflexively, buy the
time to assimilate them according to his own personal lights. The plausibility
of this kind of response, of the idea of the public figure whose public knows
more about him than he does himself, became a central question in the Iran-
Contra congressional committee hearings. There, numerous witnesses argued that the questions posed to them flowed from committee research into
their pasts so extensive that it dwarfed the capacity of personal recall to provide answers. As understood by the media, of course, the term "plausible
deniability" came to refer to the ability of official witnesses to "stonewall," to
conceal what they knew about their own recent activities from their congressional interlocutors, and to do so with some degree of plausibility. Yet their
interlocutors already had a good idea of those activities, by dint of research
and surmisal, and witnesses were compelled to acknowledge them, by force
of law. This they could avoid doing only if they could claim, with plausibility,
that their interlocutors betrayed far more knowledge about their past activities than they themselves could reasonably be expected to have had.

Plausible deniablity, in fact, set up an ironic, inverse relationship between
the extent of the research knowledge possessed by the questioner and the degree of affirmative acknowledgement given by the witness, so that the more
penetrating and esoterically detailed the information lying behind a given
question—the closer the questioner might be on the heels of the truth—the
more plausibly a witness could avoid direct confirmation or refutation by saying she could not recall. Plausible deniability became a tribute not to witnesses's ability to keep information from questioners but to the capacity of
questioners to know far more about witnesses than they themselves could
ever have been expected to retain.

Or consider, to take a different instance, the memo sent to Attorney General Edwin Meese by his friend Robert Wallach, one passage of which proposed a bribe. Days after the public had become apprised of the passage,
Meese professed that he himself still remained unacquainted with it. "The
memos were long and life is short," Michael Kinsley wrote in mock sympathy
with Meese's avowal of ignorance, "and the eye sometimes does tend to
take a short-cut across the pages of even some of the greatest classics of literature."[39] But the plausibility of this kind of response was upheld by Senator George Mitchell, otherwise one of the Iran-Contra hearings' most effective critics of the administration. Concerning the only surviving Oliver
North-John Poindexter memo, Mitchell pronounced—in a 1988 speech to
the American Bar Association—"that it was a lengthy memo. [Mention of]
the diversion [of arms money to the contras] is eight lines long, buried in
the middle of page five. It's entirely conceivable that a person reading them

would have skipped over those words, or, even reading them, not fully grasped their significance at the time."[40]

At key moments in recent democratic discourse, then, officials and candidates have shown themselves to be less in command of the recent texts of their own lives—both their private personal activities and their privy official responsibilities—than were their media or public interlocutors. While the increased transparency of an official's life might bring it ever more within the public's range of vision, its growing complexity will, at the very same time, take it further afield of his own. And it is thus no longer just an official's privacy that is challenged by the public, press, or prosecutorial desire to know more. It is the very continence of the official's persona, her self-presentation, her public identity. The advent of officials about whom—for a period of time—important facts can be known by the public, while remaining unknown to them, spells the possibility of new types of inconsistency and incoherence in public personas.

In debate over public financial disclosure we can find a particularly advanced form of this derangement in the hitherto prevailing relationship between the mental capacities of officials and their publics, and the quantity of information about officials' lives with which they both must deal. Public disclosure, of course, generally gets defended as a method for alerting the public to conflicts of interest that would otherwise remain hidden from their view, known only to officials themselves, who might then be in a position to take advantage of them. Yet consider the following two views recurrently put forward by officials, scholars, and commentators. First, in urging that confidential *private* disclosure by officials to an "independent executive unit" might be more effective than full *public* disclosure, Robert H. Freilich and Thomas M. Larson claim that "the most full public statements, if unread and unpoliced, may do less to prevent the conflicts of interest at which they are aimed, than disclosures more limited in scope or less widely published."[41] Freilich and Larson clearly—and plausibly—assume that in many cases, the mass of personal data that appears on public-disclosure forms is simply too intricate for even the broad compass of the public and media mind to digest. The paradoxical implication is that the public will know and understand more if it is told less. Or, as three congressmen put in in a 1977 House Report, "[o]ne can argue, with considerable validity, that too much disclosure may be no disclosure at all."[42] The only way to move the raw data of the officeholder's life from an *uncomprehending* to a *comprehending* public mind, in other words, may actually be to move it back from the public into the privy domain—that is, to replace unmediated public disclosure with disclosure to a confidential committee, which then refines the information and signals to the public the extent of such conflict as may exist.

Conversely, in a 1971 essay on official ethics, John Wall argued that disclosure's principal purpose is to make officeholders themselves, not the public, more "aware" of their own private interests and the ways in which they might pose a conflict. "Not all conflicts may be apparent" to the official, Wall wrote, "even if he is looking for them."[43] Indeed, as G. Calvin Mackenzie remarks in his study of the presidential appointments system, the Senate now uses "the confirmation process . . . to make [nominees for executive branch positions] cognizant of the aspects of their own backgrounds that may [place them in] conflict."[44] The purpose of the confirmation committee's very public forum is to enlighten not so much the public, but rather officeholders themselves, about their own pasts; public disclosure, as former Congressman Chet Holifield once wrote, "reminds members and spouses of the various potentials for conflict that do exist."[45] The raw financial data of their lives are likely to be so complex and recondite, evidently, that potential officeholders can move them from their *unconscious* to their *conscious* minds only by moving those data from the private to the public domain.

Together, the positions articulated by Freilich and Larson on the one hand, and Wall on the other, suggest a new doctrine. Public disclosure is not a device that makes the public more aware of conflicts that officeholders know about and would prefer to withhold. Rather, it actually makes officials themselves more aware of such conflicts while rendering the public less aware—or at least less comprehending—than might otherwise be the case. Disclosure may never "reach . . . the consciousness of the public"[46] but it may have the effect of "rais[ing] the consciousness of the filer," "calling to the conscious attention of the disclosing member himself the extent of his conflicting private interests."[47] Here, the mental compass not only of officials but also of the public itself is understood to be so limited—and the data concerning officials' lives so ramified and complicated—that the passage of those data from the private to the public domain will actually have the perverse effect of obscuring them to the public at large while illuminating them to officials. After all, if we live in a world where the public can know more about an official than he does himself, then it is not surprising that public disclosure will often inform the official more than the public.

Conclusion

Judith Shklar begins the concluding chapter of her 1984 book *Ordinary Vices* with these lines:

> This has been a tour of perplexities, not a guide for the perplexed. These chapters have been inquiries into difficulties, and they are not held together by a continuous argument moving to a destined goal . . . At most I have tried to do what I take to be the job of political theory: to make our conversations and convictions about our society more complete and coherent and to review critically the judgments we ordinarily make and the possibilities we usually see. To question our customs is not a substitute for action . . . Indeed, I cannot think why any readers of this book would ask for my advice . . . about what policies they should choose.[1]

I am borrowing these lines—although I shall modify them in a couple of ways—to open the concluding chapter of this book as well. What Shklar said in summing up what she called her "ramble through a moral minefield, not a march toward a destination"—her twisting-and-turning analysis of the perplexities of hypocrisy, snobbery, misanthropy, and treachery—captures what I have attempted in this examination of the complexities of conflicts, interests, appearances, and remedies. The last fifty years of conflict-of-interest discourse lends itself to the mode of analysis Shklar identifies, one that bends its ear to discourse's many voices rather than drowning them out with the author's own.

Yet it is not exactly the case that this book moves toward no central theme on which its various discussions are draped. That theme, however, abides not *within* but *about* conflict-of-interest discourse; it concerns the passage of "conflict" from a subjective to an objective understanding, the transformation of "interest" from an objective to a subjective conception, and the many consequences of these twin migrations.

In the realm of conflict, we have abandoned a subjective approach, one that would require us to peer into the mind of the individual official concerned, hazarding guesses as to whether he surmounted (or else surrendered to) whatever temptation he might have faced to further his own personal interests. In place of this kind of attempt to gauge whether any given official really is in subjective inner conflict—an enterprise that seems factually dubious and inconsistent with liberal legalism—we have moved toward an objective, external approach: We now prophylactically prohibit all officials from entering into an ever-increasing number of specified, factually ascertainable sets of circumstances because they *might lead* to inner conflict.

In the realm of interest, conversely, what we have abandoned precisely *is* an objective approach—one confined to pecuniary private interests that are hard, external, and visible to the naked eye. We have forsworn, as well, an objective approach to the *public* interest, a notion that our political liberalism renders dubious. Instead, we have adopted a subjective approach to both private interest and public interest. We invade the official's mind in the attempt (in any individual case) to classify various subjective traits—ideologies, predispositions, loyalties, and attachments—as impairments every bit as encumbering as pecuniary private interests while looking for a subjective conception of the public interest in what remains.

These twin impulses—conflict flying toward the objective, interest toward the subjective—lie at the heart of debate over conflict of interest in American public life, a debate which, in turn, lies at the heart of our democratic discourse. They also constitute the book's central theme, and my goal has been to explore their many implications.

Nor is it the case that I have no advice to offer, although it is not of the sort that one often finds in books on government ethics. The concluding section of Larry Sabato and Glenn Simpson's *Dirty Little Secrets: The Persistence of Corruption in American Politics* (1996), for example, is titled "Remedies." As do other such sections in other such books, it lists the authors' recommended regulatory (or deregulatory) innovations, their "program of reform." Readers looking for such a program in *this* book's chapter on Remedies would have been disappointed. It is emblematic of conflict of interest that even the material discussed under "remedies" would be part of the problem, not part of the solution.

Nevertheless, it is possible to draw some recommendations from America's fifty-year experience debating conflict of interest in public life. Yet just as I have resisted taking established positions in most of the controversies I explore, attempting instead to reframe or reinterpret them, I now offer prescriptions that elude programmatic form but rather center on narrowing the range of conflict-of-interest's various legal, moral, and political disagreements. In my analyses, I tried to hover over regulatory minutiae, descending only where necessary; here, in offering recommendations, I begin by excluding regulatory tinkering, which (however occasionally and modestly helpful) will never bring any significant resolution to conflict of interest's many controversies. Instead, if we are to ameliorate conflict-of-interest in American public life, we must engage at a deeper level. Because I have looked at the way we talk about conflict of interest, my recommendations have to do with the way we talk about conflict of interest.

As a point of departure, recall a suggestion made in the Introduction. Our debate over conflict of interest has become a crucible where legal, political, and moral arguments come together as combustible equals. Not that each kind of consideration is always present in every single conflict-of-interest debate, but no one of them faces any kind of prior restraint. In foreign-policy deliberation, by contrast, moral and political considerations usually seem more dominant than legal issues: the international legal regime, after all, does not have the status of domestic law. In constitutional discourse, legal and moral arguments are generally more welcome than anything overtly political: our judicial tradition shies away from the unabashedly political. In domestic-policy discussion, we frame legal approaches to deal with political demands while remaining reticent, after a point, to base policy prescriptions on particular moral doctrines—because our procedural-liberal tradition would not tolerate it. There are, of course, many caveats and cavils one could register to this point. But there is also, I believe, a fundamental truth to it. And if true it shows an embodied wisdom. If foreign-policy debate always had to conjure with enforceable legal regimes, if constitutional courts had to fully and explicitly calculate political consequences, if domestic policy deliberation had to deeply engage competing moral perspectives, then the result would be total deadlock—an absence of *any kind* of advance, a wholesale replaying of the same kinds of exchanges over and over . . . Just as has been the case with debate over conflict of interest in American public life.

Accordingly, my suggestion—simple to state but difficult to execute—is to surgically leech legal, political, or moral considerations, where appropriate, out of conflict-of-interest discourse. Doing so will not resolve the various debates surrounding conflict of interest any more than our foreign, constitutional, or domestic debates have been resolved. But it does promise a way, perhaps the only way, of making our government-ethics discourse less chaotic and acrimonious. I have three specific proposals.

First, consider the various categories of conflict, the various kinds of impaired mental state discussed in Part I. Impaired mental states compose the *mala in se,* the evils in themselves we seek to prohibit with conflict-of-interest law. Unfortunately, they are also legally incognizable, which is why the law focuses on objective *mala prohibita* that might simply *occasion* impaired mental states. While such *mala prohibita*—the mere possession of certain interests, the mere engagement in certain kinds of otherwise normal professional or social contact, the mere undertaking of certain kinds of otherwise permissible business activities—are legally cognizable, they are also, in and of themselves, morally innocuous. This isn't to deny that in many cases officials who commit a *malum prohibitum* also fall into the *malum in se* of a tainted state-of-mind, nor that the evidence that this has happened can be impressively suggestive. But no violator of the conflict-of-interest laws is ever—or could ever be—found guilty of a *malum in se,* a conflicted state-of-mind, because the law cannot make a crime out of states-of-mind in and of themselves. Violators, hence, can be found guilty only of a *malum prohibitum.* Although the ethics laws reap criticism for legislating morality, they in fact do just the opposite: they are, in an important way, devoid of moral content.

And yet the mere holding of certain interests while in office, or the simple engagement in particular kinds of activities upon leaving it, or the innocuous undertaking of stipulated sorts of remunerative relationships, have taken on the aura of real moral transgression. Notwithstanding that we outlaw such acts for reasons of pure legal convenience and not because they are morally wrong in themselves, committing them has nonetheless become morally stigmatizing. "In the public mind," Bayless Manning noted as long as thirty years ago, "to receive a gift or have a conflict of interest is now equated with venality."[2] Despite the fact that prophylactic law is not meant to "involve a judgment of the integrity of the official,"[3] we have come to assume that the ethics laws *are* a "moral measurement" and we therefore "place stigma" on officials who violate them."[4]

Consider another prophylactic law with which conflict-of-interest regulation is often compared: the speed limit.[5] The *malum in se* it aims to prevent—driving dangerously—is certainly a moral evil in itself. But laws that prohibit "dangerous driving" are notably vague.[6] So instead, the speeding laws erect a related *malum prohibitum*—driving over fifty-five miles per hour, say—which, though readily amenable to legal phraseology, is not in itself a moral wrong. What is more, we all realize this. That is why, in most cases, we do not stigmatize someone simply for exceeding the speed limit.[7] Going sixty is not equated with moral turpitude. But holding certain interests while being in a position to affect them *is.*[8]

The problem with conflict-of-interest law is that it has become a moral stigmatizer when, in reality, it is just law. Of course, we ought not abolish speeding laws simply because their moral content is nil, and I am certainly not saying we should do so with conflict-of-interest laws. We need conflict-of-interest laws. But, as we do with speeding laws, we should recognize them, morally, for what they are. Or, more exactly, for what they are not. "Conflict-of-interest law," as the philosopher Hadley Arkes puts it, "punishes things that are not wrong in themselves . . . it does not identify any categorical wrongdoing or situation that must of necessity lead to wrongdoing."[9] What conflict-of-interest law outlaws is "not wrongful . . . in and of itself," as the editors of the *Harvard Law Review* noted in 1981.[10] The use of the terms "wrongful in and of itself" and "wrong in themselves" is revealing. It highlights how far afield conflict-of-interest laws rest from the wrong in itself; it reminds us that the laws, in and of themselves, prohibit situations with no moral charge. We often rebuke those who wantonly use the conflict-of-interest laws as political weapons. But they would not have become such effective political weapons had they not, falsely, acquired moral warheads. In denuding the conflict-of-interest laws of the overly freighted moral charges they have acquired, we would defuse them as politically-destructive devices. If we could somehow keep in mind that these particular laws are *only* laws and not moral statements or political instruments; if we could weave the strands articulated by Arkes and the *Harvard Law Review* more tightly into our public consideration of conflict of interest, then we would have taken an important step toward making debate less needlessly rancorous than it is now.[11]

If the problems discussed in Part I, "Conflict," are fundamentally legal—involving as they do a flight from the subjective to the objective—those addressed in Part II, "Interest," are essentially moral, since they take us from the objective realm deep into the subjective. They involve us in public debates over sincerity, hypocrisy, character, principle, friendship, conviction, and self-and-other, all of which are preeminently moral topics. They always will be moral topics, and we should recognize it—especially since the temptation to address them in both legal or political terms is so compelling.

On the one hand, we devise ever-newer legal instruments to grapple with these essentially extralegal, moral questions. We dispatch U.S. attorneys, independent counsels, or congressional ethics committees to inquire into issues of character, Federal Election Commission (FEC) lawyers to divine the intent of contributors and politicians, IRS investigators to disentangle the partisan from the nonpartisan, and courts or administrative tribunals to separate good combinations-of-roles and *ex parte* contacts from bad. Many of these issues can, and must be, dealt with legally—to a point. But on any major question, U.S. attorneys, independent counsels, FEC lawyers, IRS investigators, and others will always leave a residue of unsatisfactory moral irresolution.

On the other hand, of course, there are those who, shaking their heads at such folly, insist that these issues are essentially political and should therefore be resolved politically. We should focus on officials' political records, not their private lives. We should recognize that campaign activity is red-blooded political conflict; campaign contributions, even if encumbering in the giving and the receiving, are part and parcel of democratic political communication and response.[12] We should give legislative and executive officials a freer hand in deciding the vast range of issues they confront, issues that are irremediably political and for which biased, predisposed, and favoritist approaches are appropriate, let alone unavoidable.[13] For every Senator McCain who tries to bring much of this moral terrain into the province of the law, there will be a Senator McConnell to tell us that it belongs to politics. For every Congressional Accountability Project that seeks to expand the use of the independent counsel or extend the campaign-finance laws, there is a Heritage Foundation that urges that unrestrained political argument, bargaining between interests and officials, and mutual partisan vigilance is the best, indeed the only, guarantor of good government.[14]

Obviously, law and politics have their place in these areas. But their champions make exaggerated claims for their efficacy. The questions of sincerity and hypocrisy, of principle and commitment, of sacrifice and character, of friendship and attachment—which, as suggested in Part II, are so central to our public discourse—are first and foremost *moral* issues. Whether having to do with sexual activity, business practices, or social behavior—or campaign contributions, access-granting, or *ex parte* contacts—each is linked to our unending need to descry officials and citizens as moral agents, to the quintessentially moral question of the subject and its boundaries. Such issues will always elude both legal and political resolution. Law will never tell us whether an official is sincere or hypocritical, or distinguish acceptable from unacceptable *quid pro quo*s. Nor will confining ourselves to politicians' public records and utterances, or adopting a freewheeling *realpolitik* approach to government decisions, ever leave us with the sense that no deeper issues remain to be explored. Neither is satisfactory; neither substitutes for the moral judgment on which these questions ultimately call. Officials' genuineness and their self-servingness, their views on sacrifice of and for office, their exchanges of economic and political favors in close cases: These will always impose on our moral judgment, on the faculties we use to judge the moral behavior of others. To recognize where moral issues come into play in conflict-of-interest discourse, and to acknowledge that attempts to resolve them through law or politics will never satisfy us, would also make the surrounding debate far more tractable. There is a role for serious moral deliberation about official behavior, notwithstanding our attempts to submerge it.

It would, then, help us to recognize that the objective issues of conflict are essentially legal ones, and that the subjective questions of encumbrance are unavoidably moral ones. Finally—and along similar lines—the temperature of discourse would fall if we acknowledged that the issues of appearance are purely political ones. As argued in Part III, the appearance standard holds sway in a realm not only beyond law—applying as it does to situations where no extant ethics legislation, rule, or regulation governs—but beyond established moral consensus, in that it often applies to acts whose moral status is controversial at best. The purposes of the appearance standard, accordingly, are profoundly political, meant not to remedy legal or moral but political harms, ruptures to public confidence in government, gulfs between the perceptions or sensitivities of officials and citizens. Unfortunately, prosecutors in appearance cases all too often seek legal penalties, and legal penalties inevitably come with moral stigma. Those defending themselves, for their part, insist—usually plausibly—that they have broken no law and retain a clean moral conscience. Neither recognizes that to talk appearances is to talk politics.

What would it mean to recognize that appearances take place in a realm beyond law and morality, a realm first and foremost of politics? Once in a while, discourse gives us a glimpse. As I argued in Part III, the appearance standard—notwithstanding the often compensating balm it applies to public cynicism—nevertheless creates crime without law and punishes without crime, thereby imposing antilegalistic burdens on officials. What I did not explore are those occasional cases where, in applying the appearance standard, we have displayed an interesting and equally antilegalistic tendency to exonerate without punishing, thereby helping to lift the burden. For what we are seeking in appearance cases, ultimately, is simply a reassurance, on the part of the officeholder, that his perceptions and sensibilities are in broad alignment with the public's. The appearance standard, Bayless Manning wrote on its inception thirty years ago, offers a means of enforcing our "demand that [officeholders] constantly reassure us"; hence, "preferred remedies for problems of 'appearances' should be those that amount to . . . assertions or good faith dedications—measures such as sworn statements . . . publicly conducted testimony and disclaimers."[15] Or, put another way, if in the realm of appearances to *take offense* is often to *create an offense*, and if to *accuse* is to *convict* ("innuendo," as Congressman Thomas Downey put it, "means you're guilty"), then to *confess* should perhaps suffice to *serve the sentence*.

Once again, John Tower's situation is revealing. In his memoir of the confirmation hearings surrounding his appointment as secretary of defense-designate, Tower speculates on the impact that his "role as a former consultant to defense contractors" had on his failure to be confirmed. He recalls how Senator Sam Nunn was struck by (what Nunn called) Tower's "'almost total insensitivity' to the appearance of conflict of interest" raised by Tower's consulting practice.[16] What by Tower's own account bothered Nunn, more specifically, was not the questionable *appearances* raised by Tower's record as a consultant to defense contractors *per se*—much less any *real* impropriety—but rather the "insensitivity" Tower showed toward the appearance question during his confirmation testimony.

Tower then offers his own retrospective commentary on Nunn's assessment, and his decisive point is that Nunn had earlier called him an "honest person."[17] Tower thinks he has caught Nunn in a contradiction—how could an "honest person" really be so "insensitive"?—but in fact he has profoundly misunderstood Nunn's principal concerns. On legal and moral criteria, Tower may well have been an honest man. But Nunn was looking for a political reassurance that Tower saw things the way the people's representatives did, that he perceived reality the way that much of the public does and was sensitive to norms much of the public embraces. It is unlikely that Tower would have been confirmed for other reasons. But Nunn's capacity here to break out from the legalistic and moralistic gauze surrounding appearances—his ability to recognize that an honest man (in fact, perhaps *only* an honest individual) can commit what are truly appearance violations—is as rare as an acknowledgement would have been from Tower, who, because he saw himself as legally and morally clean, refused to supply it.[18]

But assuming that all Nunn wanted was indeed a *mea culpa* from Tower, then still, would not such a request be a rather cynical one, implying, as it seems to, that officials who contravene the appearance standard should get off easy? Alternatively, is it not just a little frightening, redolent as it is of political-trial forced apologies and avowals? As argued in Part III, our insistence on reining officials within the bounds of democratic perceptions and sensitivities is neither cynical nor frightening but—although it may involve the contravention of other fundamental norms—integral to democratic politics. If the appearance standard is really meant simply to restore political communion between official and public, then neither legal penalty nor moral sanction should be necessary. And, in fact, such political communion is precisely what we do seek, or should be seeking, in many appearance cases.

In dealing with conflict of interest, we should take a leaf from our other policy debates. When it comes to the wholly objective, prophylactic way we approach conflict, we should try to scrape away some of the moral and political encrustation that now adheres to what are essentially purely legal strictures. When it comes to questions about what kinds of subjective encumbrances prey upon official judgment—interests, yes, but also biases, friendships, attachments, and loyalties—we should drain off much of the heavy-handed legal and blithe political vocabulary and recognize that the issues are essentially moral and will always require us to engage our moral judgment. And when it comes to appearance questions, which lie in a realm beyond law and moral consensus, we should drain off some of the legalistic and moralistic steam that surrounds our discourse and understand these issues for what they are: essentially political. How we would do all of this is a question I cannot answer. But five decades of experience suggest that changing the way we talk about these questions—hence understand them—is the most promising avenue for injecting some semblance of reason, decency, and closure into the never-ending stream of conflict-of-interest cases that flow at us. It offers the only lasting way of making conflict-of-interest discourse less factious and less futile.

Conflict of interest is the child of legal and political liberalism. No matter how tainted an official's subjective mental state may be, legal liberalism forbids our directly penalizing it and compels us instead to take an objective approach to conflicted judgment. Thus, we prohibit certain classes of external conduct that might simply lead officials into inner conflict, since we cannot enter into their minds and determine whether, in any given case, they will actually manage to rise above whatever personal interests they may have at stake (as undoubtedly some will do). But when it comes to determining the kinds of entities that should count as such interests in the first place, it is political liberalism that inexorably leads us to take a subjective approach. By political liberalism, I mean of course not the views that distinguish Edward Kennedy from Phil Gramm, but the very presumptions of our political order. Because political liberalism precludes our accessing an objective conception of the public interest (ask Edward Kennedy and Phil Gramm), we must reassure ourselves that officials are at least adhering to their own subjective conceptions of the public interest. And this task, in turn, requires us to go far beyond objective, hard, pecuniary interests and to ask ourselves—in any given case—which among an official's subjective beliefs, predispositions, commitments, relationships, and attachments encumber, and which contribute to, her capacity to make judgments in the public interest by her own best lights. Thanks to legal liberalism, then, we take an objective approach to conflict. Thanks to political liberalism, we take a subjective approach to interest.

Even when it comes to appearances, it is legal and political liberalism that structures the debate. Legal liberalism admonishes us not to penalize officials for appearance violations. To a legal liberal, the appearance standard creates crime without law and punishes without crime. But it is the privatizing and pluralizing traits that some philosophers associate with political liberalism— principally our own disengagement from the facts and disagreement about the norms of public life—that seem to make an appearance standard inevitable. As long as America is a liberal polity—especially one where mental states lie beyond legal sanction and the public interest lies beyond political definition—conflict of interest as we know it will always remain front and center in our public life. This leaves us no option but to change the way we talk about it.

NOTES

Introduction

1. *ABC Breaking News,* April 22, 1994, Transcript no. 143–1, p. 4.
2. Jeff Gerth, "Top Arkansas Lawyer Helped Hillary Clinton Turn Big Profit," *New York Times,* March 18, 1994, p. A20.
3. Roger Morris, *Partners in Power: The Clintons and Their America* (New York: Henry Holt, 1996), pp. 235, 310, 451 and James B. Stewart, *Blood Sport: The President and His Adversaries* (New York: Simon and Schuster, 1996), pp. 92, 417.
4. *U.S. v. Mississippi Valley Generating Company,* 364 U. S. 529 (1961) at 549–550.
5. U.S. Senate, Committee on the Judiciary, Hearings, *Integrity in Post-Employment Act of 1986,* 99th Congress, 2nd Session, April 29 and June 18, 1986, p. 21.
6. Melvin Aron Eisenberg, "The Responsive Model of Contract Law," *Stanford Law Review* 36 (1984), p. 1107.
7. Bayless Manning, "The Purity Potlatch: An Essay on Conflict of Interest, American Government, and Moral Escalation," *Federal Bar Journal* 24 (1964), pp. 252–3.
8. Bayless Manning, *Federal Conflict of Interest Law* (Cambridge, Mass.: Harvard University Press, 1964), p. 124.
9. Manning, "Purity Potlatch," p. 252.
10. See, e.g., Michael Davis, "Conflict of Interest," *Business and Professional Ethics Journal* 1 (1982), pp. 18, 23.
11. U.S. Senate, Committee on Agriculture and Forestry, *Nomination of Earl Lauer Butz to be Secretary of Agriculture,* 92nd Congress, 1st Session, November 17–19, 1971, p. 57.
12. Susan Hoekema, "Questioning the Impartiality of Judges," *Temple Law Quarterly* 60 (1987), p. 705.
13. Note, "Conflicts-of-Interests of Government Personnel: An Appraisal of the Philadelphia Situation," *University of Pennsylvania Law Review* 107 (1959), p. 994.
14. Walter Goodman, *All Honorable Men* (Boston: Little Brown, 1963), p. 118.
15. Judith N. Shklar, *Legalism: Law, Morals and Political Trials* (Cambridge, Mass.: Harvard University Press, 1964), p. 152.
16. Peter L. Strauss, "Disqualifications of Decisional Officials in Rulemaking," *Columbia Law Review* 80 (1980), p. 1037.
17. See, e.g., *Wiseman v. Spaulding,* 573 S.W. 2d 490 (Tenn., 1978). Arguably, cer-

tain procurement officials, too, operate in a realm where there are "agreed-upon ends" and it is possible to develop "results-based performance evaluation" that would substitute for certain kinds of *ex ante* conflict-of-interest controls on official judgment. This is the claim Steven Kelman advances in *Procurement and Public Management* (Washington: American Enterprise Institute, 1990), p. 91. As Kelman puts it, to develop procurement standards "is less of a political challenge than, say, developing standards for a welfare program because the evaluation of performance in computer management is less controversial" (p. 101).

18. See, for example, Melinda Ledden Sidak's review of Peter W. Morgan and Glenn H. Reynolds, *The Appearance of Impropriety in America* (New York: Free Press, 1997), in *The Weekly Standard,* September 15, 1997, pp. 37–38 and Ronald M. Levin, "Congressional Ethics and Constituent Advocacy in An Age of Mistrust," *Michigan Law Review* 95 (1996), p. 107.

19. Ronald Dworkin, *Law's Empire* (Cambridge, Mass.: Harvard University Press, 1986), p. 52.

20. Manning, *Federal Conflict of Interest Law* (Cambridge, Mass.: Harvard University Press, 1964), p. 1. Perkins chaired the New York Bar Association committee that wrote *Conflict of Interest and Federal Service.*

21. Alan Norrie, "Subjectivism, Objectivism and the Limits of Criminal Recklessness," *Oxford Journal of Legal Studies* 12 (1992), pp. 45–46.

22. A. B. Atkinson, *Social Justice and Public Policy* (Brighton: Harvester/Wheatsheaf, 1983), p. 199.

23. Michael Walzer, *Interpretation and Social Criticism* (Cambridge, Mass.: Harvard University Press, 1987), pp. 20, 22, 26.

24. Amy Gutmann and Dennis Thompson, "Moral Conflict and Political Consensus," in R. Bruce Douglass et al, eds., *Liberalism and the Good* (New York: Routledge, 1990), p. 125.

1. The Perils of Prophylactic Law

1. Moreover, in determining whether an act *exceeds* the legitimate bounds of official discretion, courts will often simply ask themselves whether there might be a rational basis for it. If so, they will uphold the act even if the officials involved executed it without, in their own minds, actually having gone through such a rational process. On this doctrine, "an agency could act irrationally on the basis of the information available to it but be upheld by a court which finds a rational basis in the information, although not necessarily the basis the agency used" (see William Funk, "Rationality of State Administrative Rulemaking," *Administrative Law Review* 43 [1991], p. 159). In investigating acts that fall *within* the bounds of official discretion, by contrast, courts (as we shall see) simply ask themselves whether the official might have been encumbered in executing it. If so they will penalize the official even if, within the workings of his own mind, he in fact overcame any such encumbrance.

2. See Association of the Bar of the City of New York, *Conflict of Interest and Federal Service* (Cambridge, Mass.: Harvard University Press, 1960), p. 19.

3. Note, "Conflict of Interests: State Government Employees," *Virginia Law Review* 47 (1961), p. 1056.

4. A.C.E. Lynch, "The Mental Element in the *Actus Reus*," *Law Quarterly Review* 98 (1982), p. 116.

5. William Blackstone, *Commentaries on the Laws of England* (Chicago: University of Chicago Press, 1979), vol. 4, p. 21.

6. Roscoe Pound, *Law and Morals* (Chapel Hill: University of North Carolina Press, 1924), p. 68.

7. Jack Maskell, *The Acceptance of Gifts by Employees in the Executive Branch* (Washington: Congressional Research Service, November 15, 1985), pp. 4–5.

8. A *malum prohibitum* is an act "not inherently immoral," but rather "an illegality resulting from positive law," whereas a *malum in se* is a "wrong in itself." See *Black's Law Dictionary,* 6th ed. (St. Paul: West, 1990), p. 959.

9. U.S. Senate, Committee on the Judiciary, Hearings, *Integrity in Post-Employment Act of 1986,* 99th Congress, 2nd Session, April 29 and June 18, 1986, p. 21.

10. Hence, the Association of the Bar of the City of New York's famous twofold observation (*Conflict of Interest and Federal Service,* pp. 3–4) that "[a] conflict of interest does not (a) necessarily presuppose that action by the official favoring one of his interests will be prejudicial to the other, nor (b) that the official will in fact resolve the conflict in favor of his personal interest if there is a conflict." We cannot tell, in other words, whether his favoring one of his interests—namely, his personal interest—will be prejudicial to the other, the public interest, because we cannot (as a normative proposition) tell what the public interest is. And we cannot tell to what extent the official may have internally resolved any conflict in favor of his personal interest, because we cannot (as a matter of fact) read officials' minds.

11. See the comments of Arthur B. Culvahouse, Jr., "Will the Ethics Reform Act Change the Way Government Conducts Business in the 1990s?," *Federal Bar News and Journal* 37 (1990), p. 418.

12. Statement of Morton H. Halperin and Jerry J. Berman on behalf of the American Civil Liberties Union, in U.S. Senate Committee on the Judiciary, Hearing, *Integrity in Post-Employment Act of 1986,* 99th Congress, 2nd Session, April 29 and June 18, 1986, pp. 193–202.

13. Bayless Manning, "The Purity Potlatch: An Essay on Conflicts of Interest, American Government and Moral Escalation," *The Federal Bar Journal* 24 (1964), p. 253.

14. Joseph S. Nye, Jr., "Corruption and Political Development: A Cost-Benefit Analysis," *American Political Science Review* 61 (1967), p. 419.

15. Robert M. Rhodes, "Enforcement of Legislative Ethics: Conflict within the Conflict of Interest Laws," *Harvard Journal on Legislation* 10 (1973), p. 376.

16. American Bar Association Disciplinary Rule 8–101 (emphases mine).

17. Apart from the problems it entails in trying to cognize the term "public interest," the ABA's (mis)understanding of the *malum in se* se implies a particular conception of the term "potential conflict of interest." If one pushes the offense forward, as would the ABA, to the point where an actual conflict of interest arises only where an official ultimately acts in a fashion contrary to the public interest,

then it is merely a *potential* conflict of interest that arises whenever an official's underlying state-of-mind is impaired. Or, put another way, it would be only a "potential" conflict of interest that arises whenever an officeholder possesses an interest that biases her official judgment. And an "actual conflict of interest" would occur only if she then ultimately acted to favor that interest to the detriment of the public interest. Indeed, the term "potential conflict" of interest is often so misused. As Marc Rodwin notes, "[s]ome observers use the term *potential conflict of interest* to refer to [what is properly understood as a] *conflict of interest,* and restrict the term *conflict of interest* to *disloyal behavior,*" a maneuver Rodwin rightly describes as inappropriate (see *Medicine, Money and Morals: Physicians' Conflicts of Interest* [New York: Oxford, 1993], p. 9). John Rohr, likewise, criticizes those who, in referring to "potential conflicts of interest," are "apparently unpersuaded of the redundancy in qualifying as potential a problem which by definition deals with potential evils" (see "Financial Disclosure: Power in Search of Policy," *Public Personnel Management Journal* 10 [1981], p. 31).

18. See, e.g., Note, "The Corporate 'Termination Bonus' for Executives Entering Government Service: Proper Government Recruiting Aid or Conflict of Interest?" *Southern California Law Review* 79 (1976), p. 849.

19. See Jeanne S. Archibald, general counsel, Department of the Treasury, *Memorandum for Robert L. Clarke, Comptroller of the Currency: Review of Your Financial Filings and Activities,* June 4, 1991 and "Mr. Clarke's Investments," editorial, *The Washington Post,* May 1, 1991, p. A18.

20. *Hall* v. *Small Business Administration,* 695 F. 2d 175 (5th Cir., 1983) at 179.

21. Morton Mintz and Jerry S. Cohen, *Power, Inc.: Public and Private Rulers and How to Make Them Accountable* (New York: Viking, 1976), chap. 18 and *Roberts* v. *Bailar* 625 F. 2d 125 (6th Cir., 1980).

22. Christine T. Sistare, "On the Use of Strict Liability in the Criminal Law," *Canadian Journal of Philosophy* 17 (1987), pp. 395–408.

23. Certainly, the meaning of the terms *strict liability, general intent,* and *specific intent* are subject to controversy. But I believe my very general use of them here is fairly uncontested. See Michael Tigar, "'Wilfulness' and 'Ignorance' in Federal Criminal Law,'" *Cleveland State Law Review* 37 (1989), pp. 527–529.

24. Rollin M. Perkins and Ronald N. Boyce, *Criminal Law,* 3rd edition (Mineola: The Foundation Press, 1982), p. 904.

25. Thomas Andrew Green, *Verdict According to Conscience: Perspectives on the English Criminal Jury System* (Chicago: University of Chicago Press, 1985), p. 308 (quoting *Observations On a Late Publication* by Martin Madan [1786]); see also James Boyd, *Above the Law* (New York: New American Library, 1968), p. 260.

26. See, for example, U.S. Office of Government Ethics Letter 94X10 and Dana Priest, "Suddenly 'Being Taken Seriously' at Office of Government Ethics," *Washington Post,* January 15, 1992, p. A22.

27. Notably, all seventeen members of Congress who were convicted of corruption in the 1980s voted for the Ethics in Government Act. See U.S. House of Representatives, Bipartisan Task Force on Ethics, *Congressional Ethics Reform,* 100th Congress, 1st Session, May 24, 1989, p. 34.

28. See, e.g., Note, "Section Six of the Office of Federal Procurement Policy Act

Amendments of 1978: A New Ethical Standard in Government Contracting?" *Cumberland Law Review* 20 (1990), p. 423, some of the discussion in *Congressional Record*, October 20, 1988, p. S17073, *U.S. v. Nasser*, 476 F. 2d 111 (7th Cir., 1973) at 118; *U.S. v. Johnson*, 419 F. 2d 56 (4th Cir., 1969) at 60.

The further that criminal prophylactic law retreats from the *malum in se*—such that violators may fail to see any moral harm in their conduct—the closer we are thus driven to require some form of *mens rea* on the part of the offender. Notably, the converse is also the case. When it comes to those criminal prophylactic laws that more closely approach the *malum in se*, our tendency is to hold offenders strictly liable. Thus bigamy, the sale of narcotics, or statutory rape—all of which are technically offenses *mala prohibita*—nevertheless come so close to the *malum in se*, to the bad to be punished, that strict liability seems suitable: After all, offenders should understand the harm they might be causing (see Glanville Williams, *Textbook of Criminal Law* [London: Stevens and Stevens, 1978], p. 912).

In this way, criminal prophylactic law not only inverts the approach we take to *non*criminal prophylactic law—where as the law retreats from the *malum in se*, as in speeding and barbecue laws, we feel *more* comfortable imposing strict liability. It also upends the approach we take to nonprophylactic criminal law, where as the law comes to embody the *malum in se*—as it does in murder, for example—we abandon strict liability and feel compelled to find *mens rea* before deeming someone an offender. "There is no offense *malum in se* without some form of *mens rea*," as Wayne R. LaFave and Austin W. Scott, Jr., put it (see *Handbook on Criminal Law* [St. Paul: West, 1972], p. 881).

29. See some of the discussion in Prepared Statement of Archibald Cox, House Committee on the Judiciary, Subcommittee on Administrative Law and Governmental Relations, Hearing, *Post-Employment Restrictions for Federal Officers and Employees*, 101st Congress, 1st Session, June 28, 1989, p. 196.

30. *United States v. Nofziger*, 878 F. 2d 442 (D.C. Cir.), *cert. denied*, 110 S. Ct. 564 (1989); see also Note, "*United States v. Nofziger* and the Revision of 18 U.S.C. §207: The Need for a New Approach to the *Mens Rea* Requirements of the Federal Criminal Law," *Notre Dame Law Review* 65 (1990), pp. 804–805. The examples I offer come from 18 U.S.C. §207, which deals with postemployment issues. But this particular dynamic between the prophylactic acts that constitute the offense, and the specifically intending mental state that characterizes the offender, pervades conflict-of-interest law more broadly. Consider 18 U.S.C. §208, which regulates self-dealing. Up until the 1962 U.S. Code amendments, officials were held responsible for "statutory violations regardless of whether [they] knew of the law or the ethical principles underlying it;" indeed for most state-level self-dealing law, "misconduct in office [was a] strict liability" affair; "intent [was] not required"; "ignorance of the law or even of the fact that one ha[d] a legally conflicting interest" was "regarded as no excuse." See James P. Clarke, "Codes of Ethics: Waste of Time or Important Control?" *Public Management* 49 (1967), p. 224; "Conflicts of Interest: State Government Employees," pp. 1045, 1059; and Harold Feinberg and Alfred A. Porro, Jr., "Ethics, Incompatibility and Conflicts of Interest of Public Officials," *Current Municipal Problems* 7 (1966), p. 403. But in 1962, 18 U.S.C. §208 was amended to "specifically require knowl-

edge before the employee [could] be penalized for acting on matters in which he [was] interested"; there now had to be "knowledge of conflict of interest." See Thomas R. White III, "To Have or Not to Have: Conflicts of Interest and Financial Planning for Judges," *Law and Contemporary Problems* 35 (1970), p. 215; Roswell B. Perkins, "The New Federal Conflict of Interest Law," *Harvard Law Review* 76 (1963), p. 1134; and Bayless Manning, *Federal Conflict of Interest Law* (Cambridge, Mass.: Harvard University Press, 1964), p. 133.

Similarly, the last few years of debate over procurement integrity was in large measure a disagreement over whether to incorporate specific-intent requirements into prophylactic conflict-of-interest law. Because "prosecutor[s] face . . . obstacle[s] in establishing a direct link between a job offer and an action by a Pentagon official to benefit a future employer," and because "without hard evidence of such cause and effect, conflicts of interest are next to impossible to prove," the Procurement Integrity Act prophylactically made it an offense for contractors to hire any officials who worked on procurements involving them. But precisely because such an offense constitutes a legal prophylaxis, not something an employer's moral intuitions could be expected to discern, "to convict in court you must prove intent"; i.e., that the employer *knowingly* hired an official who was precluded from taking the job in question. See Robert A. Kittle, "Furor Over Pentagon's 'Revolving Door,'" *U.S. News and World Report* April 29, 1985, p. 29. Finally, in light of the *Nofziger* case, Congress amended 18 USC §207(c) so that it is no longer confined to matters pending before the ex-official's former agency. The "knowledge" requirement, however, still remains for the rest of the offense.

31. See, e.g., *Commonwealth* v. *Boris,* 58 N. E. 2d 8 (1944) at 12. Only one postemployment statute, 18 U.S.C §207(a)(2), requires that an ex-official "know . . . or reasonably should know" that the matter on which she lobbies fell under her official responsibility.

32. *Congressional Record* (Senate), March 25, 1977, p. 9102.

33. Martin H. Redish and Lawrence C. Marshall, "Adjudicatory Independence and the Values of Procedural Due Process," *Yale Law Journal* 95 (1986), p. 495; Ross F. Cranston, "Regulating Conflict of Interest of Government Officials: A Comparative Analysis," *Vanderbilt Journal of Transnational Law* 12 (1979), p. 219; Ian McF. Rogers, "Conflicts of Interest: A Trap for Unwary Politicians," *Osgoode Hall Law Journal* 11 (1973), p. 542; and Robert N. Roberts, *White House Ethics: The History of the Politics of Conflict of Interest Regulation* (New York: Greenwood Press, 1988), p. 84.

34. Office of Senate Legal Counsel, *Compilation of Certain Legal Material Prepared on the Conflict of Interest Statutes,* Memorandum for Senator Saltonstall, January 16, 1953, p. 20.

35. Perkins, "The New Federal Conflict-of-Interest Law," p. 1136.

36. Anthony Lewis, "The Prosecutorial State: Criminalizing American Politics," *The American Prospect* 42 (January–February, 1999), p. 26.

37. U.S. House of Representatives, Committee on the Judiciary, Subcommittee on Administrative Law and Governmental Relations, Hearing, *Modifying the Honoraria Prohibition for Federal Employees,* 102nd Congress, 1st Session, February 7, 1991, pp. 1–14.

38. Deborah M. Levy, "Advice for Sale," *Foreign Policy* 67 (1987), pp. 78–79.
39. U.S. Senate Committee on Governmental Affairs, Subcommittee on Oversight of Government Management, Hearing, *S. 402, The Ethics in Government Act of 1993, and S. 79, The Responsible Government Act of 1993,* 103rd Congress, 1st Session, March 5, 1993, p. 152; see also Office of the Press Secretary, the White House, *President Bush's Ethics Reform Proposals,* April 12, 1989.
40. See, generally, the annual *Federal Ethics Reports* produced by the Washington Service Bureau.

2. The Topography of Conflict

1. See, e.g., Robert G. Vaughn, "Ethics in Government and the Vision of Public Service," *George Washington Law Review* 58 (1990), pp. 419, 423 and Sanford Watzman, *Conflict of Interest: Politics and the Money Game* (New York: Cowles, 1971), pp. 32–33.
2. U.S. Office of Government Ethics Letter 86X19.
3. U.S. House of Representatives, Committee on the Judiciary, Subcommittee on Antitrust, Hearing, *Activities of Peter Strobel,* 84th Congress, 1st Session, October 26–31, 1955, pp. 24–26.
4. It was no response to this problem to point out, as Hickel's brother did, that Hickel had scrupulously instructed him "to make sure that no Hickel enterprise does business" with the federal government. The problem was not self-dealing but abuse of office. See the account in Watzman, *Conflict of Interest,* p. 57.
5. David Frier, *Conflict of Interest in the Eisenhower Administration* (Ames: University of Iowa Press, 1969), pp. 79–80.
6. Beth Nolan, "Public Interest, Private Income: Conflicts and Control Limits on Outside Income of Governmental Officials," *Northwestern University Law Review* 87 (1992), pp. 57–147.
7. Association of the Bar of the City of New York, *Conflict of Interest and the Federal Service* (Cambridge, Mass.: Harvard University Press, 1960), p. 7.

3. Self-Dealing

1. U.S. House of Representatives, Committee on the Judiciary, Subcommittee on Antitrust, Hearings, *Federal Conflict of Interest Legislation,* 86th Congress, 2nd Session, May 25 and June 1, 1960, p. 611.
2. Minnesota Governor's Committee on Ethics in Government, Report (1959), p. 17.
3. Thomas L. Carson, "Conflict of Interest," *Journal of Business Ethics* 13 (1994), p. 393.
4. Roswell Perkins, "Federal Conflict of Interest Law," *Harvard Law Review* 76 (1963), p. 1129.
5. *U.S. v. Brown,* 381 U.S. 437 (1965) at 472.
6. See, e.g., Frank Anechiarico and James B. Jacobs, *The Pursuit of Absolute Integrity: How Corruption Control Makes Government Ineffective* (Chicago: University of Chicago, 1996), p. 45.

7. See 5 CFR 25305.402 (b)(1).

8. I here combine terms from both the federal self-dealing statute, 18 U.S.C. §208, and the federal self-dealing regulation, 5 CFR 2635.401.

9. U.S. House of Representatives, Committee on the Judiciary, Subcommittee on Administrative Law and Governmental Relations, Hearings, *Defense Procurement Conflict of Interest Act,* 99th Congress, 2nd Session, January 29, 20, 1986, p. 58.

10. I borrow this term from U.S. Senate Committee on Interior and Insular Affairs, Hearings, *On Melvin A. Conant To Be Assistant Administrator of International Affairs at the Federal Energy Administration* 93rd Congress, 2nd Session, 1974, pp. 172–173 (emphasis mine).

11. 305 F. 2d 197 (9th Cir., 1962) at 210.

12. See, e.g., *In Re Starr,* 986 F. Supp. 1144 (E.D. Ark., 1977), at 1154 and Judicial Conference of the United States, Committee on Codes of Conduct, Advisory Opinion No. 27, October 28, 1973 (revised July 10, 1998).

13. All nine of what Common Cause describes as the "most serious or blatant" forms of self-dealing uncovered in a series of mid-seventies GAO investigations are in fact hybrids between self-dealing and one of the other types of conflict. See Common Cause, *Serving Two Masters: A Study of Conflict of Interest in the Executive Branch* (October 1976), pp. 19–21.

14. U.S. Office of Government Ethics Letter 92X12 and Robert M. Cohen, "Reagan's Cost Control 'Bloodhounds' are Hounded by Charges of Conflicts," *National Journal,* January 15, 1983, p. 123.

15. Marver H. Bernstein, "Ethics in Government: The Problems in Perspective," *National Civic Review* 61 (1972), p. 343.

16. *Piggott* v. *Borough of Hopewell,* 91 A.2d 667 (N.J., 1952) at 670; *County of Nevada* v. *MacMillen,* 522 P. 2d 1345 (Cal., 1974) at 1348.

17. *City of Bristol* v. *Dominion National Bank,* 149 S.E. 632 (Va., 1929) at 634 and *People* v. *Darby,* 250 P. 2d 743 (Cal., 1952) at 758.

18. U.S. House of Representatives, Committee on the Judiciary, Subcommittee on Administrative Law and Governmental Relations, Hearing, *Foreign Agents Compulsory Ethics in Trade Act of 1987,* 100th Congress, 1st Session, August 6, 1987, p. 88 (remarks of Barney Frank).

19. U.S. Office of Government Ethics Letter 91X17.

20. 252 N.W. (Wisc., 1934) at 298.

21. 35 F. Supp. 102 (D.N.J., 1940) at 104.

22. *Moody* v. *Shuffleton,* 262 P. 1095 (Cal., 1928) at 1096 and *People* v. *Elliott,* 252 P. 2d 661 (Cal., 1953) at 666.

23. U.S. Senate, Permanent Subcommittee on Investigations of the Committee on Government Operations, Hearings, *Harold E. Talbott—Secretary of the Air Force,* 84th Congress, 1st Session, July 21–25, 1955, p. 199.

24. Oliver E. Williamson, *Markets and Hierarchies* (New York: Free Press, 1975), pp. 56, 72–82.

25. Perkins, "The New Federal Conflict of Interest Law," p. 1119.

26. For example, the much-discussed distinction between outside *earned* income (consulting contracts or honoraria) and outside *unearned* income (dividends and profit-sharing) maps onto the difference between abuse of office and self-dealing.

To the extent that the official's relationship with a firm takes the form of a short-term contract or honorarium, variable at the firm's behest, then if the official is in a position to benefit the firm, the situation approaches one of abuse. To the extent that it takes the form of a dividend payment—remuneration not variable at the firm's behest—then when the official is in a position to benefit the firm, the situation falls into the class of self-dealing (any advantage to the firm redounds to him directly). Where the relationship falls between these stools—where an official can affect the interests of a firm from which he receives a regular wage or salary—the situation is generally taken to be self-dealing but can be and has been treated as abuse. See, e.g., Irwin W. Arieff, "Some Members Avoid Income Limit Rule," *Congressional Quarterly Weekly Report,* September 1, 1979, p. 1843.

27. Note, "Conflict of Interests of Government Personnel: An Appraisal of the Philadelphia Situation," *University of Pennsylvania Law Review* 107 (1959), p. 1002.

28. U.S. Office of Government Ethics Letter 89X6; see also "Some Thoughts on Outside Employment," *Office of Government Ethics Newsgram,* vol. 3, no. 3, May 1986, p. 3.

29. To some, this kind of distinction makes little sense: "The rules are such," Congressman Bob Michel has said, "that we can have a million dollars of dividends [from our own interests] and still be considered honorable and ethical, but if we earn a dollar over $9,700 [from second-party interests], we are unethical" (*Congressional Record,* October 28, 1981, p. H7820).

30. Steven Lubet, "Regulation of Judges' Business and Financial Activities," *Emory Law Journal* 37 (1988), p. 21; see also George J. Stigler, "The Economics of Conflict of Interest," *The Intellectual and the Marketplace* (New York: Cambridge University Press, 1984), pp. 26–30.

4. Undue Influence

1. *Burton* v. *United States,* 202 U.S. 344 (1906) at 368; see also *U.S.* v. *Adams,* 115 F. Supp. 731 (D.N.D., 1953), *Opinions of the Attorney General* 40 (1947), pp. 533, 534, and *Opinions of the Attorney General* 42 (1962), pp. 119–120.

2. David Frier, *Conflict of Interest in the Eisenhower Administration* (Ames: University of Iowa Press, 1969), p. 95.

3. See 5 CFR 2636.305 (a)(2) Example 1; see also U.S. Office of Government Ethics Letter 81X24.

4. *Burton* at 368. While the two statutes technically do prohibit representational activity before the courts, only acts of influence before the executive branch are ever prosecuted.

5. When a critic of the federal conflict-of-interest laws wants to exemplify what he sees as their general unintelligibility, he typically turns to the two statutes governing the exertion of undue influence (see, e.g., Roswell Perkins, "The New Federal Conflict of Interest Law," *Harvard Law Review* 76 (1963), p. 1143). The first, 18 U.S.C. §203, prohibits all officials—including legislators—from performing "representational services, as agent or attorney or otherwise," before any department, agency or court in relation to any "particular matter" in which "the United States is a party or has a direct and substantial interest." It does, however, require

that the official be compensated for his representation. The second statute, 18 U.S.C. §205, prohibits an official from acting as agent or attorney in the "prosecution of a claim against the United States" and, more broadly, from doing the same for any matter in which the U.S. "is a party or has a direct and substantial interest." Eighteen U.S.C. §205 does, however, exclude legislators and requires no receipt of compensation for an offense.

6. Note, "Conflict of Interests of Government Personnel: An Appraisal of the Philadelphia Situation," *University of Pennsylvania Law Review* 107 (1959), p. 1002.

7. See U.S. Office of Government Ethics Letters 94X8 and 88X6.

8. *Burton* at 368.

9. See also *U.S. v. Johnson*, 215 F. Supp. 300 (D.C. Md., 1963) at 315, Robert S. Getz, *Congressional Ethics: The Conflict of Interest Issue* (New York: Van Nostrand, 1966), p. 16, and *Higgins v. Advisory Committee on Professional Ethics of the Supreme Court of New Jersey*, 373 A. 2d 372 (N.J., 1977).

10. *Opinions of the Attorney General* 42 (1962), pp. 119, 120.

11. *Pennsylvania Legislative Journal—House*, May 24, 1977, p. 863.

12. William G. Buss, Jr., "The Massachusetts Conflict-of-Interest Statute: An Analysis," *Boston University Law Review* 45 (1965), p. 299.

13. U.S. Office of Government Ethics Letter 90X15.

14. See also Ohio Ethics Commission, Advisory Opinion No. 89–003 (February 23, 1989), which suggests—as a remedy for undue influence—a form of recusal, albeit recusal not of the potentially encumbered but the encumbering official. The influencing official should, the Opinion states, "disqualify herself for two years from participating in [in-role] matters concerning personnel of the agency" before which she is making representations.

15. George F. Carpinello, "Should Practising Lawyers Be Legislators?" *Hastings Law Journal* 41 (1989), p. 110.

16. House Committee on the Judiciary, Subcommittee on Antitrust, Hearing, *Federal Conflict of Interest Legislation*, 87th Congress, 1st Session, June 1, 1961, pp. 672, 673.

17. See Harold J. Feinberg and Alfred A. Porro, Jr., "Ethics, Incompatibility and Conflict of Interests of Public Officials," *Current Municipal Problems* 7 (1966), p. 425.

18. Morton Rosenberg and Jack H. Maskell, *Congressional Intervention in the Legislative Process: Legal and Ethical Considerations* (Washington: Congressional Research Service, September 7, 1990), p. 3.

19. Note, "Conflict of Interests of State Legislators," *Harvard Law Review* 76 (1963), p. 1229.

20. James M. Falvey, "The Congressional Ethics Dilemma: Constituent Service or Conflict of Interest?," *American Criminal Law Review* 28 (1991), p. 372.

21. Christopher F. Edley, Jr., *Administrative Law: Rethinking Judicial Control of the Bureaucracy* (New Haven: Yale University Press, 1990), pp. 178–179.

22. Rosenberg and Maskell, *Congressional Intervention*, pp. 1, 18; U.S. House of Representatives, Committee on Standards of Official Conduct, *House Ethics Manual*, 103rd Congress, 2nd Session (April, 1992), chap. 7. Thus Senator Dennis DeConcini erred when, in explaining the representation he made to the Federal

Home Loan Bank Board, he said, "a constituent has every right to expect service from us even if the case is not a good one." See "A Standard for the Ethics Committee," editorial, *Washington Times,* December 5, 1990, p. G2.

23. See also Dennis F. Thompson, *Ethics in Congress: From Individual to Institutional Corruption* (Washington, D.C.: Brookings, 1995), p. 95.
24. Michael Waldman, "Quid Pro Whoa," *The New Republic* March 19, 1990, p. 23.
25. *House Ethics Manual,* p. 116.
26. At the state level, the legislator more resembles an ordinary citizen, which is why some states allow legislators to self-represent before their executive departments; see "Conflict of Interests of State Legislators," p. 1229.
27. U.S. Senate, Select Committee on Ethics, *Senate Ethics Manual,* 104th Congress, 2nd Session, September 1996, p. 223 and *House Ethics Manual,* pp. 239, 250; see also Minnesota Governor's Committee on Ethics in Government, *Ethics in Government* (St. Paul, January 4, 1959), pp. 51, 58.
28. Paul H. Douglas, *Ethics in Government* (Cambridge, Mass.: Harvard University Press, 1952), p. 86.
29. Robert Klonoff, "The Congressman as Mediator Between Citizens and Government Agencies: Problems and Prospects," *Harvard Journal on Legislation* 16 (1979), p. 703.
30. Jeff Gerth with Neil A. Lewis, "Widows of 3 Killed in Crash Question Senator's Effort to Limit Inspections," *New York Times,* October 16, 1994, p. A28.
31. A legislator should "not ask a regulator to withdraw a duly promulgated regulation for the benefit of one constituent." See U.S. Senate Select Commitee on Ethics, Report, *Investigation of Senator Alan Cranston,* 102nd Congress, 1st Session, November 20, 1991, *Additional Views of Senator Jesse Helms,* p. 12.

5. Abuse of Office

1. U.S. Senate, Committee on the Judiciary, Hearings, *Conflict of Interest,* 87th Congress, 2nd Session, June 21, 1962, p. 44 and House Committee on Government Operations, Report, *Avoiding Conflicts of Interest in Defense Contracting and Employment,* 88th Congress, 1st Session, November 22, 1963, p. 28. Regulations at 5 CFR 2635.101 (b)(8), (10), and 2635.701, although not using the term, prohibit abuse of office as it is commonly defined.
2. *U.S.* v. *Biaggi,* 909 F. 2d 662 (2nd Cir., 1990).
3. Paul H. Douglas, *Ethics in Government* (Cambridge, Mass.: Harvard University Press, 1952), p. 52.
4. *Biaggi,* at 682–3; see also *U.S.* v. *O'Keefe,* 825 F. 2d 314 (11th Cir., 1987) at 319–320.
5. "Model Code of Ethics for the U.S. Senate," *Hastings Center Report,* February, 1981, p. 27.
6. William Safire, "Spousal Espousal," *New York Times,* April 17, 1989, p. A19.
7. Chuck Allston, "Assessing a Day's Work," *CQ,* April 22, 1989, p. 872.
8. David Frum, "The Cabinet Clinton Deserves," *The Weekly Standard,* October 12, 1998, p. 22.
9. "Faced with the prospect that autonomous traders will experience contracting

difficulties, the parties may substitute internal organization for the market." See Oliver E. Williamson, *The Economic Institutions of Capitalism: Firms, Markets, Relational Contracting* (New York: Free Press, 1985), p. 20.

10. 807 F. 2d 1299 (6th Cir., 1986) at 1304–1305.

11. See the account in David Frier, *Conflict of Interest in the Eisenhower Administration* (Ames: University of Iowa Press, 1969), p. 16 and also New York State Ethics Commission Advisory Opinion 94-16, August 10, 1994.

12. See, as well, Judicial Conference of the United States, Committee on the Code of Conduct, Advisory Opinion 94, April 25, 1997 (revised October 27, 1998).

13. Phil Kuntz and Jeffrey A. Trachtenberg, "Democrats Criticize Gingrich Book Deal with Murdoch Firm Amid FCC Dispute," *Wall Street Journal*, December 23, 1995, p. A12.

6. Private Payment for Public Acts

1. See, e.g., *Opinions of the Attorney General* 41 (1955), p. 220; U.S. Office of Government Ethics Letter 85X19 (1985) ("there need not be a connection between the payor and the employee's agency" for a violation under Section 209). Section 209 does impose strict liability on the violator, but then again—unique among the conflict-of-interest statutes—it contains no criminal penalties.

2. Bayless Manning, *Federal Conflict of Interest Law* (Cambridge, Mass.: Harvard University Press, 1964), p. 170 and Beth Nolan, "Public Interest, Private Income: Conflicts and Control Limits on Outside Income of Government Officials," *Northwestern University Law Review* 87 (1992), p. 89 and Note, "The Corporate 'Termination Bonus' for Executives Entering Public Service: Proper Government Recruiting Aid or Conflict of Interest," *Southern California Law Review* 49 (1976), p. 861.

3. *Opinions of the Attorney General* 39 (1940), p. 501; 45 (1955), p. 5 and Paul G. Dembling and Herbert E. Forrest, "Government Service and Private Compensation: The Problem with Dollar-a-Year Men and Without Compensation Employees in the Federal Government," *George Washington Law Review* 20 (1951), p. 193. None of this is to deny that—when bribery itself looks difficult to prove—prosecutors sometimes bring Section 209 charges against an official who *is* in a position to affect the interests of the private payor.

4. Association of the Bar of the City of New York, *Conflict of Interest and the Federal Service* (Cambridge, Mass.: Harvard University Press, 1960), p. 212.

5. Ibid., p. 55.

6. "Corporate 'Termination Bonus'," pp. 843–844. In *Crandon* v. *U.S.* (494 U.S. 152 [1990]), the major Supreme Court "severance payment" Section 209 case, the issues took a different twist. *Crandon* concerned five Boeing executives who had taken lump-sum severance payments from the company immediately prior to assuming high-level Department of Defense positions in the Reagan administration. What *Crandon* illustrates is yet another way in which the dynamic of prophylaxis perversely interacts with state-of-mind considerations in conflict-of-interest law. Presumably, the purpose of 18 U.S.C. §209—which prophylactically prohibits private payments for government services—is to protect the state of

mind of the *official* concerned from encumbrances. Yet how do we determine whether the prophylactic injunction itself is being violated; how, in other words, do we determine whether any such private payment was in fact meant to underwrite the official's *public* acts and not simply to recompense his previous services as a *private* employee? The answer is that we must somehow determine the intent of the payor ("the troublesome connective language of the statute . . . appears to call for a judgment as to the subjective intention of the *payor*"; see "Corporate Termination Bonus," p. 857). Yet in having to determine the intent of the payor, we have in effect returned to the consideration of state-of-mind issues—with all their attendant difficulties—only now the mind in question is not even the mind of initial concern. Subjective inquiries of this sort being as difficult in the case of the private payor's mind as they are for the recipient official's, the *Crandon* Court thus chose to adopt its own ill-fitting objective standard for determining whether the payor intended the payment as subvention for an official act. And what objective standard did the *Crandon* Court adopt? If the payment was made at any time prior to the official's accession to office—even if the private employer knew his employee was about to assume office—then no matter how generous, it is not to be deemed to have been made "for public acts."

Long before *Crandon*, Bayless Manning speculated that one day "a court might be tempted, in view of the problem of proof, to adopt a more objective standard" instead of having to "show that the payor subjectively intended that the payment to the government employee was to be in consideration of, or for . . . government services" (see *Federal Conflict of Interest Law*, pp. 177, 176). *Crandon* is the case Manning predicted. It represents a transmutation, a three-step retreat from our concern with the original issue (the subjective state of mind of the officeholder) back to an objective way of guarding that state-of-mind (preventing private payments made for public acts), then to a subjective way of understanding that objective guard (whether it was the subjective intent of the payor to pay for public acts), then to an objective way of capturing that subjective intent (whether the payor made the payment before the official entered government service).

7. See Nolan, "Public Interest, Private Income" and National Academy for Public Administration, *The Presidential Appointment Process: Panel Discusssions on America's Unelected Government* (Washington: NAPA, November 18, 1983), pp. 12–13.

8. *Neisius v. Henry*, 5 N.W. 2d 291 (Neb., 1942) at 297.

9. Quoted in Grosvenor B. Clarkson, *Industrial America in the World War* (Boston: Houghton Mifflin, 1929), pp. 21–22.

10. Hilda R. Kahn, "Payment for Political and Public Service," *Public Administration* 32 (1954), p. 181.

11. *Congressional Record*, March 31, 1982, p. S3148.

12. See, as well, Dembling and Forrest, "Government Service," p. 177.

13. "What is Wrong with the Revolving Door?" in Barry Bozeman, ed., *Public Management: The State of the Art* (San Francisco: Jossey Bass, 1993), p. 250.

14. Association of the Bar, *Conflict of Interest*, p. 157.

15. See Seth D. Zinman, "Judging Gift Rules By Their Wrappings—Toward a Clearer

Articulation of Federal Employee Gift-Acceptance Rules," *Catholic University Law Review* 44 (1994), p. 168.

16. Alexander Trowbridge, "Thinking Ahead: Attracting the Best to Washington," *Harvard Business Review* March/April, 1985, p. 175.

17. Association of the Bar, *Conflict of Interest*, p. 7.

18. Roswell Perkins, "The New Federal Conflict of Interest Law," *Harvard Law Review* 76 (1963), p. 1137; see also W. Allen Wallis, "Comment," *The Law School of the University of Chicago Conference on Conflict of Interest*, February 20, 1961, p. 90.

19. "The Latest Meese Tale," editorial, *Washington Post*, February 1, 1988, p. A14.

7. Private Gain from Public Office

1. U.S. House of Representatives, Committee on Standards of Official Conduct, *House Ethics Manual*, 102nd Congress, 2nd Session, April 1992, p. 83.

2. Association of the Bar of the City of New York, *Conflict of Interest and Federal Service* (Cambridge, Mass.: Harvard University Press, 1960), p. 7; see also David Martin, *Participating in Privately-Sponsored Seminars or Conferences for Compensation*, U.S. Office of Government Ethics memo, October 28, 1985.

3. Dennis F. Thompson, *Ethics in Congress: From Individual to Institutional Corruption* (Washington: Brookings, 1995) p. 21.

4. Haynes Johnson, "Private Gain, Public Trust," *Washington Post*, May 14, 1986, p. A2.

5. *U.S. v. Campbell*, 684 F. 2d 141 (1982) at 148; see also *U.S. v. Brewster*, 506 F. 2d 62 (D.C. Cir., 1974) at 72.

6. Bayless Manning, *Federal Conflict of Interest Law* (Cambridge, Mass.: Harvard University Press, 1964), p. 90.

7. *Sanjour v. EPA,* 86 F. Supp. 1033 (D.D.C., 1992), *Sanjour v. EPA,* 997 F. 2d 1584 (D.C. Cir., 1992), and *Sanjour v. EPA,* 56 F. 3d 85 (D.C. Cir., 1995); see also U.S. House of Representatives, Committee on the Judiciary, Subcommittee on Administrative Law and Governmental Relations, *Office of Government Ethics Regulations on Private Travel Payments,* 102nd Congress, 2nd Session, March 5, 1992.

8. House Committee on the Judiciary, *Office of Government Ethics Regulations*, p. 98.

9. Ibid., p. 141.

10. See *Federal Travel Regulations; Acceptance of Payment from a Non-Federal Source for Travel Expenses,* 57. Fed. Reg. 52,283, 53,285 (1992), and Office of Legal Counsel, *Opinions*, vol. 5 (1981), p. 126.

11. For similar reasoning in the legislative branch, see U.S. Senate Select Committee on Ethics, *Senate Ethics Manual*, 104th Congress, 2nd Session, September 1996, p. 57.

12. 40 CFR ch. 1 3.503 (July 1, 1990, edition).

13. *U.S. v. National Treasury Employees Union*, 115 S. Ct. 1003 (1995) and Peter M. Benda and David H. Rosenbloom, "The Hatch Act and Contemporary Public Service," in Patricia W. Ingraham and Donald F. Kettl, eds., *Agenda for Excellence: Public Service in America* (Chatham, NJ: Chatham House), p. 40.

14. U.S. Office of Government Ethics, Memorandum to Designated Agency Ethics Officials, *Sanjour v. Environmental Protection Agency,* June 26, 1995, p. 2 and U.S. Office of Government Ethics, *Interim Policy on Acceptance of Travel in Connection with Certain Unofficial Teaching, Speaking and Writing Activities,* May 21, 1997.

15. See, e.g., Ann Devroy and Charles R. Babcock, "Sununu Travel Rules Tightened," *Washington Post,* June 22, 1991, p. A1 and Michael Wines, "Chief of Staff's Air Travel Practices and Questions About Their Propriety," *New York Times,* June 24, 1991, p. A12.

16. C. Boyden Gray, counsel to the president, *Memorandum for Governor Sununu, Chief of Staff to the President: Results of Our Review of Your Travel on Military Aircraft,* May 9, 1991.

17. "Mr. Espy Goes—Slowly and Expensively," editorial, *Washington Times,* October 5, 1994, p. A20.

18. Nell Henderson, "Kelly Says She Regrets Taking Fee," *Washington Post,* June 27, 1992, p. B1.

19. Gray, *Memorandum for Governor Sununu,* p. 16 and Devroy and Babcock, "Sununu Travel Rules Tightened."

20. U.S. Office of Government Ethics Letter 90X21.

21. Wisconsin Ethics Board, Opinion 332, June 5, 1986.

22. Lars-Erik Nelson, "Democracy for Sale," *New York Review of Books,* December 3, 1998, p. 9.

23. For executive officials, as Kathleen Clark notes, "travel expenses constitute forbidden 'compensation' unless the agency itself—rather than the employee—accepts them under its statutory authority." No such strictures apply to legislators. Moreover, senators may accept such private reimbursement unless the activity is "substantially recreational," and congressmen may do so as long as they are providing "substantial services" in return. Executive officials, by contrast, strain at a far tighter leash. If the activity deals with agency-related matter, then—unless the agency expressly approves—private reimbursement is forbidden. See Kathleen Clark, "Be Careful What You Accept from Whom: Restrictions on Gifts and Compensation for Executive Branch Employees," in William V. Luneberg, ed., *The Lobbying Manual,* 2nd ed. (Washington: American Bar Association, 1998), p. 248; *Senate Ethics Manual,* p. 57; *House Ethics Manual,* p. 37.

24. CFR 2635.204 (h)(2), examples 1 and 2.

25. U.S. House of Representatives, Committee on Standards of Official Conduct, *Summary of Activities: One Hundred Fourth Congress,* 104th Congress, 2nd Session, January 2, 1997, p. 58.

26. CFR 2635.808 (c).

27. *Senate Ethics Manual,* pp. 96, 98.

28. U.S. House of Representatives, Committee on the Judiciary, Subcommittee on Antitrust, Hearings, *Conflict of Interest,* 86th Congress, 2nd Session, February 26, 1960, p. 33.

29. *Senate Ethics Manual,* p. 84.

30. See, e.g., Steven Kelman, "What is Wrong with the Revolving Door?," in Barry Bozeman, ed., *Public Management: the State of the Art* (San Francisco: Jossey-Bass, 1993), p. 250.

31. Ernest Weinrib, "The Fiduciary Obligation," *University of Toronto Law Journal* 25 (1975), p. 16.

32. See, e.g., J. Patrick Dobel, "Integrity in the Public Service," *Public Administration Review* 50 (1990), pp. 354–366, H. George Frederickson, "Toward a Theory of the Public for Public Administration," *Administration and Society* 22 (1991), pp. 395–417 and Kathleen Clark, "Do We Have Enough Ethics in Government Yet? An Answer from Fiduciary Theory," *University of Illinois Law Review* (1996), pp. 57–102.

33. Alan H. Goldman, *The Moral Foundations of Professional Ethics* (Totowa, N.J.: Rowman and Littlefield, 1980).

34. Kenneth E. Goodpaster, "Business Ethics and Stakeholder Analysis," *Business Ethics Quarterly* 1 (1991), pp. 53–74.

35. See some of the discussion in Joseph A. Pegnato, "Is a Citizen a Consumer?," *Public Productivity Management Review* 20 (1997), p. 399.

36. See, for example, Terry L. Cooper, *The Responsible Administrator: An Approach to Ethics for the Administrative Role* (San Francisco: Jossey Bass, 1990), pp. 84, 107, 111.

37. See House Committee on Governmental Reform and Oversight, Subcommittee on Management, *Simplifying and Streamlining the Federal Procurement Process,* 104th Congress, 1st Session, February 28, 1995, p. 11. It is useful to contrast all of this with the reverse situation of the business manager. In government, as just noted, every client to whom the official owes ordinary-moral obligations is also part of the public to whom the official owes role-moral obligations. But in business, every shareholder to whom the manager owes role-moral obligations is also a member of the public to whom the manager owes ordinary-moral obligations. Thus, the manager may have a role-moral obligation to a particular shareholder to maximize his or her financial return, and at the same time an ordinary-moral obligation not to degrade his or her environment.

38. See, e.g., American Bar Association Committee on Governmental Standards, "Keeping Faith: Government Ethics & Government Ethics Regulation," *Administrative Law Review* 45 (1993), pp. 326–327 and Nebraska Accountability and Disclosure Commission, Advisory Opinion #117, December 2, 1988, p. 3.

39. Edwin McElwain and James Vorenberg, "The Federal Conflict-of-Interest Statutes," *Harvard Law Review* 65 (1952), p. 955.

40. I don't mean to suggest that legal paternalism is unheard of, although the number of articles on the topic is dwarfed by those devoted to medical paternalism. In his discussion of the question, David Luban offers a number of examples in which a client might be in conflict between the desire for legal victory and some other desire, opening up the possibility for paternalism should the lawyer participate in arbitrating between them. For example, a client might want to pay more alimony than he's legally obligated to because of his belief in fairness, or seek—because of his conscience—to confess to a greater offense even though the prosecution can prove only a lesser one. As Luban notes, though, the extent to which lawyers have fiduciary obligations to interests of the client other than legal victory—even in such cases—is controversial. However, the deeper question is whether the kinds of intra-client conflicts Luban describes are better understood not as conflicts between different interests the client holds, but (as Luban himself puts it) a conflict

between an interest (in legal victory) and a "value," a concern with the interests of others or society at large, both of which the client harbors. This is not nearly so much the case with intraprincipal conflicts in, say, medicine. See "Paternalism and the Legal Profession," *Wisconsin Law Review* (1981), pp. 454–493.

41. Because managers' fiduciary responsibilities extend only to the shareholder's interest in the corporation—and not otherwise to the entire range of additional interests a shareholder might harbor—managers commit fiduciary violations if they go into competition with their former companies but not if they compete with other business interests shareholders might harbor. By contrast, we do not generally condemn officials who go into private competition with a service only their former agency provides—which testifies to our tendency not to regard the government itself as the official's principal—but officials do risk attracting criticism whenever, drawing on skills or stature derived in government, they enter into competition with any other business interest an individual citizen harbors. The only exception here—the only kind of situation where courts sanction officials whose private gain from public office harms their former agency as opposed to private citizens—occurs in the case of former intelligence officers who write books that draw on knowledge and (at least in theory) classified information they derive from their government jobs. But in such cases, where the agency acts on an international, not a domestic, stage, the government itself can be said to have competitors—other governments—and hence can be deemed competitively disadvantaged by a "breached . . . fiduciary obligation." Or, put another way, in such cases the entire "national interest," not just a part of it, is arguably harmed. See *Snepp* v. *U.S., 444 U.S. 507 (1979)* at 510, 511, 512.

42. Again, the experiences of managers offers a contrast. Because managers' fiduciary responsibilities do not extend to the entire public, courts hold senior executives who compete with their (former) firms to have violated their fiduciary responsibilities no matter how much such competition might benefit society as a whole—much to the frustration of some corporate-law scholars (see Pat K. Chew, "Competing Interests in the Corporate Opportunity Doctrine," *North Carolina Law Review* 67 (1989), pp. 435–502). On the other hand, corporate-law jurisprudence is much less strict than government-ethics regulation when we move from profiting-from-position to conflict of interest. Corporate directors, with certain safeguards, are allowed to self-deal in ways that would be prohibited for government officials (see Victor Brudney and Robert Charles Clark, "A New Look at Corporate Opportunities," *Harvard Law Review* 94 (1981), p. 1028).

43. Thompson, *Ethics in Congress,* p. 51.

44. See, e.g., New York City Conflicts of Interest Board Advisory Opinion 95–92.

45. Thomas Morgan, "The Quest for Equality in Regulating the Behavior of Government Officials: The Case of Extrajudicial Compensation," *George Washington Law Review* 58 (1990), p. 489. One must be careful here, since the Judicial Conference of the United States prohibits a judge from publishing for money when the topic is "how to practice before the judge's own court, as distinguished from a judge's writing or teaching for compensation on other legal topics with respect to which the judge does not occupy a unique position by virtue of his or her own particular judgeship" (see Committee on Code of Conduct Advisory Opinion No. 87, June 30, 1992). As far as Rehnquist is concerned—and on Morgan's ar-

gument—his unique "position" refers to his position in the market: He has no private-market competitors, hence he disadvantages no one, since no one else can write "a book by the Chief Justice." But in the Judicial Conference's advisory opinion, the judge's unique position refers to his position in public office: He is one of only a few people, privileged by his position, who can talk about the inner workings of his court, hence he enjoys an unfair advantage over others who would write on the same topic. Of course, for reasons discussed in the text, the considerations that argue for an official occupying a unique private-market position may also argue for his occupying a unique public-office position.

46. William Safire, "Royalties in Office," *New York Times,* January 21, 1995, p. A23.

47. See Katharine Q. Seelye, "Murdoch, Joined by Lobbyist, Talked of Regulatory Problem at Meeting with Gingrich," *New York Times,* January 15, 1995, section 1, p. 18 and Frank Rich, "Newt's Big Buck," *New York Times,* January 5, 1995, p. A27.

48. One may query whether, in Kissinger's case, those seeking to write about diplomacy more broadly would have had to compete with him. Yet I have been unable to locate criticism launched against Kissinger's relatively personal memoirs of the sort Gingrich's more political ruminations elicited. Critics *have,* however, attacked Kissinger's consulting business and his occasional column-writing—both of which bring him more directly into confrontation with competitors—for relying on an unfair advantage derived from his having held public office (see Bruce Nussbaum, "The Big Business of Being Henry Kissinger," *Business Week,* December 2, 1995, pp. 76–77).

8. The Revolving Door: I

1. See, e.g., U.S. House of Representatives, Committee on the Judiciary, Subcommittee on Administrative Law and Governmental Relations, Hearing, *Restrictions on the Post-Employment Activities of Federal Officers and Employees,* 100th Congress, 2nd Session, May 4, 1988; Thomas D. Morgan, "Appropriate Limits on Participation by a Former Agency Official in Matters Before an Agency," *Duke Law Journal* (1980), pp. 1–63; and Gregory S. Walden, *On Best Behavior: The Clinton Administration and Ethics in Government* (Indianapolis: Hudson, 1996), pp. 15, 64, 432.

2. Steven Kelman, "What Is Wrong With the Revolving Door?," in Barry Bozeman, ed., *Public Management: The State of the Art* (San Francisco: Jossey-Bass, 1993), pp. 228, 229, 233.

3. Hence, critics have referred to the problem of ingratiation as the "*abuse* of government power in order [for an official] to ingratiate himself with a future employer," or speak of an "impropriety" in an official's exploiting "opportunities to *abuse* government power in order to ingratiate himself with a future employer" (emphases mine). See Note, "Conflicts of Interest in the Legal Profession," *Harvard Law Review* 94 (1981), pp. 1431, 1435, 1436 and Note, "Conflicts of Interest and the Former Government Attorney," *Georgetown Law Journal* 65 (1977), pp. 1034, 1039, 1049.

4. On occasion, an ingratiation situation will exhibit post-employment analogues of both abuse of office *and* self-dealing, which is not surprising since abuse and self-

dealing themselves blur into one another. So for example, while in most ingratiation situations an officeholder has the official capacity to favor a firm which then offers him a job, in a smaller subset he might approve the very government contract that creates the job itself. Here, the firm appears less as an entity preyed upon to hire the official in exchange for some governmental favor than as a conduit—a holding pen—for government funds that will directly flow to the official upon her departure from government. See, e.g., New York State Ethics Commission Advisory Opinion 98-19, November 23, 1998.

5. See, e.g., U.S. Senate, Committee on the Judiciary, Hearings, *Integrity in Post-Employment Act of 1986,* 99th Congress, 2nd Session, April 29 and June 18, 1986, p. 67 and U.S. House of Representatives, Committee on the Judiciary, Subcommittee on Administrative Law and Governmental Relations, Hearing, *Post-Employment Restrictions for Federal Employees,* 101st Congress, 1st Session, April 27 and June 28, 1989, pp. 54, 184–185.

6. "The Revolving Door—Should It Be Stopped?" (panel discussion), *Administrative Law Review* 32 (1980), p. 397 (comments of Edwin S. Kneedler).

7. Association of the Bar of the City of New York, *Conflict of Interest and Federal Service* (Cambridge, Mass.: Harvard University Press, 1960), p. 7.

8. "Conflict of Interest in the Legal Profession," p. 1433.

9. See William Safire, "Sununu Whitewash," *New York Times,* November 4, 1991, p. A19.

10. Wisconsin, Hearing, *Comments on Conflicts of Interest and Requests for Advice,* Assembly Bill 349, April 19, 1977, p. 1.

11. Edward O. Laumann, et al, "Washington Lawyers and Others: The Structure of Representation in Washington," *Stanford Law Review* 37 (1985), p. 37.

12. Morgan, "Appropriate Limits", p. 56; see also also Ronald D. Rotunda, "Introduction," Administrative Conference of the U.S., Working Conference on Ethics in Government, March 1, 1988, *Issues and Options Paper: Statutes and Regulations,* pp. 1, 4.

13. John P. Heinz et al., *The Hollow Core: Private Interests in National Policy Making* (Cambridge, Mass.: Harvard University Press, 1993), pp. 117, 119.

14. Robert B. Reich, *Tales of a New America* (New York: Times Books, 1987), p. 223.

15. Kelman, "What Is Wrong With the Revolving Door?", p. 229.

16. House Committee on the Judiciary, *Restrictions on the Post-Employment Activities,* p. 5.

17. *United States* v. *Standard Oil Co.,* 136 F. Supp. 345 (S.D.N.Y., 1955) and *Kesselhaut* v. *United States,* No. 166–74 (Ct. Cl. Tr. Div., Mar 29, 1976).

18. House Committee on the Judiciary, *Restrictions on the Post-Employment Activities,* p. 132.

19. Strictly speaking, an ex-official can act for a party whose private interests *cohere* with those of the U.S. in a particular matter—in which case he wouldn't have switched sides—and still be in violation of 18 U.S.C. §207(a)(1). For example, because of the knowledge and expertise the official derived from his substantial involvement in prosecuting a private party while in government, he might now place that party—against whom, let us assume, the U.S. is still pursuing a case—at an unfair disadvantage in suing it on behalf of another private interest as an ex-of-

ficial (see *Armstrong* v. *McAlpin,* 606 F. 2d 28 [2nd Cir., 1979]). But this, obviously, is just the kind of harm we have in mind whenever we speak of private gain from public office. In other words, as long as the violating ex-official is acting in *conformity* with U.S. interests, his only sin is "private gain from public office," which is already captured by the statutory requirement that he have been personally and substantially involved in the matter. If the requirement that U.S. interests must be at stake is to add anything to the statute, it can do so only when the ex-official is acting *against* U.S. interests—and this is why it is best understood as reflecting a concern with switching sides. For some pertinent discussion, see Ann Bradford Stevens, "Can the State Attorney General Represent Two Agencies Opposed in Litigation?," *Georgetown Journal of Legal Ethics* 2 (1989), p. 794.

20. Morgan, "Appropriate Limits," p. 39.

21. House Committee on the Judiciary, *Restrictions on the Post-Employment Activities,* p. 3; see also Manning, *Federal Conflict of Interest Law,* p. 208. Eighteen U.S.C. §207(a)(1)'s two companion statutes—18 U.S.C. §207(a)(2) and 18 U.S.C. §207(b)—do much the same thing, albeit with some small variation. Section (a)(2) varies from Section (a)(1) only slightly by requiring that the official merely have been responsible for the particular and specific matter instead of personally and substantially involved. In so doing, it simply tilts the hybrid—by comparison with (a)(1)—closer to a concern with side-switching and away from profiteering. And Section (b) restores the personal and substantial involvement requirement while explicitly prohibiting the ex-official from making use of *non*public information—thereby highlighting a concern with profiteering—but it confines itself to side-switching in treaty or trade negotiations—thereby displaying, as well, a heightened concern with disloyalty.

22. House Committee on the Judiciary, Subcommittee on Antitrust, *Federal Conflict of Interest Legislation,* 87th Congress, 1st Session, June 1, 1961, p. 70 and U.S. Senate, Committee on Governmental Affairs, Hearings, *Public Officials Integrity Act of 1977, Blind Trusts and Other Conflict of Interest Matters,* 95th Congress, 1st Session, June 7, 1977, p. 267. In fact one of the three laws, 18 U.S.C. §207(b), does extend beyond representation to cover a former official's "aiding and assisting" any person other than the U.S. concerning a treaty or trade negotiation, thus betokening a pure concern with profiting from disloyalty.

23. See, e.g., U.S. House of Representatives, Committee on Governmental Operations, Report, *Revolving Door Sunshine Act of 1993,* 103rd Congress, 1st Session, November 10, 1993, p. 7.

24. 45 CFR chap. VI (10–1–90 Edition), Section 682.20.

25. U.S. House of Representatives, Committee on Interstate and Foreign Commerce, Subcommittee on Oversight and Investigations, Report, *Impact of the Ethics in Government Act,* 96th Congress, 1st Session, May 4, 1979, p. 11.

26. U.S. Senate, Committee on the Judiciary, Report, *Integrity in Post Employment Act,* 100th Congress, 1st Session, July 7, 1987, p. 6.

9. The Revolving Door: II

1. In fact, much of the carping is directed not at the substance of the laws themselves but at the various lengths of time—one year, two years, five years, permanently—

over which they restrict the postemployment activities of the former official. There may well be something to these critiques: In absolute magnitudes some laws may be overly extensive. But relative to one another, the time limits, too, display rhyme and reason. An official's capacities to exercise influence with former subordinates or profiteer from knowledge or skills gained in office have a shelf life, lasting only as long as one's former colleagues remain incumbents and one's former files remain pending. By contrast, one can switch sides or enjoy the rewards of ingratiation—for example, be paid off for what one did in office—at an indefinite point in the future. And, indeed, the postemployment provisions roughly reflect these differences. That part of President Clinton's postemployment guidelines covering switching sides (and especially lobbying for foreign entities) permanently prohibits ex-officials from engaging in the covered activity (see Executive Order 12834, *Weekly Compilation of Presidential Documents* 29, January 20, 1993, p. 77). Similarly, 18 U.S.C. §208, which covers postemployment ingratiation, indefinitely prohibits an official from taking any job, provided he negotiated for it while possessed of the official capacity to affect the offeror's interests. By contrast, 18 U.S.C. §207(c), which covers influence, carries a time limit of two years, and 18 U.S.C. §207(a)(1), (a)(2), and (b), which cover various hybrids of profiteering and disloyalty, mix permanent with impermanent bans.

2. U.S. Senate, Committee on Governmental Affairs, Subcommittee on Federal Services, Post Office and Civil Service, Hearings, *Consultant Registration and Reform Act of 1989*, 101st Congress, 1st Session, November 17, 1989, pp. 10, 12.

3. See U.S. House of Representatives, Committee on Government Operations, Report, *Avoiding Conflicts of Interest in Defense Contracting and Employment*, 88th Congress, 1st Session, November 22, 1963, pp. 19, 26 and Charles D. Woodruff, "Organizational Conflicts of Interest—Not What It's Been Said to Be," *Public Contract Law Journal* 16 (1986/87), p. 220.

4. U.S. House of Representatives, Committee on Armed Services, Acquisition Policy Panel, Hearing, *Registration of Consultants*, 100th Congress, 2nd Session, September 23, 1988, pp. 9, 39, 47, 71.

5. John D. Hanrahan, *Government by Contract* (New York: Norton, 1983), p. 32.

6. U.S. Senate, Committee on the Judiciary, Report, *Strengthening the Criminal Laws Relating to Bribery, Graft and Conflicts of Interest*, 87th Congress, 2nd Session, September 29, 1962, p. 10 and U.S. House of Representatives, Committee on the Judiciary, Subcommittee on Antitrust, *Federal Conflict of Interest Legislation*, 87th Congress, 1st Session, June 1, 1961, p. 72.

7. Elizabeth Drew, *On the Edge: The Clinton Presidency* (New York: Simon and Schuster, 1994), p. 347.

8. President's Memorandum of May 2, 1963, Subject: Preventing Conflicts of Interest on the Part of Special Government Employees, *Federal Register* 28 (1963), p. 4539; see also 5 CFR 2641.101.

9. See Roger G. Darley, "New 'Revolving Door' Issues for Federal Officials Under the OFPP Policy Act Amendments of 1988: A Quick Overview," *Public Contract Law Journal* 18 (1988), pp. 432–445 and James W. Taylor and B. Alan Dickson, "Organizational Conflicts of Interest under the Federal Acquisition Regulation," *Public Contract Law Journal* 15 (1984/85), pp. 107–121.

10. "We Do Not Lobby"; "Ins and Outs (Cont'd)," *Washington Post,* June 10, 1994, pp. A29, A28.

11. John P. Burke, "The Ethics of Deregulation—or the Deregulation of Ethics?" in John J. DiIulio, ed., *Deregulating the Public Service* (Washington: Brookings, 1994), p. 65.

12. Philip J. Harter, "Proposed Standards of Conduct for Presidential Transition Workers," *Federal Bar News and Journal* 36 (March/April, 1989), p. 131.

13. Philip J. Harter, *Standards of Conduct for Presidential Transition Workers,* Report to the Administrative Conference of the U.S., May 1988, pp. 18–19; see also Andy Pasztor, *When the Pentagon Was for Sale: Inside America's Biggest Defense Scandal* (New York: Scribner, 1995), p. 63.

14. Harter, *Standards of Conduct,* pp. 2, 4, 20, and 23.

15. Harter, "Proposed Standards," p. 131.

16. Harter, *Standards of Conduct,* pp. 2,4.

17. Frederick C. Mosher, *Democracy and the Public Service* (New York: Oxford University Press, 1968), p. 145.

18. Especially if they are selling supplies or war materials to the military generally, or *anything* to their former branch of service. See Lisa B. Horowitz and Vernon L. Strickland, "Postemployment Restrictions on Former Military Officers," *Public Contract Law Journal* 20 (1991), pp. 637–638.

19. U.S. Senate, Committee on Governmental Affairs, Hearings, *Public Officials Integrity Act of 1977, Blind Trusts and Other Conflict of Interest Matters,* 95th Congress, 1st Session, June 7, 1977, p. 283.

20. U.S. General Accounting Office, *DOD Revolving Door,* April 16, 1987, pp. 1, 10 and Kevin J. Barry and Richard R. Kelly, "Avoidance of Post-Employment Conflicts of Interest for the Federal Employee," *Federal Bar News and Journal,* December 1986, p. 411.

21. See *Congressional Record,* November 17, 1989, p. S15672 (remarks of Senator Rudman).

22. U.S. House of Representatives, Committee on the Judiciary, Subcommittee on Administrative Law and Governmental Relations, Hearing, *Foreign Agents Compulsory Ethics in Trade Act of 1987,* 100th Congress, 1st Session, August 6, 1987, p. 31.

23. Ibid., p. 33.

24. See, e.g., Michael I. Spak, "America for Sale," *Kentucky Law Journal* 78 (1989–1990), p. 238.

25. Deborah M. Levy, "Advice for Sale," *Foreign Policy* 67 (1987), p. 76.

26. See Robert B. Reich, "Who Is Us?" *Harvard Business Review* 71 (1990), pp. 53–64. This is not to say that Reich would oppose a kind of differential treatment, but it would be one that placed greater burdens on former officials who work against the interests of American workers, not American owners.

27. Pat Choate, *Agents of Influence: How Japan Manipulates America's Economic System* (New York: Touchstone, 1990), chap. 4; see also Laura D'Andrea Tyson, "They Are Not Us: Why American Ownership Still Matters," *The American Prospect* 4 (1991), p. 37–49 and Levy, "Advice for Sale," p. 82.

28. See Note, "Attorney's Conflicts of Interest: Representation of Interest Adverse to

That of Former Client," *Boston University Law Review* 55 (1973), p. 77; *Woods v. Covington County Bank*, 537 F. 2d 804 (Alabama, 1976) at 814; and American Bar Association, Committee on Professional Ethics, Opinion No. 37 (1931). On the other hand, so-called "professional conflicts of interest" are far more likely to arise for attorneys whose clients are private entities than for lawyers who work for government. Such professional conflicts of interest crop up when an attorney either deliberately prolongs a case so as to wring out additional fees from a current client or else settles it too quickly so as to work on other files. Since government attorneys do not generally get remunerated on a fee-for-service basis, they are less likely to experience such professional conflicts of interest.

29. Jack H. Maskell, *Constitutional Analysis of 'Revolving Door' Proposal Regarding Expansion of Post-Employment Conflict of Interest Law for Federal Officials* (Washington: Congressional Rsearch Service, August 5, 1988), p. 4.

30. L. Ray Patterson and Elliott E. Cheatham, *The Profession of Law* (Mineola: The Foundation Press, 1971), p. 199.

31. Note, "Ethical Considerations for the Justice Department When It Switches Sides Deciding Litigation," *University of Puget Sound Law Review* 7 (1984), pp. 417, 421, 423.

32. Note, "Conflicts of Interest and the Former Government Attorney," *Georgetown Law Journal* 65 (1977), p. 1026; see also *In re Bruce Lindsey*, No. 98–3060 (D.C. Cir., 1998).

33. See, e.g., Jeremy Rabkin, "White House Lawyering: Law, Ethics and Political Judgments," in Cornell W. Clayton, ed., *Government Lawyers: The Federal Legal Bureaucracy and Presidential Politics* (Lawrence: University of Kansas Press, 1995), p. 107.

34. William Josephson and Russell Pearce, "To Whom Does the Government Lawyer Owe the Duty of Loyalty when Clients Are in Conflict?," *Howard Law Review* 29 (1986).

35. Robert H. Aronson, "Conflict of Interest," *Washington Law Review* 52 (1977), p. 843; see also Irving R. Kaufman, "The Former Government Attorney and the Canons of Professional Ethics," *Harvard Law Review* 70 (1957), p. 66 and Robert P. Lawry, "Confidences and the Government Lawyer," *North Carolina Law Review* 57 (1979), p. 642.

36. Note, "Toward a New Ethical Standard Regulating the Private Practice of Government Lawyers," *Golden Gate University Law Review* 33 (1983), p. 436.

37. *Armstrong v. McAlpin*, 606 F. 2d 28 (2nd Cir., 1979).

38. Note, "Conflicts of Interest and the Former Government Attorney," p. 1049 and U.S. Senate, *Public Officials Integrity Act of 1977*, pp. 222, 231.

39. American Bar Association, Committee on Ethics and Professional Responsibility, *Formal Opinion 342* (1975); Janet L. McDavid and Jack McKay, "Ex-Government Lawyers Given Freer Rein by Court," *National Law Journal*, July 26, 1982; and Lloyd N. Cutler, "Conflicts of Interest," *Emory Law Journal* 30 (1981), p. 1026.

40. Morgan, "Appropriate Limits," p. 25 and Association of the Bar of the City of New York, *Congress and the Public Trust* (New York: Atheneum, 1970), p. 115.

41. *Fleischer v. A.A.P. Inc.*, 163 F. Supp. 548, 553 (S.D.N.Y., 1958).

42. See, e.g., William L. Murphy, "Vicarious Disqualification of Government Lawyers," *ABA Journal* 69 (1983), p. 300.

Part I Summary

1. "Conflicts of Interest in the Legal Profession," *Harvard Law Review* 94 (1981), p. 1319 and Beth Nolan, "Public Interest, Private Income: Conflicts and Control Limits On the Outside Income of Government Officials," *Northwestern Law Review* 87 (1992), p. 83.
2. *U.S. v. National Treasury Employees Union*, 115 S. Ct. 1003 (1995) at 1011. The early-'90s honorarium ban, which attempted to bring a misbegotten prophylactic approach to private gain from public office—forbidding certain kinds of outside income-earning regardless of whether they bore any relationship to the official's role—was both politically and judicially repudiated. What replaced it was a more tailored (if vaguer) stricture banning honoraria in situations where the outside income-earning—writing or teaching, say—"relates to the employee's official duties"; see 5 CFR 2635.807. As the American Bar Association Committee on Government Standards puts it, "[t]he regulatory tactic of broad, prophylactic restrictions is fundamentally ill-suited to an area like outside activities, in which the ethical character of conduct is so obviously dependent upon factual context" (see "Keeping Faith: Government Ethics & Government Ethics Regulation," *Administrative Law Review* 45 [1993], p. 320).

10. Interest, Bias, and Ideology

1. See, for example, Michael Davis, "Conflict of Interest," *Business and Professional Ethics Journal* 1 (1982), pp. 18, 23; Sidney M. Davis, "Comment," *The Law School of the University of Chicago Conference on Conflict of Interest*, February 20, 1961, p. 83; G. Calvin Mackenzie, *The Politics of Presidential Appointments* (New York: Free Press, 1981), p. 98; John D. Saxon, "The Scope of Legislative Ethics," in Bruce Jennings and Daniel Callahan, eds., *Representation and Responsibility: Exploring Legislative Ethics* (New York: Plenum Press, 1985), p. 202; Harvard Business School Club of Washington, *The Businessman in Government* (Washington, D.C., May 1958), p. 26; Steven Lubet, "Judicial Ethics and Private Lives," *Northwestern University Law Review* 79 (1985), p. 1004; and U.S. Senate Committee on the Judiciary, Subcommittee on Separation of Powers, Hearing, *Nonjudicial Activities of Supreme Court Judges and Federal Judges*, 99th Congress, 1st Session, July 14, 1969, pp. 50, 52.
2. Peter Strauss, "Disqualification of Decisional Officials in Rulemaking," *Columbia Law Review* 80 (1980), p. 1006; see also Edward C. Banfield, "Corruption as a Feature of Governmental Organization," *Journal of Law and Economics* 18 (1975), p. 591 and Bob Eckhardt, "A Good Word for the Revolving Door," *The Nation*, February 18, 1978, p. 177.
3. Beth Nolan, "Public Interest, Private Income: Conflicts and Control Limits on the Outside Income of Governmental Officials," *Northwestern University Law Review* 87 (1992), p. 76 and Robert G. Vaughn, "Finally, Government Ethics as

If People Mattered: Some Thoughts on the Ethics Reform Act of 1989," *George Washington Law Review* 58 (1990), p. 514.

4. Judith N. Shklar, *Freedom and Independence: A Study of the Political Ideas of Hegel's Phenomenology* (New York: Cambridge University Press, 1976), p. 187 and *Ordinary Vices* (Cambridge, Mass.: Harvard University Press, 1984), pp. 58–78.

5. See B. Drummond Ayres, Jr., "Campaign Refrain: My Opponent's a Hypocrite," *New York Times,* November 6, 1994, p. 27.

6. U.S. Senate, Select Committee on Ethics, Hearing, *Revising the Senate Code of Official Conduct,* 96th Congress, 2nd Session, November 19, 1980, p. 84. For other suggestions that our interest in the character of politicians results from an absence of consensus on the public interest, see Gail Sheehy, *Character: America's Search for Leadership* (New York: Morrow, 1988), p. 23 and Dom Bonafede, "Ethics and the '88 Race," *National Journal,* January 8, 1988, p. 1968 (remarks of Robert Teeter).

7. Meg Greenfield, "It's Time for Some Civility," *Washington Post,* May 29, 1995, p. A15.

8. Amy Gutmann and Dennis Thompson, "Moral Conflict and Political Consensus," *Ethics* 101 (1990), p. 78.

9. Christine MacKinnon, "Hypocrisy, With a Note on Integrity," *American Philosophical Quarterly* 28 (1991), p. 327.

10. Govert den Hartogh, "Rationality in Conversation and Neutrality in Politics," *Analysis* 50 (1990), p. 205.

11. Harry Frankfurt, "Identification and Wholeheartedness," in Ferdinand Schoeman, ed., *Responsibility, Character and the Emotions* (New York: Cambridge University Press, 1987), p. 34.

12. John Rawls, *A Theory of Justice* (Cambridge, Mass.: Harvard University Press, 1971), p. 86.

13. David Bromwich, *A Choice of Inheritance: Self and Community from Edmund Burke to Robert Frost* (Cambridge, Mass.: Harvard University Press, 1989), p. 158.

11. Limousine Liberals, Country-Club Conservatives

1. Michael Arbanas, "Nice-guys Thornton, Keet, Give Personal Attacks a Try," *Arkansas Gazette,* October 1, 1990, pp. B1, B2.

2. Michael Rezendes, "Foes Say Rappaport Hypocritical on Aid," *Boston Globe,* August 25, 1990, p. 28; Steve Marantz, "Kerry Seeks Data on Subsidy," *Boston Globe,* October 11, 1990, p. 39; and Steve Marantz, "Kerry vs. Rappaport: Mud Over Matters," *Boston Globe,* October 15, 1990, pp. 1, 24.

3. E.J. Dionne, Jr., "Dole vs. Hollywood," *Washington Post,* June 6, 1995, p. A19.

4. Quoted in Craig Horowitz, "New York's Liberals Have Fallen and They Can't Get Up," *New York,* July 10, 1995, p. 46; see also James J. Cramer, "Confessions of a Limousine Neoliberal," *New York,* March 11, 1996, pp. 35–38.

5. James Fallows, *Breaking the News: How the Media Undermine American Democracy* (New York: Pantheon, 1996), p. 105.

6. Tom Wolfe, *Radical Chic and Mau-Mauing the Flak-Catchers* (New York: Farrar, Straus and Giroux, 1970), p. 43.

7. Christopher Waddell, "Hebert Ends Hunger Strike," *Globe and Mail,* April 1, 1986, p. A1.

8. See David Loth, *A History of Graft in America* (Westport: Greenwood Press, 1970), p. 291.

9. Frankfurt, "Identification and Wholeheartedness," p. 43.

10. Larry Liebart, "Lujan Looks for Ways to Promote Offshore Drilling," *San Francisco Chronicle,* April 3, 1990, p. A2.

11. Robert Pear, "Kerrey's Companies Provide Few With Medical Coverage," *New York Times,* December 28, 1991, p. A1 and Kathy Sawyer and Mark Stencel, "Chipping at Kerrey Cornerstone," *Washington Post,* December 29, 1991, p. A10.

12. Murray Campbell, "Bets Are Off in Coppsville if Voters Punish Grits," *Globe and Mail,* June 14, 1996, p. A4.

13. See Kathy Kiely, "In Safe-Water Debate, a Charge of 'Hypocrisy on Tap,'" *Houston Post,* April 20, 1994, p. A12.

14. Brian Timmons, "That's No Okie, That's My Torts Professor," *Wall Street Journal,* April 3, 1990, p. A2.

15. Lynne McFall, "Integrity," *Ethics* 98 (October, 1987), p. 7.

16. See, for example, "Democracy and Hypocrisy," editorial, *New York Times,* April 6, 1992, p. A18 and Kent Jenkins, Jr., "Fiscal Reality of Congress Sets in for Rep. Moran; Donations Bring Charges of Hypocrisy," *Washington Post,* February 11, 1991, p. D1.

17. "Honor and Hypocrisy," editorial, *Atlanta Constitution,* June 7, 1994, p. A8.

18. Bernard Williams, "Politics and Moral Character," in Stuart Hampshire, ed., *Public and Private Morality* (New York: Cambridge University Press, 1978), p. 73.

19. John M. McGuire and Bill McClellan, "Peach: Hypocrisy Not an Issue," *St. Louis Post-Dispatch,* March 15, 1992, p. 10A.

20. Hence the journalist Paul Mulshine criticized George W. Bush—who adopts a hard-line approach to drug users—not only because Bush's own indulgent personal beliefs bespoke a troubling "hypocrisy," but because they were unaccompanied by any reassuringly inconsistent personal interests. By contrast, Mulshine writes, in the period before Prohibition, "when a hard-drinking Congressman would take to the floor to inveigh against liquor, the inconsistency was obvious to all, [but] at least that Congressman was taking an action that put at risk his ready access to his drug of choice." See Paul Mulshine, "Republican Party Addicted to Drug Hypocrisy," *Minneapolis Star-Tribune,* September 28, 1999, p. 11A.

21. Howard Kurtz, "The Hounded News Hound," *Washington Post,* May 12, 1995, p. B1.

22. Stephen Chapman, "Abortion and Dan Quayle's Daughter: A Phony Issue," *Chicago Tribune,* July 29, 1992, Section 4, p. 5 and Michael Putzel, "Quayle Accused of Abortion Hypocrisy," *Boston Globe,* July 24, 1992, p. 9.

23. Timothy J. McNulty, "Bush on Abortion: Humane or Hypocritical?," *Chicago Tribune,* August 13, 1992, p. 12.

24. "Hypocrisy in the GOP," editorial, *Denver Post,* August 18, 1992, p. 6B.

25. The term "country-club conservative" enjoys broad currency in American political discourse; see, e.g., Frank Clifford, "The California Primary Race for Senate Shifting Out of Low Gear," *Los Angeles Times,* June 9, 1988, p. 3.

26. Mark Oswald, "Thornton Capitalizing on Keet's 'Boat,'" *Arkansas Democrat,* October 2, 1990, p. B7.

27. John Brummett, "Keet's Talk of Working Families and Two Boats Controversial," *Arkansas Democrat,* September 29, 1990, p. B1.

28. Jeffrey Simpson, "There's a Refreshing Voice in the NDP But It May Not Be Heard," *Globe and Mail,* August 10, 1995, p. A16.

29. Richard L. Berke, "Vox Populist: Just Regular Working Class Guys," *New York Times,* February 4, 1996, Section 4, p. 4.

30. Michael Lewis, "President and CEO," *New York Times Magazine,* February 18, 1996, p. 22.

31. Jane Coutts, "Minister's Aide Out of Job After Using OHIP Billing Data," *Globe and Mail,* December 7, 1996, p. A11.

32. Denis Donoghue, "The Politics of Homosexuality," *New York Times Book Review,* August 20, 1995, p. 26.

33. Michael Kinsley, "The Conflict of Interest Craze," *Washington Monthly,* November, 1978, p. 42.

34. Frank Bruni, "On the Trail She's Now First Mom and Wife," *New York Times,* October 13, 1996, p. A16.

35. Robin Toner, "In Final Rounds, Parties Wield Bare-Knuckle Ads," *New York Times,* October 21, 1996, p. A12.

36. George Waldon, "Ode to an Entrepreneur," *Arkansas Business,* May 6, 1991, p. 4.

37. Quoted in Julie Kosterlitz, "Fighting for Ethics: The Senate Considers the Case Against Ed Meese," *Common Cause Magazine,* April 1985, p. 42.

12. On Character in American Politics

1. For a well-wrought version of this argument, see Deborah Rhode, "Moral Character: The Personal and the Political," *Loyola University of Chicago Law Journal* 20 (1988), p. 2.

2. Michael Kinsley, "On the Zipper Beat," *The New Republic,* May 25, 1987, p. 4.

3. Quoted in John F. Kennedy, *Profiles in Courage* (New York: Harper and Row, 1956), p. 249.

4. Roger Morris, *Partners in Power: The Clintons and Their America* (New York: Henry Holt, 1996), p. 96.

5. Ibid., p. 275.

6. Ibid., p. 437.

7. John King, "Sasso, Dukakis' Trusted Corner Man," AP wire story, September 3, 1988.

8. "The Democrats in Atlanta: Transcript of the Speech by Dukakis Accepting the Democratic Nomination," *New York Times,* July 22, 1988, p. A10.

9. E. J. Dionne, Jr., "Construction Boom: It's No Accident That the GOP is Being Rebuilt by its Governors," *Washington Post,* March 14, 1999, p. B1.

10. Quoted in Ruth Marcus, "Suddenly, the President's Fate Is in Congress' Hands," *Washington Post,* September 10, 1998, p. A1.

11. Morris, *Partners in Power,* p. 56.

12. David Broder, "Should Such a President Remain?," *Washington Post,* December 11, 1998, p. A31.

13. Michael Oreskes, "That Woman," *New York Times Book Review,* April 4, 1999, p. 6.

14. George Stephanopoulos, quoted in Todd S. Purdum, "Clinton, Most Charming at a Distance," *New York Times,* September 27, 1998, p. 22 and Dee Dee Myers, quoted in Joe Klein, "Primary Cad," *New Yorker,* September 7, 1998, p. 51.

15. "Resignation the Only Responsible Option," *Atlanta Journal-Constitution,* September 12, 1998, p. 6G.

16. "Dole Cuts Senate Cord," *Boston Herald,* May 16, 1996, p. 30 and Bonnie Harris, "Dole Puts It All on the Line," *Indianapolis News,* May 17, 1996. p. A8.

17. "He's Alive! Bob Dole Gets in the Race," editorial, *Arkansas Democrat-Gazette,* May 16, 1996, p. 8B.

18. Ibid.

19. John McCain, Speech Nominating Senator Bob Dole for President of the United States, August 14, 1996.

20. Alan Ehrenhalt, *The United States of Ambition: Politicians, Power and the Pursuit of Office* (New York: Times Books, 1991), pp. 36, 274–276.

21. Richard L. Berke, "In Presidents, Virtues Can Be Flaws (and Vice Versa)," *New York Times,* September 27, 1998, p. 1.

13. Self-Generated versus Other-Imposed Encumbrances on Judgment

1. U.S. House of Representatives, Bipartisan Task Force on Ethics, Hearings, *Congressional Ethics Reform,* 101st Congress, 1st Session, May 3, 24, July 12, September 20, 1989, p. 106.

2. Quoted in Walter Goodman, *All Honorable Men: Corruption and Compromise in American Life* (Boston: Atlantic Monthly Press, 1963), p. 104.

3. Richard L. Neuberger, "When Influence Is Good—and Bad," *New York Times Magazine,* July 27, 1958, p. 9.

4. Ernest Tollerson, "Forbes, the Multimillionaire, Asks the Public for Money," *New York Times,* January 26, 1996, p. A10.

5. Eliza Newlin Carney, "The New Plutocrats," *National Journal,* August 20, 1994, pp. 1967, 1969.

6. William Greider and Thomas O'Toole, "Rockefeller Family Holdings Touch Every Economic Sphere," *Washington Post,* September 22, 1974, p. A1.

7. Jeffrey Abramson, *We, The Jury: The Jury System and the Ideal of Democracy* (New York: Basic Books, 1994), p. 100; see also Amy B. Hartmann, "Clean Sweep of the New Trial Safeguard Against Unauthorized Communications with Jury Members," *Wayne Law Review* 31 (1985), p. 1096: It is "overwhelmingly evident that a presumption of prejudice in improper contacts cases, and an actual prejudice burden in juror bias cases, can coexist within the same area of criminal procedure."

8. Peter L. Strauss, "Disqualification of Decisional Officials in Rulemaking," *Columbia Law Review* 80 (1980), p. 1044 (emphases mine).

9. Sara Greenwood Hogan, "FTC Rulemaking: The Standard for Disqualification of a Biased Commissioner," *St. Mary's Law Journal* 12 (1981), pp. 747, 739. In an influential article ("Adjudicatory Independence and the Values of Procedural Due Process," *Yale Law Journal* 95 [1986], p. 477), Martin H. Redish and Lawrence C. Marshall seem to deny this point, but in fact do not. What Redish and Marshall argue is that a decision-maker free of internal biases can sometimes make up for a hearing conducted with inadequate procedural safeguards against externally imposed encumbrances, safeguards such as the rights of notice, open record, and cross-examination. But even the full-fledged presence of such safeguards against externally imposed encumbrances, they argue, cannot overcome the ultimately skewed judgment of an internally biased decision-maker. Nonetheless, saying that an absence of externally imposed encumbrances cannot correct for inner bias where it exists is not the same thing as saying that externally imposed encumbrances such as *ex parte* contacts are *less troubling* than internally germinated biases of the same heft. Indeed, the latter will always seem closer to the legitimate formation of subjectively genuine policy views on the part of the decision-maker.

10. Hartmann, "Clean Sweep," pp. 1086, 1095.

11. U.S. House of Representatives, Commission on Administrative Review, Hearings, *Financial Ethics*, 95th Congress, 1st Session, January 13, 14, 31, February 2, 7, 1977 (remarks of David Obey), p. 125.

12. *Congressional Record*, May 27, 1982, p. S5224.

13. "The Man Behind the Voice Behind the 1994 Elections," *New Yorker*, November 28, 1994, p. 50.

14. *Quid Pro Quo* and Campaign Finance

1. Daniel Hays Lowenstein, "Political Bribery and the Intermediate Theory of Politics," *UCLA Law Review* 32 (1985), p. 819.

2. "Uncertainty as to whether [a] transaction was a bribe or simply a traditional albeit unethical political deal"—or, for that matter, an ethical political deal—dominates judicial discourse in bribery cases (Bennett L. Gershman, "Abscam, the Judiciary and the Ethics of Entrapment," *Yale Law Journal* 91 (1982), p. 1582; see also Jane Fritsch, "A Bribe's Not a Bribe When It's a Donation," *New York Times*, January 28, 1996, Section 4, p. 1). "This is not to say that bribery invariably is ambiguous," as one court put it, "but simply that when dealing with quids, quos and their relationship, there is much room for disagreement as to whether a criminal act has occurred"; see *People* v. *Cunningham*, 88 Misc. 2d 1065 (N.Y., 1976).

3. U.S. House of Representatives, Committee on the Judiciary, Subcommittee on Administrative Law and Governmental Relations, Hearing, *Lobbying Disclosure Act of 1993*, 103rd Congress, 1st Session, March 31, 1993, p. 200.

4. *U.S.* v. *Sun-Diamond Growers of California*, 138 F. 3d 961 (D.C. Cir., 1988) at 966.

5. *U.S.* v. *Brewster*, 506 F. 2d 62 (D.C. Cir., 1974) at 72.

6. Donald C. Smaltz et al., On Petition for a Writ of Certiorari in the Supreme Court of the United States, October term, 1997, *Reply of the United States*, p. 6.

7. Donald C. Smaltz et al., *Petition for Writ of Certiorari in the Supreme Court of the United States,* October term, 1997, *U.S. v. Sun-Diamond Growers of California,* p. 6.

8. Richard A. Hibey et al., On Petition for Writ of Certiorari in the Supreme Court of the United States, October term, 1997, *Respondent's Brief in Opposition,* pp. 24–28.

9. Quoted in Smaltz, Petition, p. 11.

10. 5 CFR 2623.202.

11. *U.S. v. Sun-Diamond Growers of California,* 119 S. Ct. 1402 (1999).

12. 18 U.S.C. §1951.

13. U.S. House of Representatives, Committee on Government Operations, Report, *Avoiding Conflicts of Interest in Defense Contracting and Employment,* 88th Congress, 1st Session, November 22, 1963, p. 28.

14. Hence Justice Kennedy describes extortion as a form of "abuse of office" in his concurring opinion in *Evans* v. *U.S.,* 112 S. Ct. 1881 (1992) at 1892; see also *U.S.* v. *Cerilli,* 603 F. 2d 415 (3rd. Cir., 1979) at 433.

15. This is how the dissenting Justice Thomas interpreted extortion in *Evans* v. *U.S.* at 1895.

16. Ibid. at 1889.

17. James Lindgren, "The Theory, History and Practice of the Bribery-Extortion Distinction," *University of Pennsylvania Law Review* 141 (1993), pp. 1698–1700; see also *U.S.* v. *Paschall,* 772 F. 2d 68 (4th Cir., 1995) at 71–74.

18. *U.S.* v. *Brewster* at 82.

19. Lindgren, "Bribery-Extortion Distinction," p. 1700.

20. Joseph R. Weeks, "Bribes, Gratuities and the Congress," *Journal of Legislation* 13 (1986), p. 134.

21. Commentators and courts have on occasion used contract metaphors and terminology to describe *quid pro quo.* See Fred S. McChesney, *Money for Nothing: Politicians, Rent Extraction and Political Extortion* (Cambridge, Mass.: Harvard University Press, 1997), pp. 21, 53 and *U.S.* v. *Arthur,* 544 F. 2d 730 (4th Cir., 1976) at 735.

22. I draw the term "classical" contract law from Melvin Aron Eisenberg, "The Responsive Model of Contract Law," *Stanford Law Review* 36 (1984), p. 1108.

23. Stanley D. Henderson, "Promises Grounded in the Past: The Idea of Unjust Enrichment and the Law of Contracts," *Virginia Law Review* 57 (1971), pp. 1165, 1180.

24. Ibid., p. 1161.

25. Michael D. Bayles, "Legally Enforceable Contracts," *Law and Philosophy* 4 (1985), pp. 331, 333 and Melvin Aron Eisenberg, "The Principles of Consideration," *Cornell Law Review* 67 (1982), p. 642.

26. Melvin Aron Eisenberg, "The Bargain Principle and Its Limits," *Harvard Law Review* 95 (1982), p. 742.

27. Henderson, "Promises," p. 1143.

28. Eisenberg, "The Bargain Principle," p. 745.

29. Henderson, "Promises," p. 1156.

30. Henderson, "Promises," p. 1128; see also Richard Hooley, "Consideration and

the Existing Duty," *Journal of Business Law* (1991), p. 19 and James D. Gordon III, "Consideration and the Commercial-Gift Dichotomy," *Vanderbilt Law Review* 44 (1991), p. 283.

31. Bayles, "Legally Enforceable Rules," p. 328.
32. Eisenberg, "The Responsive Model," p. 1118.
33. Ibid., p. 1107.
34. Eisenberg, "The Responsive Model," p. 1107. The classical approach, it should be emphasized, *does* contemplate the possibility that a contract could be unconscionable—that one party to a particular contract may have exerted duress or otherwise manipulated the mental state of another such that an unconscionably disproportionate, hence voidable, exchange took place. Such a possibility, however, is of a piece with classical jurisprudence's subjective approach to proportionality, in that it "depends on a determination of the parties' mental states." And it remains inconsistent with newer approaches (to be discussed below) which would void contracts on objective grounds, such as for simply failing to meet certain social or market standards of fair or proportionate exchange.
35. Bayles, "Legally Enforceable Contracts," p. 333.
36. Ibid., p. 333; see also Eisenberg, "The Responsive Model," p. 1115.
37. Gordon, "Consideration," p. 310; see also Jane B. Baron, "Gifts, Bargains and Form," *Indiana Law Journal* 64 (1989), pp. 155–203.
38. Eisenberg, "The Principles of Consideration," p. 656.
39. Eisenberg, "The Bargain Principle," p. 745 (emphasis mine).
40. Paul H. Douglas, *Ethics in Government* (Cambridge, Mass.: Harvard University Press, 1952), p. 89 and Ronald M. Levin, "Congressional Ethics and Constituent Advocacy in an Age of Mistrust," *Michigan Law Review* 95 (1996), pp. 68, 87.
41. Quoted in Burt Solomon, "Bite-Sized Favors," *National Journal,* October 11, 1986, p. 2149.
42. The Staff of Congressional Quarterly, ed., *Dollar Politics,* 3rd edition (Washington: Congressional Quarterly, 1982), p. 48.
43. John R. Wright, "Contributions, Lobbying, and Committee Voting in the U.S. House of Representatives," *American Political Science Review* 84 (1990), p. 419 and Kevin B. Grier and Michael C. Munger, "Comparing Interest Group PAC Contributions to House and Senate Incumbents," *Journal of Politics* 55 (1993), p. 621. As I noted in the Introduction, however, empirical work on the question of whether nonpropinquitous *quids* and *quos* are linked is far from univocal, which is why discourse continually falls back on the kinds of factual disagreements I analyze here. Richard A. Smith, for example, concludes his recent comprehensive review of the literature by noting that "the findings [in this area] are both conflicting and methodologically suspect, and thus ultimately inconclusive" (see "Interest Group Influence in the U.S. Congress," *Legislative Studies Quarterly* 20 [1995], p. 123).
44. Douglas, *Ethics in Government,* p. 90.
45. *U.S.* v. *Myers,* 692 F. 2d 823 (2nd Cir., 1982) at 832 and Robert W. Greene, *The Sting Man: Inside Abscam* (New York: Dutton, 1981), chap. 12.
46. *U.S.* v. *Kelly,* 539 F. Supp. 363 (D.D.C., 1982) at 371, 373 and *U.S.* v. *Williams,* 305 F. 2d 603 (2nd. Cir., 1983) at 616.

47. Quoted in Congressional Quarterly, *Congressional Ethics: History, Facts, Controversy* (Washington: Congressional Quarterly, 1992), p. 119.

48. Donna Fenn, "Using Husbands as Business Cards: Political Wives in Compromising Positions," *Washington Monthly*, June 1982, p. 42.

49. See also *U.S. v. Arthur* and *U.S. v. L'Hoste*, 609 F. 2d 796 (5th Cir., 1980) at 833.

50. U.S. House of Representatives, Committee on Standards of Official Conduct, Report, *Investigation of Financial Transactions Participated In and Gifts of Transportation Accepted by Representative Fernand J. St. Germain*, 100th Congress, 1st Session, April 1987, p. 2.

51. Amitai Etzioni, *Capital Corruption: The New Attack on American Democracy* (San Diego: Harcourt, Brace, Jovanovich, 1984), p. 71.

52. Eisenberg, "The Responsive Model," p. 1109.

53. Gordon, "Consideration," p. 310.

54. Steven Chibnall and Peter Saunders, "Worlds Apart: Notes on the Social Reality of Corruption," *British Journal of Sociology* 28 (1977), p. 146.

55. *Congressional Record* (Senate), May 4, 1994, p. 5163.

56. See the account in Chibnall and Saunders, "Worlds Apart," pp. 146–147.

57. Francis X. Clines, "Map of Campaign Finance Trail Leads to Labyrinth," *New York Times*, July 16, 1997, p. A11.

58. Baron, "Gifts," p. 196; see also William Ian Miller's "Requiting the Unwanted Gift," in *Humiliation: And Other Essays on Honor, Social Discomfort and Violence* (Ithaca: Cornell University Press, 1993), especially p. 23.

59. Ross F. Cranston, "Regulating Conflict of Interest of Public Officials: A Comparative Analysis," *Vanderbilt Journal of Transnational Law* 12 (1979), p. 245 and Comment, "Questioning the Impartiality of Judges," *Temple Law Quarterly* 60 (1987), p. 704.

60. See the discussion at *Congressional Record*, May 4, 1994, p. S5166. Indeed, as Susan Rose-Ackerman notes, officials may be *more* inclined to enter into *quid pro quo* relationships with friends than with strangers, because they "will be less likely than strangers to reveal the corrupt deal or to renege on the agreement." See Susan Rose-Ackerman, *Corruption and Government: Causes, Consequences and Reform* (New York: Cambridge University Press, 1999), p. 98.

61. On pettiness, see Charles Krauthammer, "Jim Wright and the Real Corruption in Washington," *Washington Post*, April 21, 1989 ("I am as titillated as the next pundit by corruption on a grand scale, but corruption on this scale I find sad"). On greed, see Susan Rose-Ackerman, *Corruption: A Study in Political Economy* (New York: Academic Press, 1978), p. 50 and John T. Noonan, *Bribes* (New York: MacMillan, 1984), p. 697.

62. Lowenstein, "Political Bribery," p. 819.

63. Eisenberg, "The Responsive Model," p. 1109.

64. *Quid pro quo* is a "mental crime," the sort of offense where, as A. C. E. Lynch puts it, "the mental element is part of the *actus reus*"; it is not a more "orthodox" kind of offense where "the mental element is merely a requirement of *mens rea* vis à vis its *actus reus*." See "The Mental Element in the *Actus Reus*," *Law Quarterly Review* 98 (1982), p. 116.

65. See "Political Bribery and the Intermediate Theory of Corruption," *UCLA Law Review* 32 (1985), p. 798; see also William Welch III, "The Federal Bribery Statute and Special Interest Campaign Contributions," *Journal of Criminal Law and Criminology* 79 (1989), p. 1363 and Joseph R. Weeks, "Bribes, Gratuities and the Congress," p. 133.

66. See Kathleen Clark, *Paying the Price for Heightened Ethics Scrutiny: Legal Defense Funds and Other Ways That Government Officials Pay Their Lawyers*, Washington University School of Law Working Paper No. 97–3–2 (1997), p. 31 and Jim Sasser, "Learning from the Past: The Senate Code of Conduct in Historical Perspective," *Cumberland Law Review* 8 (1977), p. 378.

67. See Ellen Miller, *Speaking Freely* (Washington: Center for Responsive Politics, 1998), pp. 7, 8.

68. For a different but (I think) not incompatible interpretation of some of these situations, see Dennis F. Thompson, *Ethics in Congress: From Individual to Institutional Corruption* (Washington: Brookings, 1995), pp. 113–114.

69. *D.C. Federation of Civic Associations* v. *Volpe*, 459 F. 2d 1231 (D.C. Cir., 1971) at 1246, 1250, 1261.

70. Lowenstein, "Political Bribery," p. 828.

71. Ibid., p. 807.

72. Lowenstein ("Political Bribery," p. 827) illustratively reports that when the California Marshalls' Association was accused of making unethical contributions to the speaker of the state assembly, the president of the association said, "We're just participating in the legislative process." "A naive observer," Lowenstein pointedly comments, "might have imagined that campaign contributions were part of the electoral process"; see also Weeks, "Bribes, Gratuities and the Congress," pp. 127, 145. Along similar lines, Rep. William M. Thomas notes that "PACs have given up the attempt to change who is in the seat but now simply influence the person in it." See U.S. House of Representatives, Committee on House Administration, Hearing, *Campaign Finance Reform*, 102nd Congress, 1st Session, March 22, 1991, p. 41.

73. *Buckley* v. *Valeo*, 424 U.S. 1 (1976) at 21, 38, 58.

74. Richard L. Hall and Frank W. Wayman, "Buying Time: Moneyed Interests and the Mobilization of Bias on Congressional Committees," *American Political Science Review* 84 (1990), pp. 799, 802–803.

75. Richard A. Smith, "Advocacy, Interpretation and Influence in the U.S. Congress," *American Political Science Review* 78 (1984), p. 59.

76. Likewise, lobbying that *is* meant to move legislators—but on an array of issues, not just one—is also treated relatively more benignly. To the extent that lobbyists engage in "general advocacy," as opposed to lobbying on a specific bill or case, they escape what regulation there is. In defending himself from charges of abusing his relationship with Vice President Al Gore, Roy Neel—Gore's former chief of staff and now a telecommunications-industry lobbyist—said, "I have had discussions with the Vice President in general terms on telecommunications policy. . . . But I do not lobby him on any single issue related to our industry." See Don Van Natta, Jr., "Gore Is Finding Insider Image Tough to Shake," *New York*

Times, October 31, 1999, Section 1, p. 24; see also Comment, "Federal Lobbying Disclosure Legislation," *American University Law Review* 26 (1977), p. 1014.

77. Heinz Eulau and John D. Sprague, *Lawyers in Politics* (Indianapolis: Bobbs Merrill, 1964), p. 19.

78. U.S. House of Representatives, Committee on Standards of Official Conduct, *House Ethics Manual,* 102nd Congress, 2nd Session, April 1992, p. 54.

79. Rev. Rul. 78–248, 1978–1 C.B. 154, Situation 4.

80. Committee on House Administration, *Campaign Finance Reform,* pp. 18, 32.

81. Frank J. Sorauf, *Inside Campaign Finance Reform: Myths and Realities* (New Haven: Yale University Press, 1992), pp. 199, 208, 228; see also David Frum, "An End to Money Grubbing: Changing the Campaign Finance System," *The Weekly Standard,* January 15, 1996, p. 25: "The chairman of Exxon might give $1,000 to a candidate because he agrees with the candidate's views . . . The various energy industry PACs, however, distribute their largesse on the crassest quid pro quo basis . . . When reformers allege that the system of financing congressional elections has deteriorated into legalized bribery, they come uncomfortably close to the truth."

82. An irony emerges at this point in the rhetorical landscape. Because groups that rely on public funding or tax exemptions cannot advocate for a candidate—only for a particular issue position—their advertisements can never say "elect" or "defeat" candidate X. If they wish to come right up to the line without crossing it, they will conceive ads that espouse a particular side of a policy question, identify a candidate who is opposed, and instead of saying, "Defeat Congressman Foley," they will say, "Ask Congressman Foley to change his mind." In other words, in order to avoid taking an electoral approach to voters, they will advocate that voters take a legislative approach to candidates. (See Lisa Rosenberg, *A Bag of Tricks: Loopholes in the Campaign Finance System* [Washington: Center for Responsive Politics, 1996], pp. 2–3.) The converse regime, I emphasize, applies in the converse context: not where citizens draw on their own private resources to engage officials through gifts, contributions, lobbying, or voluntarism, but where officials draw on public resources to engage citizens through (for example) the use of the frank or various tax-exempt foundations they may happen to control. That is, officials who engage citizens in these ways enjoy greater political and judicial approval precisely to the degree that their intent *is* to move citizens' opinions on particularistic issues. And they run a greater risk of disapproval—in using the frank or their own foundations—precisely to the extent that they intend to reinforce citizens' perspectives on holistic political doctrines or partisan platforms. Whereas we prefer citizens to take an electoral and not a legislative approach when intervening with politicians, in other words, we prefer politicians to take a legislative and not an electoral approach when intervening with citizens.

On franking, see James A. Gardner, "The Use and Abuses of Incumbency," *Fordham Law Review* 60 (1991), p. 247 ("the public will by law pick up the tab for material mailed for legislative purposes . . . but not for material mailed for the purpose of campaigning") and *Rising* v. *Brown,* 313 F. Supp. 824 (C.D. Cal., 1970), where the court held that Congressman George Brown's "sudden departure in his brochure from the environmental interest of his subcommittee to his views on the war"—in other words, from a particularistic issue-oriented toward a totalistic platform-oriented communication—"suggests a dual [legislative/electoral] purpose," hence franking the brochure was illegal. On tax-exempt foundations, see Lee A. Sheppard, "Is Gingrich's Think Tank Too Partisan for Exemption?," *Tax Notes*, December 5, 1994, p. 1175 (such foundations must not engage in "the reinforcement of an interested citizen's initial support") and the comments of Gingrich aide Jeffrey Eisenach who, in rebutting charges that foundations allied with Newt Gingrich supported a television program targeted to "Republican-leaning audiences," insisted instead: "I think it energized a lot of people to think differently about public policy problems" (see Jackie Koszczuk, "All Eyes on the IRS as Agency Looks Into Gingrich Case," *CQ*, February 22, 1997, p. 477).

83. Quoted in Ellen Miller, *Speaking Freely* (Washington: Center for Responsive Politics, 1998), p. 63.

84. Agenda-framing, of course, can also involve the opposite: manipulating the agenda to ensure that an issue never comes up for consideration at all. As I suggest below, however, because the agenda-manipulating legislator acts less as a decision-maker than as an advocate, and also because agenda-manipulation operates at a meta-level (its concern is not with biased consideration of policy questions but with the biased consideration of what questions are to be considered in the first place), it is generally treated as the least troubling, if not a totally untroubling, form of *quo*.

85. See, e.g., "Money Begets Access, and Access Begets Influence," in Miller, *Speaking Freely*, pp. 61–89 and John W. Kingdon, *Agendas, Alternatives and Public Policies* (Boston: Little, Brown, 1984), p. 1.

86. See, generally, Thompson, *Ethics in Congress*, pp. 117, 184–190.

87. *U.S. v. Myers*, 692 F. 2d 823 (2nd Cir., 1982) at 853–860.

88. This is an impressionistic statement on my part, but I believe any fairly comprehensive reading of public debate would find many more references to a concern with access-granting as a *quo* than with agenda-manipulation. To illustrate: Ellen Miller's *Speaking Freely*, a book in which former congressmen ruminate on the ethical dilemmas they faced in office, has a section on access-granting but none on agenda-manipulation; see likewise Dan Clawson et al., *Dollars and Votes: How Business Campaign Contributions Subvert Democracy* (Philadelphia: Temple University Press, 1998), pp. 63–106.

15. Spousal Interests

1. Richard L. Neuberger, "When Influence is Good—And Bad," *New York Times Magazine*, July 27, 1958, p. 9.

2. For example, the *House Ethics Manual* replicates the spirit if not the letter of most regimes in requiring a spouse to disclose her assets unless the official has no knowledge of them, will not benefit from them, and did not transfer them to the spouse in the first place. See also Center for Responsive Politics, *The Impact of Financial Disclosure on Spouses* (Washington, 1985), p. 13.

3. For a good overview, see Alfred S. Neely IV, *Ethics in Government Laws: Are They Too Ethical?* (Washington: American Enterprise Institute, 1984), p. 9.
4. "Hillary the Pol," *New Yorker,* May 30, 1994, p. 90.
5. See, e.g., *Githens* v. *Butler County,* 165 S.W. 2d 650 (Missouri, 1942).
6. U.S. House of Representatives, Commission on Administrative Review, Report, *Financial Ethics,* 95th Congress, 1st Session, February 14, 1977, p. 5 and Note, "Fighting Conflicts of Interest in Officialdom," *Michigan Law Review* 73 (1975), p. 780.
7. W.D. Parker, *Commission of Inquiry into the Facts of Allegations of Conflict of Interest Concerning the Honourable Sinclair M. Stevens* (Ottawa: Minister of Supply and Services, 1987), p. 355.
8. Note, "Conflicts of Interest and the Changing Concept of Marriage: The Congressional Compromise," *Michigan Law Review* 75 (1977), p. 1654.
9. William Safire, "Spousal Arousal," *New York Times,* September 24, 1984, p. A19.
10. Flora Lewis, "Politicians Are People," *New York Times,* August 7, 1994, p. A25.
11. Donna Fenn, "Using Husbands as Business Cards: Political Wives in Compromising Positions," *Washington Monthly,* June 1982, pp. 40–44 and Deborah Baldwin, "After the Election: It's Hard Being Married to a Politician, Especially in Washington," *Common Cause,* March/April 1987, pp. 22–23.
12. *Association of American Physicians and Surgeons* v. *Clinton,* 997 F. 2d 898 (D.C. Cir., 1993) at 904; see also remarks of Senator John Glenn, *Congressional Record,* April 2, 1993, p. S4449.
13. The District Court, from whose ruling Hillary Clinton had appealed, not only held that she remained outside the ambit of the president's official role, it for that reason ruled against her. See *Association of American Physicians* v. *Clinton,* 813 F. Supp. 82 (D.D.C., 1993).
14. Peter Beinart, "Take This Wife, Please," *The New Republic,* July 5, 1999, p. A4.
15. Irwin N. Gertzog, *Congressional Women: Their Recruitment, Treatment and Behavior* (New York: Praeger, 1984) p. 25.
16. Quoted in William Claiborne, "Mary Bono Adjusts to the Political Spotlight," *Washington Post,* April 6, 1998, p. A4.
17. Fenn, "Using Husbands," p. 42.
18. Baldwin, "After the Election," p. 25.
19. Jenet Conant, "The Ghost and Mr. Giuliani," *Vanity Fair,* September 1997, pp. 154–172.

16. Combination of Roles and *Ex Parte* Contacts

1. *Ward* v. *Village of Monroeville,* 409 U.S. 57 (1972) at 93.
2. *Pangburn* v. *Civil Aeronautics Board,* 311 F. 2d 349 (1st Cir., 1962) at 356.
3. John R. Allison, "Combination of Decision-Making Functions, Ex Parte Communication, and Related Biasing Influences: A Process-Value Analysis," *Utah Law Review* (1993), p. 1173; see also *Withrow* v. *Larkin,* 421 U.S. 35 (1975) at 37–38 and *Cinderella Career and Finishing Schools, Inc.* v. *FTC,* 425 F. 2d 583 (D.C. Cir., 1970) at 590.
4. Allison, "Combination of Decision-Making Functions," pp. 1171, 1172.

5. Kenneth Culp Davis, *Administrative Law and Government,* 2nd ed., (St. Paul: West, 1975), p. 185; see also U.S. House of Representatives, Committee on Interstate and Foreign Commerce, Special Subcommittee on Legislative Oversight, Hearing, *Administrative Process and Ethical Questions,* 85th Congress, 2nd Session, November 18, 1958, p. 202.

6. Allison, "Combination of Decision-Making Functions," p. 1138; see, e.g., *American Telephone and Telegraph* v. *FCC,* 499 F. 2d 439 (2d. Cir., 1971).

7. Combination of roles is most troubling in judicial or quasi-judicial contexts but provokes concern as well in quasi-legislative and even legislative decision-making. For example, the venerable delegate-trustee debate—over whether the legislative roles of advocacy for the constituency and decision-making in the public interest encumber one another—is a combination-of-roles issue.

8. Davis, *Administrative Law,* p. 186. While their potential for perturbing official judgment grows as the official role in question moves toward the judicial end of the spectrum, *ex parte* contacts provoke concern in legislative or rule-making situations as well. Consider, for example, the controversy that erupts whenever lobbyists for one side in a policy controversy are invited—behind closed doors—to help draft legislation (see, e.g. Neil A. Lewis, "Rules Regulating Oil Industry Are Mired in a Debate on Ethics," *New York Times,* June 27, 1999, p. 19). In what follows, I abstract from any (quasi-)judicial-(quasi-)legislative differences, which in any case are differences in degree. For examples of *ex parte* concerns experienced in all three branches, see *Home Box Office, Inc.* v. *FCC,* 567 F. 2d 9 (D.C. Cir., 1977); Note, "Ex Parte Communications During Informal Rulemaking," *Columbia Journal of Law and Social Problems* 14 (1979), pp. 269–308; Paul R. Verkuil, "Jawboning Administrative Agencies: Ex Parte Contacts by the White House," *Columbia Law Review* 80 (1980), pp. 970–971; *National Advertisers, Inc.* v. *FTC,* 617 F. 2d 611 (D.C. Cir., 1979) at 633; and Glenn T. Carberry, "Ex Parte Communications in Off-the-Record Administrative Proceedings: A Proposed Limitation on Judicial Innovation," *Duke Law Journal* (1980), p. 65.

9. Peter L. Strauss, "Disqualification of Decisional Officials in Rulemaking," *Columbia Law Review* 80 (1980), p. 1044.

10. See *Federal Trade Commission* v. *Cement Institute,* 333 U.S. 683 (1948) at 684; *Home Box Office* at 57; and Michael Asimow, "When the Curtain Falls: Separation of Functions in the Federal Administrative Agencies," *Columbia Law Review* 81 (1981), p. 725.

11. *U.S.* v. *Grinnell,* 384 U.S. 563 (1966); see also *Amos Treat Co.* v. *Securities and Exchange Commission,* 306 F. 2d. 260 (D.C. Cir., 1962).

12. See, generally, U.S. Senate, Committee on the Judiciary, Subcommittee on Separation of Powers, Hearings, *Nonjudicial Activities of Supreme Court Justices and Other Federal Judges,* 91st Congress, 1st Session, July 14, 15, 16, September 30, 1969.

13. Indeed, the distinction between advocatory and advisory officials frequently blurs indelibly in any given case. See, for example, Davis, *Administrative Law,* pp. 182, 186–187; Asimow, "When the Curtain Falls," pp. 759, 775, 785, 788–789, 795–796; and *Action for Children's Television* v. *FCC,* 564 F. 2d 458 (D.C. Cir., 1977) at 477.

14. *Action for Children's Television* v. *FCC* at 477; see also Cornelius J. Peck, "Regulation and Control of Ex Parte Communications with Administrative Agencies," *Harvard Law Review* 76 (1962), pp. 246, 249.

15. W. Warfield Ross, "Congress Should Act to Restrict Ex Parte Contacts Within Agencies," *National Law Journal* 21 (1979), p. 22.

16. *Hercules, Inc.* v. *Environmental Protection Agency*, 598 F. 2d 91 (D.C. Cir., 1978).

17. Or, alternatively, an exchange between the decision-maker and other agency officials might be sufficiently constructable as an extension of her own mental processes to invite charges of combination-of-roles but sufficiently extrinsic to her own mental processes that *ex parte* concerns also emerge. See *ATT* v. *FCC*, 499 F. 2d 439.

18. Many "arguments and proposals," as Cornelius J. Peck noted many years ago, "do not distinguish clearly between the problem of separation of functions and the different though related problem of ex parte communications"; see "Regulation and Control," p. 258.

19. Nathaniel L. Nathanson, "Report to the Select Committee on Ex Parte Communications in Informal Rulemaking Proceedings," *Administrative Law Review* 30 (1978), p. 580.

20. Steven Lubet, "*Ex parte* Communications: An Issue in Judicial Conduct," *Judicature* 74 (1990), p. 100.

17. Hold the Interest, Vary the Role

1. "Senator Kerr Talks about Conflict of Interest," *U.S. News and World Report*, September 3, 1962, p. 86.

2. Peter L. Strauss, "Disqualification of Decisional Officials in Rulemaking," *Columbia Law Review* 80 (1980), p. 1037.

3. For other examples of the Kerr argument, see George F. Carpinello, "Should Practicing Lawyers be Legislators?," *Hastings Law Journal* 41 (1989), p. 92, Lloyd N. Cutler, "Balancing the Ethics Code," *Washington Post,* March 13, 1989, p. A15, and U.S. Senate, Select Committee on Ethics, Hearing, *Revising the Senate Code of Official Conduct Pursuant to Senate Resolution 109,* 96th Congress, 2d Session, November 18, 1980, p. 18 (testimony of Hadley Arkes).

4. U.S. Senate, Committee on Labor and Public Welfare, Subcommittee to Study Senate Concurrent Resolution 21, Hearing, *Establishment of a Commission on Ethics in Government,* 82nd Congress, 1st Session, June 22, 1951, p. 123.

5. Theodore J. Lowi, *The End of Liberalism: Ideology, Policy and the Crisis of Public Authority* (New York: Norton, 1969), pp. 96–97. The question here, of course, is not whether the official's advocatory role itself encumbers him in his judging role (or vice versa); this is a conflict-of-roles question, and an age-old one in the legislative context. Here, the question is to what extent the possession of pecuniary interests helps the official in the one role but not the other.

6. See, e.g., New York State Bar Association, Committee on Professional Ethics, Opinion 589 (1988) and Kirsten L. Christophe, "The Common Practice of At-

torneys Sitting on Clients' Boards of Directors Creates Ethical and Practical Pitfalls," *National Law Journal,* September 15, 1997, p. B5.

7. See, e.g., Amy Keller, "Faircloth Attacked for Pork, As in Pigs," *Roll Call,* February 13, 1995, p. 1.

8. See the remarks of Daniel H. Lowenstein, U.S. House of Representatives, Commission on Administrative Review, *Financial Ethics,* 95th Congress, 1st Session, January 13, 14, 31, February 2, 7, 1977, p. 125.

9. For a good discussion of the distinction between narrow and polycentric legislative advocacy—or between representing constituents' "private troubles" and their "political opinions"—see Donald D. Searing, "The Role of the Good Constituency Member and the Practice of Representation in Great Britain," *Journal of Politics* 47 (1985), p. 370.

10. Strauss, "Disqualification," p. 1001.

11. Carpinello, "Should Practicing Lawyers be Legislators?," p. 91.

12. State of New Jersey, *Report of the Legislative Commission on Conflicts of Interest to the Senate and General Assembly of the State of New Jersey,* December 31, 1957, p. 14.

13. Carpinello, "Should Practicing Lawyers be Legislators?," p. 92; see also U.S. House of Representatives, Committee on Standards of Official Conduct, *House Ethics Manual,* 102nd Congress, 2nd Session, April 1992, p. 21 and Barry McGill, "Conflict of Interest: The English Experience," *Western Political Quarterly* 12 (1959), p. 822.

14. Ronald M. Levin, "Congressional Ethics and Constituent Advocacy in an Age of Mistrust," *Michigan Law Review* 95 (1996), pp. 5, 8.

15. Jeffrey H. Birnbaum, "Arctic Alaska and Rep. John Miller Face Scrutiny Over 1990 Sinking of Fishing Ship in Bering Sea," *Wall Street Journal,* April 10, 1991, p. A24; see also Jane Fritsch, "Senator's Proposal to Aid Timber Company Assailed," *New York Times,* June 18, 1996, p. A10.

16. American Bar Association Committee on Government Standards, "Keeping Faith: Government Ethics and Government Ethics Regulation," *Administrative Law Review* 45 (1993), p. 299.

17. *Congressional Record,* June 16, 1983, p. S8508.

18. Ibid., p. S8508.

19. *Congressional Record,* October 38, 1981, p. H7825; see also U.S. House of Representatives, Committee on Rules, *Hearings and Markup on House Resolution 287,* 95th Congress, 1st Session, February 23, 1977, pp. 47, 121 and Association of the Bar of the City of New York, *Congress and the Public Trust* (New York: Atheneum, 1970), p. 68.

20. *Congressional Record,* March 28, 1979, p. S6529.

21. *Congressional Record,* October 28, 1981, p. H7824.

22. Hanna Pitkin, *The Concept of Representation* (Berkeley: University of California Press, 1967), pp. 144–167 and William T. Bianco, *Representatives and Constituents* (Ann Arbor: University of Michigan Press, 1997), p. 24.

23. *Congressional Record,* October 28, 1981, p. H7828.

24. Ibid., p. H7283.

18. *De Minimis*

1. Office of the Senate Legal Counsel, *Compilation of Certain Legal Material Prepared on the Conflict of Interest Statutes* (memorandum for Senator Saltonstall), January 16, 1953, p. 20; see also U.S. House of Representatives, Committee on Standards of Official Conduct, Hearing, *Standards of Official Conduct*, 90th Congress, 1st Session, September 14, 21, and 27, 1967, p. 250.
2. Roswell B. Perkins, "The New Federal Conflict-of-Interest Law," *Harvard Law Review* 76 (1963), p. 1136.
3. *Congressional Record* (Senate), August 7, 1970, p. 27798 (remarks of Senator Bayh); see also May 5, 1994, p. S5229 (remarks of Senator Feingold).
4. Comment, "Federal Lobbying Disclosure Legislation," *American University Law Review* 26 (1977), p. 989.
5. *Congressional Record*, March 3, 1982, p. S1465. The subjective approach to pecuniary interest that Heflin here advances—on which something can be encumbering as long as the official concerned believes it has market value or at least has a "value to others" (see *U.S. v. Sheker*, 618 F. 2d 607 [9th Cir., 1980] at 609)—differs from the "subjective" approach that prevails in abuse of office and articulated in *U.S. v. Gorman* (discussed in chap. 5). There, the issue is whether something has value to the official herself that goes *beyond* its market value, for which the official has already made just recompense.
6. Note, "Conflict-of-Interests of Government Personnel: An Appraisal of the Philadelphia Situation," *University of Pennsylvania Law Review* 107 (1959), p. 994; see also 5 CFR 2640.301(4).

Part II Summary

1. Roswell B. Perkins, "The New Federal Conflict of Interest Law," *Harvard Law Review* 76 (1963), p. 1136.
2. *Foster v. City of Cape May*, 26 Atl. 1089 (N.J., 1897).

19. The Meaning of "The Appearance of Official Impropriety"

1. All quotations here are from 692 F. 2d 1129 (7th Cir., 1982) at 1131, 1132.
2. *Wathen v. I.R.S.*, 557 F. 2d 1191 (Ct. Claims, 1975).
3. Executive Order 12674, 101 (n).
4. Judith N. Shklar, *Legalism: Law, Morals and Political Trials* (Cambridge, Mass.: Harvard University Press, 1964), p. 152.
5. The Supreme Court, for example, has recently declined to rest decisions about the applicability of criminal-procedural safeguards on the question of whether "the punishment arose in a criminal or a civil proceeding. It found such an approach was too 'abstract' and not adequately responsive to 'humane interests.'" See Mary M. Cheh, "Constitutional Limits on Using Civil Remedies to Achieve Criminal Objectives: Understanding and Transcending the Criminal-Civil Law Distinction," *Hastings Law Journal* 42 (1991), pp. 1330, 1350 and also Kenneth

Mann, "Punitive Civil Sanctions: The Middleground Between Criminal and Civil Law," *Yale Law Journal* 101 (1992), pp. 1801, 1842–1843.

6. John C. Coffee, Jr., "Paradigms Lost: The Blurring of the Criminal and Civil Law Models—and What Can Be Done About It," *Yale Law Journal* 101 (1992), p. 1878.

7. Nigel Walker, *Punishment, Danger and Stigma: The Morality of Criminal Justice* (Oxford: Basil Blackwell, 1980), p. 4.

8. For a discussion of the stigmatizing "personal effects" of appearance findings on the lives of officials, see Suzanne Garment, *Scandal: The Culture of Mistrust in American Politics* (New York: Times Books, 1991), chap. 10.

9. Mann, "Punitive Civil Sanctions," p. 1811.

10. See Coffee's discussion of a version of the appearance standard in "Paradigms Lost," pp. 1878–1879, 1890–1892.

11. Richard L. Berke, "Congress Questions Its Own Policing Act," *New York Times,* June 15, 1990, p. A13.

12. See, for example, Archibald Cox, "Ethics in Government: the Cornerstone of Public Trust," *West Virginia Law Review* 94 (1991–1992), pp. 281–300.

13. Arthur H. Miller and Ola Listhaug, "Political Parties and Confidence in Government: A Comparison of Norway, Sweden and the United States," *British Journal of Political Science* 20 (1990), p. 358.

14. Seymour Martin Lipset and William Schneider, *The Confidence Gap: Business, Labor and Government in the Public Mind* (New York: Free Press, 1983), pp. 76, 79.

15. Norbert Schwartz and Herbert Bless, "Scandals and the Public's Trust in Politicians: Assimilation and Contrast Effects," *Personality and Social Psychology Bulletin* 18 (1992), pp. 574, 577.

16. John Dunn, "Trust and Political Agency," in Diego Gambetta, ed., *Trust: Making and Breaking Cooperative Relations* (Oxford: Basil Blackwell, 1988), pp. 75, 80.

17. Brief for Respondent Joan Bray, *Nixon v. Shrink Missouri Government PAC,* U.S. Supreme Court, October term, 1998, No. 98-963, p. 46.

20. The Legalistic Attack on the Appearance Standard

1. See U.S. Department of Justice, Office of Professional Responsibility, *Review of the Independent Counsel's Inquiry into Certain Activities of Attorney General Edwin Meese III,* (Washington, D.C., October 28, 1988).

2. David E. Rosenbaum, "The Mysterious Chemistry That Turns Whiff into Stench," *New York Times,* March 13, 1994, Section 4, p. 6.

3. See the testimony of Michael Josephson, U.S. Senate, Committee on Governmental Affairs, Subcommittee on Oversight of Government Management, Hearing, *Tenth Anniversary of the Ethics in Government Act and Reauthorization of the Office of Government Ethics,* 100th Congress, 2nd Session, April 12 and 13, 1998, p. 174 and Robert H. Aronson, "Conflict of Interest," *Washington Law Review* 52 (1977), p. 847.

4. U.S. House of Representatives, Committee on Government Operations, Report,

Exemptions from Conflict-of-Interest Statutes in Defense Employment, 86th Congress, 2nd Session, July 1, 1960, p. 8.

5. *Wild* v. *U.S.,* 692 F. 2d (7th Cir., 1982) at 1137; see also 1135.

6. Federal Register 57, p. 35008; see also "Take the Money, Dr. Sullivan," editorial, *New York Times,* March 27, 1989, p. A16.

7. As the Office of Government Ethics itself acknowledged, such a "reference to the perspective of a reasonable person with knowledge of the relevant facts" has the effect of "temper[ing] the appearance standard" (see U.S. Office of Government Ethics, *Proposed Regulations,* July 21, 1991, p. 6).

8. U.S. Senate, Committee on Governmental Affairs, Subcommittee on Federal Services, Post Office and the Civil Service, Hearing, *The Department of Defense: The Consultant Game,* 100th Congress, 2nd Session, July 8, 1988, p. 14 (comments of Senator Carl Levin) and the testimony of Dennis F. Thompson, U.S. House of Representatives, Bipartisan Task Force on Ethics, Hearing, *Congressional Ethics Reform,* 101st Congress, 1st Session, May 24, 1989, p. 115.

9. Josephson Institute for the Advancement of Ethics, *Preserving the Public Trust: Principles of Public Service Ethics* (Marina del Rey: Josephson Institute, 1990), p. 2.

10. U.S. House of Representatives, Committee on Interstate and Foreign Commerce, Subcommittee on Oversight and Investigations, *Conflict of Interest on Regulatory Commissions,* 95th Congress, 1st Session, May 23, 24, June 2, 1977, p. 61 and Eugene B. McGregor, Jr., "The Great Paradox of Democratic Citizenship," *Public Administration Review* 44 (Special Issue) 1984, p. 127.

11. Nathan Lewin et al., Counsel for Attorney General Edwin Meese III, *Response to the Report of the Office of Professional Responsibility,* January 16, 1989, pp. 1–3.

12. U.S. Office of Government Ethics Letter 86X5.

13. U.S. House of Representatives, Committee on Standards of Official Conduct, Hearings, *Standards of Offical Conduct,* 90th Congress, 1st Session, August 16, 17, 23, 24, September 14, 21, 27, 1967, p. 119.

14. "The issue of vagueness really does not differ from the issue of retroactivity: in both cases the determination of the precise limit between what is punishable and what is not is determined *post factum* . . . in this sense, a vague law is an *ex post facto* law." See Bostjan M. Zupancic, "On Legal Formalism: The Principle of Legality in Criminal Law," *Loyola Law Review* 27 (1981), pp. 423, 424.

15. *Connally* v. *General Construction Co.,* 269 U.S. 385 (1926) at 391.

16. Richard H. Fallon, Jr., "Making Sense of Overbreadth," *Yale Law Journal* 100 (1991), p. 903.

17. Steven D. Smith, "Rhetoric and Rationality in the Law of Negligence," *Minnesota Law Review* 69 (1984), p. 298.

18. Senate Ethics Committee, *Revising the Code,* p. 25 ("we're talking about giving people advance warning in areas that may be on the borderline of criminality").

19. Dennis F. Thompson, *Political Ethics and Public Office* (Cambridge, Mass.: Harvard University Press, 1987), p. 137.

20. See Charles Krauthammer, "Jim Wright and the Real Corruption in Washington," *Washington Post,* April 12, 1989, p. A20.

21. See some of the discussion in Thompson, *Political Ethics,* pp. 129–140.
22. See, for example, *Masino* v. *U.S.,* 589 F. 2d. 1048 (Ct. Cl., 1978).
23. *Wild* at 1137.
24. Stuart Taylor, Jr., "Life in the Spotlight: Agony of Getting Burned," *New York Times,* February 27, 1985, p. 24; see also Thompson, *Political Ethics,* p. 139.
25. *Congressional Record,* November 20, 1991, pp. S17177, 17178.

21. The Political Justification for the Appearance Standard

1. Cass R. Sunstein, "On Analogical Reasoning," *Harvard Law Review* 106 (1993), p. 743.
2. Ibid., p. 745.
3. Judith N. Shklar, *Legalism: Law, Morals and Political Trials* (Cambridge, Mass.: Harvard University Press, 1964), p. 152.
4. Ibid., pp. 152–3.
5. Ibid., p. 152.
6. Ibid., p. 162.
7. Ibid., pp. 202, 205.
8. John Calvin Jeffries, "Legality, Vagueness, and the Construction of Penal Statutes," *Virginia Law Review* 71 (1985), p. 383.
9. Similarly, "in Nazi Germany the Catholic Boy Scout organization was dissolved on the basis of a decree outlawing communist activities . . . [For Hitler,] 'objectively' Catholics [were] communists, even if 'subjectively' this might not quite be the case" (*Legalism,* p. 205).
10. Ibid., p. 203.
11. Ibid., p. 202.
12. Ibid., p. 202.
13. Ibid., pp. 166, 164, 162.
14. Ibid., p. 162.
15. Ibid., p. 166.
16. Ibid., p. 220.
17. Owen Fiss, "Objectivity and Interpretation," *Stanford Law Review* 34 (1982), p. 748.
18. See, e.g., U.S. House of Representatives, Bipartisan Task Force on Ethics, *Congressional Ethics Reform,* 100th Congress, 1st Session, May 24, 1989, p. 78.
19. U.S. House of Representatives, Committee on the Judiciary, Subcommittee on Administrative Law and Governmental Relations, Hearing, *Lobbying Disclosure Act of 1993,* 103rd Congress, 1st Session, March 31, 1993, p. 196.
20. See *Legalism,* p. 170 and Meg Greenfield, "Private Lives, Public Values," *Newsweek,* May 18, 1987, p. 92.
21. Michael Oreskes, "Congress: The Man Facing the Ethics Inquiry Is a Bold Risk-Taker Out of Step With His Time," *New York Times,* May 22, 1989, p. B6.
22. James C. Wright, Jr., *Reflections of a Public Man* (Fort Worth: Allied Printing, 1984), p. 84.
23. John J. Fialka, "Sen. Johnston's China Advocacy Raises Eyebrows," *Wall Street Journal,* April 22, 1994, p. B6.

24. "Two Trials for Speaker Wright," editorial, *The New York Times,* April 24, 1989, p. A18 (emphasis mine).

25. Michael Kinsley, "Now that We Know Meese's Standards," *Washington Post,* July 21, 1988, p. A23.

26. *Legalism,* p. 170.

27. *State v. Kuehnle,* 88 Atl. Reporter 1085 (N.J., 1913); see also some of the discussion in Appellant's Brief, *U.S. v. Rostenkowski,* U.S. Court of Appeals for the D.C. Circuit, Nos. 94–3158, 94–3160, December 20, 1994, p. 28.

28. Alan Norrie, "Subjectivism, Objectivism and the Limits of Criminal Recklessness," *Oxford Journal of Legal Studies* 12 (1992), p. 533 and Jeffrey Toobin, "Humility and Justice: What People Do Is a Lot Clearer Than Why They Do It," *New Yorker,* April 1, 1996, pp. 7–8.

29. William Galston, *Liberal Purposes: Goods, Values and Diversity in the Liberal State* (New York: Cambridge University Press, 1991), chap. 10.

30. Bruce Ackerman, *We The People,* vol. 1, *Foundations* (Cambridge, Mass.: Harvard University Press, 1991), p. 234.

31. George Kateb, "The Moral Distinctiveness of Representative Democracy," *Ethics* 91 (1981), p. 358.

32. See, e.g., Stephen Macedo, *Liberal Virtues: Citizenship, Virtue and Community in Liberal Constitutionalism* (Oxford: Clarendon Press, 1990), pp. 272, 276.

33. Ronald Beiner, *Political Judgment* (Chicago: University of Chicago Press, 1983), pp. 148, 82, 85, 131–132.

22. Recusal, Divestiture, Balance, and Disclosure

1. Or, to take another example, consider the speeding laws, where the *malum prohibitum* is driving over fifty-five miles per hour, and the *malum in se* driving dangerously. Speeding laws come with penalties (fines) but also license revocations (preventives). Of course, license revocations have a punitive effect as well, since they are visited only on violators. But then again, it is only by violating the law that one identifies herself as a member of the class of speeders, whereas no comparable legal violation is necessary to identify oneself as an official.

2. G. Calvin Mackenzie, *The Politics of Presidential Appointments* (New York: Free Press, 1981), pp. 107–108.

3. Hastings Center, "Model Code of Ethics for the United States Senate," *Hastings Center Report,* February 1981, p. 21.

4. Peter L. Strauss, "Disqualifications of Decisional Officials in Rulemaking," *Columbia Law Review* 80 (1980), p. 1037.

5. Association of the Bar of the City of New York, *Conflict of Interest and Federal Service* (Cambridge, Mass.: Harvard University Press, 1960), p. 204.

6. *Berger v. U.S.,* 255 U.S. 22 (1920) at 35.

7. Robert Vaughn, *Conflict of Interest Regulation in the Federal Executive Branch* (Lexington, Mass.: Heath, 1979), pp. 54–55; see also *Fritz v. Gordon,* 517 P. 2d 911 (Wash., 1974) at 926 and National Municipal League, *Model State Conflict of Interest and Financial Disclosure Law* (New York: Sowers, 1979), p. 19.

8. Gabriele J. Paone, "Contending with Organic Law: Conflict of Interest Prohibi-

tions at the U.S. Department of the Interior," *Office of Government Ethics Newsgram*, vol. 2, no. 4, November 1985, p. 2.

9. See the testimony of Alan B. Morrison, Director of Litigation for Public Citizen, in U.S. Senate, Committee on Governmental Affairs, Hearing, *Public Officials Integrity Act of 1977, Blind Trusts and Other Conflict of Interest Matters*, 95th Congress, 1st Session, June 7, 1977, p. 218.

10. U.S. Senate, Select Committee on Ethics, Hearing, *Revising the Senate Code of Official Conduct Pursuant to Senate Resolution 109*, 96th Congress, 2nd Session, November 18, 1980, pp. 106–107.

11. U.S. Office of Government Ethics Letter 93X21.

12. Steven Lubet, "Regulation of Judges' Business and Financial Activities," *Emory Law Journal* 37 (1988), pp. 16–17, 21.

13. U.S. Office of Government Ethics Letter 90X1.

14. Quoted in Howard Kurtz, "Gingrich-Murdoch Meeting Renews Calls for Probe of Book Deal," *Washington Post*, January 15, 1995, p. A9.

15. Burt Solomon, "A Question with No Good Answers: Who'll Pay Clinton's Legal Bills?," *National Journal*, May 21, 1994, p. 1203. At the time, a knowledgable lawyer suggested to Solomon that "the only way to assure the public that [Clinton's] legal defense fund is 'blind' is to put a judicious Republican"—he proposed "Kenneth Starr, a former Solicitor General"—"in charge of it."

16. Note, "The Disqualification of Administrative Officials," *Columbia Law Review* 41 (1941), p. 1384.

17. See, e.g., Bernard Schwartz, "Bias in *Webster* and Bias in Administrative Law— The Recent Jurisprudence," *Tulsa Law Review* 30 (1995), pp. 461–484.

23. What Is a Balanced Committee?

1. Congressional Research Service, *The Federal Advisory Committee Act Sourcebook: Legislative History, Texts and Other Documents*, 95th Congress, 2nd Session, 1978, pp. 288–289.

2. Although FACA's balance provision literally requires committees to be representative of all "points of view relevant to their functions," the aim of each party in any given balance case has become simply to ensure representation of all interests the committee directly affects. Congress, courts and litigants, in other words, have simply taken "'a direct interest' as proxy for a point of view so that judicial review would be available" (see *Public Citizen* v. *National Advisory Committee on Microbiological Criteria for Foods*, 886 F. 2d 419 (D.C. Cir., 1989) at 423, 427). Also, because most committees operate according to supermajority or other consensual decision-making norms, groups seeking representation rarely ask for more than one or two seats even on bodies that might otherwise consist of over a hundred private-sector members. See Eric Glitzenstein and Patti Goldman, *The Federal Advisory Committee Act at the Crossroads* (Washington: Public Citizen, 1989), p. 33.

3. Defendant's Opposition to Plaintiff's Motion for a Preliminary Injunction, *National Treasury Employees' Union* v. *Reagan* (D.D.C., February 12, 1988), pp. 2–3.

4. *National Anti-Hunger Coalition* v. *Executive Committee of the President's Private Sector Survey on Cost Control*, 557 F. Supp. 524 (1983) at 526, 528.

5. Memorandum in Support of Plaintiff's Motion for a Preliminary Injunction, *National Treasury Employees' Union* v. *Reagan*, Civil Action No. 88–086 (D.D.C., February 5, 1988), p. 17.

6. *National Anti-Hunger Coalition* v. *Executive Committee* at 528.

7. *Public Citizen* v. *National Advisory Committee* at 430.

8. Plaintiff's Reply Memorandum in Support of Their Motion for a Preliminary Injunction, *Public Citizen* v. *National Advisory Committee on Microbiological Criteria for Foods* (D.D.C., July 27, 1988), p. 8.

9. Memorandum in Support of Plaintiff's Motion for a Temporary Restraining Order, *Pension Rights Center* v. *Advisory Council on Employee Welfare and Pension Benefit Plans* (D.D.C., March 14, 1986), p. 19.

10. Proceedings, *National Anti-Hunger Coalition* v. *Executive Committee of the President's Private-Sector Survey on Cost Control*, 557 F. Supp. 524 (February 17, 1983), p. 55; see also Proceedings, *National Anti-Hunger Coalition* v. *Executive Committee of the President's Private-Sector Survey on Cost Control*, 711 F. 2d 1071 (D.C. Cir., July 20, 1983), pp. 83, 30 ("[f]or every one of those groups to be seated [we would require] an Executive Committee of thousands of members").

11. *Public Citizen* v. *National Advisory Committee* at 426, 427.

12. Plaintiff's Reply, p. 4.

13. Proceedings, 711 F. 2d 1071 (D.C. Cir., July 20, 1983), pp. 66, 56.

14. Jeremy Rabkin, *Judicial Compulsions: How Public Law Distorts Public Policy* (New York: Basic Books, 1989), p. 75.

15. Ibid., p. 10.

16. Transcript of Preliminary Injunction Before the Honorable John Garrett Penn, United States District Court Judge, *Public Citizen* v. *National Advisory Committee on Microbiological Criteria for Foods* (D.C. Cir., November 18, 1988), p. 26.

17. Joseph Vining, *Legal Identity: The Coming of Age of Public Law* (New Haven: Yale University Press, 1978), pp. 149, 155.

18. John Burnheim, *Is Democracy Possible? The Alternative to Electoral Politics* (Berkeley: University of California Press, 1985), pp. 195, 112.

19. Plaintiff's Reply, pp. 7, 8 and Memorandum in Support of Plaintiff's Motion, pp. 3, 15, 16.

20. U.S. Senate, Committee on Government Operations, Report, *The Federal Advisory Committee Act*, 92nd Congress, 2nd Session, September 7, 1972, p. 5.

21. Proceedings, 557 F. Supp. 524, p. 60. Groups here can be understood to argue that the quasi-legislative realm ought to be a functionally representative one. "[B]y not requiring each citizen to sort out his whole philosophy of life," as Elaine Spitz puts it, "a functional system divides up a person's interests for him, giv[ing] him a chance to choose meaningfully"; see Spitz, *Majority Rule* (Chatham, N.J.: Chatham House, 1984), p. 43.

24. Disclosure and Its Discontents

1. U.S. House of Representatives, Committee on Post Office and Civil Service, Subcommittee on Human Resources, Hearing, *Effects of Federal Ethics Restrictions on*

Recruitment and Retention of Employees, 101st Congress, 1st Session, June 13, 1989, p. 173.

2. U.S. House of Representatives, Committee on the Judiciary, Subcommittee on Administrative Law and Governmental Relations, *Post-Employment Restrictions for Federal Officers and Employees,* 100th Congress, 2nd Session, May 4, 1988, pp. 112, 122.

3. *Congressional Record* (Senate), February 3, 1975, pp. 2019, 2039.

4. *Congressional Record* (Senate), January 27, 1971, p. 725 (comments of Senator Spong).

5. Erwin G. Krasnow and Richard E. Lankford, "Congressional Conflicts of Interest: Who Watches the Watchers?" *Federal Bar Journal* 24 (1964), p. 278.

6. See also Joseph S. Clark, "Some Ethical Problems of Congress," *Annals of the Academy of Political and Social Science,* January 1966, p. 20 and George A. Graham, *Morality in American Politics* (New York: Random House, 1952), p. 245.

7. *Congressional Record* (Senate), February 3, 1975, p. 2039.

8. U.S. House of Representatives, Committee on Standards of Official Conduct, *Standards of Official Conduct,* 90th Congress, 1st Session, August 16, 17, 23, 24, September 14, 21, 27, 1967 (comments of Rev. John M. Wells), p. 288.

9. U.S. Senate, Committee on the Judiciary, Subcommittee on Improvements in Judicial Machinery, Hearing, *Judicial Disqualification,* 93rd Congress, 1st Session, July 14, 1971, and May 17, 1973, p. 74.

10. Linda K. Lee, "Conflict of Interest: One Aspect of Congress' Problems," *George Washington Law Review* 32 (1964), p. 971.

11. Josephson Institute for the Advancement of Ethics, *Preserving the Public Trust: Principles of Public Service Ethics* (Marina del Rey: Josephson Institute, 1990), p. 12; see also John W. Wall, "Public Officials: The Constitutional Implications of Mandatory Public Financial Disclosure Statutes, and a Proposal for Change," *Law and the Social Order* (1971), p. 10 and Presidential Commission on Federal Ethics Law Reform, *To Serve with Honor: Report and Recommendations to the President* (Washington: Government Printing Office, 1989), p. 81.

12. Michael Kinsley, "The Conflict of Interest Craze," *Washington Monthly,* November 1978, pp. 42, 44.

13. U.S. Senate, Committee on the Judiciary, Subcommittee on Separation of Powers, Hearing, *Nonjudicial Activities of Supreme Court Justices and Other Federal Judges,* 91st Congress, 1st Session, July 15, 16, September 30, 1969, pp. 61, 302, 420–421.

14. Ibid., p. 429.

15. Peter L. Strauss, "Disqualifications of Decisional Officials in Rulemaking," *Columbia Law Review* 80 (1980), p. 1005.

16. *Cinderella Career and Finishing Schools* v. *FTC,* 425 F. 2d 583 (1970) at 590.

17. *Association of National Advertisers* v. *FTC,* 627 F. 2d 1151 (1979) at 1195 (Judge MacKinnon, dissenting in part and concurring in part); see also *Mackler* v. *Board of Education of the City of Camden,* 108 A. 2d 854 (N.J., 1954) at 857.

18. For a discussion of this problem in the legislative setting, see Richard L. Hall and Frank W. Wayman, "Moneyed Interests and the Mobilization of Bias in Congressional Committees," *American Political Science Review* 84 (1990), p. 801.

19. Steven Lubet, "Judicial Ethics and Private Lives," *Northwestern University Law Review* 79 (1985), p. 989.

20. *Congressional Record* (Senate), January 27, 1971, p. 725.

21. Wall, "Public Officials," p. 111 and John P. Burke, "The Ethics of Deregulation—or the Deregulation of Ethics," in John J. DiIulio, Jr., *Deregulating the Public Service* (Washington, D.C.: Brookings, 1994), p. 71.

22. Ruth Gavison, "Privacy and the Limits of the Law," *Yale Law Journal* 89 (1980), pp. 452–454.

23. Colloquium, "Will the Ethics Reform Act Change the Way Government Conducts Business?," *Federal Bar News and Journal* 37 (1990), pp. 415, 418 (comments of Norman J. Ornstein and Arthur B. Culvahouse, Jr.).

24. *Congressional Record* (Senate), May 4, 1994, p. S5153.

25. U.S. Senate, Select Committee on Ethics, Special Counsel Report, *Investigation of Senator David F. Durenberger*, 101st Congress, 2nd Session, July 10, 1990, p. 9.

26. David Grann, "Prosecutorial Indiscretion," *The New Republic*, February 2, 1998, p. 21.

27. Bill Miller, "As Espy Trial Ends, Its Insight Into Gifts and Favors Is Murky," *Washington Post*, November 23, 1998, p. A21.

28. Michael Kelly, "The Company He Keeps," *Washington Post*, November 24, 1999, p. A23.

29. Answer to Complaint, *U.S.* v. *Samuel R. Berger*, (D.D.C., November 10, 1997), pp. 3, 4 and Susan Kavanagh, "Berger Agrees to Conflict-of-Interest Settlement Under 18 U.S.C. §216," *Federal Ethics Report* (Washington: Washington Service Bureau), December 1997, pp. 14–15.

30. Andrew Stark, "Under the O . . . Oops!," *Saturday Night*, February 1996, p. 24.

31. See *Bullock* v. *Carter*, 495 U.S. 134 (1972) and *Lubin* v. *Parish*, 415 U.S. 709 (1974).

32. See, e.g., *Shelton* v. *Tucker*, 364 U.S. 479 (1960) and *NAACP* v. *Alabama*, 357 U.S. 449 (1958).

33. Administrative Conference of the United States, *Ethics in Government*, Proceedings of a Working Conference, Washington, D.C., March 1, 1988, pp. 29, 30, 37; see also Lloyd N. Cutler, "Balancing the Ethics Code," *Washington Post*, March 13, 1989, p. A15.

34. Administrative Conference, p. 44 (comments of Fred F. Fielding); see also California Assembly, Committee on Governmental Organization and Financial Disclosure, Hearing, October 30, 1969, p. 28.

35. Thomas D. Morgan, "Public Financial Disclosure by Federal Officials: A Functional Approach," *Georgetown Journal of Legal Ethics* 3 (1989), p. 238.

36. U.S. Senate, Committee on Governmental Affairs, Subcommittee on Oversight of Government Management, Hearing, *Tenth Anniversary of the Ethics in Government Act and Reauthorization of the Office of Government Ethics*, 100th Congress, 2nd Session, April 12, 13, 1988, p. 107; see also *Congressional Record* (House), March 20, 1970, p. 8439.

37. U.S. Senate, Select Committee on Ethics, Hearing, *Revising the Senate Code of Official Conduct Pursuant to Senate Resolution 109*, 96th Congress, 2nd Session, November 18, 1980, p. 111.

38. Eleanor Randolph, "Plagiarism Suggestion Angers Biden's Aides," *Washington Post*, September 13, 1987, p. A6.

39. Michael Kinsley, "Another Fine Meese," *The New Republic*, February 22, 1988, p. 4.

40. See Andrew Stark, "The Man Who Knew Too Little: Now We Have More Facts About Public Figures Than They Have About Themselves," *Washington Post*, April 1, 1990, p. C5.

41. Robert H. Freilich and Thomas M. Larson, "Conflicts of Interest: A Model Statutory Proposal for the Regulation of Municipal Transactions," *UMKC Law Review* 38 (1970), pp. 373, 399; see also House Committee on Post Office and Civil Service, *Effects of Federal Ethics Restrictions on Recruitment and Retention of Employees*, p. 144.

42. U.S. House of Representatives, Committee on the Judiciary, Report, *The Ethics in Government Act of 1977*, 95th Congress, 1st Session, November 2, 1977, p. 102. Consider that the U.S. Office of Government Ethics' *Public Financial Disclosure: A Reviewer's Reference* is itself over 250 pages long.

43. Wall, "Public Officials," p. 109.

44. G. Calvin Mackenzie, *The Politics of Presidential Appointments* (New York: Free Press, 1981), p. 105.

45. Chet Holifield, "Conflicts of Interest in Government-Contractor Relationships," *Federal Bar Journal* 24 (1964), p. 308.

46. Joel L. Fleishman, "The Disclosure Model and Its Limitations," *Hastings Center Report*, February 1981, p. 17.

47. Note, "Conflict-of-Interests of Government Personnel: An Appraisal of the Philadelphia Situation," *University of Pennsylvania Law Review* 107 (1959), p. 1021; see also David H. Martin, "From an Ethical Viewpoint," *Office of Government Ethics Newsgram*, vol. 3, no. 2, February 1986, p. 2.

Conclusion

1. Judith N. Shklar, *Ordinary Vices* (Cambridge, Mass.: Harvard University Press, 1984), p. 226.

2. Bayless Manning, "The Purity Potlatch: An Essay on Conflicts of Interest, American Government, and Moral Escalation," *The Federal Bar Journal* 24 (1964), p. 247.

3. Donald E. Campbell, Acting Director, Office of Government Ethics, *Acceptance of Food and Refreshments by Executive-Branch Employees*, October 23, 1987, p. 8; see also June E. Edmondson, "And Gifts and Travel for All," *Federal Bar News and Journal* 37 (1990), p. 405.

4. U.S. House of Representatives, Committee on the Judiciary, Subcommittee on Antitrust, Hearing, *Federal Conflict of Interest Legislation*, 82nd Congress, 2nd Session, March 2, 1960, p. 333 and U.S. Senate, Committee on Governmental Affairs, Subcommittee on Oversight of Government Management, Hearing, *Ethics in Government Act Amendments of 1982*, 97th Congress, 2nd Session, April 28, 1982, p. 50.

5. See, e.g., Jerome Frank, *If Men Were Angels* (New York: Harper and Row, 1942), p. 151 and U.S. Senate, Committee on Labor and Public Welfare, Subcommittee

322 | Notes to Pages 266–270

to Study Senate Concurrent Resolution 21, Hearing, *Establishment of a Commission on Ethics in Government,* 92nd Congress, 1st Session, June 20, 1951, p. 61.

6. Unless, of course, they are given some form of "objective" definition, which often means turning them into heightened speeding laws ("dangerous driving laws" prohibit "grossly excessive speed"; see Robert S. Shiels, "Dangerous Driving in Scotland," *Journal of Criminal Law* 58 (1994), pp. 248–249).

7. Rollin M. Perkins and Ronald N. Boyce, *Criminal Law,* 3rd ed., (Mineola, N.Y.: Foundation Press, 1982), p. 880.

8. See, e.g., U.S. House of Representatives, Committee on Rules, Hearings and Markup, *Financial Ethics,* 95th Congress, 1st Session, February 23, 24, 1977, p. 41.

9. U.S. Senate Select Committee on Ethics, Hearing, *Revising the Senate Code of Conduct Pursuant to Senate Resolution 109,* 96th Congress, 2nd Session, November 18, 1980, p. 17.

10. Note, "Developments in the Law: Conflicts of Interest in the Legal Profession," *Harvard Law Review* 94 (1981), pp. 1269, 1473–1474; see also *U.S. v. Brown,* 381 U.S. 437 (1965) at 453.

11. This is not to deny that there may be a moral obligation to obey any law simply *because* it's law and regardless of its proximity to or distance from any moral content. Certainly, some theorists reject the idea that we labor under a moral obligation to obey any law just because it's law, without further inquiry (see, e.g., M. B. E. Smith, "Is There a Prima Facie Obligation to Obey the Law?," *Yale Law Journal,* vol. 82 [1973], p. 956). But to avoid opening that can of worms here, I'll simply restate my point. Regardless of whether there exists a moral obligaton to obey all law—such that any offender deserves *some* moral stigma—there attaches, or should attach, an additional moral stigma proportional to the extent to which a law rests closer to the *malum in se* than the *malum prohibitum* end of the spectrum. In other words, the typical conflict-of-interest violator—while he should be punished—should bear the same moral stigma as the typical speeding-law offender, however much stigma we think that should be.

12. Kathleen M. Sullivan, "The Law: Put Politics Back Where It Belongs," *Washington Post,* January 3, 1999, p. C4.

13. For effective statements of this position, see Stephen Gottlieb, "The Dilemma of Election Campaign Finance Reform" and Martin Shapiro, "Corruption, Freedom and Equality in Campaign Financing," *Hofstra Law Review* 18 (1989), pp. 213–200, 385–394.

14. See, e.g., Congressional Accountability Project, *Personal Use of Campaign Funds,* September 25, 1994, and Heritage Foundation Issue Bulletin #230, "Repealing the First Amendment," March 13, 1997.

15. Manning, "Purity Potlatch," pp. 244, 255.

16. John Tower, *Consequences: A Personal and Political Memoir* (Boston: Little Brown, 1991), p. 301.

17. Ibid., p. 301.

18. John P. MacKenzie, "The Appearance of Honor," *New York Times,* March 7, 1989, p. A24.

INDEX

Abramson, Jeffrey, 149
Abscam affair, 161, 202
Absolute test, 201–202
Abuse of office, 7, 37–39, 40, 60–67;
  distinction from other offenses, 47–50, 61–
  65, 67, 74, 96–97, 154, 280n26;
  examples, 7, 37, 38, 60, 62, 63, 66–67;
  remedies, 239–240
Access-granting, 175, 176, 177, 307n88
Accountability, 11, 236
Ackerman, Bruce, 231
Actus reus, 22, 31, 167
Adams, Sherman, 66
Adham, Sheik Kamal, 98–99
Administrative Procedure Act, 184
Advocacy roles: advocatory or advisory
  officials, 309n13, 310n5; vs. judging roles
  of legislators, 190–200
Agencies: combination of roles, 184–185,
  187; *ex parte* situations, 187
"Agency" understandings of public office,
  236
Agenda-shaping, 175, 176, 177, 307nn84, 88
Allison, John R., 184–185
American Bar Association, 24, 25, 275n17,
  296n2
American Civil Liberties Union, 24, 25
Amoco Corporation, 256
Analogy, use explained, 223–224
Anonymous contributions, 208–209, 219
Appearances of official impropriety, 9–10, 13,
  17; legal retroactivity, 10, 209–212, 217–
  221, 227–228, 269, 314n14; a political
  (not legal or moral) issue, 207–208, 211–
  212, 217, 223–232, 268–271;
  prejudgment, 10, 209–212, 213–217, 221,
  226–227, 231; and *quid pro quo,* 221–222;
  self-dealing, 44–45; and strict liability,
  229–230; vs. real official impropriety, 208,
  213–214; vs. temptation, 25–27

Aristotle, 232
Arkes, Hadley, 266–267
Association of American Physicians v. *Clinton,*
  181, 183, 308n13
Association of the Bar of the City of New
  York, 275n10
Atkinson, A. B., 14
Atlantic Richfield (ARCO), 37
Avco Manufacturing, 47–48, 49, 61, 64, 65,
  66

Baker, Howard, 198–199, 200
Balance of interests, 10–11, 235–236, 237,
  238, 240, 241–242; committees, 243–249,
  317n2
Baron, Jane, 164
Bayles, Michael, 157, 158–159
Bazelon, David, 170
Begala, Paul, 107
Begich, Peggy, 182, 183
Beinart, Peter, 182
Beiner, Ronald, 232
Bellew, Murl, 58–59
Berger, Sandy, 256
Bernstein, Marver H., 45
Biaggi, Mario, 7, 37, 60, 61, 64
Bias, 5–6, 119–122, 127–128, 149–150,
  185–186, 241; journalists, 252–253;
  judges, 254. *See also* Hypocrisy; Lobbying
Biden, Joseph, 23, 259
Blackstone, Sir William, 22
Blair, James, 1, 2
Blankley, Tony, 240
Blind trust, 240–241
Bono, Mary, 182
Bribery: compared with abuse of office, 49,
  61, 62–63; compared with undue
  influence, 48, 49; criminal type of *quid pro
  quo,* 7, 38, 39–40, 154, 155, 178, 301n2;
  definition of bribery/*quid pro quo,* 7, 39,

323